'A strong cadre of leaders [...]
complex and fast changing e[...]
practical book shows how to build such a cadre of a leaders'

*Alain Bejjani, Chief Executive Officer, Majid Al Futtaim Holding*

'Transformation means changing at scale starting with leaders. Our organization – like many – has limited resources and this book really showed me how we could use time and money effectively to create better leaders everywhere that counts'

*Andrea Clemente, HR Latin America Whirlpool Corporation*

'There are hundreds of magic recipes in the market about the "most important attributes of great leaders", but most of them provide only limited help to translating these lessons into concrete leadership growth programmes across the whole organization. This book is very different. It integrates the teaching on very thoroughly researched, highly practical and wide-ranging leadership development approaches with a fictitious implementation story, which stays entertaining until the very end'

*Bernd Uhe, Global Head of Human Resources, Pictet Group*

'I find this book very illuminating. It is one of the best pieces I read about leadership since *Leadership at Scale* is a unique blend of cutting edge, field-tested research on developing the right leadership at scale, and a roadmap to make it happen in practice. The book is both: a state-of-the-art reference for the different research findings on Leadership and a practical handbook of how to make sustainable and lasting change happen. It has everything for firms and their leaders to cope with today's increasingly complex, volatile and hence challenging world'

*Bruno Pfister, Chairman of Rothschild Bank AG*

'Most leadership development programs disappoint or are being canceled to generate quick savings, leaving many organizations short of capable leaders. Yet, building leaders is one of the key priorities for organizations in today's dynamic and complex environment. This book shows how firms can develop a leadership culture that can help them thrive and prosper'

*Daniel Vasella, M.D., Chairman and CEO Emeritus Novartis AG*

'Today many organizations are trying to simplify and become more dynamic. However, decentralizing decision power and engaging all members of large organizations requires building more and stronger leaders. *Leadership at Scale* is a practical guide to do so'

*Mario Greco, Chief Executive Officer, Zurich Insurance Group*


'Large-scale organizations present particular challenges. At the NHS, Europe's largest employer, all 1.3m staff are potential leaders. This deeply-researched book shows how to work at scale, to simplify, concentrate and sustain leadership development for large organizations: it tells us who to develop and why, how and for how long, and in what ways. As a practical guide it is invaluable'

*Professor Nicki Latham, former COO Health Education England (NHS), responsible for the NHS Leadership Academy*


'To institutionalize themselves organizations need a leadership culture. This book shows compellingly and practically how to do it. A worthwhile read!'

*Nicolas Pictet, Senior Partner, Pictet Group*


'A first class template demonstrating how to use superior leadership to drive performance in large organizations'

*Paul Myners (Lord Myners), former FTSE100 Chair and Treasury Minister*


'The core principles outlined in this book are relevant for all organizations, regardless of size, industry or strategy. In a more and more digitized world this book should be required reading in particular for young leaders'

*Rolf Dörig, Chairman of the Board of the Swiss Life Group and Adecco*

'An organization with better leaders will invariably have better results. This practical guide shows you how to develop your leaders by focusing on what drives performance and on what people can learn easily and quickly on the job. The authors show how this approach can work for many leaders right across your organization'

Stuart Rose (Lord Rose), Chairman, Ocado PLC

'While there are many books about individual leadership development, the new focus here is on improving leadership effectiveness across a whole organization, based on your specific context and strategy. This book will show you a theoretically sound but still pragmatic way to improved leadership effectiveness'

Prof. Dr. Thomas A. Gutzwiller, Partner, GW Partners AG, and Professor in Corporate and Leadership Development at the University of St. Gallen, Executive School of Management

'Leadership is our most valuable resource to drive positive change in business and society. *Leadership at Scale* is a comprehensive, academically thorough, and yet practical guide on increasing leadership effectiveness across a large organization, not only for the top leaders, but for all employees. I look forward to applying the principles in our organization'

Vasant Narasimhan, M.D., Chief Executive Officer, Novartis AG

# Leadership at Scale

# Leadership at Scale

*Better leadership, better results*

## CLAUDIO FESER,
## MICHAEL RENNIE
## & NICOLAI CHEN NIELSEN

This edition first published in Great Britain by Nicholas Brealey Publishing in 2019
An imprint of John Murray Press

An Hachette company

First published in hardback in Great Britain by Nicholas Brealey Publishing in 2018

1

*British Library Cataloguing-in-Publication Data*
A catalogue record for this book is available from the British Library.

ISBN 978 1 47369 604 4
UK eBook ISBN 978 1 47368 419 5
US eBook ISBN 978 1 47369 001 1

Every reasonable effort has been made to trace copyright holders, but if there are
any errors or omissions, Nicholas Brealey will be pleased to insert the appropriate
acknowledgement in any subsequent printings or editions.

Printed and bound by Clays Ltd, Elcograf S.p.A.

John Murray Press policy is to use papers that are natural, renewable and recyclable
products and made from wood grown in sustainable forests. The logging and
manufacturing processes are expected to conform to the environmental regulations of
the country of origin.

Nicholas Brealey Publishing
John Murray Press
Carmelite House
50 Victoria Embankment
London, EC4Y 0DZ, UK
Tel: 020 3122 6000

Nicholas Brealey Publishing
Hachette Book Group
Market Place Center
53 State Street
Boston, MA 02109, USA
Tel: (617) 263 1834

www.nicholasbrealey.com

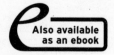

# Dedication

For Evelyne, Dario, and Alessio, for your understanding,
support, and love.
*Claudio*

For my mother Patricia who through her values and love
inspired my lifelong interest in leadership.
*Michael*

For Samira, for your unwavering support and love, and for
always believing in me.
*Nicolai*

# Contents

# Acknowledgements

This book is the result of a broad effort, and draws on insights and extensive contributions from over 30 senior McKinsey leadership development practitioners globally. Below are the key contributors, and specific chapter authors are also acknowledged at the beginning of each chapter.

## Core contributors

**André Dua** is a Senior Partner in McKinsey's New York office. He is a founder of McKinsey Academy, the founder of McKinsey's Higher Education Practice, and the founder of McKinsey's State and Local Government Practice.

**Andrew St George** is a writer, academic, and advisor to McKinsey. He has written ten books in linguistics, communications and management, including *Royal Navy Way of Leadership* for UK Naval Command. He works internationally with commercial organizations, public services, and governments.

**Arne Gast** leads the Organization Practice across Asia-Pacific, based in McKinsey's Kuala Lumpur Office. He is the co-founder of Aberkyn, McKinsey's special 'home' for transformational facilitation that has grown into eight global hubs over the last few years.

**Bill Schaninger** is a Senior Partner in McKinsey's Philadelphia office. He is Chairman of Integrated OrgSolutions, and leader of McKinsey's Global Talent Management Practice, working with a globally diverse client portfolio.

**Charlotte Relyea** is a Partner in McKinsey's New York office and leader of McKinsey Academy. Prior to leading McKinsey Academy, Charlotte was a co-leader of McKinsey's Client Capability Building initiative, and a leader in McKinsey's Tech, Media, Telecom and Marketing and Sales practices.

**Chris Gagnon** is a Senior Partner in McKinsey's Dallas office. Chris leads McKinsey's Organization Practice in North America and co-chairs the Practice globally. His work with clients focuses on integrated 'Organization Strategies' that combine culture, talent, leadership, design and change management.

**Cornelius Chang** is an Associate Partner based in Singapore, leading McKinsey Academy for Asia. He has supported numerous leadership, talent, and culture and change engagements across a wide range of industries globally.

**David Speiser** is a Partner in McKinsey's Zurich Office and leads McKinsey Academy's 'Executive Programmes'. He serves leading companies in multiple industries on strategy, organization, and mergers and acquisitions, resource allocation and leadership development.

**Emily Yueh** is a Partner based in McKinsey's New York office and is a leader in McKinsey Academy. She focuses on organizational, executive leadership development and performance transformation work for leading financial institutions, pharmaceuticals and educational institutions.

**Faridun Dotiwala** is a Partner who leads McKinsey's Human Capital practice in Asia. His work is in the area of leadership development, establishing corporate academies, CEO and top team development and alignment and shaping large scale culture shifts in organizations.

**Filippo Rossi** is a Senior Partner in McKinsey's Paris Office, and has over 20 years of consulting experience relating to lean methodologies, primarily within the heavy industries. Filippo leads McKinsey's Healthy Lifestyle initiative, covering the four main pillars of nutrition, exercise, sleep and stress management.

**Florian Pollner** is an Expert Partner in McKinsey's Zurich Office. Florian leads McKinsey's Leadership and Learning client service across EMEA, and is co-founder and EMEA lead of McKinsey Academy, McKinsey's dedicated Leadership Development entity.

**Gautam Kumra** is Managing Partner of McKinsey's India office, based in New Delhi. He led the Firm's Organization Practice in Asia and was one of the leading thinkers behind the Firm's research and insights on transformational change.

**Gemma D'Auria** is a Partner in McKinsey's Middle East Office, where she leads the Organization Practice. She has designed and helped launch multiple large-scale leadership development efforts and corporate academies in the region, reaching thousands of leaders.

**Haimeng Zhang** is Senior Partner in McKinsey's Hong Kong office, and leads the Asia-Pacific Organization Practice. He supports multinational clients on organization topics including top team effectiveness, leadership development program design and HR transformation.

**Johanne Lavoie** is a Partner in McKinsey's Canadian practice and Master Expert in leadership. She recently authored Quarterly articles on Inner Agility and artificial intelligence, the book *Centered Leadership: Leading with Clarity, Purpose and Impact*, and a TEDx on integrating movement and stillness in disruptive times.

**Julia Sperling** is a Partner in McKinsey's Frankfurt Office. As an MD and neuroscientist, Julia leads McKinsey's work on applying modern adult learning techniques grounded in neuroscience in leadership development programmes.

**Mary Andrade** is the Director of the Learning Design and Development Center of Excellence at McKinsey, and is based in Amsterdam. She is pioneering 21st century learning methodologies, approaches, and design for McKinsey and the learning industry.

**Michael Bazigos** was formerly Vice President of McKinsey's OrgSolutions, and co-led the Organizational Science Initiative. He has published widely in professional and business journals including *McKinsey Quarterly* and *Journal of Leadership Studies*.

**Mike Carson** is a Partner in McKinsey, and a founder of Aberkyn, leading the growth of Aberkyn's global network of local hubs; he is based in London and Amsterdam.

**Michiel Kruyt** is a Partner and one of the leaders of the Organization Practice of McKinsey. Michiel is a co-founder of Aberkyn, McKinsey's 'home' for change leaders, and currently co-leads it.

**Nick van Dam** is a Partner and Global Chief Learning Officer at McKinsey, based in Amsterdam. He is an internationally recognized advisor, author, speaker and thought leader on Corporate Learning and Development.

**Ramesh Srinivasan** is a Senior Partner in the New York Office of McKinsey. Ramesh leads McKinsey Academy, and is Dean of the Bower Forum, McKinsey's program for CEO learning

## OTHER CONTRIBUTORS

This book has involved a large number of additional contributors. There are too many to mention individually here, but we would like to especially thank: Allen Webb, Allison Thom, Amadeo Di Lodovico, Ashley Williams, Anne Blackman, Claudette Lucien, Els van der Helm, Erica Rauzin (who edited the fictional story), Fernanda Mayol, Jacqueline Brassey, Judith Hazelwood, Kayvan Kian, Linda Hovius, Malvika Singh, Mary Meaney, Nikola Jurisic, Rik Kirkland, Rob Theunissen, Roland Slot, Sahar Yousef, Scott Keller, Tim Dickson, Venetia Simcock and the McKinsey editorial production team (Gwyn Herbein, Dana Sand, Katie Turner, Sneha Vats, Belinda Yu, and Pooja Yadav).

# Introduction: Leadership that really drives performance

*Andrew St George, Claudio Feser, Michael Rennie, Nicolai Chen Nielsen*

Why this book? | Why leadership matters | The organizational leadership challenge | Meeting the organizational leadership challenge: leadership at scale | What does impact look like? | Structure of this book

In this book, we will use a fictional company called New Classic Look clothing (NCL) to illustrate a leadership development journey in practice. Carolyn Randolph is the CEO of NCL, a specialized clothing company based in Shanghai. The company had grown quickly under her leadership, was operating in over 50 countries, and had amassed a yearly revenue of $6 billion. The stock had outperformed the market in recent years, and shareholders expected the growth to continue. Ever since the head of design had retired last year, however, NCL struggled to stay up to date with the latest trends in the fast-changing market. Carolyn felt that the company required a comprehensive revamp in order to stay relevant.

In our story the company executives recently finalized an ambitious strategy to reignite growth, but Carolyn had her doubts about their ability to execute it. The executive team seemed jaded and out of touch with the dynamic market they operated in, and Carolyn did not feel that the company had a strong 'leadership bench' to take over in the future. In a bid to enable the strategy and help NCL reach its performance objectives, Carolyn decided to launch an ambitious leadership development programme.

Carolyn is not alone. Many executives we work with feel they have a leadership gap in their organization, with negative performance implications. In addition, many organizations struggle to bridge this gap. We find that **a large proportion of leadership development initiatives do not achieve the desired outcomes and do not result**

**in enhanced performance**. Making this link, while critical, is difficult to do in practice. We will be re-acquainted with Carolyn, her executive team, and NCL in Part 2 of this book, where we will follow their leadership development journey in detail, and see how NCL is able to increase its leadership effectiveness across the organization, to help enable the overall company strategy.

## *Why this book?*

**Leadership increases value by driving performance**, pure and simple. Every day throughout a large organization, hundreds of leaders make thousands of decisions; these decisions involve millions of interactions; and each of these can either support or harm the main effort of the organization. So it makes sense for an organization to guide their people in interactions in a way that aligns behaviour with strategy and purpose. Great organizations understand the primacy of the relations that its leaders – at all levels – have with those around them.

Yet a new leadership challenge has emerged: organizations consistently state that they lack the required leadership to execute their strategies, despite collectively spending billions of dollars on leadership development globally. Perhaps your organization is one of them: you understand the need for effective leaders, and yet the development programmes you run are not delivering what you need of them?

We wrote this book in order to develop more and better leaders in organizations. We focus on *leadership at scale*, on leadership development across an organization. We have found that most of today's leadership development approaches in organizations – while important for selected individuals – simply do not work for organizations as a whole.

We know what works and we practise what we preach. McKinsey & Company is one of the world's largest leadership factories. Internally, we invest over $500 million each year in building our own knowledge and leaders. We have seen more of our alumni go on to be chief executives of other companies than any other management consulting firm, and indeed any other firm: currently more than 450 McKinsey alumni are leading billion-dollar organizations, in addition to the many alumni who are high-ranking officials in public office. What we practise within, we apply to our professional engagements. We serve

88 of the Fortune 100 companies, half of which on human capital and leadership topics. McKinsey – a 'top five' global leadership development institution – conducts over 100 leadership development programmes globally per year.

We constantly review and measure what we do for clients; and we research widely. In this book, we have combined data from over 375,000 employees in 165 organizations, new research from over 500 executives, years of practical experience, as well as our own internal approach to developing our people, to crack the code for developing leadership at scale that *really* drives organizational health and performance. Our approach rests on the idea that leadership excellence matters profoundly, more than previously thought, in terms of both organizational health and performance. We offer a **systematic and fact-based approach towards developing leadership across the entire organization**, in order to really move the needle on performance. Leadership at scale is the answer.

This book is the product of hundreds of colleagues and friends from McKinsey and beyond, who have come together to integrate and advance our latest thinking on leadership to better serve our clients on the topic. We are proud of our insights, but also know that leadership is an unfolding science that continuously yields new data on how humans, organizations and society work.

We wrote this book for a broad, global audience of current and future leaders. It is relevant for anyone leading an organization, department, or team, as well as for individuals who want to improve their knowledge of leadership and understand how they can perform better on the job. It will help executives and current leaders take a critical look at their leadership development approach, understand how to better link leadership with the overall strategy, and drive performance through leadership effectiveness. For leadership development practitioners (for example, the chief human resources officer (CHRO) or head of learning and development), there is significant detail to provide a roadmap for implementation as well. For individuals and aspiring future leaders, the book provides a broad background on **the importance of leadership in organizations and what good leadership looks like**, what works and what does not in terms of becoming a better leader, and the specific skills that are needed to succeed in today's organizational environment.

The book is applicable to businesses, non-profit organizations and governments. We also see a benefit in using the book as a textbook on applied leadership courses at universities or business schools.

Our hope is that this book will, first of all, help you create higher performing, healthier and more sustainable organizations. Beyond that, we hope that the science and practice of great leadership will ripple throughout society itself. Some say that the world is in a 'crisis of leadership',[1] and we believe in advancing the pursuit of excellent leadership as a noble goal in and of itself.

## Why leadership matters

Effective leadership is important for organizations, and leadership development is often the top human capital priority of CEOs and a top three priority overall.[2] No surprises here. But how much does leadership really matter? We show that leadership excellence matters profoundly, more than perhaps previously thought, in terms of both organizational performance and health. First, leadership effectiveness matters *directly* to *performance*. It is measured – discretely – by a range of metrics relating to observed organizational practices, and is a predictor of future performance. **The better the leadership effectiveness, the better the organizational performance**. Companies with top-quartile leadership effectiveness have on average a 3.5 times greater total return to shareholders (TRS) than companies with bottom-quartile scores, over a three-year period.[3] Organizations that invest in developing leaders during significant transformations are 2.4 times more likely to hit their performance targets.[4] So, leadership effectiveness can be measured independently – and has a positive impact on – organizational performance.

Second, *health* (which we define as an organization's ability to align, execute and renew itself) sustains exceptional performance over time. (We define the components of organizational health in more detail in Chapter 1.) For over ten years, we have measured health through the medium of the Organizational Health Index (OHI), and have accumulated a database of over 5 million respondents across all geographies and sectors. We find that health is one of the best predictors of future performance. Health encompasses a number of highly desirable organizational qualities that include strategic alignment, talent retention, energy, purpose, commitment, innovation, direction, accountability and external orientation. We show that **leadership effectiveness is itself a key driver of organizational health**, and that it is extremely rare to achieve top-quartile health without top-quartile leadership effectiveness.

## The organizational leadership challenge

Leadership has been studied for thousands of years, and there has historically been a great admiration for heroes, and the great men and women in history. Over the last century numerous schools of leadership have emerged. Scholars talk about the 'romance of leadership',[5] and the larger-than-life quality that the term often assumes. It has been found, for example, that people have a tendency to explain poor company performance on uncontrollable or external events, while good performance is credited to the foresight and quality of leadership.[6]

Today, there is no lack of leadership advice on the market. There are hundreds of university (and corporate) courses on the topic alone. A plethora of leadership coaches and niche consultancies have emerged. A quick internet search on the topic yields several hundreds of thousands of articles, books and videos, many of them published within the past few years.

So it should be simple for organizations, right? Unfortunately, this is not the case. Organizations are drowning in leadership advice (and it's not helping them), and are smothered by theoretical jargon. We have found that there is a double gap, and it is a big one. We call it the *organizational leadership challenge.*

First, leadership is often the number one human capital priority for CEOs (and a top three priority overall), and our latest research showed that a third of organizations do not feel they have the quality and quantity of leaders to execute their strategies and performance objectives. An additional third of organizations state that they do not have the leadership capacity needed to take them through the next three to five years, beyond the near-term strategy and performance objectives.[7]

Second, depending on context, between 50 and 90 per cent of leadership development interventions are not successful, a finding consistent across multiple sources. For example, our recent survey of executives found that only 55 per cent believe their leadership development efforts meet and sustain the desired objectives. Indeed, when looking only at those who 'strongly agree', the proportion drops to around 11 per cent.[8] In another study, three-quarters of the nearly 1,500 senior managers at 50 organizations interviewed were dissatisfied with their organization's learning and development function.[9] And only 7 per cent of senior managers polled by a UK business school think that their companies develop global leaders effectively.[10] It is clear that there is a huge problem. (Another interesting discrepancy is that leaders overwhelmingly over-estimate their effectiveness at leading and the effectiveness of their leadership development efforts, compared to the views of those they lead.)

Organizations are certainly attending to the gap by spending money on leadership development. One study reported that in 2017, US companies spent, on average, $1,075 per learner compared with $814 per learner in 2016 on capability building.[11] A large portion of this spend is on leadership-related development (more than $50 billion by some accounts[12]), with a typical four-week executive leadership course costing $40–50,000 for tuition only ($2–2,500 per day).[13] This points towards billions of dollars wasted, with little or no impact.

These two conundrums go hand in hand and lead to a double whammy: organizations do not have the leadership capacity they need now or in the future, and they are not successful when trying to develop more and better leaders.[14] Perhaps your organization is one of them: you understand the need for effective leaders, and yet the development programmes you run are not delivering what you need of them.

Some claim that the leadership industry has failed.[15] While this is a strong assertion, we do agree that better leadership development is needed. There are three main reasons for why this is the case. First, the majority of the leadership literature targets individuals, focusing on how to increase the effectiveness of one or a few individuals. The literature often talks about the key behaviours that leaders need to display, for example: authenticity, decisiveness and strategic thinking. While improving the effectiveness of individual leaders is important, an incremental 'bottom-up' approach is not sufficient in today's fast-paced markets when entire organizations need to adapt quickly to new realities. To truly increase their leadership effectiveness fast, organizations must think at a much larger scale, and respond in a coordinated, system-level manner.

Second, leadership research often is 'one-size-fits-all', that is it typically focuses on leadership qualities that cut across a sample of high performing organizations. While such cross-cutting leadership qualities are undoubtedly important, they miss the important question of what was different between the organizations, but still effective. To increase leadership effectiveness at scale, organizations must understand and develop the leadership behaviours that matter to their specific contexts.

The third reason for the organizational gap in leadership effectiveness is that leadership is widely seen and mostly written about as a soft discipline, often with limited hard data. A lot of research is based on anecdotal evidence, or small sample sizes. The industry is highly fragmented with few performance standards (besides reputation), and anyone can in theory set up a leadership development practice overnight. What is needed is more science and more rigour.

## Meeting the organizational leadership challenge: leadership at scale

We know from our research and our experience what works. Our approach begins with enabling organizations to increase their leadership effectiveness *at scale* across the organization, to really drive performance. Scale implies touching a critical mass of leaders and employees to reach a tipping point – after which point the change becomes self-sustaining and the organization fundamentally changes how it leads.

The need to develop leaders at pace and scale has never been more acute, as we live in an era of accelerating change and uncertainty. In large organizations several hundreds if not thousands of leadership decisions are made each day. As an organization grows (or shrinks) it must change with the times, and rises and falls as a result of the quality of the decisions it makes.

There are multiple levers that executives can use to improve leadership effectiveness, including leadership development programmes, talent acquisition, promotions and dismissals, succession planning, and even organizational structure and process changes. We focus on leadership development interventions, as this creates meaningful near term changes in leadership effectiveness (besides, perhaps, drastic hiring and firing decisions). As such, **the focus of the book is on increasing leadership effectiveness of an organization as a whole, through leadership development interventions** (the focus is not on developing individual leaders, although this is of course part of a whole-system effort). We have set about this in three ways:

1 We offer clear insights based on proprietary research data from hundreds of leadership development practitioners and participants. Coupled with the latest neuroscience of adult learning, this illustrates the **key success factors of leadership development interventions.** We tested over 50 key actions to discover what really matters. We present our **four key principles related to:**

   i focusing on the critical shifts that drive disproportionate value

   ii engaging a critical mass of leaders through breadth, depth and pace

   iii architecting programmes for behavioural change using modern adult learning principles grounded in neuroscience

   iv integrating the programmes in the broader organizational system and measuring the impact of the programmes.

   However, there is no 'silver bullet' – organizations must do many things right in order to succeed. With this approach organizations can flip the odds of success of leadership programmes from an average of approximately 10–50 per cent to almost 100 per cent. Leadership development is very much a science, and **we show how to move from insight to action and really make the change happen at scale, across the whole organization.**

2 Related to the principle of focusing on the critical behaviours that really matter for a particular organization, we offer an updated review of situational leadership. Situational leadership is by no means new and has been recast or reinvented by many studies related to contingency or contextual leadership.[16] However, for first time, we have been able to set effective leadership in a precise organizational health context defined through data in a practical way. **Our latest research shows the specific**

**behaviours an organization should develop to increase its leadership effectiveness, given the organizational context.** In addition, we discuss the mindsets and skills organizations should foster, to best support the desired behaviours.

This latest research breaks new ground by isolating the characteristics that make for effective leadership under any circumstances, in terms of not only behaviours but also mindsets and skills. The research pinpoints those (behaviours, mindsets and skills) that are best suited to discrete stages of an organization's development. In effect, our research renders pointless the academic debates about whether exemplary leadership is situational or normative. The data clearly reveals that it can be both, in different contexts, and all the time *depending on the context*. We can also illuminate, with some certainty, those behaviours that consistently undercut the long-term health of an organization as well as those that hurt the organization in particular situations.

For example, we have found that organizations with bottom-quartile organizational health (the least healthy) should focus more on fact-based decision-making and solving problems effectively, while organizations with top-quartile health (the healthiest) should focus on motivating and bringing out the best in people. (We discuss organizational health and how to measure it in more depth in Chapters 1 and 2.) These insights can help organizations adopt the leadership behaviours fit for their specific context, to best drive performance.

3　We show how to create system-wide change. We set out the 4Ds (Diagnose, Design & Develop, Deliver, Drive Impact) – stages that characterize the leadership development programmes we run. At each stage we show how the programme works by linking to the broader organizational context, and by addressing the importance of talent acquisition, succession planning and performance management. Leadership development is only one of the many tools available to executives. Others, such as talent acquisition, succession planning and performance management are equally important, and often run in parallel with leadership development efforts, as part of a broader initiative.

**With this knowledge, you can take a comprehensive approach to increasing the leadership effectiveness in your organization.**

Some will say that the key success factors listed above are already known. The question then becomes why do organizations not adopt them? There could be three main reasons:

- There could be a short-term orientation and lack of sustained focus from CEOs and Boards. It is easier to focus on a few, high-profile and visible interventions that deliver immediate feedback (such as executive programmes) than to design and sustain an integrated programme over a period of time.
- CHROs/CLOs may need to focus on simplifying their message and ensuring an even stronger focus on linking leadership development and organizational results.
- Third, it may be that – as is with any organizational effort – bringing an idea to life is often much more difficult than generating the idea in the first place. Knowing what best practice leadership development looks like does not guarantee a successful implementation.

Interestingly, we also find that organizations typically have learning and development budgets available for leadership development – the money is there. The imperative is therefore to spend this budget more effectively (not necessarily to earmark new funds for leadership development) in order to generate a better return on the investment.

## *What does impact look like?*

When done correctly, leadership development interventions can have a profound impact. The impact is two-fold:

- increased leadership effectiveness improvements
- business impact across the organization.

In the short term, we often see profound shifts in the leadership effectiveness evaluations of participants, for example measured through a 360-degree feedback survey at the beginning and end of a programme. In addition, we also often see significant performance improvements stemming from the on-the-job 'breakthrough projects' conducted by the participants. For example, a global chemicals producer rolled out a global leadership transformation across 200+ plants, leading to an annual net income increase of more than $1.5 billion (from a market cap starting point of approximately $40 billion).

Another example is from an energy and construction company that rolled out a seven-month leadership programme for 30 senior leaders and 200 middle managers. The impact from projects above and beyond the normal work of participants resulted in an incremental revenue of more than $250 million (almost 3 per cent of revenue).

Longer term, successful organizations are able to sustain the shifts in leadership effectiveness by **expanding the initiative to all levels of the organization** and, through this, generate additional business impact. One large insurance company in Asia, for example, ran a six-month leadership development programme for 'pivotal leadership positions', consisting of four Vice Presidents, 33 Regional Managers, and 210 Office Heads. Positive behavioural changes were observed in 70 per cent of the participants. Further rollout across the organization led to a 25 per cent improvement in core business KPIs, and also helped turn around 30 office branches that were previously not meeting their performance targets. Common for all the companies was an underlying increase in organizational leadership effectiveness. We include case studies throughout the book to help illustrate the concepts, both short snippets as well as longer, more in-depth examples.

## Structure of this book

This book has three parts:

- **Part 1 (Chapters 1–6):** we define leadership and the mindsets and behaviours required for effective leadership at scale for a given context; and we discuss our leadership development philosophy and the guiding principles of our approach.
- **Part 2 (Chapters 7–12):** we outline our approach in more detail with case examples and an extended fictional case (based on our collective experience) of CEO Carolyn

Randolph and her company. We felt this was the best way to show how a leadership development programme looks from the outside and feel from the inside.

- **Part 3 (Chapters 13–14):** we look at some of the questions that might arise from our approach to whole-system development.

The research and methodology supporting our views can be found in the Appendices. An outline of the book is provided below.

## PART 1: LEADERSHIP DEFINED

### CHAPTER 1: THE FOUNDATIONS: CONTEXT, EXPERIENCE AND MINDSET

Leadership has been studied for thousands of years, and a multitude of definitions and schools exist. After studying, practising, and developing leadership for many years, we define leadership in terms of a set of observable behaviours, which are affected by the context, skills and mindset of the leader. We know what makes a great individual leader and great leadership, and focus on both the organizational context and the individual context to produce insights on *leadership at scale*.

### CHAPTER 2: THE LEADERSHIP AT SCALE DIAMOND

We discuss our different pillars of leadership knowledge, including our latest research, and introduce our four core principles of leadership development, which jointly constitute the leadership at scale diamond.

### CHAPTER 3: CORE PRINCIPLE 1: FOCUS ON THE CRITICAL SHIFTS

Different organizational contexts present different leadership challenges. We review different lenses to identify the leadership behaviours that will be most effective, including the primary lens of organizational health. Armed with our latest research with over 375,000 data points, we show the specific leadership behaviours that can help an organization transition to higher stages of health, depending on the health quartile that the organization is in.

## CHAPTER 4: CORE PRINCIPLE 2: ENGAGE THE ORGANIZATION

Too often, leadership development efforts are sporadic and episodic. We discuss the importance of developing a critical mass of leaders through sufficient breadth (who must be reached), depth (how intensely must they be reached) and pace (how quickly should interventions be rolled out).

## CHAPTER 5: CORE PRINCIPLE 3: ARCHITECT PROGRAMMES FOR BEHAVIOURAL CHANGE

Programmes must be designed not just for knowledge acquisition or skill building, but to maximize behavioural change on the job. This requires more than classroom learning which, for leadership development purposes, is well and truly dead. We present the seven adult learning principles based on neuroscience that organizations should adopt in leadership development journeys.

## CHAPTER 6: CORE PRINCIPLE 4: INTEGRATE AND MEASURE

Capability building only forms 25 per cent of the required effort to make leadership at scale succeed. Successful programmes involve the whole organization. Measurement of these programmes is essential. We discuss communication, role-modelling, measurement and system reinforcement to sustainably shift organizational ways of working.

# PART 2: OUR APPROACH IN PRACTICE

## CHAPTER 7: A ROADMAP FOR SUCCESSFUL LEADERSHIP DEVELOPMENT

There are many ways to implement a leadership development intervention – what is key is that the four principles outlined are adhered to. We outline our typical approach in practice, framed around four main steps: Diagnose, Design & Develop, Deliver, Drive Impact. For each stage, we outline the typical outputs and how to get there.

## Chapter 8: Meet Carolyn Randolph

Here we introduce our fictional story of New Classic Look clothing (NCL), which is facing a leadership crisis. The organization embarks on a leadership development journey across the organization, in order to improve organizational health and reach its performance objectives.

## Chapter 9: Setting the leadership aspiration

Too many leadership development interventions start with a bottom-up 'needs analysis', and completely miss the link to strategy. We show here how to translate your strategy into required leadership qualities and capabilities through a leadership model, and define the aspired business outcomes as a result of the intervention. Thereafter comes assessing the current leadership strengths and gaps, as well as the root causes, which is a critical prerequisite prior to designing the programme. At the individual level, this includes understanding the mindsets that account for why leaders behave the way they do today, and how the mindsets and behaviours need to change in the future, based on the leadership model ('from–to' shift).

## Chapter 10: Designing the roadmap

Our research shows that designing a successful leadership development intervention requires multiple sources of input, including 'end-users', external best practices and design expertise. In addition, it is critical to design the 'learning transfer' up front, that is the process of putting learning to work in a way that improves performance.

## Chapter 11: Delivering the Leadership Peak Programme

Neuroscience informs the latest thinking on how to help adults learn and change their behaviour. In addition, technology is playing a huge role in redefining the delivery of programmes, and best practices include gamification, on-demand learning and daily 'triggers' to participants.

## Chapter 12: Driving impact

More than a quarter of organizations do not measure the return on leadership development. We show how to measure return on investment (ROI) with the same rigour as other initiatives across three dimensions: participant assessment, behavioural change and business performance. In addition, it is critical to adapt formal HR systems to reinforce the leadership model (for example, performance evaluation, compensation, succession planning) and to use 'graduates' to build future leaders and embed desired leadership expectations further down the hierarchy.

# PART 3: FREQUENTLY ASKED QUESTIONS

## Chapter 13: FAQs on leadership development

Questions include the return on investment, how leadership development differs across organizational levels and industries, and the importance of recruiting.

## Chapter 14: FAQs on trends relevant to leadership

Questions include defining the most critical leadership behaviours in the future, how millennials differ (and what to do about it), whether men and women lead differently and how technology is changing leadership development.

# APPENDICES

These include supporting material for our situational leadership research, an elaboration of the skills and mindsets that can underpin each leadership behaviour, and details on how to boost individual learning and performance.

We hope this book is an insightful and enjoyable read and contributes to enhanced leadership effectiveness and performance in your organization.

# PART I
# Leadership defined

# I

# The foundations: context, skills and mindsets

*Andrew St George, Claudio Feser, Michael Rennie, Nicolai Chen Nielsen*

Why leadership matters | Leadership is manifold, and so is leadership theory: a short review | Summary

'Anyone can hold the helm when the seas are calm', said Publilius Syrus over 2,000 years ago. In organizational life today, there are few calm seas, few periods without turmoil. A good captain has the capacity to apply his or her refined judgement in uncertain situations and to encourage others to follow; then to learn from the experience and be ready for the next storm. Leadership matters, and organizations must find and develop that quality in their people to outlast and overcome those stormy seas.

This chapter introduces the foundations of our thinking on leadership and leadership development. First, we illustrate the link between leadership effectiveness and organizational health and performance. Second, we give a brief history of leadership development theories and philosophies. Third, we present our definition of leadership and its implications for organizations and leadership development.

## Why leadership matters

We know from our research and our practice that **the best-performing organizations transcend others in terms of their leadership**. At its best, great leadership can achieve extraordinary results. And at its worst, poor leadership can derail teams, organizations and even nations. The evidence for this has long been intuitive, and visible to the discerning observer: it is possible to feel within minutes of visiting an organization whether it is ill or well (and even ill- or well-led).

But this feeling is of little use unless there is data to support the insight and turn it into value-adding and actionable advice.

Anecdotally, there are a multitude of reasons why leadership matters: more clarity about direction, better plans, faster execution, better talent development and so on. These elements fall broadly into both organizational performance and organizational health. When reviewing the importance of leadership, it is therefore important to address both concepts. We will review each in turn.

## Leadership drives performance

**Leadership effectiveness has a strong correlation with performance directly.** Companies with top-quartile leadership outcomes on the McKinsey Organizational Health Index (there will be more on the OHI in the next chapter) have 3.5 times greater average total return to shareholders (TRS) than companies with bottom-quartile leadership outcomes, over a three-year period. When we looked at 14 individual leadership behaviours (more on the specific behaviours in the next chapter), we found that companies with top-quartile results for the leadership behaviour scores have between 1.4 and 7.2 times greater average TRS than companies with bottom-quartile scores, depending on the behaviour being looked at. For example, when looking at the ability of organizations to problem-solve effectively (one of the leadership behaviours we tested), companies in the top quartile on problem solving have a 6.6 times greater average TRS than companies in the bottom quartile on that behaviour.[1]

Other studies back up these results: organizations performing in the top quartile on overall leadership effectiveness (leadership outcome) outperform bottom-quartile companies by nearly 2 times on EBITDA (earnings before interest, tax, depreciation and amortization).[2] Organizations that invest in developing leaders during significant transformations are 2.4 times more likely to hit their performance targets.[3] And leaders who have developed a core of self-mastery feel 4 times as prepared to lead amidst change and are 20 times more likely to be satisfied with their leadership performance.[4]

## Leadership matters to health

**Leadership matters to organizational health.** Organizational health is the ability of an organization to align, execute and renew itself to sustain

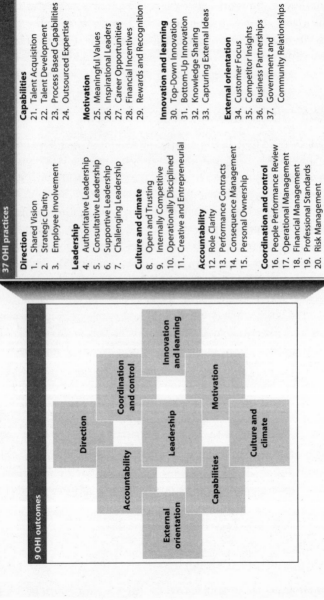

**9 OHI outcomes**

**37 OHI practices**

**Direction**
1. Shared Vision
2. Strategic Clarity
3. Employee Involvement

**Leadership**
4. Authoritative Leadership
5. Consultative Leadership
6. Supportive Leadership
7. Challenging Leadership

**Culture and climate**
8. Open and Trusting
9. Internally Competitive
10. Operationally Disciplined
11. Creative and Entrepreneurial

**Accountability**
12. Role Clarity
13. Performance Contracts
14. Consequence Management
15. Personal Ownership

**Coordination and control**
16. People Performance Review
17. Operational Management
18. Financial Management
19. Professional Standards
20. Risk Management

**Capabilities**
21. Talent Acquisition
22. Talent Development
23. Process Based Capabilities
24. Outsourced Expertise

**Motivation**
25. Meaningful Values
26. Inspirational Leaders
27. Career Opportunities
28. Financial Incentives
29. Rewards and Recognition

**Innovation and learning**
30. Top-Down Innovation
31. Bottom-Up Innovation
32. Knowledge Sharing
33. Capturing External Ideas

**External orientation**
34. Customer Focus
35. Competitor Insights
36. Business Partnerships
37. Government and Community Relationships

FIGURE 1.1 Organizational health is defined through nine outcomes, driven by 37 management practices

exceptional performance over time. Organizations with poor health typically face stark challenges, for example: lack of direction, customer losses, low employee morale, loss of talent and lack of innovation. On the other side, organizations with great health are typically performing extremely well, leading in their industry, gaining share in the market, attracting great talent and working with engaged, motivated employees.

At McKinsey & Company we measure organizational health with the Organizational Health Index (OHI), a metric based on nine outcomes (which measure perceptions of effectiveness), and 37 management practices (which measure frequency of each practice) (See Figure 1.1).

For more than fifteen years, we have compiled over 1 billion data points from more than 5 million respondents across more than 1,700 organizations. These organizations are spread out globally in over 90 countries, with all regions almost equally represented. Our research in the past decade shows that the OHI score of an organization is a strong predictor of shareholder returns. Organizations with high OHI scores tend to produce high levels of shareholder returns in the three years subsequent to the measurement of the OHI score.

The effectiveness of leaders in an organization strongly correlates with the OHI score of that organization. The $R^2$ is 0.78, meaning that the leadership outcome explains almost 80 per cent of the variance in the overall health scores – see Figure 1.2.

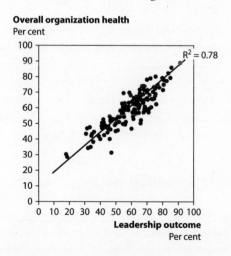

FIGURE 1.2 Overall organizational health

There is a significant difference between the likelihood that companies with a specific leadership level have top-quartile overall health: it is virtually impossible to have top-quartile health if leadership effectiveness is in the fourth quartile or third quartile, while only 27 per cent of companies with second-quartile leadership effectiveness have top-quartile health. This number jumps to 65 per cent for top-quartile companies in terms of leadership for exceeding the 25 per cent proportion of top-quartile health companies, conferring a 240 per cent advantage (see Figure 1.3). Leadership is thus clearly a key component of organizational health.

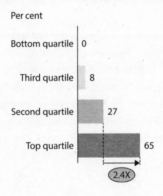

Per cent

| Bottom quartile | 0 |
| Third quartile | 8 |
| Second quartile | 27 |
| Top quartile | 65 |

2.4X

FIGURE 1.3 Likelihood that companies with specified leadership level have top-quartile overall health

Hence we have seen that **leadership effectiveness is a clear driver of overall organizational performance and health**. So, what leadership behaviours are the best, under what circumstances, and how can organizations develop these behaviours at scale? This is the subject of the following chapters. Before we address these questions, it is important to understand the different leadership theories that exist, as well as how we define leadership and the implications this definition has on leadership development.

## *Leadership is manifold and so is leadership theory: a short review*

What makes a good leader? Ask any five experts what makes a good leader, and chances are you will get six answers: Aspiration. Inspiration. Imagination. Creativity. Authenticity. Integrity. Perhaps anything goes. It's now time for a reality check. There's good news, and there's bad. The bad news: we don't have a one-word answer. The good news: we have found the stepping-stones that empower organizations to develop leadership that is more effective, right across the organization.

Leadership has been a subject of investigation since the dawn of democracy in ancient Greece. Some 2,500 years ago, Plato's *Republic* sparked a furious debate among the citizens of Athens. His rigorous rules for the selection and education of the guardians of the ideal state were as controversial then as they are today. Overnight, leadership had become the talk of the town.

Today, colleges and universities in the US alone offer hundreds of degree programmes in leadership. Amazon lists more than 60,000 book results on the topic.[5] In 2016 the word 'leadership' was mentioned in US news headlines more than 25,000 times,[6] up from just a few hundred in the 1990s. Once again, leadership is the talk of the town.

In an effort to bring some measure of order to this rich discussion, we have identified five principal schools of leadership. While this break-down is obviously a simplification, we believe it is an instructive one.

- **Traits-based leadership.** According to this theory, leaders are born, not made. Proponents of innate leadership believe that immutable personality traits, such as intelligence or character, determine an individual's leadership effectiveness and performance. One of the more popular versions of this school of thought is the 'Great Man Theory', developed by the Scottish scholar Thomas Carlyle in the Victorian era. Carlyle was convinced that the history of the world was 'the biography of great men' (he does not include women). It may well be that some individuals are more inclined to lead (and lead well) than others; but the limitation of this theory lies in its determinism: unless you are born a great leader, you never will become one.

- **Behavioural leadership.** This theory is based on the assumption that leadership is action rather than character. Leaders become leaders not by birth, but by the power of the behaviour they display. Rooted in nineteenth century behavioural psychology, this theory postulates that effective leadership is defined by a set of ideal behaviours. For instance, a strong leader may be someone who develops a compelling vision, acts courageously and takes decisions quickly. The drawback of this theory is its assumption that the same set of behaviours is optimal in all circumstances. But in a concrete business situation, some abstractly defined 'ideal behaviour', whatever it may be, could prove irrelevant or even detrimental to the leader's intent. It is hard to refute the idea that all leadership involves interaction and exchange between people, and therefore that all leadership is about behaviours; however, there is no one-size-fits all model, and behaviours have to be apt and appropriate in order to be effective.

- **Situational leadership**. According to this theory, great leadership arises only in response to specific situations. Its followers are convinced that different real-life situations call for different traits or behaviours in a leader; they deny that leadership is based on any single optimal psychographic profile or set of ideal behaviours. This theory draws on empirical research suggesting that someone who is a leader in one situation might not necessarily fill this role in others. Situational theories of leadership enjoy great popularity in practice. Their main drawback is their assumption that leaders can adjust their style according to the situation – that when circumstances or teams change, leaders can easily change their behaviours accordingly. In reality, even the finest leaders may have a hard time adapting to a changing environment or new types of challenges.[7]

- **Functional leadership**. This theory construes leadership as a combination of specific skills that help groups of individuals become effective as a team. These skills enable the leader to perform essential functions, such as monitoring, organizing, coaching, motivating and intervening. Proponents of functional leadership consider both behavioural and situational factors, suggesting that leaders should devise their courses of action in light of the specific requirements of a given organizational unit. The limitation of this theory is twofold. First, many of its opponents regard it as overly simplistic, since it reduces leadership to a technique or set of techniques. Secondly, real-life leaders often find it difficult to match the right approach to the right needs, to inflect their style to suit the needs of different groups, or both. In this respect, functional leadership theories resemble situational leadership theories.[8]

- **Psychological leadership.** This type of theory recognizes the fact that the path to great leadership is riddled with obstacles, and that many leaders feel they are less effective than they believe they could and should be. In response, the proponents of psychological leadership argue that leaders must accomplish self-mastery by exploring the driving forces of ineffective leadership behaviour and tackling their inner resistance to change. Critics of psychological leadership theory note that it relies on inference and interpretation rather than observation and measurement, and that it may be dangerous in the wrong hands. Because it uses introspection and self-examination, psychological leadership development requires practitioners with deep psychological expertise and experience.

In addition to these schools where ideas on leadership have coalesced, there has been a substantial body of work from numerous different angles. There is a great deal of literature from individual (often successful) leaders, who share their experiences. There are sector-based analyses – for example from the military – as well as regional studies that dive into cultural differences. More recently, gender based studies have emerged, which explore the differences and similarities between women and men.

All these theories have limitations as they try to explain leadership through a single lens, be it character, behaviour or situation. Therefore modern leadership models take several angles to address the practical definition of leadership. For example, the 'Be + Know + Do' model of leadership[9] of the US Army is essentially interdisciplinary in that it focuses on character and traits (Be), skills (Know), and behaviours and action (Do), and draws on a clear sense of behaviours in context. The 'Be + Know + Do' model derives from several of the schools (innate, behavioural, situational). The point here is that **no one model or theory can carry the whole field.**

While we believe in the value of Occam's Razor – the principle that the simplest scientific explanation is usually the best – we also find that each of these schools (while adding an important angle) falls short of the manifold reality of organizational leadership we encounter in our work. We also take account of the individual variance we find. We serve many of the world's most distinguished leaders, and we find that no two are alike. Some are introverts, others extroverts. Some lead by doing; some are great at bringing out the best in others. Some thrive on detail, others on the big picture. Yet these wildly different individuals are all great leaders in their respective fields. In real life, all kinds of people excel and succeed as leaders.

Any theory should explain the past and help predict the future: such a thing is unlikely with a one-dimensional and static view of leadership. Instead, **we take a view that is expressed through research, informed by real work engagements and the results we have achieved internally as well as with clients**. No one answer fits all occasions, and equally no model is either robust or flexible enough to compass the many variables at work. The appeal of a 'Both/And' approach is more attractive as leadership challenges become more complex.

Bear in mind that we have at all times an organizational perspective: we think in terms of leadership within and across an organization, not solely of individual leadership. To increase the leadership effectiveness of an organization as a whole, it is imperative that **executives think at an organizational, system-wide level**, and the approach one takes to do this differs markedly from that of increasing the effectiveness of individual leaders.

Our definition of organizational leadership builds on several schools of thought and is pragmatic. We take inspiration from multiple schools and advocate an approach that is comprehensive and practical. In fact, we do not propose a new model of leadership. Rather, we build on existing thinking. Our definition of organizational leadership is thus as follows:

> Leadership is a set of behaviours that in a given context align an organization, foster execution and ensure organizational renewal. These behaviours are enabled by relevant skills and mindsets.

Our definition draws on all the schools of leadership thinking: behavioural (behaviours and skills), situational (in a given context), functional (aligning, fostering execution and renewing), and traits based and psychological (mindsets). It builds on existing work in the leadership literature. Gary Yukl, for example, categorizes individual leaders as task-oriented, relationship-oriented, change-oriented, and external, and stresses the situational variables alongside the importance of behavioural flexibility, i.e. the importance of adapting one's leadership behaviours to certain situations. This is in a long tradition of situational leadership thinking, exemplified in the work of Ken Blanchard or John Adair that emerges from military practice[10] yet is explored further through our research and practice on what really works 'in the field'. Figure 1.4 summarizes our model of leadership, incorporating the four key elements of context, behaviours, skills and mindsets.

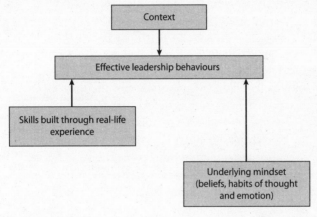

FIGURE 1.4 Four key elements of leadership

We believe leadership comes alive in the behaviours that are used, felt and observed across an organization. These seen and felt behaviours are where we have placed our main research effort (beginning with 24 leadership behaviours in the next chapter). Our research shows that the context defines which behaviours are most desired and most effective. We take these observed behaviours as our units of analysis, and the organization's health (and the industry and economy in which it operates) as the primary context in which that behaviour is expressed. Our emphasis is on improving leadership effectiveness at an organizational level to help achieve organizational performance goals. Broadly, there are four premises in our view of organizational leadership.

# 1 Leaders align, execute and renew

**Leadership is expressed in action.** For us, this takes the form of *alignment*, *execution* and *renewal*. Leaders make decisions about people and direction (we call this *alignment*); they see that their intent is carried out (we call this *execution*), and they think about the next evolution of activity (we call this *renewal*). This cycle of alignment, execution and renewal may take place over the short term (in the event of a crisis) or the long term (in the event of a shift of circumstance or priority).

All leadership therefore seek to achieve these three things in concert. There are many ways to express this triad – alignment might well include visioning and inspiring people; execution might well involve organizing and measuring performance; and renewal might well entail a leadership approach that values creativity, innovation, adaptation, learning and development.

We want to highlight the importance of the third element *renewal*, which is represented in our definition by the last three words, the *constantly changing environment*. Organizational contexts have and will always be ever changing, and a key element of leadership is thus to display resilience and agility in order to continue to thrive.[11] We have previously shown that organizations and teams must demonstrate all three dimensions by emphasizing different elements of organizational health (see Figure 1.5), and it is only natural that leaders help bring these outcomes about.

# 2 All leadership takes place within a context

Our definition pays close attention to how **leadership behaviours differ according to the specific context.** This comes to bear in two ways:

1 The context of each organization differs in terms of industry, maturity, geography, general business performance, and so on. Each context, at an organizational level, thus requires different behaviours.

2 Organizational strategies typically emanate from the top down to the rest of the organization, often through explicit Key Performance Indicators (KPIs) and clearly defined boundaries. Hence the common goal around which to align will vary

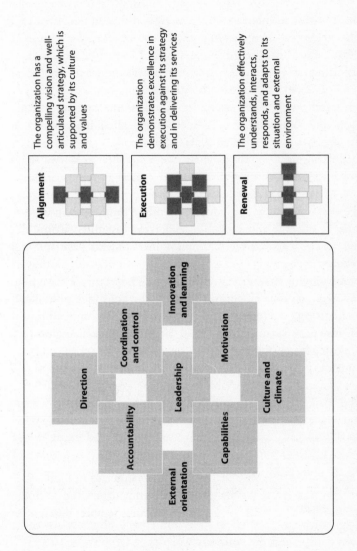

**Alignment**

The organization has a compelling vision and well-articulated strategy, which is supported by its culture and values

**Execution**

The organization demonstrates excellence in execution against its strategy and in delivering its services

**Renewal**

The organization effectively understands, interacts, responds, and adapts to its situation and external environment

Direction

Coordination and control

Innovation and learning

Accountability

Leadership

Motivation

External orientation

Capabilities

Culture and climate

FIGURE 1.5  Alignment, execution and renewal as measured by organizational health outcomes

greatly from one department to the next, meaning that the specific contexts *within* an organization have a bearing on the most relevant behaviours to display.

Would you trust a physician who prescribes the same treatment to all patients, regardless of their symptoms? Probably not. We strongly believe that there is no such thing as standard leadership behaviour that works irrespective of contextual factors, such as corporate strategy or the level of hierarchy of a given position.

Our research with Egon Zehnder International, an executive search firm, illustrates this point. By matching Egon Zehnder's management appraisals of more than 5,500 senior leaders with McKinsey's 'Granularity of Growth' database, we were able to isolate the impact of leadership on growth in terms of total return to shareholders. We have found that leadership quality matters. Executives at top-performing companies display stronger leadership profiles than those at other companies. But, more importantly, we found that different contexts require different combinations of leadership competencies.[12]

Let's take growth strategies as an example. Thought and business leadership help commercial companies make the bold moves that let them excel at mergers and acquisitions; for example, the strongest predictor of growth through M&A turned out to be market insight. In contrast, people leadership and organizational savvy are more conducive to organic growth, which involves succeeding through superior execution of a given strategy. Achieving organic growth takes leaders who excel at developing organizational capability and display team leadership. These insights are in line with the work of Ralph Stogdill, a pioneer of situational leadership theory. In his influential review *Personal Factors Associated with Leadership* he found that few, if any, leadership skills are universally applicable.[13] Hence the contextual awareness and the ability of a leader to adapt his or her behaviours appropriately is critical for successful leadership.

Take the chief executive of an American energy utility. When the market was deregulated, the company was plunged into the most serious financial crisis of its history. The CEO helped transform the organization from a denizen of the regulated age into a competitive player in a liberalized global market. He is convinced that leadership should be a function of economic reality: 'You have to put things in the context of a business model. Who are your real customers? Can you grow the business? What kind of partner do you need to make it work? What do you really do? And where should that work be done?'[14] The executive in question has since been named 'one of the best-performing CEOs in the world' by Harvard Business Review.

Our experience shows that highly successful executives typically think about a range of dimensions to determine the relevant context for effective leadership in a given case, for example:

- **Landscape**: what are the characteristics of the industry and competitive arena?
- **Mandate**: who are the stakeholders, and what do they expect?
- **Strategy**: what is the company, or business unit, trying to achieve?
- **Organization**: what are the structures, processes, systems and culture like?
- **Team**: what is the team like in terms of skill, will and psychological makeup?

## 3 Skills built through real-life experience enable effective leadership behaviours

Would you get on a plane piloted by an aviation expert who has logged zero flying hours? Would you buy tickets to the concert of a band that has never actually played together? We would not. Of course, you can learn to fly a plane in a simulator. You can learn to play the guitar by watching virtual tutorials. All this is true – up to a point. Sooner or later, you have to take your plane off the ground, get up on stage with the band.

The ability to display effective leadership behaviours in a given situation depends on having the right *skills* (and experience, which we count as an accumulation of skill). Leadership skills are the leadership lessons and wisdom that individuals have accumulated through formal training and on the job learning. Skills cannot be developed solely by reading about them; and learning can only be accelerated to a certain extent. As Henry Mintzberg said, 'Leadership, like swimming, cannot be learned by reading about it'.[15] It is undoubtedly important to receive the right training and best practises as a foundation for any skill-building effort. However, successful leaders are sure to hone their new skills in the context of actual business assignments – and are seen doing it.

In any given situation, a leader either has the right skills or does not, in which case the organization will have to take a risk and support the individual in developing these skills. In a low-risk situation, such as restructuring a small department, this may not be an issue at all, but in a high-risk situation, such as the acquisition and integration of a major competitor, it could be favourable to have individuals who have prior experience and skills learned from a similar initiative. Alternatives to developing leaders in their place could be to transfer leaders from within the organization, or to hire them from the outside, and then either on a permanent or temporary basis.

Leaders define goals, attract talent, assign responsibility, monitor target achievement and make decisions. In this respect, we follow the behavioural school: leadership is something you do.[16] The important thing is that you do it, rather than just pretend to. Even after very basic training sessions, adults typically retain just 10 per cent of what they hear in classroom lectures, versus nearly two-thirds of what they learn by doing (more on this in Chapter 5). Furthermore, burgeoning leaders, no matter how talented, often struggle to transfer even their most powerful workshop experiences into changed behaviour on the front line.

Over the course of almost a decade, we have accompanied dozens of senior leaders who made transformational change happen in a wide range of national cultures, industries and organizations. They have restructured international conglomerates, turned around companies on the brink of bankruptcy, steered former monopolies through deregulation, and helped reinvent entire national economies. Despite the diversity of their assignments and the lessons they learned along the way, they all agree on one thing: these lessons could only be learned in real life. There is no exercise, no handbook, and no training programme that will prepare you for the real thing. As Marvin Bower, McKinsey's Managing Director from 1950 to 1967, put it: 'The only training for being a CEO, is being a CEO.'

In short, **great leaders' skills are forged on-the-job,** and the experience and skills that leaders have accumulated help them display more effective leadership behaviours.

## 4 Leaders must develop the right mindsets based on introspection and self-awareness

Leaders are often required to adapt their behaviour to a new assignment, expand their knowledge to make sense of a change in context, or enhance their skill set as they take a new role. But in some cases, a more fundamental kind of development is called for. Think of an executive who moves into a board-level position, takes on an assignment in an entirely new corporate culture, or assumes a position of leadership in a situation of extreme uncertainty. According to our research, those who are most satisfied with their performance as leaders are those who excel at knowing and mastering themselves. They have the ability to regulate their own energy, tap into their personal sources of meaning and strength, overcome fears and connect with others.[17]

These and similar capabilities are unlike the kinds of skills learnt from a textbook. Collectively, they constitute what we think of as the hidden layer of leadership. This line of thought is inspired by psychological theories of leadership.[18] While behaviour can be observed and knowledge can be communicated, psychology remains hidden beneath the surface. We use the metaphor of an iceberg; behaviours are 'above the water' and constitute only 20 per cent of what there really is. Below the water lie mindsets and beliefs, values, and needs and fears. See Figure 1.6. The reason we focus on mindsets is because **mindsets ultimately drive behaviours**. Hence, in the same way that ensuring leaders have the right experiences and skills for a given context, it is critical to understand and address what lies beneath the waterline in order to bring out the desired leadership behaviours.

There is ample literature that illustrate the power of mindsets and underlying needs and fears, including Kegan and Lahey's *Immunity to Change*, Mitroff and Linstone's *The Unbounded Mind*, Senge's *The Fifth Discipline*, Dweck's *Mindset: The New Psychology of Success*, Russo and Schoemaker's *Decision Traps and Winning Decisions*, and Gallwey's pioneering work in *The Inner Game*.[19] In addition, recent breakthroughs in neuroscience are explaining, by taking into account neuroplasticity (the brain's ability to reorganize itself by forming new neural connections throughout life – we will review this in more depth in

Chapter 5), how adults learn, the role our emotions play, and how we form new habits.

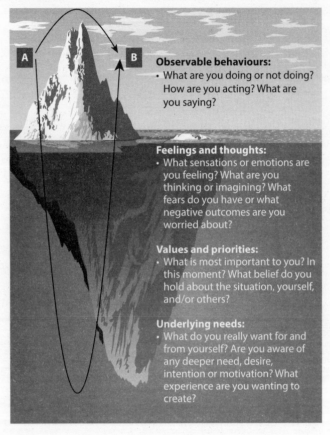

**Observable behaviours:**
• What are you doing or not doing? How are you acting? What are you saying?

**Feelings and thoughts:**
• What sensations or emotions are you feeling? What are you thinking or imagining? What fears do you have or what negative outcomes are you worried about?

**Values and priorities:**
• What is most important to you? In this moment? What belief do you hold about the situation, yourself, and/or others?

**Underlying needs:**
• What do you really want for and from yourself? Are you aware of any deeper need, desire, intention or motivation? What experience are you wanting to create?

FIGURE 1.6 Mindsets drive behaviours

Variations of 'iceberg coaching' are common among executive coaches and some psychologists. The main idea is to identify the set of strongly held core beliefs that drive the behaviours above the water-line. Often, these core beliefs are unconscious for the individual, and it is only through careful questioning and reflection that they emerge. These core beliefs are, in turn, driven by a set of underlying needs and fears. For example, many young employees may not automatically ask their leaders for help if stuck on a problem. Indeed, some may go out of their way to *hide* the fact that they are stuck, instead spending many hours late in the evening trying to crack it themselves. They may have a limiting belief that *asking for help is seen as a sign of weakness*. If we dig a little deeper, we may often find an underlying belief that *asking for help will lead to a poor performance rating*, triggered by fear of a poor evaluation. This, in turn, could be triggered by a fear of failure, perhaps due to pressure at home, from peers, or from the employee himself or herself. (The iceberg model is a simplified version of a psychological model of elements that trigger behaviour. In reality, there are other elements to consider as well [personality traits, motivation, etc.])

Although some of these elements below the waterline are formed early in life and may be hard to change, we find that awareness alone often goes a long way toward increasing leadership effectiveness. Awareness helps us understand the unconscious roots of our behaviour, making them accessible to conscious reflection and careful evolution. Our research on organizational health shows that **making one's mindset the subject of conscious scrutiny is an indispensable prerequisite of leadership effectiveness.** Only about a third of over 2,500 executives in our sample said that their organization's transformations explicitly assessed the mindsets that would need to change to reach their goals. Those that did so were 4 times more likely to be successful.[20]

Take as an example a professional-services business that wanted senior leaders to initiate more provocative and meaningful discussions with the firm's senior clients. Once the trainers looked below the surface, they discovered that these leaders, though highly successful in their fields, were instinctively uncomfortable and lacking in confidence when conversations moved beyond their narrow functional expertise. As soon as the leaders realized this, and went deeper to understand why, they were able to commit themselves to concrete steps that helped push them to change.

A major European industrial company, meanwhile, initially met strong resistance after launching an initiative to delegate and decentralize responsibility for capital expenditures and resource allocation to the plant level. Once the issues were put on the table, it became clear that the business-unit leaders were genuinely concerned that the new policy would add to the already severe pressures they faced, that they did not trust their subordinates, and that they resented the idea of relinquishing control. Only when they were convinced that the new approach would actually save time and serve as a learning opportunity for more junior managers – and when more open-minded colleagues and mentors helped challenge the 'heroic' leadership model – did the original barriers start to come down and decentralization start to be implemented.

One would think that, given the pertinence of this, leaders would have ample tools and training to help them understand their own and others' mindsets in order to identify and shift limiting beliefs. Sadly, we find that this is not the case. There is still much work to be done in organizations to help leaders shift behaviours in themselves and in others by using tools such as iceberg coaching and self-reflection. Identifying some of the deepest, 'below the surface' thoughts, feelings, assumptions and beliefs is too often shirked in development programmes.

This is an important point for context-specific leadership. Organizations that wish to foster certain leadership behaviours must proactively foster the underlying mindsets most conducive to carrying out those behaviours. This starts by identifying the aspired mindsets. Thereafter organizations must assess current mindsets in the organization, draw a link to the desired mindsets (what we call the 'from–to' shifts) and design the interventions to create the shift. We will discuss our approach in more detail in Part 2 of the book.

From the perspective of leadership development, self-knowledge is essential in several ways. First, it is a source of insight: exploring our character or psychological makeup helps us understand what we thrive on and what we value. Secondly, it is a source of strength: a clear sense of how we are wired helps us apply our unique traits and talents to the tasks we face. Thirdly, it is a source of social competence: self-awareness lets us realize how we differ from other people, helps us see others for who they really are, and lays the foundation for collaboration.

While there may not be any particular type of personality predestined for leadership, we find that great leaders are often acutely aware of their unique traits and talents, and of how they can use these to everyone's advantage. The ability of a leader to understand his or her underlying mindsets, focus on strengths and shift limiting beliefs is thus a core enabler of effective leadership behaviours. Great individual leaders are willing to confront the inner barriers that sometimes keep them from realizing their full leadership potential. This is why it is better to create awareness rather than prescribe behaviour, and help leaders build on their strengths – rather than compensate their weaknesses, in the context of their work. **We firmly believe that a leader's most powerful tool is neither a formula nor a checklist, but an open mind.**

The focus on behaviours, skills and mindsets is another way of casting the relationship between the three elements in 'Be + Know + Do' schools of leadership thinking.[21] The skills and mindsets are vital here, because they bridge the gap between knowing and doing. They are not necessarily natural to the workplace. They need to be learned, practised and mastered.

In addition, it is important to note another implication of our definition: that **leadership is relevant at all levels of the organization**. We do not discriminate in terms of hierarchy of leaders, managers, supervisors and front-line employees. At every level of the organization there are leadership opportunities and prerequisites to succeed. For the organization as a whole, leadership at all levels is thus not only relevant but critical in driving performance. In a typical organization, the leadership/executive team makes only a fraction of the leadership decisions on a daily basis, and it is the cumulative sum of better leadership at all levels that really moves performance.

No organization can survive with inadequate leadership. Leadership is a key enabler of financial and non-financial organizational performance. It is a complex topic, however, and is often romanticized. It appears to have many truths, depending on where you look, and you would be hard pressed to find someone who does not have an opinion about the topic.

## Summary

This chapter has laid the foundations for us to explore what constitutes effective leadership, and what organizations can do to improve leadership development. We have reviewed the history of leadership and looked at five different schools of thought. We find that leadership development does not fall into one or two categories but is very much an 'and'. By combining the different theories with proprietary research, our own leadership experiences developing consultants, and hundreds of client engagements, we have defined a unique perspective on leadership (and a definition) that is pragmatic – allowing us to understand what really drives leadership effectiveness at an individual and an organizational level.

In sum, our perspective on leadership posits three things. First, effective leadership at an organizational level is about behaviours that ensure alignment, execution and renewal. Second, the specific behaviours required are defined by the organizational context. Third, these behaviours are enabled by the right skills and the right mindsets. Organizations must understand their context and the resulting behaviours that are required, and put in place the skills and mindsets *at scale* in order to drive effective leadership.

In the following chapters, we will review the research and practice that underpin our approach to develop the right leadership behaviours (defined by context), and the underlying skills and mindsets required.

# 2

# The Leadership at Scale Diamond

*Gautam Kumra, Michiel Kruyt, Ramesh Srinivasan*

Our pillars of knowledge | Our latest research on leadership
development | Our core principles: the Leadership at Scale Diamond

We base all that we do on a set of clear and straightforward principles adduced from our extensive practice, theoretical knowledge, and
repeated research and testing in the field. In terms of leadership development, we think of *whole system development* in order to create or
**enhance leadership effectiveness at an organizational level at the
right pace and scale.** Progress towards this goal is most often measured through an organization-wide tool such as the Organizational
Health Index (OHI), outlined earlier.

Increasing the effectiveness of individual leaders is, of course, a positive enabler and outcome of this process, but it is not the issue that
we address here (that is an individual goal, and there are other ways of
reaching it). This chapter reviews our pillars of knowledge, our four
principles of leadership development (jointly defined as the *Leadership
at Scale Diamond*), and shows how the principles fit together in an integrated system. The next four chapters elaborate on each principle in
more detail.

It is important to bear in mind that the primary goal of any leadership development intervention is enhanced performance through
organization-wide leadership effectiveness. Structured leadership
development programmes are one of several ways to achieve this,
and it is what concerns us here. However, a key success factor in
creating leadership effectiveness is to take a holistic approach, organization-wide, including not only leadership development but also
succession planning, mobility, recruiting and so on. Part 3 of the
book (Frequently Asked Questions) focuses on these other important

interventions; these are by no means secondary, but are not the prime focus of this book.

## Our pillars of knowledge

Leadership development is both an art and science, populated (over-populated, one might say) by many theories and ideas. Where is one to start looking, when so much material exists? Furthermore, what should one do when different theories seem to contradict one another?

Within leadership development, we know that our core principles must be expressed together, and that to remove or underplay one or more is to risk a less than ideal outcome. Where, then, do we derive our leadership development principles from, and what supports and nourishes them?

Our core principles are based on a combination of experience and knowledge, a form of practical wisdom. We showed in Chapter 1 that we apply a multi-faceted, practical approach when defining leadership, drawing on different schools of thought. The same holds true when we shape our leadership development principles. We draw on a large number of theories, and combine the best of these with our practice, in a pragmatic manner.

We regularly review and draw on the latest leadership theories and trends globally, with a critical eye focusing on the material that is credible and backed by science. We reviewed the different schools of leadership theory in Chapter 1. In addition, we are adaptive and pro-active, and not only incorporate new research where relevant, but also regularly challenge our own thinking through our internal knowledge network and external advisory boards.

We draw heavily on *organizational science*. McKinsey's research into organizations provides a deep and actionable link between leadership effectiveness, organizational health and performance. Our situational leadership research (introduced in this chapter and the next) helps determine what is needed in a given context, while our leadership development, OHI, and transformational change initiatives provide a fact-based methodology to creating and sustaining successful change programmes. In addition, our 'OrgSolutions' team bridges the gap between organizational topics and science in numerous other domains, including 'people analytics' through big data, and the Organizational Science Initiative. We regularly and habitually take the temperature and measure the heartbeat of leadership development across sectors and geographies, and beyond our already international and diverse clients.

We apply the latest insights from *neuroscience* in terms of adult learning principles, positive psychology, mindfulness-based development techniques, as well as how to manage personal energy to maximize learning. We draw from in-house neuroscientists and our dedicated Firm Learning team, as well as external experts and advisors.

We constantly gather feedback on *what works in practice*, through our more than 100 leadership development engagements per year globally. A key pillar of knowledge is thus our learning as practitioners, which is growing rapidly each year. In addition, we regularly host multi-client executive forums across a broad set of domains, including the Bower Forum for CEOs, Executive Transitions Masterclass for CXOs, the Change Leaders Forum and Centred Leadership Programme for senior leaders, and the Young Leaders Forum for mid-tenure leaders. Each year, we host over 60 forums, engaging over 1,000 leaders from more than 350 organizations across more than 60 countries.

Finally, in line with our multi-faceted approach, we have developed *multi-disciplinary approaches* in philosophy, spirituality, psychology, development theory, anthropology, morals and values when they are required to make the necessary leadership shifts.

Two areas in particular are worth highlighting:

1 An increasing body of research is showing the link between an organization's stage of development and leadership effectiveness within it. An increasing portion of our work with organizations and individuals focuses on the deeply held beliefs and underlying mental blocks that get in the way of personal and professional unfolding.

2 We have experienced a growing trend among especially late-tenured CEOs toward more profound questioning and deep reflection. Here, we often turn to philosophical and spiritual teachings.

## *Our latest research on leadership development*

We mentioned the *organizational leadership challenge* in the introduction to the book: a third of organizations do not feel they have the quality and quantity of leaders to execute their strategies and performance objectives. In addition, a third of organizations state that they do not have the leadership capacity needed to take them through the next three to five years, beyond the near-term strategy and performance objectives.[1] Equally troubling, only approximately 55 per cent of executives say that their leadership development interventions in their organizations meet and sustain the intended objectives. Indeed, when looking only at those who 'strongly agree', the proportion drops to around 11 per cent.[2] In other words, organizations do not feel they have the leadership required now or for the future, and they are not able to plug the gap.

We test and refine our approach from time to time, covering a broad range of topics related to enhancing leadership effectiveness.[3] We have also previously discussed that at an organizational level, **leadership development requires a systematic approach**. Our research on why leadership development programmes fail, for example, pinpointed four key pitfalls – overlooking context, decoupling the effort from real work, underestimating mindsets, and failing to adequately measure results.[4]

In 2016 we expanded this research and tested a comprehensive set of 50 leadership development actions in the field, with over 500 executives and leadership development practitioners globally. An explicit research design choice was to aim for comprehensives – hence the large number of 50 actions tested – in order to cover all the actions we felt could be necessary for leadership development success. This latest research adds to our existing stock of knowledge, and enables important insights into making leadership development interventions work in organizations. There are three key insights, at an aggregate level.

1 **Leadership development at scale requires a systematic approach that covers four key areas.** When we looked at the results, we found that some actions matter much more than others, and that these are truly critical to programme success. For example, organizations that have successful leadership development interventions are 8.1 times more likely to focus on the most critical leadership behaviours that really matter to performance, based on fact-based research, compared to organizations whose

leadership development interventions are not successful. (Successful leadership development programmes were defined as those that achieved and sustained the desired objectives of the programme.)

We also saw that the most critical actions clustered into four main themes: **contextualizing the programme based on the organization's position and strategy, ensuring that the interventions cover the whole organization, designing for behavioural change and learning transfer by using the latest adult learning principles, and integrating the efforts into the broader organization.** These themes are consistent with other leadership development research we have undertaken – as well as what we see in practice. Figure 2.1 shows the ten most important leadership development actions, grouped around the four main themes. Each multiple shows how many times more likely a leadership development programme is successful and sustained, when applying the key action. The implication for organizations is that they must be sure to cover all four areas when devising a leadership development programme.

2　There is no 'silver bullet'; **succeeding is rather about doing many things right.** There is a clear correlation between leadership development actions and programme success rates. In Figure 2.2 the $x$ axis is the number of actions and the y-axis is the success rate; the curve shows the increasing effect of the number of actions taken. As such, successfully organization cover not only the four main areas mentioned above, but also ensure depth of actions within each one.

It is worth pointing out that: first, the chances of success do not rise above 30 per cent until around 24 key actions are taken; second, over 40 key actions must be taken to increase chances of success to 80 per cent; and third, as mentioned above, organizations that do all 50 actions increase their success rates to 99 per cent.

3　The third insight is simply that **our approach works.** We found that a subset of the organizations we surveyed were consistently able to achieve and sustain their leadership development objectives, through a comprehensive and best practice approach employing all 50 actions. These organizations were able to 'flip

## Increase in likelihood of using key actions, top 10

| Key themes | Factor | Increase in likelihood of using key action[1] |
|---|---|---|
| Leadership development interventions are contextualized based on the organization's position (OHI) and strategy | Focuses on the most critical leadership behaviours that really matter to performance, based on fact-based research | 8.1 |
| | Determines how the mindsets and behaviours need to change in the future, based on the leadership model | 5.5 |
| | Has translated its strategy into the required leadership qualities and capabilities through a leadership model | 5.4 |
| Leadership development interventions cover the whole organization | Ensures leadership development interventions cover the whole organization and designs programmes in the context of the broader leadership development strategy | 6.9 |
| | Ensures that its leadership strategy and leadership model reaches all organizational levels | 6.4 |
| Leadership development interventions leverage latest adult learning principles[2] | Actively encourages individuals to practice the new behaviours that will contribute to being a better leader | 6.1 |
| | Leadership development programmes link content to projects (either individual or group) that stretch participants and require them to apply their learnings in new settings over an extended period of time | 4.6 |
| Leadership development interventions are embedded into the formal and informal mechanisms of an organization | Reviews current formal/informal mechanisms for building leadership skills, prior to building a leadership development intervention | 5.9 |
| | Adapts formal HR systems to reinforce leadership model/the desired behaviours (e.g., recruiting, performance evaluation, compensation, succession planning) | 5.6 |
| | Top team role models desired behaviours in the context of leadership programmes e.g., by acting as programme faculty, project sponsors, mentors, or coaches | 4.9 |

[1] How many times more likely an organization with a successful leadership development intervention applies the action, compared to organizations with unsuccessful leadership development interventions

[2] Other important factors were including individual fieldwork between forums (3.6x), being strengths based (3.4x), coaching (3.2x), and addressing mindsets (2.9x)

FIGURE 2.1  Ten most important leadership development actions

the odds' of success, from just over 50 per cent to almost 100 per cent. This makes sense, given the hypothesis driven nature of the research itself, but is nonetheless an assuring confirmation that our approach works. (Note: successful leadership development programmes were defined as those that achieved and sustained the desired objectives of the programme – including respondents that 'agree' and 'strongly agree').

**Success of leadership development programmes[1]**

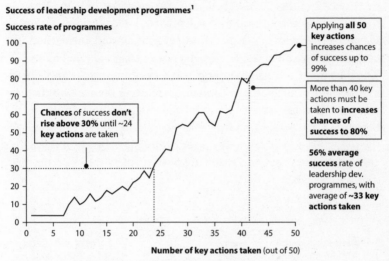

<sup></sup>[1] Leadership development programmes that were 'somewhat' or 'very' successful on both performance and health dimension; moving average of five actions.

FIGURE 2.2 More than 40 key actions must be taken to increase chances of success to 80 per cent

## Our core principles: the Leadership at Scale Diamond

We now move to the core principles that underpin our approach, and which must always hold true for a leadership development to be successful. They are informed by our recent research discussed above – which pinpointed the four key areas and depth of actions required for leadership development at scale – yet build on this through many other sources. **The core principles we outline below are shaped by what we know from past and recent research, see in the field, and sense as individual practitioners** dealing with individual clients around the world. They derive from known causes and rational deduction, and have been developed through many years' research, practice and refinement. Like any good theoretical model, they not only help explain 'what is going on' but also predict what is needed in the future.

They bring together our thinking on the topic, and form the bedrock of our leadership development approach (which we outline in more detail in Part 2 of the book). They relate to the 'what' (context-specific shifts), 'who' (engaging the organization), and 'how' at the individual and organizational levels (architecting programmes to maximize behavioural change, and integrating and measuring). We collectively call these the *Leadership at Scale Diamond* (see Figure 2.3). The 'Diamond' is a constant loop – as an organization is implementing the four principles, it is constantly adjusting them along the way: it is a continuous, never-ending process. As context shifts, so do the behaviours, skills and mindsets that organizations need to foster. In the following sections, we set out our thinking on each of these four core principles, while the following four chapters elaborate on them in further detail.

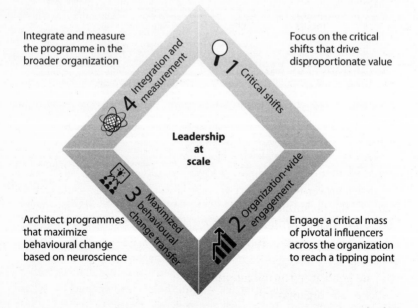

Integrate and measure the programme in the broader organization

4 Integration and measurement

Focus on the critical shifts that drive disproportionate value

1 Critical shifts

**Leadership at scale**

3 Maximized behavioural change transfer

2 Organization-wide engagement

Architect programmes that maximize behavioural change based on neuroscience

Engage a critical mass of pivotal influencers across the organization to reach a tipping point

FIGURE 2.3 The Leadership at Scale Diamond

## Core Principle 1: Focus on the critical shifts that drive disproportionate value

*Link leadership development to the organizational context and strategy and focus on the three to five shifts (behaviours, skills and mindsets) that will have the biggest impact on performance.*

In our latest research, we learned that **leadership development is often disconnected from the organization's position and strategy**. The executives told us that often their organizations have not translated their strategy into required leadership skills through a leadership model specific to their needs. Instead of focusing on the critical leadership capabilities that really matter to performance, many organizations use generic and broad leadership competency models.

What we often find is a long list of leadership standards, an over-complex web of dozens of competencies and corporate-values statements. Each is usually summarized in a seemingly easy-to-remember way (such as the 3Ss or 4Ts, or as a mnemonic); each on its own terms makes sense. In practice, however, what managers and employees often see is an 'alphabet soup' of imperatives that are neither specific enough nor ordered by priority.

But successful organizations do not make up leadership mantras or do leadership development for the sake of it. They link leadership development to the organization's strategy. **When leadership development is properly linked to strategy, the outcomes are appreciably better**. In our research we found that organizations which were successful at leadership development were 8.1 times more likely to **focus on the most critical leadership behaviours that really matter to performance** than those who do not.

When planning a leadership development initiative, organizations should ask themselves a simple question: *What, precisely, is this programme for?* If the answer is to support an acquisition-led growth strategy, for example, the organization will probably need leaders brimming with ideas and capable of devising winning strategies for new or newly expanded business units. If the answer is to grow by capturing organic opportunities, the organization will probably want people at the top who are good at nurturing internal talent.

Once an organization has defined its leadership aspirations, linked to the context, it is time to prioritize. Organizations cannot do everything, so they are best served by attending to what really matters, the three to five most critical behaviours (and skills and mindsets) to support and further their strategy. Indeed, our ongoing transformational change research and experience show that to be successful during change programmes, organizations should focus on the three to five most critical shifts. This was also consistent with our latest research – where we found that organizations with successful leadership development interventions were 3.2 times more likely to focus on these three to five critical shifts – and also very much in line with what we see in practice. Too often, organizations try to do too many things at once, meaning that the key shifts don't materialize and stick.

But on which behaviours should an organization focus? That's the question we asked ourselves when kicking off a large scale study about situational leadership. In a study done in 2016 – surveying 375,000 people in 165 organizations – **we found that only a few leadership behaviours drive organizational performance, and that these behaviours vary by context**. For instance, a turnaround crisis requires different leadership capabilities than an expansion and growth phase.

Specific behaviours (and skills and mindsets) are not enough, however. In today's environment, strategy sometimes changes rapidly. A new technology and new competitor can throw a well performing organization into a turnaround crisis over a short period. What is needed in addition to context-specific behaviours is adaptability, i.e. the mental flexibility to be able to adapt to different situations and adjust behaviours rapidly; and not just in individual leaders but in sufficient numbers across an organization. Being adaptive requires a high degree of self-awareness and a learning mindset. We have found that leaders who are self-aware and who have a learning mindset are 4 times more prepared to lead amidst change. In the next chapter, we detail the specific behaviours, skills and mindsets that are most effective in different contexts, as well as our approach to developing adaptability in leaders.

## Core Principle 2: Engage a critical mass of pivotal influencers across the organization to reach a tipping point

*Organizations must ensure sufficient breadth, depth and pace in order to change leadership behaviours across the organization, and to give all employees an understanding of what great leadership looks like.*

Today many leadership development programmes are episodic and focus on only a subset of the organization. What is needed to sustainably shift leadership behaviours across an organization is a combination of breadth, depth and pace.

First is breadth. In our research, we found that organizations with successful leadership development interventions were 6.9 times more likely to ensure leadership development interventions cover the whole organization and design programmes in the context of the broader leadership development strategy. We also found that successful organizations are 6.4 times more likely to ensure that their leadership strategy and model reaches all levels of the organization than those who do not.

In practice, this means reaching a critical mass of pivotal influencers at all levels of the organization quickly. **A critical mass of pivotal influencers displaying a new behaviour is needed to reach a tipping point, where the change becomes self-sustaining and the organization is transformed.** The tipping point required depends on many factors (including the stickiness of the message, and the degree of interaction between agents), and tipping point theory across fields such as epidemiology, sociology, and marketing indicate that 10–30 per cent of a population must change behaviour or become infected in order for the change to become irreversible. In our experience, reaching up to 10–30 per cent is not needed across a full organization; what is needed is to reach a critical mass of the pivotal influencers, who people in the organization look to for cues on what matters to be successful (or survive) in the organization. Pivotal influencers are able to influence the behaviours of others in the organization, due to their role, a trusted relationship, or character. They include top layers of management – CEO, N-1, N-2 (and subsequent levels below CEO) – top talent, influencers and pivotal roles (for example, branch managers, plant managers). We find that reaching 5–15 per cent of the organization is needed, depending on the organization (for example, size, industry, number of spans and layers).

Second is depth. **Building a repertoire of leadership capabilities takes time.** A new behaviour that is practised repeatedly develops into a capability, a competence. But most leadership development programmes do not think about leadership development as multi-year or multi-decades journeys in which several competencies are built over time. Instead, most leadership development programmes are typically of short duration – a few weeks to several months, sporadic and piecemeal. Moreover, many tend to focus on the 'flavour of the year', on whatever aspect of leadership that is perceived to be most fashionable now. The consequence is that new insights and behaviours never develop into competencies.

Third is pace. We find that **quicker is better** – as a rule of thumb, if employees in the organization have not seen meaningful change as a result of the leadership development intervention 6–9 months after it is announced, they will typically begin to start questioning its value to the organization and to them. As such, it is usually beneficial to start not only with the top layer (N-1s) but also their direct reports, typically at the director or VP level.

Organizations such as professional services or the military understand that leaders must be apprenticed and grown from within their organization. They therefore devote time, energy, people and money to develop their leaders over long periods. This approach produces a sustained developmental journey for the individual leader, a planned and secure supply of leaders for the organization, and an organization-wide leadership culture. In Chapter 4, we outline in more detail how organizations can think about breadth and depth in order to ensure system-wide leadership change.

## Core Principle 3: Architect programmes that maximize behavioural change based on neuroscience

*Design interventions with an explicit focus on helping individuals become 'better at their daily jobs' using the latest principles linked to neuroscience, to maximize the value and organizational impact of what is taught and learned.*

Adult learning is a term that has been long established. The differentiating factor here is the focus on designing interventions with an explicit goal of transferring the maximum amount of learning to the daily work of individuals, and on using the *latest* adult learning principles, grounded in neuroscience.

Many leadership development interventions today build on an archaic understanding of training. Every successful leader, when asked about how he or she learned to lead, would tell stories of having mastered difficult situations and having led through adversities – which then ultimately helped the leader become better at their daily jobs. That is because leadership capabilities (like any other capabilities) are built when people have to deal with a problem in practice in a specific context. When someone discovers a new behaviour to cope with a demanding situation, and when he or she practises the new behaviour in his or her daily work over time it becomes a capability. However, that is not how most leadership development programmes work. Many, if not most, still rely on a 'teacher and classroom' (facilitator and workshop) model, with limited improvement in how leaders go about their daily work.

Instead, **we design interventions explicitly around achieving the maximum degree of learning transfer**. Learning transfer is the process of developing knowledge or skills in one context that improve a person's performance in another context. We leverage the latest neuroscience to achieve this. Neuroscience has achieved significant breakthroughs in the past 20 years in terms of our understanding of the brain and of how adults learn. We know, for example, that neuroplasticity (the ability of the brain to form new neural pathways and functions) is no longer limited to childhood, but rather continues throughout one's life.[5] We also know more about how to explicitly enhance learning transfer in adults, and the implications it has on leadership development initiatives. In essence, there are seven adult learning principles that we regularly adopt:

- Stretching participants outside their comfort zones
- Using self-directed learning and self-discovery
- Applying on-the-job learning to form new skills through repetition and practice
- Providing a positive frame to link positive emotions to learning
- Ensuring the interventions are strengths-based
- Addressing underlying mindsets (whole-person approach)
- Using reflection and coaching to ensure feedback loops

Our latest research on leadership development backs this up. We found that organizations with successful leadership development interventions are 6.1 times more likely to actively encourage individuals to practise the new behaviours that will contribute to being a better leader than unsuccessful organizations.

Another key success factor related to adult learning was that organizations linked content to projects (either individual or group) that stretched participants and required them to apply their learnings in new settings over an extended period of time (multiple of 5.4×). Other important actions (outside of our top 10 list) were including individual fieldwork between forums (3.6×), being strengths-based (3.4×), coaching (3.2×), and addressing mindsets (2.9×). Taken together and designed correctly, these interventions result in a high degree of learning transfer.

In addition **there are numerous best practices based on neuroscience that organizations can adopt to boost not only learning but also employee productivity in general.** These are related to multi-tasking, mindsets, biases, mindfulness and bodily health. We will elaborate on the above elements in Chapter 5.

## Core Principle 4: Integrate and measure the programme in the broader organization

*Organizations must ensure that the broader ecosystem directly supports and reinforces the shift in behaviours, skills and mindsets that the leadership development programme promotes.*

Many leadership development programmes are *isolated initiatives*, disconnected from other management interventions that aim at transforming an organization. Recently we attended a discussion in which a head of Learning and Development had been delegated the task to build leadership capabilities, and was now required to show results. However, building new leadership capabilities entails changing and learning new behaviours. Few people change behaviours when they simply receive training. This head of Learning and Development was not set up for success, as the responsibility was not coupled with a broader mandate to tweak other organizational elements. Indeed, we sometimes see culture initiatives and other health interventions being run completely separately from leadership development, which not only diminishes the effectiveness of each initiative but can, in worst case scenarios, confuse employees.

Most people change behaviour and learn new competencies if their superiors explain and role-model these new behaviours, and if incentives systems and the model and culture of an organization reinforce those behaviours. **To create lasting impact at scale, organizations must adapt the systems, processes and culture to enable the leadership programme**. However and unfortunately, most leadership development interventions are not embedded in an overall approach that includes these elements, but are run as isolated initiatives.

Our research suggests that leadership development is most successful if it is embedded in a set of organizational interventions that include – in addition to leadership development interventions – three elements:

- Senior leaders across the organization (especially the CEO and executive team) role-model those behaviours. We found that organizations with successful leadership development programmes were 4.9 times more likely to have senior leaders role-model desired behaviours in the context of the leadership programmes (for example, by acting as programme faculty, project sponsors, mentors, or coaches), than organizations with unsuccessful leadership development programmes.
- The organization communicates, fosters understanding and creates conviction for the desired leadership behaviours and competencies, across the organization, in a structured and deliberate way.
- Formal mechanisms such as the performance management system, the talent review system, and the organizational structure and key processes reinforce the required changes in competencies. In our work we found that organizations with successful leadership development programmes are 5.6 times more likely to adapt their formal HR systems to reinforce the leadership model/the desired behaviours (for example, recruiting, performance evaluation, compensation, succession planning), than organizations with unsuccessful leadership development programmes. An additional action linked to this (outside the top 10) was ensuring programme objectives, metrics, tracking mechanisms and governance are clearly formulated and in place, which had a multiple of 3.3.

# Case study: Building a culture of great moments

## Context and challenge

One of the largest and most prominent conglomerates in MENA, with a presence in 16 markets and about 45,000 employees across 12 different businesses, defined a long-term strategic direction and a new operating model that entailed a significant shift in the role of the holding company (corporate centre) as well as a need to identify and groom existing and future leaders across the group. In addition, the organization struggled with disjointed cultures across the various operating companies and an insufficient pipeline of future leaders, and aspired to improve its organizational health in order to sustain performance in the long-term and ensure the company remained 'fit for purpose'.

## Approach

From the outset, the initiative was set up as a joint, strategic partnership between McKinsey and the client organization. We started by conducting a roadshow to visit and benchmark leading corporate academies globally, and thereafter designed the blueprint for a state-of-the-art Leadership Institute: The Leadership Institute would be the incubator of top talent and the engine to supply the future leadership pipeline, the custodian of the organization's culture and values, and provide world-class training and development to address the most critical leadership needs across the group.

We defined a detailed Leadership Model linked to the vision and strategic objectives of the organization, and to its transformation agenda. There were six leadership model themes in total, including 'Thinks Customer', 'Thinks Group' and 'Develops Talent'. The Leadership Model themes were broken down into observable behaviours by organizational level, and integrated into the talent development and performance management frameworks across the organization. We thereafter designed and launched five transformational programmes, which focused on top talent across the group. Each programme was tightly linked to the leadership model, and made relevant to the specific organizational challenges the participants faced. In parallel, we developed internal facilitation capacity and capabilities within The Leadership Institute to sustain and scale the transformation.

Finally, the Institute activated an organization-wide culture programme including a very successful onboarding for new hires, and launched an international speaker series and other community-building initiatives to energize the top talent cohort and the broader organization.

## Impact

The impact of The Leadership Institute was far reaching, and significant progress was achieved in a short amount of time. In the first three years, The Leadership Institute reached more than 400 top talent in leadership journeys, 900 new joiners in a 3-day onboarding programme, 19,000 frontline employees in a one-day induction programme, and 4,000 employees through culture-shaping initiatives. Programme feedback was consistently favourable, with a 9.3 out of 10 average rating for leadership programme effectiveness.

At an organizational level, The Leadership Institute helped achieve a 14 percentage point increase in the OHI score for the company within the first three years, moving the organization from third quartile to the middle of the second quartile. The leadership outcome on the OHI was a big driver, increasing 13 percentage points in the same period, from fourth to second quartile. At an individual level, participant feedback emphasized the 'life changing' impact of the programme, and top talent across the group highlighted the programmes as a primary reason for their continued excitement and commitment to the organization.

## Reflection

One of the critical success factors was the unwavering commitment of the CEO and executive team to the talent agenda, which enabled the mobilization of the entire group (people and resources) to launch The Leadership Institute in record time.

While moving quickly, however, the launch was never a rushed endeavour; from the outset, we ensured that we approached the development with a long-term view in mind. We also spent time prior to launch on designing and ensuring top team involvement and alignment on the leadership model, and subsequent programme design.

Another important success element was that The Leadership Institute involved the whole organization. In addition to the top team going through leadership programmes and role-modeling the change, the Institute launched an onboarding programme that 'retroactively' reached all existing employees as well as new employees. Furthermore, the Institute launched culture programmes that embedded the leadership model and values into the organization, ensuring that the Institute was able to provide not only a pipeline of future leaders, but also be the custodian of the organization's culture and values, and enable the strategy more broadly.

## An integrated system

The four principles outlined in this chapter inform an integrated system for leadership development. **Our research and experience shows that all four principles must be present in order to increase the leadership effectiveness across an organization.** Even if three of the four principles are adhered to, the leadership development impact is often severely compromised. In addition, the core principles are part of a continuous process. As context shifts, so do the behaviours, skills and mindsets that organizations need to foster.

There are many different ways to put a leadership development intervention into practice (for example, the number of forums days, the exact learning modules used, the facilitators deployed, on-site or at a remote location). Budgets often put a constraint on the solution space available. However, what is key is to incorporate the four principles in the programme, and this applies at all organizational levels and for all budget levels. Doing this should greatly enhance the chances that the interventions are successful and that the changes are sustained.

It is important to note that while the basis of our knowledge stays broadly the same, the stock of knowledge is continuously growing. So when the facts change, we alter our thinking. We regularly update our findings, and conduct new research to test, refine or validate our approach. However, these principles have been formulated to stand the test of time, and also to be flexible enough to incorporate new knowledge as it emerges.

The specific behavioural shifts that hold true for Core Principle 1 will change as new research is conducted and as the organizational contexts continue to shift. Technology, in particular, is a cross-cutting theme which has important implications on each of the four core principles, which we highlight in the subsequent chapters. To give a flavour, in Core Principle 1, technology is becoming an increasingly important part of the leadership development curriculum, as organizations can no longer ignore the opportunities and threats from for example, advanced analytics and digitization. In Core Principle 2, technology is becoming a key means to identify the top talent of an organization and to reach a 'critical mass' during the programme itself, for example through mobile apps and virtual reality. The adult learning approaches to maximize learning transfer, which underpin Core Principle 3, will evolve as we gather further evidence on how the brain learns, and as we develop new technologies for delivery (for example, wearable tech for instant feedback). And technology will enable new ways to integrate and normalize the leadership development programmes (Core Principle 4). However, in all instances the core principles themselves continue to hold true.

## Summary

The four principles make up the *Leadership at Scale Diamond*, which forms the basis of our leadership development efforts. The next four chapters will outline in more detail each principle, including our latest research and thinking on each topic. Part 2 of the book will thereafter illustrate how we integrate and implement the four principles during a leadership development intervention.

# 3
# Core Principle 1: Focus on the critical shifts

*Bill Schaninger, Chris Gagnon, Haimeng Zhang, Michael Bazigos*

Why context-specific critical shifts? | Opening up the black box of organizational contexts | The leadership behaviours that really matter | Transitioning between contexts: adaptive leadership | The critical enablers: skills and mindsets | Implications for leadership development

In the opening chapter, we showed that leadership effectiveness correlates strongly with organizational performance. We defined leadership as a set of behaviours that inspire and align a group of people to successfully execute a common goal in a constantly changing environment. In other words, **leadership is about alignment, execution and renewal, at scale.** We saw that the ability of leaders to display effective behaviours is driven by their ability to understand and adapt to the context, their skills and on-the-job experience, and their mindset. In the previous chapter, we stressed that organizations must foster these behaviours, mindsets and skills *at scale*, in order to foster effective leadership that truly drives performance. We laid out the *Leadership at Scale Diamond*, with the first core principle centred on the critical shifts linked to context that really drive performance. Here, we go one level deeper and discuss the specific behaviours, skills and mindsets that matter.

First, we discuss the importance of this core principle and what often happens when it is not present. Second, we open up the black box of context. We know that organizations must align, execute and renew, but we will see that the degree and approach to doing this differs by their context. We review the different potential organizational contexts one could explore, and zoom in on organizational health as a valuable lens of looking at context. Third, we review the 'situational-leadership staircase', where we outline the behaviours that are most effective for organizations, by health context. We find that there are both *baseline* behaviours, which should be applied within any context, and *situational* behaviours, whose effectiveness are context-specific. We discuss how organizations can 'move up the ladder' and increase their leadership effectiveness. Fourth, we review the importance of adaptability in order to effectively transition between different contexts. Fifth, we explore the underlying enablers of skills and mindsets that best support the desired behaviours, by context. Finally, we discuss the implications for leadership development programmes in practice.

## Core Principle 1: Focus on the critical shifts that drive disproportionate value

Link leadership development to the organizational context and strategy, and focus on the three–five shifts (behaviours, skills and mindsets) that will have the biggest impact on performance

### *Why context-specific critical shifts?*

We showed in our *McKinsey Quarterly* article from 2014 that overlooking context is a key reason that leadership development programmes fail.[1] Our latest research backs this up: we saw that organizations that had successful leadership development interventions were 8.1 times more likely to focus on the most critical leadership behaviours that really matter to performance, based on fact-based research. Of the organizations that were successful, 73 per cent applied this action, compared to 9 per cent for organizations that did not have successful leadership development interventions. In other words, there were virtually no organizations that did not do this action that had successful leadership development interventions.

Other key actions from our research include: translating the organization's strategy into the required leadership qualities and capabilities through a leadership model (5.4× more likely to be carried out by organizations that had successful leadership development interventions), determining how the mindsets and behaviours need to change in the future, based on the leadership model (5.5×), and the organization tailors the intervention based on organizational context in terms of content and delivery (4.2×). It is worthwhile noting that in addition to behavioural shifts, we see the importance of focusing on the underlying skills and mindsets needed to support the behaviour as well. Hence a discussion of context-specific shifts covers behaviours, skills and mindsets.

Our experience backs this up. Too many training initiatives we come across rest on the assumption that one-size-fits-all and that the same group of skills or style of leadership is appropriate regardless of strategy, organizational culture, or CEO mandate. Many popular books on the traits of successful companies are likewise broad in their recommendations. Instead of focusing on the critical leadership capabilities that may really matter to performance, many individual leaders and organizations as a whole use generic and broad leadership competency models.

For example, the CEO of a large European services business we know had an outstanding record when markets were growing quickly, but failed to provide clear direction or to impose financial discipline on the group's business units during the most recent economic downturn. Instead, he continued to encourage innovation and new thinking – hallmarks of the culture that had previously brought success – until he was finally replaced for underperformance.

In the case of a European retail bank anxious to improve its sales performance, the skill that mattered most (but was in shortest supply) was the ability to persuade and motivate peers without the formal authority of direct line management. This art of influencing others outside formal reporting lines runs counter to the rigid structures of many organizations. In this company, it was critical for the sales managers to persuade the IT department to change systems and working approaches that were burdening the sales organization's managers, whose time was desperately needed to introduce important sales-acceleration measures. When managers were able to focus on changing the systems and working approaches, the bank's productivity rose by 15 per cent.

The second part of this core principle attends to the behavioural shifts that really matter. Organizations should not only map out the leadership behaviours that will enable their strategy, but must also prioritize and focus on three to five key shifts at a time. Organizations with successful leadership development interventions were 3.2 times more likely to focus on these critical shifts. This is consistent with our transformation change research, and also with what we see in practice. Too often, organizations try to do too many things at once, meaning that the key shifts don't materialize and stick.

## *Opening up the black box of organizational contexts*

The idea of situational leadership is not new. It is widely understood that consensus-driven leadership is not what is needed when the house is burning down; venture capitalists will know that the passionate founder who leads a start-up through its meteoric early years is no sure bet to lead it for the long term. However, most of the literature we see today that focuses on the organization as context offers one-size-fits-all prescriptions, for example advocating integrity, relentlessness and humility in leaders. To attain the highest level of leadership effectiveness, organizations are counselled to create a leadership cadre that replaces departing leaders with perfectly moulded successors.

No doubt, these qualities are important. But that research lens was trained on commonalities among high-performing organizations, thereby missing what was different between them but still effective. Identifying and explaining the commonalities of organizations tends to be easier than identifying factors that explain their variations. For this, it is important to first identify relevant organizational contexts, and thereafter have a robust method to analyse both the commonalities and differences.

## The research questions

After reviewing the existing literature on leadership effectiveness at an organizational level, we became curious about two questions. First, how do organizations *lead*? The organizational culture literature has long established that collective behaviours of people often pervade organizations and their units – either by design or by evolution – and become their signature brand. Those behaviours become understood by many as the way we work – an aspect of organizational culture – which can differ substantially across organizations. Ask yourself: *How would I describe my organization's ways of working?*

Our research tells us this applies to leadership behaviours as well, and our experience confirms it. Measurements from organizational survey data support the view that organizations differ in their mix of leadership behaviours. Distinct and reliably different patterns of leader behaviour are apparent; and these patterns are pervasive enough to be obvious to the front line staff. Studies that focus their analyses on individual leaders would miss those broad, organization-level patterns.

Those patterns shape employees' experiences and expectations of leaders right down to the front line, where value is created or lost daily during myriad 'moments of truth'. While many commentators are drawn instinctively to leadership behaviours at the top (which are no doubt important), the visibility and effectiveness of particular leadership behaviours at the front line is among the greatest risks to, or opportunities for, long-term value creation. These findings led to the assertion that it is only by developing effective *leadership at scale*, at all levels and among all employees, that organizations can truly drive performance.

The second question we looked at was as follows: *Is there 'one right way', or is leadership situational for organizations?* It is reasonable to expect that leadership behaviours required for a company challenged to survive and with declining workforce motivation may well differ from those required to avoid complacency when a company is doing well. 'One right way' approaches are normative and, more often than not, miss the mark when circumstances differ.

But which behaviours are best for which situations (or contexts)? And what does 'context' mean? What are its parameters? That is, how exactly do we know when that we are in a particular context? Finally, how can we tell that a context has changed enough to emphasize different behaviours?

A modest history of contingency research in the leadership literature implicates situational factors. However, these invariably focus on teams, not organizations, defining the situational contingency variously as leader-member relationships and task structure,[5] 'subordinate maturity',[6] decision making,[7] to give three notable examples. There are many others, yet our question remained unanswered. Was there a set of behaviours that applied at the broader level of large unit or enterprise that varied under specified parameters or contexts?

## Organizational health as context

There are many lenses through which to view context, for example in terms of industry, company life cycle/maturity, organizational size, ownership structure, geography, and general organizational/financial performance. In addition, there is the context within organizations, for example its strategy, its structure, its people, or even the specific function or department at hand.

Each one of these contexts will require different behaviours for effective leadership. Let's take the industry context, as an example. In oil and gas, it might be fruitful for leaders to emphasize operational excellence and safety standards; while in professional services a firm might emphasize more knowledge sharing and apprenticeship. Indeed, we have shown this to be the case with hard data, in terms of general organizational health. We have identified four 'recipes' – made up of a coherent set of management practices that complement one another[8] – and found that organizations that strongly align to one of the four organizational health recipes are 5 times more likely to have top-quartile health than organizations that only have weak alignment.[9] There are dominant recipes in every industry. So organizations have a strong starting point about where to focus their energy if we take the industry as context. One could easily imagine that these more desirable management practises hold true for leaders in these organizations and industries as well.

Other contexts similarly have important nuances. In ownership, a family-owned business will require different leadership behaviours from a publicly listed company or from an organization that has been bought by a private equity investor. In culture, differences are undoubtedly pertinent, and a good portion of literature already exists on the topic. In strategy, a growth strategy will require different behaviours than a consolidation (or retrenchment) strategy. And in operations, the nature of leading a finance department is likely to be different from leading a marketing department.

In addition, there are bound to be certain normative qualities, such as demonstrating a concern for people, offering a critical perspective, having integrity and being ethical, which will always be part of what makes a great leader. Organizations should of course take these timeless qualities (as well as industry, geographical, department and other contextual nuances) into account when developing more effective leadership. This is also something we do, when we devise the content for leadership development programmes for clients.

However, we find that one context proves to be the most insightful in terms of pinpointing the most common leadership challenges that organizations face, and in determining the behaviours that most foster leadership effectiveness: *organizational health*. There are three reasons why this is the case.

1 **Organizational health cuts across all other elements.** All organizations (public, commercial, governmental) have better or poorer health, regardless of industry, ownership structure, geography and so on. Indeed, organizational health can be measured at a business unit or department level as well, as long as there are sufficient data points. The resulting leadership challenges and critical behaviours also cut across other contexts and are thus widely applicable.

2 **Health is robust.** To model what other successful organizations do, for example by emulating the leadership behaviours of the best performing companies in the industry, is no guarantee of success. In addition, if the focus is on financial performance alone and the fastest growing or most profitable organizations are exemplars, there could be many hidden influencers (for example, industry or company life cycle) to distort the results. Health, on the other hand, has a clear link to both financial and non-financial performance.

3 **Health is actionable.** It has a very clear end state, as organizations aspire to become top quartile, and at some point top decile. This gives a laser-like focus on using leadership (in conjunction with other initiatives) not only to increase the leadership effectiveness outcome but also to transition to higher levels of overall health. We have seen countless examples of organizations using health to spur on leaders – at all levels of the organization – towards greater and higher achievements.

As such, **we treat organizational health as the primary context to identify the leadership behaviours that will be most effective, and overlay these with secondary lenses such as those described above.** We can take a global view, informed by work we do over long periods and across many sectors. In addition, normative qualities are embedded both at the organizational level (when mapping behaviours to enable a strategy) as well as at the individual level (for example, when developing individual development plans).

## How healthy is your organization?

To make the insights in this chapter applicable, leaders must have an accurate sense of how healthy their organizations are. Developing such a view is easier said than done: it's natural for leaders to overestimate the health of their organization and the effectiveness of their leadership, given the way many of them identify with their companies and roles.

In our experience, too many executives default to describing their organizations as good striving to be great.[10] But this can't be true; by definition, more organizations can't be above the median line of organizational health than below it. When we examine survey data through the lens of the different levels of an organization, we find that leading executives typically have more favourable views of its health than do its line workers – who are, after all, much closer to the true centre of gravity.

What's more, surveys, interviews, and a significant amount of honest self-reflection all go into more robust assessments of organizational health. Since a rigorous self-diagnosis isn't always possible, we've developed some rules of thumb, such as those depicted in Figure 3.1. These move beyond guesswork and provide a more informed sense of what it feels like to be in one type of organization or another.[11]

The above assessment is of course only an indication of an organization's health, but provides a level of grounding for the rest of the chapter.

Now that we have established health as the context, let us move now to **the behaviours that really matter within each health quartile**, and the resulting leadership challenges that organizations face.

## *The leadership behaviours that really matter*

To explore the effectiveness of specific leadership behaviours at organizations in different states of organizational health, we tested 24 leadership behaviours along the key leadership categories of alignment, execution and renewal. These 24 behaviours included the four leadership styles that we always include in OHI assessments (authoritative leadership, consultative leadership, challenging leadership and supportive leadership)[12] and 20 new leadership behaviours. We surveyed more than 375,000 people from 165 organizations across multiple industries and geographies – creating the largest database of its kind. Drawing on our own work experience and on evolving academic insights we tested the 24 leadership behaviours to see if they passed strict criteria in terms of situational leadership.

Our second research question – *Is there 'one right way', or is leadership situational for organizations?* – was answered clearly by our analysis.

| How healthy is your organization? | Disagree or strongly disagree | Neutral | Agree or strongly agree |
|---|---|---|---|
| Leaders communicate a clear and compelling vision of where the organization is headed, how to get there, and what it means for people | 0 | 5 | 10 |
| Leaders in the organization ensure individuals understand what is expected of them, have sufficient authority and feel accountable for delivering results | 0 | 5 | 10 |
| Leaders consistently measure and manage business and risk, and act to address problems when they arise | 0 | 5 | 10 |
| Leaders engage with important external stakeholders (customers, suppliers, partners, and others) to more effectively create and deliver value – both now and in the future | 0 | 5 | 10 |
| Leaders use effective leadership styles to shape the actions of people in the organization to drive high performance | 0 | 5 | 10 |
| Leaders encourage and harness new ideas, including everything from radical innovation to incremental improvement, so the organization can effectively evolve and grow over time | 0 | 5 | 10 |
| Leaders ensure the institutional skills and talent are in place to execute the strategy and create competitive advantage | 0 | 5 | 10 |
| Leaders develop employee loyalty and enthusiasm, and inspire people to exert extraordinary effort to perform at their very best | 0 | 5 | 10 |
| Leaders in the organization cultivate a clear, consistent set of values and working norms that foster effective workplace behaviour | 0 | 5 | 10 |
| **Total** | | | |

| Scoring legend: | |
|---|---|
| **Organizations whose members overwhelmingly respond like you...** | **Score** |
| ... are healthy (among the top quartile), and can expect to achieve and sustain performance and create surplus value over the long term | 70–90 |
| ... enjoy good but not great health (second quartile from top), but can achieve health and ultimately market rewards over a 1-2 year period | 60–69 |
| ... are below average in health (third quartile from top), but can leverage specific strengths to accelerate their journey to health and performance. | 50–59 |
| ... are in the bottom quartile of health, but can make faster gains than other companies provided they quickly identify and take action on performance and health priorities. | 0–49 |

FIGURE 3.1  McKinsey 'Organizational Health' Quiz

The analysis yielded what we call a leadership staircase – a pyramid of behaviour analogous to Maslow's hierarchy of needs.[13] For the interested reader, Appendix 1 provides additional details on our approach.

In the leadership staircase (see Figure 3.2) some kinds of behaviours are always essential. We call them the baseline leadership behaviours, and there are four in total. Shoring these behaviours up serves to keep organizations from sliding into trouble, but in themselves they do not differentiate between mediocre and top performance. Leaders need competence in additional behaviours – above and beyond the baseline – to help their organization climb the staircase. We call them situational leadership behaviours, and there are 11 in total.

Our research suggests that in order to move the health of an organization from fourth to third quartile, the most effective forms of situational leadership behaviours are those which are often associated with a directive, 'top-down' leadership style: making fact-based decisions, solving problems effectively, and focusing positively on recovery. It appears that those behaviours are most needed when an organization is in dire straits.

In order to move an organization's health further up into the second quartile it appears that leaders should focus on those behaviours which are often referred to as 'execution-oriented': keeping groups on task, employing strong result orientation, clarifying objectives and consequences, and seeking different perspectives. In addition, it is important to build in speed and agility, and this often follows once execution has been nailed. These 'execution-oriented' and 'agility-related' behaviours do not substitute for the 'top-down' behaviours that were prevalent in the third quartile. They come on top. The leadership staircase implies that every step builds on the previous one.

Moving further up in the leadership staircase toward building a top-quartile organization – an organization that innovates, outperforms its competitors, engages its employees, attracts great talent, and outperforms stakeholders' expectations – requires leaders to add behaviours that are often described as 'inspirational': motivating and bringing out the best in people, and modelling organizational values.

In summary, organizations at the bottom of the health spectrum must build leaders that can assertively put an organization back on track, then establish a solid execution engine to get results and build in speed, and finally inspire employees and help them reach their full potential. In addition, the four baseline behaviours should be present at all times, from the very beginning. The full staircase is shown in Figure 3.2. This staircase model aligns squarely with our own real-world observations. See Figure 3.3 for a detailed description of each of the baseline and situational behaviours.

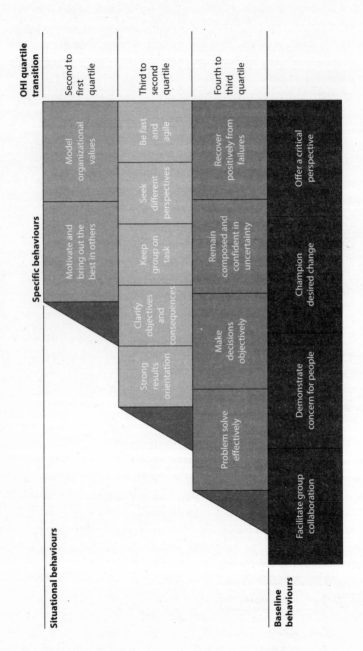

FIGURE 3.2 The situational leadership staircase

| | Leadership behaviour | Description |
|---|---|---|
| **Second to first quartile** | Motivate and bring out the best in others | • Challenge employees to do more than they thought was possible and find ways to make work more meaningful for their employees |
| | Model organizational values | • Clearly communicate a set of values that are personally meaningful to employees and challenge employees to live up to the organization's values and norms |
| **Third to second quartile** | Strong results orientation | • Emphasize the importance of efficiency and productivity and prioritize the highest value work |
| | Clarify objectives and consequences | • Translate their vision for the company into specific strategic goals and milestones with clear links between performance and consequences |
| | Keep group on task | • Operate with discipline and rigor and closely monitor performance |
| | Seek different perspectives | • Encourage employees to (i) contribute ideas, (ii) engage key external stakeholders when needed, (iii) import 'best practices' and (iv) solicit feedback from customers |
| | Be fast and agile | • Act or adjust quickly to new ways of doing things when faced with new challenges and new problems |
| **Fourth to third quartile** | Problem solve effectively | • Effectively solve difficult problems |
| | Make decisions objectively | • Exercise good judgment by making quality and informed decisions based on facts, data, and analytics |
| | Remain composed and confident in uncertainty | • Remain calm and clear-headed when faced with daunting challenges, in order to more effectively guide the organization in times of challenge or ambiguity |
| | Recover positively from failures | • Quickly recover from setbacks and failures and treat them as an opportunity to learn |
| **Baseline** | Facilitate group collaboration | • Encourage different parts of the company to work together to make improvements to the organization, creating a sense of teamwork and mutual support throughout the company |
| | Demonstrate concern for people | • Build a positive environment characterized by team harmony, support, and caring for employees' welfare |
| | Champion desired change | • Drive innovation in the company and champion changes to improve how the company operates |
| | Offer a critical perspective | • Devote sufficient attention to considering how the company can do things differently, challenge assumptions and question the status quo |

FIGURE 3.3  Baseline and situational leadership behaviours

In addition, we identified certain 'negative differentiators'. Organizations in higher health quartiles emphasize these behaviours less than the organizations in health quartiles below them, from a ranking point of view (the absolute numbers were still higher, meaning that organizations in higher quartiles still exhibit this behaviour more than organizations in lower quartiles).

When applying these findings, we always counsel organizations to work on all leadership behaviours; the ranking simply helps prioritize within those.

The organizational context changes constantly and so can organizational health. Effective situational leadership adapts to these changes by identifying and marshalling the kinds of behaviour needed to lead more effectively and thereby move an organization from its present state to a stronger, healthier one. In the following section, we look at the different leadership behaviours that are most effective for different stages of health, and how organizations can transition between health quartiles.

Let's now look at the staircase and the transitions from step to step in more detail.

## Making the transitions on the staircase

It is important to note the behaviours at different steps of the situational leadership staircase are both cumulative and sequential. Organizations embarking on a health journey must first master the behaviours at the bottom, and move up as their organizational health shifts. Organizations beginning at a higher level of health must be sure to master (and sustain) the baseline behaviours as well as the behaviours in the lower health quartiles before beginning to work on their context-specific behaviours. The reason for this is that the staircase shows the *relative emphasis* of different behaviours in different contexts. Organizations should ideally display all 15 leadership behaviours at any given time (or as many as possible), yet with differing degrees of emphasis depending on their context.

### BASELINE BEHAVIOURS

For companies at every level above the truly dysfunctional, a set of threshold forms of baseline behaviours appears to be essential. Others may also be called for, depending upon an organization's state of health, but the following practices are appropriate no matter what a company's health may be:

- effectiveness at facilitating group collaboration
- demonstrating concern for people
- championing desired change
- offering critical perspectives

The absence of such fundamentals of healthy interpersonal interaction invites disorder; shoring up these behaviours, on the other hand, serves to keep organizations from sliding backward into trouble. But in themselves, they don't spell the difference between mediocre and top-tier organizational health. Organizations need additional practices to climb the staircase.

## DIGGING OUT (FOURTH QUARTILE TO THIRD QUARTILE)

Organizations in the bottom (fourth) health quartile face stark – even existential – challenges, such as low levels of innovation, declining customer loyalty, wilting employee morale, the loss of major talent and critical cash constraints. Typically, these companies lack some or even all of the baseline forms of behaviour. Implementing the full complement is essential. But under trying conditions, our research suggests, the most effective forms of leadership behaviour are:

- making fact-based decisions
- solving problems effectively
- focusing positively on recovery
- remaining calm and confident in uncertainty

Ironically, these additional behaviours are often the opposite of what distressed organizations actually do. Leaders at too many bottom-quartile companies, in their urgency to act, seek quick top-down fixes (such as replacing senior executives one or more times) but forego granular, fact-based analyses or well-rooted strategies.

This is bad news, because some of these common behaviours were found to be negative differentiators. Specifically, we found one that passed all our criteria: *challenging leadership.* This calls for leaders to get employees to do more than they thought possible. Unfortunately, its overuse in low health environments is counterproductive. The analogy is that the patient is too sick for the medicine: a marathon is no cure for a broken leg.

No doubt it's dangerous to draw too many lessons from well-known historical examples: memory is selective. Yet we're struck by the parallels between these findings and the experiences of IBM in the early 1990s and of Continental Airlines later that decade. When Lou Gerstner, hired from the outside, took over as the new chairman and CEO of a then deeply troubled IBM, he prioritized clear, fact-based problem solving. One measure of this mandate was his insistence that the executive team essentially abandon slide presentations and submit plans in jargon-free prose. He also refused to accept the idea that the company's decline, partition, or even liquidation was inevitable. The ability to see the facts clearly and to demonstrate resilience helped Gerstner and his team to break a long downward slide, reconsider a product category previously dismissed as obsolete, and turn what many had presumed to be an inevitable asset breakup into a new trajectory for growth. The leadership's mindset, moreover, became ingrained in the enterprise; members of Gerstner's team who rode out the reorganization bought into his practices, and passed many of them on to their own working teams.

So too at Continental Airlines: in the late 1990s morale had been so broken that workers were reportedly tearing the Continental logo off their uniforms to avoid being recognized as company employees off the job. As part of the company's turnaround, members of the new leadership team embraced effective attitudes and behaviours, drilled down to assess profitability on a route-by-route and flight-by-flight basis, and took decisive action grounded in reality. In fact, this uncompromising focus on facts led then COO Greg Brenneman to discover, over Thanksgiving, that the company would run out of cash in less than two months. With spirited resilience, the leadership team eliminated unprofitable routes, implemented specific initiatives for recovery (such as bonuses for on-time departures), and brought a loss maker into the black within 12 months.[14]

## MOVING ON UP (THIRD QUARTILE TO SECOND QUARTILE)

Our research and experience suggests that a major differentiating leadership characteristic of companies on the upswing is the ability to take practices that are already used at some levels of the organization and use them more systematically, more reliably, and more quickly. This shift calls for behaviour that places a special emphasis on:

- keeping groups on task
- orienting them toward well-defined results
- clarifying rewards, objectives and consequences

Such situations also favour leaders who:

- embrace *agility* (speed, stability, flexibility)
- seek *different perspectives* (best practices, internally and externally) to help ensure that their companies do not overlook possibly better ways of doing things.

But under these circumstances, qualities such as the ability to motivate and bring out the best in others and to model company values found at the top tier of organizational health typically have a less pronounced effect.

We also found two negative differentiators. First is *remaining composed and confident in uncertainty*, which is in fact one of the positive differentiators in the jump from fourth quartile to third. However, as organizations increase in health and move into both the second quartile as well as the first, the operating environment typically becomes less uncertain, and hence there is less of premium of focusing on this behaviour. Second is *consultative leadership*, which includes soliciting employee feedback and giving employees autonomy – things are moving faster, there is a premium put on speed, so there is less time to consult.

The jump from the third quartile to the second quartile is an important and a difficult one. It is the only transition that has a negative correlation in terms of similarity between the quartiles. (The correlation between Q4 and Q3 is 0.67, between Q3 and Q2 it is -0.71, and between Q2 and Q1 it is 0.37.) What this means is that a fundamental behaviour and mindset shift is required, with an emphasis on many behaviours not previously emphasized. While effective leadership in the third quartile requires more hands-on, fact-based decision making and problem solving, in the second quartile leadership requires much more empowerment and accountability of employees. This empowerment consists of both the carrot and the stick, while fostering the best practices from within and outside the organization. Leaders transitioning to second-quartile behaviours often struggle with letting people 'run with it' without getting stuck in the day-to-day operations.

A US-based financial-services company we know supplies a practical example. Its leadership aspired to strengthen the organization's financial performance, innovate in the core business, and use an integrated package of health, performance, and leadership initiatives to capture more value at risk. At the outset, this company's organizational health was in the third quartile – below the median. Key challenges included a lack of clear objectives or accountability (highlighted by committees with muddled or overlapping missions; poor development and career opportunities for high performers; and weak management of financials, operations and risk (reflected, among other ways, by the absence of robust metrics). Exacerbating these problems, the leadership's approach to running the company was pervasively top down.

To meet the challenges, the leaders implemented an integrated set of health and performance initiatives – for example, they developed clear standards and outcomes to clarify day-to-day tasks. The company made its objectives (and the consequences of not achieving them) transparent by articulating a forceful strategic vision marked by specific operating goals and milestones. The leadership also aimed to foster bottom-up, employee-driven solutions and actively encourage new perspectives. Although many things went right for this company beyond its walls, these internal moves undoubtedly strengthened it, and the results were tangible. Within two years, it had achieved its top line objectives in health, performance, and leadership, and its stock price had increased by 250 per cent.

## TO THE TOP (SECOND QUARTILE TO FIRST QUARTILE)

Finally, there is the jump from the second quartile to the first – the summit of achievement. Here there are two main behaviours that really make a difference:

- Motivate and bring out the best in others
- Model organizational values

At this level of organizational health, individuals are typically high performing, self-driven and self-governing. The leader's role is to inspire, motivate and coach people to reach ever higher levels of performance. Much like personal coaches to elite athletes, leaders at this level do not necessarily need to have all the answers, but they must show employees how to find them.

The organizational mission, vision and culture becomes an increasingly important driving force the more healthy an organization becomes, and it is critical that leaders role-model the aspired behaviours and foster understanding and conviction among employees, through consistent communication.

This transition has only one negative differentiator, but it is an interesting one: **Clarify objectives, rewards and consequences**. It is interesting because this is a positive differentiator in the transition between the third quartile and the second quartile. What we found is that this leadership action has exhausted its utility after second-quartile health is attained, and that continued emphasis thereafter is counterproductive for employees. Employees in organizations with top quartile health are well aware of what the objectives are – often they are responsible for setting them – and they are also clear about the performance management system. In addition, they are anyway often intrinsically motivated to do the job at hand, and emphasizing external rewards, including financial ones, can have negative effects on their motivation.[15]

## WHY NOT START AT THE TOP?

If identifiable forms of leadership behaviour are associated with companies in the higher quartiles, can an organization in the lower quartiles simply apply them immediately and leap to the top? Our research and experience suggest that attempts to do so typically end poorly. **Emphasizing the kinds of behaviour that are not attuned to an organization's specific situation can waste time and resources and reinforce bad behaviour.** Worse, it can make an upgrade to a higher health quartile even more difficult. This makes intuitive sense: the leaders of a company in deep trouble should not prioritize, for example, modelling organizational values, a first-quartile behaviour.

We observed one cautionary example at a joint venture that ended badly for a number of related health, performance and leadership reasons. Its board installed a highly charismatic leader with an outsized focus on top quartile-style motivational behaviour. He travelled globally with his chairperson, for example, touting the joint venture's 'premium on innovation' and declaring that despite its merger-like characteristics, there was a 'job for everyone' who was passionate about its vision. Unfortunately, at the time of these pronouncements, the organization had done little groundwork on critical issues of integration, including the difficult how-to's of harmonizing disparate IT systems and organizational cultures. Both legacy organizations responded by continuing to execute and perform as if nothing had changed. There was evidence they hoped that nothing ever would.

The joint venture responded to missing its first-quarter targets by setting even more ambitious ones. It handed accountability to the executive responsible for sales and marketing, but no root-cause analyses were undertaken. When it discovered a cash crisis, it made no credible efforts to craft a practical response; instead, the top executive continued to trumpet his mission throughout his global visits. But a 'job for everyone' fell victim to the joint venture's alarming cash position, which forced mass layoffs, and with them came the end of the leadership's credibility. The venture was dissolved after just over a year of misguided operation.

## Link to adult development

The leadership development staircase and our broader research and practice on leadership development are consistent with the theories of adult development. We found through the leadership staircase that leaders in organizations must manage a number of key shifts to move from bottom to top quartile health: first is a need to assertively (and perhaps in a top down fashion) put the organization back on track. Second is the imperative to create an execution and results-oriented engine, and to build in speed and agility. And third, leaders must move towards a more inspirational, coaching-oriented and participative form of leadership, in order to bring out the best in others. These transitions require significant shifts in terms of the behaviours and mindsets on the part of the leader.

These three shifts point in a similar direction to the basic stages (levels, structures) of adult development, or consciousness. For example, the research on cognitive development describes the transition towards logic and then increasingly abstract levels of reasoning.[16] The research on self-related stages describes (very broadly) the shifts from survival, towards results and achievement, and then collective meaning and service.[17] The link is illustrated even more clearly when looking at specific development models, covering both the individual and the collective, from Maslow in the 1940s to Kegan and Lahey and Laloux in the 2010s.

In addition, our research specifies that it is not possible to skip stages, and a shift to a higher stage requires that the previous stage is transcended and included (and not dropped). Adult development theory posits a similar narrative of progress that is an incremental journey, where one stage must be completed before one can embark on the next. For the interested reader, we refer to the sources listed in the references at the back of the book.

## Transitioning between contexts: adaptive leadership

**Effective leadership in different organizational contexts requires different behaviours, skills and mindsets.** In a static world, the insights from the previous sections would provide an effective range of behaviours as needed: determine the context and display the relevant behaviours. However, we do not live in a static world: far from it. Wherever we look, we see the world changing. New technologies are rendering business models obsolete, increased interconnectedness is amplifying the effects of global shocks, and demographic shifts are creating new consumer and employee groups – each with different demands. For organizations, contexts will continue to shift in the future, and as a result those organizations will move in and out of different health quartiles – likely in a downward fashion if they fail to react. **Leaders must thus have the mental flexibility to be able to adapt to different situations and adjust their behaviours rapidly.** We call this *adaptive leadership*.

Adaptive leadership requires increased self-awareness and the right mindset for learning. It is thus a supplement to both the baseline and situational leadership components that we reviewed in the previous chapters – while baseline and situational leadership help you lead effectively within a given context, adaptive leadership helps you transition between contexts quickly and effectively.

Adaptive leadership seems simple enough in theory, but is often much more challenging in practice, especially in high-paced environments. In this chapter we review the trends relevant to leadership in organizations, and the implications they carry for leaders. We then discuss the need for adaptive leadership, and review how we build adaptability through our Centred Leadership approach.

## A new industrial revolution

The world is becoming more complex, and with it the requirements for organizations to thrive and the leadership needed to do so. In the past, organizations could hold on to proprietary advantages for longer, business activities were primarily local, and the pace of business was slower. Commercial companies, for example, often operated in one or a few industries, and their organizational contexts were relatively stable.

However, the world has changed dramatically, and is now more short term, more global, faster and more unstable. As a result, in the past 20 years we have seen organizations facing increasing challenges to maintain performance, and as a result the demands on leaders has grown. The velocity of value creation and disruption is increasing, fuelled in large part by an increase in knowledge creation and sharing. (For example, while it took a typical Fortune 500 company around 20 years to reach a market cap of a billion dollars, successful new organizations are now able to reach the milestone within a few years.) The estimated lifespan of a Fortune 500 company has gone from 90 years in 1935, to 30 years in 1975, to 14 years in 2010. The number of positions reporting to the CEO has gone from five in 1990 to ten today. The proportion of international business activities has risen from 33 per cent in 1990 to 66 per cent in 2018. While response times of up to 48 hours were previously deemed acceptable, today a response time of two or three hours on critical issues is often expected.[18]

What does the future hold? We know that the world is changing, but will it really be that different from before? We believe it will. Our research and interviews with leaders globally highlight five main trends that are relevant for organizations and for the leadership required to succeed.

1 **Increased interconnectedness.** The world is becoming increasingly connected, whether measured by internet statistics, global trade, or company supply chains. These trends can be a boon but they also act as an amplifier for shocks.

2 **The rise of emerging markets.** Based on current projections, by 2050 the emerging seven economies (China, India, Brazil, Russia, Indonesia, Mexico and Turkey) will be over 50 per cent larger than the G7 (US, Japan, Germany, UK, France, Italy and Canada) at market exchange rates.[19]

3 **The changing nature of capitalism.** We are seeing a rise in alternative ownership structures, growing resource scarcity, and increasingly demanding consumers and customer centricity.

4 **Technological disruptions.** Technological innovations are advancing faster than ever in a non-linear fashion, and will shape organizations across all industries and lead to new business models, shifting profits and new labour markets.

5 **Marked demographic shifts.** These are leading to an increase in the proportion of elderly (categorized as over 65 years of age) globally, primarily in developed countries, and simultaneously a rise in the proportion of Millennials and Generation Z in the workforce.

Each of the above trends is important in and of itself. Each requires leaders to master new behaviours, skills and mindsets. For example, organizations will need to adopt a more systematic approach to understanding potential shocks, increase sustainability as a business imperative, up their 'technology quotients' across the organization, and align their people processes with the demands of new generations.

However, when taken together, the implications of these trends are even more profound. Compared with the Industrial Revolution, the current change is happening ten times faster and at 300 times the scale, or roughly 3,000 times the impact.[20] Indeed, we are operating in what some call a 'post-VUCA' (volatile, uncertain, complex and ambiguous – a term originally used in the military in the 1990s) world, and are in the midst of a new industrial revolution. We believe that complexity will only increase in the future, at an increasing rate given the velocity of change, and this has important implications for organizations and their leaders.

## The need for adaptive leadership

Previously, organizations might stay in a certain context (for example, turnaround or rapid growth) for an extended period – meaning that the behaviours, experiences and mindsets needed were relatively stable, and familiar to their leaders. However, the accelerating scale and pace of change has increased the movement of organizations between different contexts within a much shorter space of time. At any given moment, approximately one in three organizations will be undergoing some kind of significant restructuring. A third of these efforts last more than two years.[21] Indeed, many organizations often find themselves in different situations at the same time across business units and/or geographies.

This new organizational reality means that **leadership matters more than ever, and its importance for organizational performance will only increase in the future.** Leaders today operate in a multi-speed and multi-competitive environment simultaneously. How can they remain active and creative in this environment?

We believe that **leaders must be adaptive, able to rapidly understand their context and tailor their leadership style accordingly.** The analogy is that of a decathlete, who combines power, agility and technique to compete across ten separate disciplines. In practice, adaptive leaders display a broader range of behaviours, drawing on a more comprehensive set of skills, and accessing greater self-awareness to achieve peak performance.

Our McKinsey research supports the primacy of adaptive leadership. Our research on 21st-century leadership, with interviews of over 100 CEOs, charts a rapidly changing world, and finds the leaders must be able to step back, 'see with a telescope and a microscope', to make decisions under increasing uncertainty. For example, Carlos Ghosn, Chairman and CEO of Renault-Nissan, highlighted the importance of adapting one's strategy in the face of external shocks:[22]

> We need to be more prepared for external crises, where it's not the strategy of the company that is in question; it's the ability of leaders to figure out how to adapt that strategy. We are going to have a lot more of these external crises because we are living in such a volatile world – an age where everything is leveraged and technology moves so fast. You can be rocked by something that originated completely outside your area.

Other interviews stressed the importance of humility and openness to change as key success factors for adaptive leadership.[23]

At an organizational level, our transformational change research shows that organizations that manage the change effort with rigour, building up a cadre of change leaders and shifting mindsets in the organization to adapt to the desired new state, are twice as likely to succeed than organizations that don't manage the change effort rationally and scientifically.[24] We have found similar findings on the importance of adaptive leadership and adaptive organizations in academia and other applied research as well.

Linking back to our framework of organizational context, **adaptive leadership can be seen as the ability to move quickly and effectively between different contexts.** These contexts include organizational health (for example, in the case of company with multiple operating divisions at different stages of health), but also a broader array of micro and macro contexts. For example, we discussed above the different behaviours needed in organizations in all four health quartiles. Leaders can use adaptive leadership to rapidly adapt to changing health quartiles, or to simultaneously lead business units, departments, or teams that are operating at different levels of health.

Professor Ron Heifetz has carried out extensive research on 'Adaptive leadership'.[25] Heifetz focuses on how to manage the complexity and pace of continual change while also being able to improve daily effectiveness. He shows that leaders must increasingly be able to solve adaptive challenges – which require new ways of thinking and learning to be solved, rather than technical challenges – which can be solved through linear problem solving and known solutions. Heifetz also coined the terms 'balcony and dance', urging leaders to 'step up on the balcony' once in a while in order to gain perspective on the bigger picture, to increase their leadership effectiveness. Another example of research on adaptability is from the Leadership Circle, which shows that leadership development must (at a minimum) keep pace with the rate of change. Leaders whose mental 'operating systems' are more developed than the world around them are able to lead more creatively (rather than reactively), with significantly higher business performance as a result. The research shows that the average Creative score in businesses in the top decile in terms of performance was 80 per cent, while the average Creative score in the bottom decile was 30 per cent.[26]

Finally, one executive search agency drew on research and thousands of executive assessments to identify the leadership traits and skills that were most fundamental to senior-level executive success. They found that the ability to drive change is key, as well as the humility and self-awareness to adapt one's view as new insights are learned.[27] Adaptability was furthermore found to hold true at the organizational level as well.[28]

For individuals, too, adaptive capabilities are increasingly important. People stay in their jobs on average 4.2 years according to a 2016 survey[29] (meaning that people today hold up to ten jobs in their life-time), with a higher degree of geographic and industry variation. In addition, in the near future, it is estimated that over one-third of skills (35 per cent) considered important in today's workforce will have changed.[30] In order to stay relevant, individuals will therefore be forced to upskill themselves. Adaptive leadership, and the mental awareness and flexibility it entails, is a critical enabler.

## Building adaptability through Centred Leadership

At McKinsey, we build adaptability through our *Centred Leadership approach*. Centred Leadership helps people lead from a core of self-mastery, across five key dimensions (see Figure 3.4). Our Centred Leadership research, conducted for more than ten years with more than 5,000 executive data points and hundreds of in-depth interviews to date, shows that Centred Leaders (defined as leaders who master all five elements of Centered Leadership) feel four times more prepared to lead amidst change and are almost 20 times more likely to be satisfied with their leadership performance and life overall.[31]

The Centred Leadership approach focuses extensively on building self-awareness including understanding one's strengths and weaknesses, the impact of one's behaviours on others, and one's personal values and beliefs. It also emphasizes the ability to frame and re-frame situations in order to change one's thoughts and behaviours to be more effective and to bring out your 'best self' more.[32] Below we describe each element that Centred Leaders master in order to build adaptability.

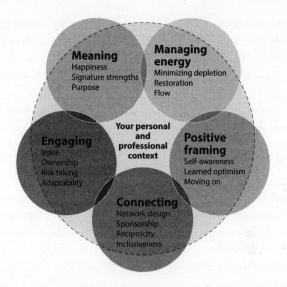

FIGURE 3.4 The Centred Leadership approach

- **Meaning:** Meaning is the anchor of Centred Leadership and the most powerful factor. Why is meaning important for leaders? Studies have shown that among professionals, meaning translates collectively into higher productivity, lower turnover and increased loyalty. The individual benefits include greater job satisfaction and feelings of transcendence (in other words, contributing to something bigger than yourself generates a deeper sense of meaning, thereby creating a virtuous cycle). It begins with happiness, as meaningful engagement offers lasting fulfilment. Second, it taps into our core strengths. Finally, it helps us lead with purpose, which in turn inspires conviction, courage and confidence we may not realize we have. We help leaders find meaning through guided visualizations, identifying strengths, and reflecting on peak experiences.
- **Positive Framing:** We see the world through invisible 'frames' of our own making, and the ways we view the world and process experiences can influence professional outcomes. For example, many studies suggest that optimists see life

more realistically than pessimists, a frame of mind that can be crucial to making the right business decisions. Optimists, research shows, are not afraid to frame the world as it actually is – they are confident that they can manage its challenges and move their teams quickly to action. By contrast, pessimists are more likely to feel helpless and to get stuck in downward spirals that lead to energy-depleting rumination. Framing builds the self-awareness to see ourselves both 'on the balcony and in the dance'. This allows us to step back, pause and shift our perception of the situation, allowing us to shift our reactions to them as well. We help leaders understand their frames and how they can shift them consciously through iceberg coaching, reflecting on needs and fears, and through learned optimism, among other techniques.

- **Connecting:** People with strong networks and good mentors enjoy more promotions, higher pay, and greater career satisfaction. It is essential to build relationships, trust and a meaningful community that can help you develop to your full potential. The key elements are network design, sponsors, reciprocity and inclusiveness. Those who are connected in this way with others feel a sense of belonging, which makes their lives meaningful. As Mark Hunter and Herminia Ibarra have noted in the *Harvard Business Review*, what differentiates a leader from a manager 'is the ability to figure out where to go and to enlist the people and groups necessary to get there.'[33] It is vital to have individual relationships with senior colleagues willing to go beyond the role of mentor – someone willing to stick out his or her own neck to create opportunity for or help a protégée.

- **Engaging:** Many people think that hard work will eventually be noticed and rewarded. That can happen – but usually doesn't. Engaging is about a range of behaviours (clear voice, posture, establishing commitments) to create a strong presence. Those who are fully engaged in work have aligned their intentions, attention and emotions; they speak clearly and are happy to take responsibility. In these ways, their hard work is noticed and valued. We help leaders engage by writing down personal commitments, prioritizing what they will and won't do, and creating personal 'mini boards' to hold themselves accountable.

- **Managing Energy:** Work doesn't have to be exhausting. Managing your energy involves being aware of what activities deplete you, how you can restore your energy, and how you can be in a *flow* state more often, to reach peak performance. Mihály Csíkszentmihályi, a founder of positive psychology, studied thousands of people, from sculptors to factory workers. He found that those who frequently experienced *flow* (a sense of being so engaged by activities that you don't notice the passage of time) were more productive and derived greater satisfaction from their work than those who did not. Further, it energized rather than drained them. Important techniques for energizing include mapping out your sources and uses of energy (different for introverts and extroverts), identifying energy boosters, and through mindfulness.[34]

This book will not focus on the Centred Leadership elements in detail (the interested reader can refer to *Centered Leadership* by Joanna Barsh and Johanne Lavoie, published in 2014). The focus here is on how Centred Leadership builds adaptability – crucially through self-awareness and having an open mind for learning – and the implications for leadership development.

Organizations can build adaptability by having a strong growth culture and expecting (or demanding) that their employees continuously develop while at the same time equipping employees with the right skills and mindsets to do so.[35] This includes supporting employees, for example by a feedback culture, by leaders personifying the behaviours, or by aligning the incentive systems of the organization. When we design leadership development programmes, we acknowledge the importance of adaptability, with an important focus on exploration and reflection, embedding Centred Leadership elements throughout. Our programmes invariably have a strong foundation of knowing oneself, and are typically built up from 'Leading Self', then 'Leading Others', then 'Leading Organizations', and finally 'Leading Change'. This will be further detailed in Part 2 of the book.

Building adaptability should not be confused with the behaviours, skills and mindsets required in each individual health context. Rather, they are elements that can help leaders transcend the requirements for effective leadership within different organizational contexts at a micro and a macro level. As such, adaptive leadership helps leaders not only in terms of shifts across health quartiles, but also more broadly when entering new and different contexts, and for general 'future-proofing' of organizations.

## *The critical enablers: skills and mindsets*

We saw in Chapter 1 that **effective leadership behaviours require contextualization, the right skills and the right mindsets**. Earlier in this chapter, we described the specific leadership behaviours that are most effective in different contexts, and which can help a transition into higher stages of organizational health – comprising four baseline leadership behaviours and 11 situational behaviours, spread out across the four health quartiles. We also discussed the importance of fostering adaptability. The focus was on behaviours, and on the behavioural shifts required.

Any behaviour, however, is nourished by the right skills and the right mindset – without these enablers, it is challenging to carry out the behaviours effectively and sustainably. For each behaviour in the situational leadership staircase and for adaptability (and for any other leadership behaviour that an organization is trying to foster), identifying and embedding these types of mindset shifts and skills are key components of our leadership development curriculum in practice. Below we provide illustrative examples of how this could look for the first baseline behaviour identified above: *facilitating group collaboration effectively*. For the interested reader, Appendix 2 has a more comprehensive overview of potential skills and mindsets that could help foster the baseline behaviours, situational behaviours and adaptive leadership.

We focus on being practical rather than theoretical, with concrete and real-world skills and mindsets to cultivate, in order to foster the desired behaviours. It should be noted, however, that the examples we give are illustrative and not definitive. They are based on our experience and typical observations, and should be taken as a starting point. We do not claim to be comprehensive, and acknowledge that a great deal of additional research and tools exist for the behaviours that we discuss. In practice, additional design and tailoring takes place when we embed skill-building elements and mindset shifts into a leadership development programme, drawing from a broad range of sources.

## Skills and mindsets for facilitating group collaboration effectively

The first baseline behaviour is facilitating group collaboration effectively. This is one of the most fundamental leadership behaviours, and its importance is most evident in its absence. It could require a number of key mindsets:

- 'Teamwork leads to better outcomes than the sum of individuals working in isolation.'
- 'We need to have a common direction and be able to rely on one another to achieve it.'
- 'People have different preferences and working styles (each of which are equally valid), and not everyone is like me.'
- 'Meeting preparation is important but not enough – I also need to ensure collaboration and creativity in the context of the meeting itself, as well as rigorous follow-up.'

Coupled with this are a number of skills. We lay out six of these below.

1 **Group collaboration and team formation.** Leaders may not always have the luxury of choosing their teams, but it is critical nonetheless to understand the skills required for the task at hand and whether the current team members have them.
2 **Ability to create joint accountability and commitment.**
3 **Understanding of team dynamics,** and how to make different working preferences gel into a high performing teams. Tools such as the Myers–Briggs Type Indicator (MBTI) or the Big Five personality traits may be helpful for the leaders to understand and appreciate differences in individuals' inclinations and behaviours. The MBTI measures personal preferences across four dimensions: extroversion vs. introversion, sensing vs. intuition, thinking vs. feeling, and judging vs. perceiving. The Big Five personality traits measures one's Openness to experience, Conscientiousness, Extraversion, Agreeableness and Neuroticism, often

shortened to the acronym OCEAN. Both have a rigorous paid version as well as more simple, free online assessments.[36]

4   Leaders must be able to **establish a culture where honest dialogue is possible**, and where conflicts are resolved quickly and effectively.

5   Leaders must be able to **negotiate fair (and ideally win–win)** *outcomes*. A practical resource is *Getting to Yes*, which includes tools such as 'separating the people from the problem', 'focusing on interests, not positions', 'inventing options for mutual gain', and 'using objective criteria'.[37]

6   Finally there are **practical skills in running meetings effectively** that can support a leader in facilitating group collaboration. Running effective meetings sounds like a trivial issue, but oftentimes we see one or more key elements missing. Running effective meetings includes meeting preparation (sending a meeting invitation with an agenda, ensuring that the right people are present), preparing the key facts to support decision makers on the decisions required, an ability to foster collaboration, creativity and fun in the meeting itself, capturing and disseminating minutes of the meeting/action items, and following up.

Our leadership-in-context research outlined the specific behaviours that are most effective for different health contexts – which we typically apply as the primary lens when identifying the critical behaviours to enable an organization's performance. In addition, we discussed the importance of adaptability. In this section, we discussed the importance of the underlying skills and mindsets that are linked to these behaviours, and provided an example for one of the baseline behaviours. Appendix 2 has additional examples for the remaining situational and adaptive leadership behaviours.

## *Implications for leadership development*

For leadership development interventions, the context-specific shifts based on health, as well as the elements of Centred Leadership, are only guide rails. The leadership staircase is not a prescriptive manual for effective leadership. Context is broad, and exceptions abound; and for these reasons, principles must always be tempered and augmented by practice. We therefore look at the organization-specific context and the behaviours that matter most for that organization when designing leadership programmes in practice – for example its industry context and 'recipe', its stage of growth, and its aspirations and strategy.

We treat health as the primary lens through which to view leadership behaviours, but always overlay these secondary lenses. We also consider other leadership development theory in addition to the leadership staircase, where relevant. For example, the psychological leadership school has shown a strong link between stage of development (or level of consciousness) with leadership effectiveness – so organizations can benefit from embedding elements in the programme to help individuals develop their mental complexity in this regard. In addition, proponents of moral universalism could push to include values and ethics, such as integrity, honesty and professionalism. Additionally, we take into consideration the enduring importance of building adaptability, and framing programmes along the 'lead self, lead others, lead organizations, lead change' spectrum.

A more recent, but increasingly important and fast moving crosscutting influence is that of technology. We already discussed technology as one of the forces that is increasing the velocity of value creation and disruption, necessitating adaptability among leaders. However, technology itself is an increasingly important part of leadership development curriculum, as it is presenting unique leadership challenges in its own right. For example, we know that 50 per cent of all activities performed by humans today could be automated in as little as the next ten years – using technologies that are already existing.[38] It is therefore a powerful lens through which to see leadership development. Workplaces are becoming increasingly distributed: we are moving from linear value chains to horizontal platforms to any-to-any ecosystems; and many organizations are moving from doing everything in-house to outsourcing increasingly value-adding activities to third parties, for example R&D activities in pharmaceutical companies. And there is a new gig economy emerging, built around value-creating interactions that quickly adapt to new needs and ideas, often with asset light business models.[39] This has led to disruption in many industries.

For example, the world's largest accommodation provider owns no rooms, the world's largest taxi company owns no cars, and one of the world's largest retailers owns no warehouses. In the next decade, organizations will need to develop a high number of leaders who are adept at managing and influencing this technology revolution. These leaders must understand the implications of technology on their business models. They need empathy for people going through this shift – who will often be increasingly anxious – and they need to be able to inspire employees during the transformation.

The end result of reviewing different influences and identifying the critical behaviours for an organization's strategy is typically a leadership model, often consisting of 10–20 behaviours across three to six key themes. The leadership model should then be tailored to different career paths (for example, generalist and expert) and adapted to different organizational levels (for example, individual contributor, general manager, executive). We will discuss the creation of a leadership model in more detail in Part 2 of the book.

Equally important is the focus on a few critical shifts. Once an organization has defined its leadership model (in terms of desired behaviours), it is time to prioritize. What works best in practice is a focus on three to five big shifts over a 12–18-month period. Once the priority behaviours have been adopted across the organization, new priorities can be established. In parallel, however, the original behaviours should continue to be reinforced for at least another three years, to make the change sustainable. In later chapters in Part 2, we discuss how this can be achieved.

Once the priority behaviours have been identified, we spend time up front identifying the skills and mindsets that are required to help enable the desired behavioural shifts. It may seem obvious, but these skills and mindsets – and the behaviours they help produce – are often most apparent in their absence. What would it be like to try to run an organization that lacked the ability to 'offer a critical perspective' for example? Decisions would be inaccurate, partial, inward looking, and prone to 'groupthink' or other forms of bias. This would be an organization that was collectively incapable of basing its decisions on known causes derived from rational deduction.

Additionally, it is important to reiterate that the priority shifts (behaviours, skills and mindsets) must be adopted across the whole of the organization and not just by the top team or in certain parts. Individuals will benefit from leadership development (and not only at work but also beyond, in social and community life) but the organization is the chief beneficiary. **If each organization fosters these** behaviours at scale, it will generate benefits at scale in all manner of conversations, interactions and decisions that go far beyond the leadership development intervention.

Organizations that correctly identify and prioritize the key behaviours, skills and mindsets that will best enable their strategy reap the benefits of more effective leadership.

## Case study: Building new capacity by releasing leadership potential

### Context and challenge

In 2011, a mobile-phone provider in Asia – serving nearly 35 million subscribers – faced a typical leadership problem. This, as the CEO noted, was a lack of leadership capacity across the whole organization: 'Every time we looked into reorganization or a new business opportunity, we would be looking at the same 20 people to run it. In a company of more than 5,000 employees, it just couldn't stay that way.' And equally, there was no succession plan to identify or supply talent from within to fill crucial leadership roles.

The challenge was therefore a need for leadership of scale and depth. An initial assessment showed a gap on both counts: within two to three years, 80 additional leaders capable of leading growth or turnaround initiatives needed to be found; and the performance of another 80 had to be improved significantly. This situation was not unique to this kind of organization, or to the sector.

The gap would not only be filled through leadership development programmes. There was broad acknowledgement that the organization had to prepare the ground for nurturing leaders more broadly: recruiting, succession planning, talent development and performance management all needed improvement, with accountability and ownership for talent and leadership development among the top team.

# Approach

The first step was to define a 'profile of success' for leadership in the organization. A set of leadership competencies were developed through external benchmarking, structured interviews and top team engagement, analyzing and linking to the strategic value drivers, and reviewing the existing competencies used in the talent management system. The joint McKinsey and client team developed a detailed Leadership Model with seven themes: Execution Excellence, Entrepreneurial, People Orientation, Customer Orientation, Innovation, Personal Values, and Strategic Thinking. The leadership model competencies were translated into specific, observable behaviours, and integrated into the broader talent management systems:

- **Recruiting:** The leadership competencies became an important part of the assessment, and also became the catalyst for a referral programme for senior leaders to identify and nominate promising external talent
- **Performance management:** To accompany the increased focus on development, performance management was revamped and shifted from a KPI-based discussion to a more holistic discussion that focused not only on what had been achieved, but also how it had been achieved
- **Talent management principles:** The leadership model itself had a People Orientation theme, highlighting the importance of taking accountability for people development. The leadership model revamp was used as an opportunity to truly shift ownership of people development from HR to all leaders in the organization
- **Talent development:** The organization designed and launched a set of six to nine-month programmes to grow high potential staff into more effective organization leaders, at different organizational levels

# Impact

After less than two years, the initiative had achieved successes across three levels.

1 **Improved performance**: 100 per cent of participants and their superiors stated that the programme boosted their leadership capabilities, their ability to deliver business results, and their readiness for higher-level roles. This sentiment was further echoed in talent reviews by the organization's senior leaders at the closure of each programme. Less than a year from the completion of their programme, one in three participants shifted into a new or expanded role and used these improved skills to boost its performance

2 **Strength in depth**: Internal successors were identified for the majority of positions, two participants of the Executive Development Programme had joined the senior leadership team, and other graduates were leading the initiatives that the organization had to deprioritize in 2011 due to the lack of leaders. The CEO said: "hopefully even the future CEO can come from that group."

3 **Increased employee engagement**: All participants found that their experience with the leadership programs increased their engagement toward the organization; the programmes met its promise to invest in its people. This helped the organization to curb attrition among middle managers and young high performers that had provided a challenge at the outset.

# Reflection

Not all leadership development initiatives embrace the fact that it takes more than a set of programmes to increase leadership effectiveness. The organization developed a leadership model that was used as a catalyst to shift the talent development system more broadly, embedding it into recruiting, performance management, leadership development programmes, as well as top team ownership for talent development.

Moreover, the experience here showed that the leadership development journey does not end after nine months. Instead, supportive relationships are maintained and former cohorts are involved in subsequent tracks as mentors and co-faculty. Regular sessions of an open leadership circle continued to challenge participants and help to spread the lessons of the programme into the broader organization.

In light of the initiative's success, this organization raised its aspirations. Leadership development was not just about filling a gap; instead, it wanted to become an exporter of talent to the wider conglomerate. Furthermore, the programmes became the flagships of the Organization's University, a centre for executive learning.

## Summary

In the opening chapter we defined leadership as **a set of behaviours that in a given context align an organization, foster execution, and ensure organizational and personal renewal.** These behaviours are supported by relevant skills and mindsets. This definition shapes the fundamentals of the 'what' of a leadership development intervention. First, effective leadership at an organizational level is about behaviours that ensure alignment, execution and renewal. Second, the specific behaviours required are defined by the organizational context (which each organization must understand, and the most important of which is organizational health). Third, these behaviours are enabled by the right skills and the right mindsets, which must also be explicitly built during a leadership development intervention.

With regard to context, we saw that what links organizations most usefully across sectors and regions, and over time is the state of their health. As such, we treat organization health as the primary context to identify the leadership behaviours that will be most effective, and overlay these with secondary, organization-specific lenses.

In a static world, the situational leadership staircase as well as other context specific behaviours would provide an effective toolbox for executives to adapt their behaviours as needed. However, the world is far from static, and we saw that a more a dynamic view of leadership, appropriate to the accelerating pace of global change, is needed. This environment demands a broader range of behaviours and experience from leaders. Contexts can blur together or can shift rapidly, and leaders must be able to rapidly adapt. Adaptability is not a substitute for context-specific leadership, but rather an enabler, allowing leaders to move in and out of different context while remaining effective. As such, we have developed three categories of leadership behaviours:

- **Baseline behaviours**: these apply within any context
- **Situational behaviours**: their effectiveness is context-specific
- **Adaptive behaviours**: these help you move between
  different contexts

These lenses typically culminate in a leadership model, which specifies the leadership behaviours that are most critical to achieve the organizational strategy. Organizations should focus on three to five critical shifts at a time, in order to make the change sustainable. In addition, organizations must identify the underlying enablers of skills and mindsets that best support the desired behavioural shifts.

Now that we have outlined 'what' should be the focus during a leadership development intervention, the next question, then, is 'who' to target. This is the focus of our next chapter.

# 4

# Core Principle 2: Engage the organization

*André Dua, Charlotte Relyea, David Speiser*

**Why organizational journeys?** | **Elements of engagement:
breadth, depth, pace** | **Implications for leadership development** | **The
increasing velocity of journeys** | **A short note on resourcing**

Today many leadership development programmes are *episodic* – they focus
on only a subset of the organization, and do not move quickly enough.
Sustainably shifting leadership behaviours across an entire organization,
however, requires an effort of the right breadth, depth and pace. Any leadership development programme must **bring about change across an
organization, not merely in isolated parts, and reach a critical mass
of pivotal influencers across all levels of the organization quickly.**
In order for this to happen the programme must be appropriate to the
organization and rationally conceived and executed; moreover, it must be
culturally attuned to the organization. Its acceptance (and therefore success) depends on a general understanding across the organization of what
great leadership looks like, and, for some, what the best leadership feels like.

Our Core Principle 1 attends to the critical shifts in a leadership development programme and links these to the organizational context and to
the creation of value; in essence, this is the 'what' of the leadership development programme. Core Principles 3 and 4 deal respectively with the 'how'
of leadership development at the individual and the organizational level.

Here, in Core Principle 2, we look at the 'who' of leadership development. This principle is based on the concept of *engaging the organization*. It addresses the matter of who should participate in leadership
development, under what conditions, how often, and for how long.
This is the way that the organization engages individuals across its
structure (we call this breadth), the nature, frequency and duration of
the development (we call this depth) and the speed at which the programme is initiated and rolled out (we call this pace).

## Core Principle 2: Engage a critical mass of pivotal influencers across the organization to reach a tipping point

Organizations must ensure sufficient breadth, depth, and pace in order to change leadership behaviours across the organization, and to give all employees an understanding of what great leadership looks like

## *Why organizational journeys?*

Why, then, is it necessary for an organization and its leadership development programmes to engage closely and mutually? There are two bodies of evidence that show the importance of engagement and the organization-wide view that it implies: our research, and our experience in delivering leadership development programmes (equally we note where a lack of these can disable or render ineffective the best-intended of programmes).

First, the research. There are several striking insights from our research that inform the elements that make up what we might characterize as the *organizational journey in leadership development* – in other words, how does the organization engage with its leaders and influencers over time? Those organizations that succeed in their efforts are much more likely (a likelihood measured in multiples of 5 to 7 times) to structure their leadership development programmes along the thinking that we set out as the organizational (as opposed to individual) journey.

For example, we know that organizations with successful leadership development interventions are 6.9 times more likely to cover the whole organization and design programmes in the context of the broader leadership development strategy. We also know that organizations with successful leadership development programmes are 6.4 times more likely to ensure that their leadership strategy and model reaches all levels of the organization.

This idea of what we might call an organizational journey for all participants is supported by two more data from our research:

organizations with successful leadership development programmes are 4.6 times more likely to assess the leadership status gap (and the reasons for it) at all levels of the organization; and organizations with successful leadership development programmes are 4.9 times more likely to model the desired behaviours in their top teams and beyond, as senior people become formally and informally involved (as speakers, faculty, mentors) in the development programme.

The above points cover the importance of 'breadth' (that is, ensuring the leadership development interventions reach a critical mass of influencers in the organization). In addition, research shows what that adequate 'depth' (in terms of how people are engaged on a leadership programme) is required for a sufficient amount of time. Capabilities are not built overnight, and people need sustained time and touch points to develop them.

Unfortunately, the vast majority (81 per cent) of leadership development programmes take place over 90 days or less; and a mere 10 per cent run for more than six months.[1] Organizations are spending too little time over too short a period on leadership development, which does not allow participants to reflect on and trial their new skills, and time for the supportive effect of cohort-behaviour to have an impact. The impact shows: 41 per cent of successful leadership development programmes are over two months, while only 25 per cent of unsuccessful programmes have a similar duration, and successful programmes are on average more than 35 per cent longer duration than unsuccessful ones.[2]

Second, what we know from our practical experience. The most impactful leadership programmes that lead to a visible shift in daily leadership behaviours and bottom line impact always entail *organization-wide thinking*. These programmes reach far into the structure and culture of the organization, initially focusing on a critical mass of leaders, and over time reach a tipping point and shift the behaviours of all employees. To do this, the programmes also have sufficient depth and pace, with 12–18 months spent on each wave of desired shifts in order to ensure real transformation. We even see some organizations where leadership development is never an 'intervention' but rather a part of the steady state business processes. GE, for example, equates leadership to the 'plumbing in a house', and leadership development therefore occurs on an ongoing basis, with a clear leadership journey for top talent at all levels of the organization.

Unfortunately, we often see the opposite: leadership development is delegated many levels down the organization, without the necessary support from senior organizational leaders; the top managers do not 'walk the talk' and either disengage personally or embark on a superficial leadership journey themselves. We see leadership development efforts that are narrow in application across the organization and are shallow for the individual: cohort-specific episodes instead of organization-wide engagement.

Organizations such as professional services or the military understand that leaders must be apprenticed and grown from within their organization. **They devote time, energy, people and money to develop their leaders (and influencers) over long periods.** This approach produces a sustained developmental journey for the individual leader, a planned and secure supply of leaders for the organization, and an organization-wide leadership culture.

## Elements of engagement: breadth, depth, pace

A number of factors readily emerge in successfully engaging the organization. We see repeatedly the effect of a 'critical mass' where sufficient numbers of leaders and influencers are behaving in ways consistent with the desired strategy – setting the way for others. Equally we see the importance of sufficient range and density of leaders from disparate parts of the organization behaving in new ways such that their own new behaviours are reflected back at them – their sense of themselves as changing derives from seeing others' positive reactions to them. (The opposite reaction bears significant risk – we sometimes see leaders returning from a programme full of energy, only to be disappointed by the lack of enthusiasm shown by those colleagues who did not join the programme for the new way of working; these leaders often revert back to their old way of working, lose enthusiasm and, in the worst cases, leave the company.)

Moreover, there have to be sufficient numbers of more senior leaders who can talk about change that the leadership development programme is bringing about; they will play a role in the formal processes (performance review, staff appraisal, 360-degree review) that reinforce the new leadership behaviours. Their roles also contribute the broader culture that sustains the changes brought about by the programme. There is, for example, a positive effect of cohort classes as sufficient leaders across the organization meet and form working relationships with each other based on a common leadership development experience.

The journey must be pursued with sufficient intensity and over sufficient duration as well. Many leadership development programmes are episodic and sporadic, for example covering only one cohort (or one individual) at a time, for a two-to-three-week period. We see such episodic and sporadic leadership development efforts fail not only because they are undertaken without being part of a broader effort, but also because the components of the programme are insufficient in themselves to bring about meaningful change. Additionally, interventions should have adequate pace and energy. If not, momentum is lost, learning is squandered, and the broader organization can become frustrated by the lack of visible change.

As such, engaging the organization entails three elements:

- **breadth** (the numbers of those involved in a programme)
- **depth** (the frequency and nature with which participants are involved and kept involved)
- **pace** (the speed of the initial rollout of the programme).

These three elements help ensure the intervention transforms a critical mass; and this critical mass then creates a tipping point in behavioural change across the organization. In practice, this means transforming a critical mass of leaders (through breadth, depth and pace) at all levels within an organization. When sufficient numbers of leaders display the new behaviours, a tipping point is reached, the change becomes self-sustaining and the organization is transformed. We discuss the three elements of depth, breadth and pace in more detail below.

## Breadth

The breadth of a leadership development programme is the extent to which it involves people across and down the organization. The key question here becomes: *How much is enough?* There are many ways to answer this. One of them is through the lens of network theory, an interdisciplinary body of work that unites thinking from maths and physics, anthropology, social science, communications and, above all, epidemiology. They can be applied to all spreading phenomena in biological, digital and social networks. The organization is a complex mix of the latter two.

In networks there are many determinants of size, speed and quality. Network size can be measured by nodes and network thinkers tend to distinguish between static networks like railways and scale-free networks like the internet. Network speed (or speed of growth or information within a network) can be thought about in terms of epidemiology: here, network thinkers arrive at a transmission or diffusion rate based on probability of infection and frequency or density of connection, and in terms of susceptibility and recovery rates. And in terms of network quality, social networks theorists tend to talk of weak ties, structured holes, super-spreaders. Often the most engaging thinking bridges the disciplines, so a physicist can write of contagion: 'in scale free networks even if a virus is not very contagious, it spreads and persists'.[3] A network view of the organization can really help shape how we think in practical terms about the organizational journey.

Social change theory that derives from evolutionary theory and sociology is another way to see the element of breadth, and can augment thinking about why as well as how change takes place.

Yet another way of thinking rests on looking at the moment that a critical mass is reached in a network: Malcolm Gladwell's synthetic view in *The Tipping Point* focuses on 'the moment of critical mass, the threshold, the boiling point'.[4] He coins the phrases the 'Law of the Few', the 'Stickiness Factor' and the 'Power of Context', which deal with the messenger, the message and the context respectively.

Other bodies of thought focus on team or individual agency. John Kotter's long-standing work on organizational change, for example, posits that all change must be led by a team that has the right amount of power, expertise, credibility and leadership.[5] As for individual agency, it is now possible through measurement of communications and network analysis, to map the extent and value of an individual's interactions.[6]

We have looked at the individuals who make up the network that might carry a message. How does the nature of the message itself affect how far (and fast) it travels? The idea of 'stickiness' here is important,[7] alongside the extent to which a leadership change message is radical, conservative, expected or unexpected. Here, more traditional corporate communications thinking has a bearing on how the leadership development programmes are advertised and launched on the organization.

Anthropological thinking can add value here, drawing on the idea of a message, behaviour or style that spreads from person to person within a culture – a meme – that takes on an independent life (rather like a gene in genetic theory) and is shaped by variation, mutation, competition or inheritance.

Another element that plays a vital role in the leadership development journey is the state of the organization. Here, the urgency, the timing, the resources, the physical disposition and the state of readiness of an organization can all enable or disable a leadership development effort.

The nature of an organization, and its sector, can have a marked influence on how successful a leadership programme might be: for example, public sector organizations tend to have different governance structures that promote wide (and time-consuming) consultation; FMCG organizations tend to drive change quickly and see the immediate results of changes; and extraction and utilities organizations have operational and safety priorities that might have a practical effect on how and when a cohort can be assembled.

Equally, organizations vary in size and in the disposition of their workforce; retailers and manufacturers tend to have a smaller critical mass as a percentage of the overall workforce; knowledge-based organizations, which tend to have high degrees of autonomy throughout the workforce (indicating a high degree of leadership at all levels) and tend to have a higher critical mass that must change.

Together, these three perspectives – messengers, message and context – make up the full picture in thinking about reach. Larger organizations (30,000–50,000 people) typically work with a top 250–750. This is around 1 per cent of their organization, a manageable size for 'senior leadership' positions. However, we find that this is not enough; while critical, it does not go deep enough into the organization. In our experience we find that 5–15 per cent is needed, depending on the organization. This is also roughly what constitutes 'top talent' across all levels in many organizations.

However, it makes sense to consider again the purpose of any leadership development programme: is it to develop all leaders, or only those leaders who are in roles that produce value, or who are vital to operations? In a properly staffed organization all leaders have a role to play, but perhaps not equally vital at all times. Similarly, it can be argued that only a subset of leaders actually need the development programme, because – as numerous studies have shown – only truly excellent leaders matter as they drive a disproportionate amount of performance and impact.[8] The question is therefore: *How do you move individual leadership excellence to overall organizational leadership effectiveness?* The answer – the organizational journey – is to ensure an organization-wide understanding of what great leadership looks like. The remaining 85–95 per cent of employees then have clear role models in terms of the desired leadership behaviours, and their understand and adoption of these behaviours can be further supplemented by targeted capability building efforts, communication and incentives alignment (more on this in Chapter 6).

Leaders change roles, too. So we believe that the purpose of any leadership development programme should be to increase leadership effectiveness across the organization. Leadership development, then, must start at the CEO and top leaders, but then move down to the 5–15 per cent pivotal influencers in the organization. Pivotal influencers are able to influence the behaviours and thinking of others in the organization, due to their role, a trusted relationship, or character. These influencers include the CEO and top team, top talent, influencers and pivotal roles (such as branch managers and plant managers), which may not necessarily be high in the organizational hierarchy. Timing and positioning are vital: starting at the top is sufficient at the outset, but you need to rapidly move through the organization.

However, some people are more influential than others, and change happens best when the most influential are appropriately distributed: not too thinly to be lone voices, and not too densely to become a choir without an audience. There is therefore a need for pockets of critical mass equally across hierarchies. In every unit/critical area, there is a minimum group that can support each other (with sufficient power – here tipping point theory and social change theory apply). For example, at one multinational organization with 50,000 employees, we engaged the top 2,000–3,000. Half of those 50,000 were actually engaged in operations and not in the customer-facing roles we sought to influence; hence were engaging around 10 per cent of those we sought to influence.

# Depth

The organizational journey cannot be developed overnight. Building a repertoire of leadership capabilities takes time. A new behaviour must be practised repeatedly in order to develop into a capability, a competence. But most leadership development programmes do not think about leadership development as multi-year or multi-decades journeys in which several competencies are built over time. Instead, most leadership development programmes are typically of short duration – a few weeks to several months, sporadic and piecemeal. Moreover, many tend to focus on the 'flavor of the year', on whatever aspect of leadership that is perceived to be most fashionable now. The consequence is that efforts are not aligned to the critical shifts that will improve performance, and new insights and behaviours never develop into competencies.

The depth of a leadership development programme suggests a longitudinal approach: *How often and to what extent are individuals reached by the programme?* A typical leadership development programme might draw together a cohort of people for classroom forums. But this is to see learning in a narrow way. Participants learn primarily by doing. So we tend to look at leadership development from the perspective of what can be achieved through daily work rather than through non-work. Learning is working and working is learning; therefore to account for learning on the job we say the ideal time is 250 days given that there are appropriate interventions and curriculum content. Leadership, after all, is learned through leadership, not sitting in a class. In fact, we are in training 100 per cent of our time. If we want to be successful in growing leaders, we need to make sure our learning interventions are embedded into our work. They are coached on the job. They can take a digital course to help them on a problem they have at the job. They then solve the problem and, in and by doing so, learn new skills, including those of leadership. This learning on the job ideally sits within a culture of delegation and support, so that people develop on a daily basis. We will return to the link between leadership development and culture in Chapter 6.

While embedding a culture of development ('250 days of learning') is an important foundation to think about leadership development (and learning in general), many organizations benefit from additional, more structured leadership development interventions – for example when rolling out a new or revised leadership model. While 'stretch' accounts for the learning that takes place within work, it is also vital to allow time for reflection and peer learning in order to consolidate the progress that has been made. In addition, the time on a development programme spent in classroom or more formal locations can provide new ideas and stimulate the other portions of learning.

The question then becomes: what does this journey look like? As we discussed in the previous chapter, the leadership model should be adapted to different organizational career paths and levels. An individual on a specific career path should have a clear view of the leadership expectations as they become more senior in the organization. In parallel, the leadership development interventions to help them meet these expectations should follow suit. This often manifests itself in a multistage journey. For example, one organization delineates its major 'leadership pipeline' along four main stages: manager, general manager, director and VP. Each stage on average takes four to six years. New top talent at each stage (for example new hires or people who have been promoted) go through a structured leadership development intervention, while other top talent who have already completed the stage's main leadership programme are given stretch assignments on the job, mentoring and formal yearly 'refreshes'.

To be more precise, **within each stage on a leadership journey, we advocate a field, forum and coaching approach over an extended period of time**, covering learning on the job (field), work-based projects (field), structured reflection and stimulation (forum) in an environment discreet from work, and coaching and mentorship (coaching). What we typically see working well in terms of days (broadly speaking) is roughly three to five forums each of which are two or three days with fieldwork and coaching in between, for the main part of a leadership programme. This should then be supplemented with yearly refreshes of the content and of the expectations of the leaders. We will elaborate on the specific mechanisms to make learning interventions successful, in the next chapter.

## Pace

The pace of a leadership development programme is the speed at which it is rolled out across the organization. Here, we mean the pace in terms of reaching broadly throughout the organization, not in terms of the speed for each individual. In general we find that faster is better.

We mentioned in the last chapter that priority shifts should be focused on for 12–18 months. This typically starts by engaging the leaders over six to nine months, and then quickly trickles down to the rest of the organization as well over the subsequent six to nine months. As a rule, we find that if within six to nine months of launching a programme the people at the lower levels of the organization see or feel a change as a result of the leadership development programme, they will typically be convinced and see it as a success. What is critical here is that a holistic change approach is used, touching all four quadrants of the Influence Model (more on that in Chapter 6). For the top leaders and pivotal influencers, role-modelling and symbolic actions are key.

The reverse is also true. If after the first six to nine months little or nothing has happened, people lose heart; worse, they may see the whole programme (and its instigators and advocates) as a failure. It is therefore very risky to go slow. We often see this in practice, unfortunately.

Organizations make choices about pace based on a variety of factors. We find that pace, depth and breadth often depends on capacity or money, which are often not the right boundary conditions; it is better to think in terms of risk of remaining in the present state, or the danger of promoting a disadvantageous leadership style, or the problems of failing to attract and retain talent.

Organizations often feel there is a delivery risk inherent in moving faster: how can we possibly make the practical and budget arrangement this quickly? However, that risk is over-estimated while risk of failure is under-estimated. 'Wait and see' we have found, is dangerous. Equally, annual budget allocation can be dangerous as it can lead to an erratic and unpredictable start-stop sequence inimical to organization-wide development.

For speed, leadership development must start at the top (level 1) of the organization. But it should also start with level 2 (and involve level 1) in order to get breadth quickly, while also involving the top and seeking to engage the critical 'Sergeant-Major' layer quickly who are often more involved in the actual operations of the daily business.

For example, when a national military organization of 80,000 staff launched its new leadership ethos plan, it assembled 800 senior officers (or 1 per cent of the organization) in one venue on one day, and from there rolled out the initiative immediately to its sergeant-majors (each responsible for 120 staff) and from them to its sergeants (each responsible for 35 staff) without any delay.

Other organizations set strict time limits. One started its leadership development programme from first principles and set a deadline of six weeks to develop and start delivering it. Their view was that after the six-week development time, if the programme worked, they would pilot it in any of the 100 countries in which they operated, and roll it out.

Whatever the intrinsic quality of any programme, it must have impact and effect change; and these are best achieved through larger numbers of people. Simply put, **if enough people change their behaviour as leaders, the programme succeeds; conversely, if too few change, the programme fails**. Moreover, these phenomena are not confined to leadership development programmes; they exist in any organizational change efforts.

## Implications for leadership development

The principle of engagement affects the way that programmes are planned, designed, delivered and established in the organization. We look at these steps in detail in Part 2. A sense of the undertaking and the effort required – the journey – should shape all thinking. The effort should be informed by a sense of current leadership capacity and future needs, usually best in the form of a gap analysis. It should also be informed by the intrinsic needs of the leadership development programme itself: enough individuals have to change their way of thinking and behaving for the change to become widespread enough.

To make this work, organizations must secure the full commitment of top management to drive development of the leadership effort, align top-management fully behind mutually agreed leadership gap, connect and communicate clearly to the organization, ensure top-management role-models the desired leadership mindset and behaviours, and ensure that members of the top team are willing to go on a leadership journey themselves.

We see five main implications of Core Principle 2.

1  The leadership path should be outlined from entry level to the executive team, regardless of whether the organization includes only a subset of employees or all employees on such a leadership journey. Each rung of the ladder should furthermore have

its own learning pathway, and there should be a clear structure for individuals within the journey.

2 During leadership development interventions, or at other inflection points such as promotions or job movements for leaders, there must be provision for leadership development for sufficient individuals. 5–15 per cent of the workforce should be on a specific leadership development programme during a change effort (as part of the longitudinal learning journey outlined above). Whether or not such development interventions are mandatory will depend on the culture and purpose of the organization; at any rate, they should be attractive enough to pull in participants either by means of their intrinsic value or by means of their reputation.

3 New content and curriculum should be designed to achieve the greatest breadth across the organization; this in turn will reach the critical mass of leaders. The content should be adjusted and tailored to each level, but it must have a broad appeal, application and acceptance. For example, say an organization chooses to focus on empowerment as a theme during a leadership development programme. The content must be tailored to each level, covering the specific behavioural expectations at each level. This will give everyone in the organization a sense of what great leadership looks like and how it is expressed for them specifically.

4 The organization must build up a delivery engine geared towards breadth, depth and pace. Technology plays a key role in enabling this. The latest learning systems – for example laptop based interactive video conferences, virtual reality headsets and mobile applications – can enable a significant yet effective reach across the organization, at a low cost. In addition, building up a programme delivery infrastructure is key to reach scale, for example through a 'train the trainer' approach and using 'power mentoring' (where five mentees each become mentors to five more colleagues).

5 The journey should run at pace. All the programmes' design and content should allow for both the short-term and long-term facets of the programme. This means that the initial (say,

nine-month) roll-out should not find itself exhausted too soon; and also that a yearly 'booster' should be conceived to allow for new thinking, new technology, changing organizational context and most importantly the developed learning and potential of the participants. The programme should continue to stretch the participants.

## *The increasing velocity of journeys*

While thinking of engagement in terms of an organizational journey may already be a big step for some organizations, the buck does not stop there. Any discussion and implication of organization journeys must take into account the surrounding trends for organizations. And the trends are demanding. Building on the 'new industrial revolution' discussion in the previous chapter, skills are decaying more quickly than before – see Figure 4.1.[9] It is estimated, for example, that 65 per cent of children entering primary school today will end up working in new job types that do not yet exist.[10]

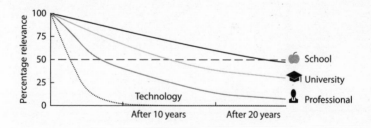

FIGURE 4.1 The degree to which different types of knowledge stay relevant over time

As such, all organizations must renew their development activities periodically. But when and how is this best done in terms of the organizational journey? Does a period of activity draw to a close before another begins? Or do many journeys start simultaneously? A helpful way to think about these questions is through the concept of an S-curve. The S-curve model was developed in the 1960s, and its proponents claim it is one of the best models to understand a non-linear world. It has been applied broadly, for example in regards to organizational life cycles, innovation and general skill-building.[11]

Let's apply this to learning. When people enter a new role, for example, they are faced with many new demands and stakeholders, representing a new curve. Capabilities must be built. At the beginning, they go through a steep learning curve in which their knowledge and skills rapidly increase. However, the business impact of their performance is typically low. Gradually their development and business impact accelerates as they gain competence and confidence in the role, until they reach an inflection point. After being in a role for a certain period of time people reach the upper, flatter part of curve, where learning and development have stagnated, tasks have become habits, and business impact has slowed significantly.[12] As a result, the best time to initiate the second curve is before the peak of the existing one, while the organization has the resources to start something new. Start the second curve too early, and the benefits of the first are squandered; too late, and the resources and impetus are gone – see Figure 4.2.[13]

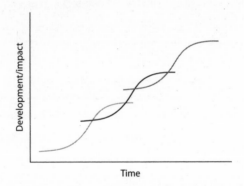

FIGURE 4.2 The S-curve model

Regarding leadership development, the curve represents the natural life of a programme. The next curve should thus be planned and launched while things are going well. The implications of an increasingly complex world and an accelerating rate of skills decay are shorter cycles between each curve. This implies more breadth (more employees need to be trained), more depth (more intensity and more frequent touchpoints for development), and faster pace of rollout (the rate of learning and skills acquisition is becoming an increasingly important competitive advantage). This means more, not less, leadership development in the future. Similarly, the notions of continuous learning and adaptability are becoming more important, for all employees.

For leadership development practitioners, the implications are that leadership development must become agile and quick to react to changes in the external environment. It also implies greater emphasis on on-the-job learning (which we discuss in the next chapter), and a greater emphasis on embedding interventions into a broader culture of learning and leadership (which we discuss in Chapter 6).

---

## Case study: Change leadership at pace and scale

### Context and Challenge

Our client, a global leader in innovative pharmaceuticals and consumer health products is one of *Fortune* magazine's 'Most admired companies', a global leader in innovative pharmaceuticals and consumer health products, with over 50,000 employees in over 140 countries. It faced a fundamental challenge in the form of a 'patent cliff' with several of its major products about to go off patent. In response, the organization launched a new strategy to drive future growth, with a differentiated approach in its core business areas – moving to a model more dependent on 'speciality' products. It implemented a new organization structure which aligned the commercial organization with the new strategy, streamlined R&D, and improved efficiency in shared services. Finally, it invested in capability building in areas that would be critical to the future success of the strategy.

However, the company had two significant challenges. The company's own employee engagement survey indicated that the company was a heavily performance-focused, IQ-driven organization, which was weak at leading change at scale, empowering its people and engaging the hearts and minds of its employees. Additionally, the new strategy would play out in very different ways in its different markets. In some developed markets, it would essentially mean massively downsizing large parts of the business, while in some emerging markets, the aim would be to double the same business within five years. To fuse the strategic intent with the varying dynamics in the different markets, it was vital to achieve full buy-in for the transformation among the company's top leaders globally.

# Approach

Our role was to help the organization's leaders understand the strategy and be able to communicate clearly and succinctly what it meant to their divisions and teams, empower them to develop strong local strategies consistent with the company strategy, and help them plan how to roll out the change with a much greater focus on engaging their people.

To support the organization's leaders in implementing the new strategy and new organization structure, we set up a central Project Management Office (PMO) and launched multiple initiatives, including creating an integrated change story and communication plan, re-tweaking performance targets, putting in place on-going role-modelling from senior leaders, and activating a network of change agents. In addition, we rolled out the Change Accelerator programme across the organization's top leadership, in order to increase change readiness.

The programme consisted of two-day workshops to tackle the barriers to transformation, ongoing check-ins with senior leaders on their initiatives, and feedback and coaching sessions from trained facilitators to the leaders. Velocity was key in order to achieve success, and the programme had breadth, depth, and pace: the programme was rolled out to over 120 countries globally within 6 months, reaching over 1,000 leaders. Each country had a differentiated approach based on their size, complexity, and change readiness. The scale and pace was achieved by training 70-80 internal facilitators to support the rollout.

The first workshops focused on the new strategic direction, what it meant to be a change leader, engaging and motivating employees through identifying their sources of meaning, and prioritizing the key mindset and behaviour shifts that had to happen (e.g. increased customer centricity). Approximately 18 months after the first workshops, a second series of workshops were rolled out to the same population group, also within 6 months. These workshops focused on helping leaders fully embed the new behavioural shifts, and working through in detail the implications for organizational structure and the skills required to implement the strategy. Approximately two years later, a third series of workshops was rolled out, at the same pace. The focus of these workshops was on re-energising the organization and on further training in change management skills.

## Impact

The workshops, combined with the regular check-ins and feedback sessions, provided continuous support for senior leaders to implement the new strategy and way of working. The programme built change capabilities in all leadership teams across business units and functions in 120+ countries. The program achieved extremely high scores (9/10 for content, and for faculty), and participants emphasized that the programme helped shift mindsets, delivered actionable insights, and energized the team. At an organizational level, the company outperformed the industry over the 5 year period when the programme was being rolled out in terms of total returns to shareholders, and also increased sales by ~25%, moving the organization to the second largest in the industry.

## Reflection

There were four elements which contributed to the broad success of the programme. First, while certain initiatives previously had allowed countries to 'opt-out', meaning that not all countries were covered, this leadership development effort was non-negotiable. The programme was rolled out in a very disciplined and systematic way, and covered all leadership teams in the company. Second, the programme was tightly linked to strategy and to the business objectives, and was not 'change management for the sake of it'. In fact, the positive feedback from the first countries created a positive buzz in the organization, and a strong "pull" for the programme. Third, the programme facilitators did not just come from HR or the Organizational Development (OD) department. The central PMO also trained up business leaders across the globe, which led to the workshops having both the change management and business side of things front and center. Finally, the programme was rolled out at a rapid pace in short bursts, which not only had a positive impact on the local businesses, but also led to employees globally *feeling* and *seeing* the change shortly after hearing about the transformation – thereby greatly boosting morale and belief in the new direction.

## A short note on resourcing

A common question we get revolves around costs. Surely a leadership programme that engages such a large number of people will be prohibitively expensive? We find that this does not have to be the case. Learning and development budgets often have enough scope to reach sufficient leaders in the right way, if done accurately. **In other words, the money is there, but needs to be spent in the correct way.**

Here is an example: large organizations typically spend around $800 per employee on training (in general, not just leadership development).[14] A 10,000-person organization will then have a yearly training budget of approximately $8 million. For an organization of this size, a programme should seek to reach 5–15 per cent – or around 1,000 people overall (the faster the better). If within those 1,000 there are 20 per cent (200) on a structured programme at any time, of around eight days: that makes 1,600 days of formal programme per year. Our experience shows a design and delivery cost for fully tailored programmes of approximately $2000 per forum day equivalent (including forum, fieldwork and coaching), equal to around $3.2 million.

The remaining 800 leaders could be engaged through online learning and one-day boosters. Assuming two days of contact per person, at a cost of $500 per day per person (lower due to technology plus in-house facilitators), that amounts to $0.8 million.

The other 9,000 employees in the organization are reached (in terms of leadership) through on the job coaching by their managers, reinforcing mechanisms, and 'seeing what good looks like' by leaders in the organization. They can potentially also be reached through technology, which – once developed – can have a marginal cost close to 0. We will discuss this in more detail in Chapter 6.

The total is thus approximately $4 million on leadership development of the top 10 per cent, or about half of a typical training budget. The other half can then be used for in-house staff costs and technical/functional skills. Interestingly, we find that organizations typically have learning and development budgets available for leadership development – the money is there. The imperative is thus to spend this budget more effectively, and not necessarily to earmark new funds for leadership development.

## Summary

Is engaging the leadership with the organization development effort relevant for all organizations? Of course there will be nuances, but if the goal is to improve organization-wide leadership effectiveness, then the answer is yes.

Organizations must engage a critical mass of excellent leaders and influencers in order to change leadership behaviours at the appropriate level, and to give everyone in the organization an understanding of what great leadership looks like. Ideally this begins with the top team. They must be willing and able to embody and explain what great leadership looks like. The organizational journey – with its elements of breadth, depth and pace – is one on which the whole organization embarks. Without it, leadership development interventions become sporadic and episodic, and without lasting impact across the organization. We also saw the decreasing 'cycle times' between required skill refreshes. Organizations that engage mutually with their leadership development efforts tend to think in terms of continuous development, for all people, at all times.

# 5
# Core Principle 3: Architect programmes for behavioural change

*Filippo Rossi, Julia Sperling, Mike Carson*

Neuromyths and the importance of modern adult learning | The
readiness of the brain to learn | The seven adult learning principles |
Boosting individual learning and performance | Implications for
leadership development

We now move from the 'what' and 'who' of leadership development at
scale to the 'how'. This chapter deals with the 'how' related to individual learning, while the next chapter deals with the 'how' at an organizational level.

At an individual level, how should organizations think about structuring a leadership development intervention, with maximum learning transfer? How can they ensure that the leadership development
initiatives are effective for the participants and improve their ability to
go about their daily work? There is no shortage of leadership advice
out there. The genuine thirst for explanations of brain functions was
fuelled in recent decades by the advances in cognitive neuroscience. In
an unprecedented manner this field has united scientists from infor-
matics, physics, engineering, biology and psychology to medicine
around a common mission.

The most prominent driver of the exponential growth in knowledge was the use of brain imaging techniques like functional magnetic
resonance imaging (fMRI). Starting from the first pioneering days in
the 1980s, the number of scientific publications using fMRI has grown
rapidly, with 28,600 peer-reviewed publications in 2013,[1] compared
to only 200 in 1983. The required imaging devices are readily available in clinical settings and allow researchers to measure a proxy for
brain activity indirectly. The resulting data can then be linked back to
concurrent behaviour of subjects during the experiments.

As a result, we have achieved significant breakthroughs in the past 20 years in understanding the brain and how adults develop. We know, for example, that neuroplasticity (the ability of the brain to reorganize itself by forming new neural connections and functions throughout life) is no longer seen as limited to childhood; in fact it continues throughout one's life. We also know more about how to enhance the transfer learning interventions to on-the-job impact, and the implications this has for leadership development.

Adult learning as a theory and practice is not new. The formal term is 'andragogy', first used in 1833 by Alexander Kapp. Malcolm Knowles made significant contributions to the field in the late 1960s and 1970s, and others have since continued developing the field. What is different today is the emphasis on *modern* adult learning principles, grounded in a much deeper understanding of our brain and how adults learn; and this leads to more specific ways to embed the methods in leadership development.

This chapter reviews the importance of applying modern adult learning principles, the neuroscience behind the readiness of the brain to learn, discusses the seven modern adult learning principles that we apply in our leadership development approach to maximize learning transfer, and discusses other ways that organizations can enhance individual learning and performance in general. Finally, we review the implications for leadership development initiatives.

## Core Principle 3: Architect programmes that maximize behavioural change based on neuroscience

Design interventions with an explicit focus on helping individuals become 'better at their daily jobs' using the latest principles linked to neuroscience, to maximise the value and organizational impact of what is taught and learned

### *Neuromyths and the importance of modern adult learning*

As insightful and valuable as the new insights based on neuroscience have been, the dissemination and often lay interpretation have led to many misconceptions of how the human brain works. These misconceptions also found their way into the corporate world and influenced the design and application of behavioural change and life-long learning efforts and the way executives think about their brain functions.

For example, we were told that human beings are either 'left-brained' hence logical or 'right-brained' hence emotional; or that we use only 10 per cent of our brain capacity at any point in time; or that we learn significantly better in our preferred learning style (for example, audio, visual); or that there are critical periods in childhood, after which there is no hope for future learning.

A recent survey discovered the existence of these myths even in the thinking of teachers.[2] Over 90 per cent of the teachers in the UK and Netherlands do believe in the single preferred learning style hypothesis and 50 per cent of them in the 10 per cent brain utilization assumption. Many of these claims are misconceptions – something we refer to as 'neuromyths' – and there are many more to mention.[3]

**Avoiding these neuromyths, and applying modern adult learning principles based on neuroscience is critical because it has a material impact on whether individuals successfully change behaviour or not.** Research shows, for example, that only 10 per cent of participants can recall the content of classroom lecture after three months, compared to a 65 per cent recall rate for participants undergoing action learning (telling, showing and experiencing).[4] A similar example is the rule of thumb of 70:20:10, popularized in the 1990s. Executives were asked to report how they believed they learned best, and the results indicated that approximately 70 per cent of learning comes from on-the-job training, 20 per cent comes from mentoring and coaching, and 10 per cent comes from classroom and online training.[5]

Our latest research on leadership development backs this up. We found that organizations with successful leadership development interventions were 6.1 times more likely to **actively encourage individuals to practise the new behaviours that will contribute to being a better leader.** Another key success factor related to adult learning that successful organizations were more likely to apply was **linking content to projects (either individual or group) that stretched participants and required them to apply their learning in a new setting over an extended period, such a model was 5.4 times more likely to feature in a successful leadership development programme than in an unsuccessful one.** be successful. Other important actions more frequently applied in successful leadership development organizations were *including individual fieldwork between forums* (3.6×), *being strengths based* (3.4×), *coaching* (3.2×) and *addressing mindsets* (2.9×).

The global training market is estimated to be worth over $350 billion. **Organizations can simply not afford to base their learning interventions on inaccurate and no longer up-to-date assumptions.** Having 90 per cent of employees losing the content they've learned in training within three months is simply not an option; and eliminating these neuromyths is essential in advancing leadership development and the organization as a whole. **Nonetheless, we find that many organizations apply an outmoded approach to learning and leadership development.** One study found that Fortune 500 companies focus 55 per cent of their learning and development allocation in classroom training, 25 per cent in coaching and mentoring, and 20 per cent in on-the-job training (see Figure 5.1).[6]

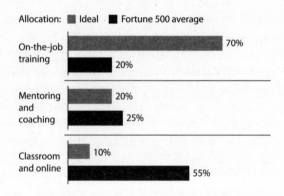

FIGURE 5.1  Main ways to develop talent

In practice, we also see this to be the case. Oftentimes, employees are allocated a learning and development budget and asked to pick from a predefined 'course catalogue' or menu of courses they would like to go on. These courses are neither tailored to the employee, nor directly address the daily tasks the employee needs to perform. As we will see later in the chapter, enabling self-directed learning can enhance learning transfer, yet the learning content must be within the contours of the critical shifts, which we outlined in Core Principle 1.

We also sometimes see organizations spend the majority of their leadership development budgets on sending a select number of top talent to executive programmes overseas. There is often a disconnect between what participants learn and what they apply when they are 'back' in their offices.

The natural question is *why* do organizations not apply a more holistic approach to developing leaders, if the facts are clear? We believe there are three primary reasons:

1 Some organizations may not be fully aware of the latest adult learning principles and how to design an intervention explicitly around the goal of maximizing learning transfer.
2 Some organizations may be aware, but underestimate the importance or magnitude of the difference in impact between different approaches.
3 Some organizations may indeed be looking for best practice approaches, but are unable to find the right suppliers (at the right cost) to implement them.

We find that many leadership development companies in the market are simply not geared to deliver tailored content, at scale, in the right way. To give a few examples – leadership development solutions should be customized to the specific organizational challenges at hand (Core Principle 1); scalable to reach the right critical mass, at the right pace, in the organization (Core Principle 2); delivered just-in-time; employ a whole-person approach that address underlying mindsets; and be on the job against real business challenges. However, what we often see is one-size-fits-all, standardized courses; one-time programmes for individuals or one cohort; courses delivered 'just-in-case' (up-front, with limited clarity on what learnings participants will need when and in which context); a focus on only functional skills; and programmes that are 'off the job', based on case studies and classroom lectures.

Based on a comprehensive literature review below we describe the latest neuroscientific insights on how our brain learns. Bridging the gap between the popular neuromyths and a vast corpus of knowledge gathered in the last decades is no trivial task; the stock of knowledge is growing rapidly. However, we believe that the key concepts provide a helpful lens for organizations today.

## The readiness of the brain to learn

Before we move to our core principle in practice, it is useful to discuss briefly the neuroscience behind the brain's readiness to learn. There is, for instance, a neuromyth we call 'the critical window of childhood'. Most of us have heard about critical windows, meaning that in the first years of infancy the majority of the brain's development occurs. After this period, or so the assumption too often goes, the trajectory of human development is deemed to be more or less fixed. This misconception is a distortion of the observation that for the primary senses like vision and hearing, as well as for primary language acquisition, a lack of appropriate sensory input in the critical temporal windows will deter the development of these senses or the ability.[7]

This assumption of expanding findings into all areas of human development has even led to the Heckman model[8] (describing a postulated return on investment on every $1 spend for education/ learning) with the outcome that beyond the age of three the return on all learning decays exponentially.

However, besides the exceptions mentioned above, the brain is indeed able to reorganize itself by forming new connections throughout life based on appropriate stimuli – a phenomenon known as neuroplasticity. The scientific proof behind neural pathways' ability to change is not new (the first evidence emerged in the 1920s through Karl Lashley's work) but it gained wide acceptance among neuroscientists only in the 1970s. Today, neuroplasticity is no longer contested, and there is increasing evidence that many areas of the brain remain 'plastic' well into adulthood.[9]

It is clear, however, that the brain does not automatically form these pathways – the right stimulus and attention are needed in order for adults to attain new skills and therefore display new types of behaviour (for leadership development). The next section addresses how organizations can structure learning interventions.

## The seven adult learning principles

It seems axiomatic to say that adults learn best when they are treated as adults; the question is, how can this be achieved? Equally it is safe to say that the age of one-way classroom learning died long ago; what has replaced it? A modern field and forum approach is good, but not the fullest answer to both these questions. What is required is a more holistic approach to driving change through learning.

**Organizations must take into account the spectrum of how the adult brain learns.** We synthesize this imperative into seven main adult learning principles. Leadership development efforts must:

1 stretch participants outside their comfort zones
2 use self-directed learning and self-discovery
3 apply on-the-job learning to form new skills through repetition and practice
4 provide a positive frame to link positive emotions to learning
5 ensure the interventions are strengths-based
6 address underlying mindsets (whole-person approach)
7 use reflection and coaching to ensure feedback loops

We review each principle below, and the underlying neuroscience behind them.

## 1 STRETCH PARTICIPANTS

**Adults learn best when they are stretched outside their comfort zones**, in what we call the learning zone (see Figure 5.2). This is because development through establishing new neural pathways comes through doing a different activity (a new language, a musical

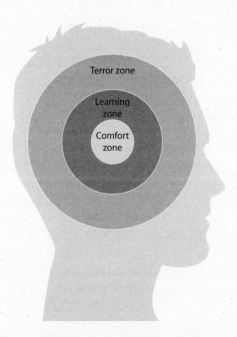

FIGURE 5.2 The learning zone

instrument, a new sport) and/or through doing habitual activity differently.[10] Our comfort zone, learning zone and terror zone represent increasingly anxious places; Robert Yerkes and John Dodson showed, for example, that learning performance is optimal when our level of anxiety is neither too low nor too high – i.e. in the middle.[11] We therefore advocate an approach that stretches participants, putting then under stress without placing them in their terror zone.

In practice, this requires challenging tasks that are 'just' outside the range of participant skillsets, but which the participant would be able to grow into and achieve with sufficient support. These tasks should ideally be customized to each individual (for example, through an individual development plan), so they address their own development needs. The tasks can both be in the context of forums (for example, facilitated self-reflection, problem solving in a group setting, presenting in front of a group) as well as in the context of the daily job (for example, doing a task for the first time, with the support of one's manager).

## 2 SELF-DIRECTED LEARNING

**Another important element is that participants direct their own learning/self-discovery.** Adults are autonomous and self-directing, meaning that they live under a large degree of self-governance and to their own laws, beliefs and values. Allowing them to direct their own learning therefore enhances motivation.

In addition, given greater choice and autonomy, an individual learner will choose (more accurately than a teacher, say) exactly when, where and how they wish to learn. Learning therefore takes place in the right way for each individual, from 'push' to 'pull', which enhances the overall learning effectiveness.

Another neuromyth we often see is the theory that people are either dominantly analytical (and left brained) or more creative (and right brained). However, this either/or dichotomy is false. The two hemispheres of the brain are linked and communicate extensively together; they do not work in isolation. The simplistic notion of a false binary has led, in many businesses, to the misconception that each one of us has a strictly preferred learning style and channel. Recent studies have flatly disproved this idea. Learning delivered in multiple modalities for example, audio-visual stimuli consistently provided better results than learning in a single sensory modality (for example, only audio). While self-directed learning helps boost learning for the individual learner, leadership development initiatives should still seek to engage all the senses.[12]

In practice, organizations can allow participants to set their own learning goals, embed exploratory elements into the learning process (for example, allowing participants to discover, reflect, and act on their strengths and development areas) and self-directed elements (for example, online modules outside of structure forums). Organizations can structure the overall programme on an 'opt-in' basis (i.e. not making the programme mandatory but requiring participants to sign-up) and make certain programme elements such as coaching optional (and thus requiring participants to set up coaching times themselves).

Coupled with a desire for autonomy and flexibility, adults have a desire to understand the benefits and value of a learning intervention. Organizations must therefore also ensure the programme value and link to the job is clearly communicated and practised (see the next adult learning principle below).

As mentioned earlier, self-directed learning must be within the boundaries of the overall organizational priorities. There must be central, strategic curation, to ensure that the learning is linked to the critical shifts linked to what matters most for the organization (outlined in Core Principle 1).

With choice comes responsibility for absorbing the learning (when needed professionally and matched to a personal schedule). We therefore remain as flexible as possible (within the boundaries of a programme) about how participants learn, the manner of delivery, and the timing of any tasks, readings or assignments, but are sure to track progress (for example, course completion rates) as well as learning absorption (for example, through manager feedback or 360-degree review). It is critical that organizations hold participants accountable for their own learning.

## 3 ON-THE-JOB LEARNING AND REPETITION

**Adults learn best when they learn on the job using and developing their work skills.** This is because the brain can form and strengthen new neural pathways. Regular practice of a skill leads to expansion of the skill related network of a functional area, for example, the hand representation of a violin player or the size of a brain region of London taxi drivers dedicated to memory (hippocampus).[13] In other words, neurons that fire together wire together.[14] The reverse is also true. The brain has an active 'pruning process', where only the neural connections and neural pathways that are frequently activated are retained. We all know the feeling of losing a certain skill (for example, a language, or ability to play an instrument) that we have not used for a period of time.

We therefore always include dedicated and structured fieldwork in our leadership development approach, alternating between on-the-job application of new skills, coupled with more formal learning sessions (for example, forums or online modules). On-the-job application of skills could be achieved in the context of one's daily work, and/or through 'breakthrough projects' that are above and beyond daily tasks, for example a specific initiative in the context of a broader transformation.

We firmly believe that **learning is working and working is learning**. Learning forums are highly interactive and engaging (and hard work!), while participants are expected to apply what they learn and practise in their daily jobs, resulting not only in enhanced learning but also in organizational impact – which should be ultimately goal of any learning intervention.

## 4 Positive context

Research has shown that in all mental activities emotions and cognition are inextricably linked.[15] Although there are specialized modules in the brain for both emotions and executive functions, they heavily interact and influence each other. Hence, **we cannot speak about learning without considering its emotional context**.

Long before the advent of cognitive neurosciences, Plato hypothesized the link between learning and emotion: 'all learning' he said, 'has an emotional base'. More recently, neuroscience has shown that emotionally arousing events or material (pleasant or unpleasant) that activate the amygdala correlate highly with subsequent recall.[16] With regard to learning environments, a large number of studies have shown that positive emotions can enhance learning, while negative emotions (for example, being fearful of making a mistake) are ambivalent to learning or can, in the worst cases, diminish learning.[17]

In addition, studies in animals and humans have shown that positive events and rewards are associated with the release of a substance called dopamine in our brain, which greatly aids memory formation[18] and makes us want to experience more of these events.[19] Embedding learning itself in a pleasant and rewarding environment with clear rewarding milestones will therefore increase our appetite for learning in general and motivates future learning.

Creating a positive context also enables participants to take bigger risks, which, as discussed in the first adult learning principle regarding stretching participants, allows them to move outside their comfort zones and into the learning zone. We find that participants need to feel encouraged and supported to take these plunges. As such, it is a paradox of creating a secure environment in order for participants to leave their comfort zones. We find this to hold true not only in learning settings, but also among effective teams in practice. We commonly do a 'peak performance' exercise in workshops to pinpoint the characteristics of high performing teams – one of the key elements that emerges is that people on teams that experience 'peak performance' feel encouraged and supported, which allows them to take more risks and push the boundaries of performance.

For leadership development in practice, this means creating a safe space for learning, where participants are able to take risks and discuss potential concerns. To do this, it can be helpful to establish ground rules at the beginning of learning sessions, for example, regarding confidentiality, not passing judgement, and supporting fellow participants. Additionally, it goes without saying that learning interventions benefit from being fun and relaxed, and it is important to ensure a good fit between facilitators, coaches and organization.

## 5 Strengths-based (without ignoring development areas)

It is imperative that people focus on their strengths, not weaknesses when developing their leadership effectiveness. A study of two bowling teams at the University of Wisconsin illustrates the importance of focusing on strengths. In the study, the team that was coached using video tapes of their successes improved twice as much as the team that was shown only their mistakes.[20] There are four main reasons why strengths-based development is more effective.

First, because for a given amount of energy, adults derive greater benefits from building on a strength than from correcting a development area. In other words, the improvement in a strength will be higher than the improvement in a development area for the same unit of energy. During the course of our life, we constantly develop new neural pathways when engaging in activities. We develop strengths in the areas of the brain that have had the most synaptic connections. This implies that where we have a 'strength', as an adult, there are a lot of synaptic connections. As the synapses begin to develop and become strengthened, the brain requires less energy to activate those specific neurons, compared to forming new ones – this is why people often say that their strengths come more naturally to them.[21] We therefore focus our learning and development on building on existing strengths (assuming that these are in line with the required leadership behaviours of the organization).

Second, adults tend to give greater emphasis to negatives than to positives (known as 'risk aversion'), up to three to five times as much in some cases.[22] There is therefore a need to counteract the inordinate impact of negative information ('you are poor at listening', for example) by emphasizing a strength ('you are good at understanding others'). This means, for example, that during a feedback session, a leader should emphasize an employee's strengths three to five times more than development areas – otherwise the employee will remember only the development areas.

Third, focusing on strengths often leads to more positive experiences and success stories; this releases dopamine and ensures continued motivation to learn. In addition, studies have shown that 'winning' gives momentum and velocity for further wins.[23] For example, when training for a 10km race, building up endurance and experiencing a series of smaller successes (for example, 4km, 6km, 8km) builds momentum and prepares the body physically and mentally for bigger tasks ahead. While there is also the risk of becoming overconfident and becoming too risk-loving, this is perhaps less relevant in learning environments.

The final reason that leadership development interventions should be strengths-based is not linked to neuroscience, but is important for the overall organizational context. We know that *spiky leaders* (leaders who are exceptional in a handful of competencies, average or deficient in others) are much more important to overall company performance than *all-rounders* (leaders who are good in most competencies, average in others, with no deficiencies). There are twice as many more spiky leaders in top-quartile organizations compared to second-quartile organizations.[24] Another study of almost 20,000 employees across 34 organizations in 29 countries showed that performance was 21–36 per cent higher in companies where managers emphasized strengths.[25]

Our transformational change approach echoes these sentiments, and finds that organizations that focus on both strengths and weaknesses are more successful than organizations that focus only on strengths or only on weaknesses.[26] In a learning context, interventions should clearly map out the strengths of individuals and ensure that personal development plans focus on these strengths. In parallel, it is also important to ensure that people do not ignore relevant areas of improvement, if these do not meet a minimum bar.

## 6 THE UNDERLYING MINDSET

The sixth key adult learning principle is addressing the underlying mindsets that enable the desired change – what we term a 'whole-person approach' to leadership development. This is because our behaviours are driven by our thoughts, which in turn are driven by our underlying values and beliefs, as described in Chapter 1. **Understanding one's underlying beliefs is a pre-condition to removing many of the roadblocks not only to learning but also to behavioural change.** These are elements of a whole-person approach, and build on the psychological school of adult development (for example, outlined by Robert Kegan and Lisa Lahey in *Immunity to Change*).[27]

Conventional skill-building approaches invariably focused on what the leader should know (for example, the frameworks and professional skills relevant for the job). This was later coupled with what the leader should do (i.e. focusing on the practical behaviours that can be identified, learned and practised).

A whole-person approach, on the other hand, also focuses on who the leader should be. It focuses on identity and authenticity, and on consciously developing the self to develop a leadership personality. This is typified in the 'Be + Know + Do' models of leadership development. It includes uncovering what is getting in the way of behavioural changes (for example underlying mindsets and root perspectives) to help leaders permanently shift how they act at work. Research and practice show clearly that participants in a whole person programme are more likely to experience relevant and lasting personal change and develop authentic and effective leadership.

# 7 FEEDBACK (AND REFLECTION)

Finally, **any successful leadership development programme must include sufficient measurement and feedback loops to participants,** to enhance the learning process. We distinguish between two types of feedback.

*External feedback* from our surroundings is a critical for three main reasons:

1 External feedback gives the brain direction so it knows where to focus. In addition, the feedback can help raise awareness levels among the participant, which helps them realize what they could do more of or do differently.

2 Feedback can be a source of motivation. People with a growth mindset see challenges as positive, and use the gap between where they are now and where they want to be to spur them on. (The reverse is also true, as people with a 'fixed' mindset can view feedback as threatening and demotivating. It is thus essential that learning interventions foster the right development environment and emphasize the importance of having a growth mindset.)

3 The feedback gives the facilitators and programme designers an indication of where people are in the learning process. They can thereafter increase or decrease the learning complexity to ensure that participants stay in the 'learning zone' and do not get either comfortable or terrified.

*Internal feedback* has to do with metacognition and the process of 'thinking about thinking'. This includes how we reflect on our thinking process and development. Studies have shown that people who are more introspective have more grey area in the prefrontal cortex, a region of the brain linked to the evolutionary development of humans. This suggests that introspection aids in the learning process.[28] In the learning context, asking oneself a set of questions on a regular basis in a reflective environment can aid the learning process, for example:

- Am I aware of my strengths and development areas?
- Am I focusing on the right combination of my strengths and development areas?
- What is working well for me in the learning process? What could be improved?
- Am I applying my learnings? If not, how can I do so?

As such, we always recommend including coaching as part of leadership development efforts (with a coach, a manager/mentor, or at a minimum in peer groups among the programme cohorts). In addition, we build in time for participant reflection during the programme, and use learning journals to capture a participant's thoughts and reflections.

---

## Case study: From mindfulness and mysticism to the bottom line

### Context and challenge

In 2012 McKinsey began working with a large pharmaceutical company (with over 20,000 employees in 25 countries and a turnover of over $2 billion). The challenge was to make leadership throughout the organization an aspiration for all employees rather than a role for some. The existing development programmes were more instructional than transformational, and it was the latter that was seen as necessary to give employees the space, autonomy and mindset to flourish at work and therefore better serve their patients.

### Approach

The programme focused on personal transformation, addressing inner mindsets and bodysets to bring about change. The Firm worked with change leaders to overturn impediments to change, and the programme became, in the client's words, 'so wildly successful that we ran many batches after', scaling from batches of 25 to batches of 50 over three years. In addition, the program is now run entirely by the client through their internal team. At each stage the work deepened so that participants *master the inner game in order to be better equipped to play an effective outer game*. In essence, this was a spiritual journey linked to tangible business impact.

Personal transformation lay at the heart of the programme. It is through personal transformation that the client was able to

---

build a culture that embodied the brand values of 'empathy' and 'dynamism'. Here, personal transformation was closely linked to organizational transformation.

For example, leaders worked on gaining in confidence and developing a compelling leadership presence; connecting to a deep sense of purpose; overcoming the grip of anger or rage; connecting with people on the basis of empathy and trust; overcoming fear (of failure/mediocrity/loss of image); operating with a winning mindset; and moving from a 'logic only' or 'data driven' approach to combining intuition and logic to create breakthrough results.

The programme evolved to become the flagship leadership development programme for the top four levels of leadership. The sole objective of the programme was to get promising senior leaders in the organization to connect with and operate from their full potential and link it to business impact. It followed the philosophy of *Lead Self – Lead Others – Lead Business* and draws inspiration and practices from many bodies of work (Eastern spiritual traditions and mysticism, Immunity to Change, Mindfulness, Somatics, Non-Violent Communication, Theory U, Social Presencing Theatre, Gestalt etc.) to create a strong pipeline of leaders across the organization.

Leaders were supported, even after the formal completion of the programme, through a strong alumni programme that helped them stay on the journey of self-growth and transformation.

## Impact

The programme had three outcomes: first, at a personal level, leaders at the organization were able to overcome limiting mindsets and bodysets and to become more effective (pursuing excellence from a space of joy rather than stress or fear, better decision making, self-expression, confidence, inspiration, people development etc). Second, in groups, the programme brought about deep collaboration across borders. And, third, across the organization the programme created a culture of deep connection and empathy (greater patient-centricity) and led to an impact of $125 million improvement in its first three years.

The programme's success prompted the C-Suite to undertake a 12-month developmental journey to bring about 'alignment and resonance' in the top team to deliver on the business mission of 'providing affordable and accessible medicines to all'.

This in turn evolved from a programme into a whole agenda, a movement which encompasses the top team, senior leadership across BUs and functions and the broader organization, all addressed through different interventions, with the intent to unleash individual potential that would fold in to organizational potential.

As the organization's CHRO observed: 'In all these years, I am yet to see a leadership agenda that is so closely tied with the organizational vision, that uses personal transformation to guarantee business impact. The results over four years are there for all to see.'

# Reflection

The leadership development intervention was a success because it addressed the whole person. While many programmes are skills-focused (what the leader should know and do), this programme also touched on who the leader should be. In addition to learning business skills such as delegation, problem solving, and managing change, leaders also developed a deeper personal awareness, explored how to leverage their strengths, and built empathy in order to connect more deeply and emphatically with their colleagues. Furthermore, the programme included structured breakthrough projects, so that participants grew in the context of business challenges. While the real business results were measured, the real focus was on how participants were able to achieve them. The programme was unequivocal in its focus on personal growth, and also ensured that the skills and qualities that were developed were those demanded for specific situations that the participants were facing.

## *Boosting individual learning and performance*

What is good for learning is typically also good for enhancing the performance of employees in general. For example, stretching employees into the learning zone will likely lead to better business results in a shorter amount of time. Giving employees autonomy (within boundaries) and creating a positive context will likely enhance motivation and quality. Matching employee strengths with the tasks at hand will inevitably be beneficial to results.

In the same way, there are other elements beneficial to both learning and day-to-day performance. We do not categorize them as 'adult learning principles', but organizations would nonetheless undoubtedly benefit from taking them into account. We highlight five of these elements:

- **Single-tasking:** the brain does not multi-task well. Brain scans show that irrespective of what a person is doing, generally the whole brain is active. Hence eliminating multi-tasking is critical for learning new things, as well as carrying out tasks effectively and efficiently.
- **Growth mindsets and awareness of stereotype threats:** The mindset of a person has a clear impact on a person's ability to learn and perform. For example, Female Asian-American students reminded of their Asian heritage performed much better in a subsequent math exam compared to a group which was reminded on the stereotype that 'math is hard for girls'. In addition, fostering a growth mindset, with a positive attitude towards oneself and learning, improves one's ability to overcome challenges and learn.[29]
- **Elimination of biases:** All humans have biases, some of which reduce decision-making effectiveness – for example the 'confirmation bias' or 'availability bias'.[30] Organizations can counter these biases through interventions at the individual level (for example, feedback and reflection) and organizational level (for example, adaptive decision-making processes).
- **Maintaining a healthy lifestyle:** That sleep, exercise and nutrition are important is not new information for anyone

reading this book. What is different now, with the advent of more advanced fMRI techniques, is our ability to measure the magnitude of the impact of bodily health on our ability to carry out cognitive tasks and learn new ones. Organizations can no longer afford to treat bodily health as a 'nice to have' but should offer relevant programmes and policies to ensure employee welfare. These elements are not meant to be comprehensive; they do not cover, for example, interventions based on positive psychology or spirituality; however, they offer they key building blocks to maintaining a healthy lifestyle. This includes stress management, as well as ensuring sufficient down time ('recovery') for employees.

- **Meditation and mindfulness:** Neuroscience shows a link between meditation and mindfulness, and improved performance, learning and general well-being. As a result, numerous organizations have given employees opportunities to benefit from mindfulness and meditation, for example, through structured programmes and setting up meditation rooms.[31]

Appendix 3 has additional details on each of the above elements, including the neuroscience behind each one.

## *Implications for leadership development*

When designing and delivering leadership development interventions, and focusing specifically on how to influence the behaviours of individuals, organizations would benefit from an overarching focus on maximizing learning transfer. In practice, this means applying the seven adult learning principles outlined in this chapter. As a reminder, these are: stretching participants, including self-directed elements, ensuring a positive context, making the development strengths-based, including on-the-job learning and repetition, addressing mindsets, and including feedback and reflection. We already discussed some of the practical implications of the principles earlier in the chapter. We will also see in Chapter 7 (our approach) and Part 2 of the book (our approach in practice) how we design leadership development interventions and embed adult learning principles in practice.

**Technology plays a key role in applying the adult learning principles effectively**: mobile-based applications with a library of relevant and self-paced modules can help enable self-directed learning. Wearable technology can be used to provide instantaneous feedback, for example on how much people are speaking (useful if the wearer is trying to speak more or less in group settings) and on voice intonation and emotions (useful if, for example, the wearer is trying to change their presence or negotiation style). Push messages and daily reminders can enable 'deliberate practice', on-the-job application and repetition. Gamification and social learning networks can provide a more positive context. One app, for example, gives points when modules are completed (increasing motivation to complete the modules) and when participants 'check-in' with one another at work and discuss the learning programme (increasing the motivation to go from virtual to physical networks). These points can then, in turn, be used to unlock new learning modules or other features. Earning 'badges' after completing courses are another way to promote learning, and also serve the useful function of broadcasting to the wider learning group (or organization as a whole) when certain skills have been developed. And virtual reality (VR) is pushing the boundaries of addressing mindsets, uncovering biases, and simulating on-the-job application of new behaviours. VR has long been used in areas like the army and pilot training (usually, where real-life drills entail danger, it makes sense to practise in VR). Now, however, VR is making inroads into leadership development. For example, Stanford's Virtual Human Interaction Lab uses virtual reality simulations to help participants build empathy by allowing learners to experience the life of someone else by 'walking a mile' in their shoes, prior to simulated social interactions.[32]

**Of the seven adult learning principles, we emphasize here the importance of on-the-job application and shifting mindsets.** If we recall our definition, leadership is about behaviours, which are supported by the right skills and the right mindset. It is worth looking at these two components in further detail, as they are critical to individual behavioural change, yet often lacking in leadership development programmes that focus heavily on classroom learning.

First, the application of the skills in project-work during the course of the programme is important. This will result in an optimum blend of learning at work, feedback and reflection, in-class courses and reading.

However, there are dangers. One is how to relate what is learned to what is done at work; the risk is that these will become and remain 'decoupled'. When planning the programme's curriculum, therefore, organizations face a delicate balancing act. On the one hand, there is value in off-site programmes (many in university-like settings) that offer participants time to step back and escape the demands of a day job. On the other hand, even after very basic training sessions, adults typically retain just 10 per cent of what they hear in classroom lectures, in contrast to nearly two- thirds when they learn by doing. Furthermore, burgeoning leaders, no matter how talented, often struggle to transfer even their most powerful off-site experiences into changed behaviour at work.

The answer sounds straightforward: tie leadership development to real on-the-job projects that have a business impact and improve learning. However, it's not easy to create opportunities that simultaneously address high-priority needs – say, accelerating a new-product launch, turning around a sales region, negotiating an external partnership, or developing a new digital-marketing strategy – *and also* provide personal development opportunities for the participants.

A medical-device company got the balance badly wrong when one of its employees, a participant in a leadership-development programme, devoted long hours over several months to what he considered 'real' work: creating a device to assist elderly people during a medical emergency. When he presented his assessment to the board, he was told that a full-time team had been working on exactly this challenge and that the directors would never consider a solution that was a by-product of a leadership-development programme. Given the demotivating effect of this message, this entrepreneurial employee soon left the company.

In contrast, one large international engineering and construction player built a multi-year leadership programme that not only accelerated the personal-development of 300 mid-level leaders but also ensured that projects were delivered on time and on budget. Each participant chose a separate project: one business-unit leader, for instance, committed his team to developing new orders with a key client and to working on a new contract that would span more than one of the group's business lines.

These projects were linked to specified changes in individual behaviour – for instance, overcoming inhibitions in dealing with senior clients or providing better coaching for subordinates. By the end of the programme, the business-unit head was in advanced negotiations on three new opportunities involving two of the group's business lines. Feedback demonstrated that he was now behaving like a group representative rather than someone defending the narrow interest of his own business unit.

Moreover, evolving more effective leadership requires changing individual behaviour. Nevertheless, although most organizations recognize that this also means adjusting underlying mindsets, they are too often reluctant to address the root causes of why their leaders act the way they do. Doing so can be uncomfortable for participants, programme trainers, mentors and bosses – but if there is not a significant degree of discomfort, the chances are that the behaviour won't change. Just as a coach would view an athlete's muscle soreness as a proper response to training, leaders who are stretching themselves should also feel some discomfort as they strive for new levels of performance.

Identifying some of the 'below the surface' feelings, assumptions and beliefs is usually a precondition of behavioural change – one too often shirked in development programmes. Promoting the virtues of delegation and empowerment, for example, is fine in theory, but successful adoption is unlikely if the programme participants have a clear 'controlling' mindset (*I can't lose my grip on the business; I'm personally accountable and only I should make the decisions*). Some personality traits (such as extroversion or introversion) may be difficult to shift, but people *can* change the way they see the world and their values.

Here again, mindsets take time to discover, challenge and change. We saw in the previous chapter that over 80 per cent of programmes run for three months or less, and only 10 per cent run for more than six months. This is a huge roadblock to sustaining shifting mindsets and behaviours among people.

In terms of enablers, there is also often room for improvement. For example on bodily health, in particular the role of sleep, exercise and nutrition, and without going into great detail, there are a number of things organizations can do to encourage healthy choices by employees. Organizations can combat lack of sleep by giving employees sufficient time for learning interventions, to avoid them being done late at night. They can include sleep management, exercise and nutrition tips in training curriculums (interestingly, 70 per cent of the leaders in our survey said that sleep management should be taught in organizations). We published a number of practical tips in a recent *McKinsey Quarterly* article on sleep.[33] Organizations can make adjustments in terms of travel policies, working norms (for example, expecting email responses 24/7 vs. 'blackout' times for email), mandatory work-free vacations, flexible working hours, 'nap rooms' in the office, discounts to gyms or creation of a workout room onsite, providing showers for those who cycle or run to work, and improving the quality of food available (in canteen, lunch vouchers, vending machines).

Now, it is worth mentioning that the biggest gap in adopting healthy choices is often less about knowing what to do, and more about making the desire to change stick. Numerous studies have shown that individuals do not change their lifestyle (for example, giving up smoking, eating more healthily and beginning to exercise more), even when it is a question of life or death. In these cases, what is required is often uncovering and shifting deep-seated inhibitions to change, and practising the new behaviours for six–nine months to make them sustainably shift.[34] Enabling these shifts are a central part of an effective programme.

---

## Case study: Accelerated Development Programme with customized digital learning platform

### Context and challenge

The organization is a leader in chemicals and agribusiness with revenues of over $10 billion annually; it is headquartered in Europe, with over 25,000 employees globally.

Its challenge was to develop leaders across the organization to enable acceleration of business growth; it needed its future business to have greater balance between excellent technical and people skills, to be self-driven and agile learners, and to be able to work across the organization through cross-functional collaboration. Its objective(s) in engaging McKinsey were: to develop 100 high-potential future leaders and to accelerate their readiness for critical higher-level roles.

# Approach

McKinsey designed a 14-month Accelerated Development Programme (ADP) that ensured sustained behavioural change and business impact through a full suite of development interventions:

- **Learning in forums**: multi-day experiential workshops, and self-paced digital learning courses
- **Applying learning in fieldwork**: Exercises in which participants apply learnings from forums in their daily jobs, business challenge for participants to hone their new skills, and structured mentoring programme for participants to practice developing more junior colleagues
- **Feedback, self-reflection and coaching**: 360-degree leadership assessment, leadership (executive) coaching sessions, business coaching, virtual peer coaching, and individual development planning sessions

Across all the programmes, the learning experience was expressed as a series of eight journeys: understanding self; the leader's mindset and perspective; understanding the organization; constructive challenge and continuous improvement; becoming an agile leader; growing personal resilience; strengthening people; and growing leaders. The different learning interventions were staggered throughout the journey, and ensured a holistic, intense and memorable experience for participants.

A tailored digital platform underpinned the learning journey for participants. In addition to being a one-stop shop for participants with a chronological view of all elements of the programme, it also enabled participants to share their interesting content with peers, and for programme owners to communicate with the participants and keep them engaged.

# Impact

The programme is currently in its first year, and has so far received very positive feedback from participants, including:

- 97% rating for value for time spent in programme
- 95% rating on ability to put into practice what was learnt
- 98% recommendation rating to peers and colleagues

The above scores are some of the highest we have received globally, in particular the dimension regarding the ability to put into practice what was learnt. Equally positive feedback came from the client sponsor as well as Learning and Organizational Development (L&OD): 'Having worked with numerous vendors in my past 15 years in this field, I believe McKinsey today has one of the most advanced products on the market and offers probably the most complete leadership development service to global organizations.'

# Reflection

Digital tools allow organizations to take user engagement and application of new leadership skills to the next level. The integrated platform for the Accelerated Development Programme greatly increased participant engagement, as they quickly became part of an online global community, where they could access programme content, receive programme communication, and interact with senior leaders and fellow participants.

In addition, the platform provided a clear overview of the full suite of programme elements and provided timely nudges to participants on upcoming milestones, ensuring that participants were able to carve out time from their busy schedules to complete programme elements in between the structured forums. What often happens for leaders is that business realities take over outside of workshops, and engagement falls away. However, 80 per cent of the learning happens on the job, and the digital platform helped ensure that participants applied what they learned, received feedback from multiple sources, and reflected on their progress – ultimately driving sustainable behavioural change.

## *Summary*

This chapter has run through the third core principle of leadership development at scale, covering the 'how' of a leadership development intervention in regards to individual learning effectiveness. The chapter highlighted that the human brain remains 'plastic' well into adulthood, and discussed the seven key adult learning principles that we regular apply in leadership development to bring about changes in individual behaviour.

We also discussed the fact that many adult learning principles are not new, yet a large degree of organizations do not apply them, or at least not in a holistic manner. The natural question is *why* do organizations not apply a more holistic approach to developing leaders, if the facts are clear? We discussed three main reasons: not being aware of the principles, not understanding the magnitude of importance of the principles, and understanding them yet unable to find the right suppliers to implement them.

The next chapter outlines our Core Principle 4: putting in place a system that enables, supports and reinforces the leadership programme by integration and measurement. This principle also deals with the 'how' of leadership at scale, yet at an organizational level.

# 6

# Core Principle 4: Integrate and measure

*Arne Gast, Faridun Dotiwala, Gemma D'Auria*

Why is system integration important? | Integrating the change through
the Influence Model | Measuring impact | The link to organizational
culture | Implications for leadership development

In the last chapter, we saw that the human brain remains plastic during
adulthood, and we reviewed modern adult learning techniques. We
discussed the importance of applying these learning methods during a leadership development programme in order to shift behaviours
sustainably. However, formal training/capability building is only one
component of a system-wide change effort. In order to shift behaviours across an organization, more is needed.

This chapter reviews the importance of embedding the desired
behavioural changes in the broader organizational system, which we
do through the Influence Model (discussed below). This encompasses
not only capability building, but also role-modelling, fostering understanding and conviction, and aligning HR and people systems. In
addition, it includes measuring the progress and adapting as needed.
Finally, we illustrate the implications for leadership development and
how this could look in practice.

## Core Principle 4: Integrate and measure the programme in the broader organization

Organizations must ensure that the broader ecosystem directly
supports and enables the shift in behaviours, skills and mindsets
that the leadership development programme promotes

## Why is system integration important?

During our research for this book we considered the question *Do organizations lead?* We answered this with a resounding 'yes' – see Chapter 3. In the same way, one could ask whether organizations have distinct cultures (contexts) that are self-sustaining and self-perpetuating. Numerous researchers find that this is indeed the case. More importantly for leadership development, studies have shown that people adapt to their environments, and that their behaviours are at least in part due to the context they are in.[1] Changing the context, or system, therefore changes people's behaviours.

As such, if leadership programmes are treated as *isolated initiatives*, they will never succeed in shifting and maintaining the behaviours of the leaders and broader organization. **To create lasting impact at scale, organizations must adapt formal and informal mechanisms to enable the leadership programme.** This could include 'harder' elements such as a revised performance management system, performance evaluation, compensation, and internal mobility and succession-planning, as well as the 'softer' elements of feedback, non-financial rewards such as recognition, and praise, and the overall way employees interact and work.

Like many other of our core principles, the importance of integrating and measuring is most apparent in its absence. One of the most frustrating situations leaders face, having learned new things and grown during a programme, is to return to a rigid organization that not only disregards their efforts for change, but also actively works against them. This recalcitrance could take many forms: unsupportive superiors who do not espouse new and different behaviours, HR systems that do not reward (or may even penalize) new leadership behaviours such as empowerment and experimentation, and innovation, and processes and authority thresholds that do not enable certain behaviours (for example, customer centricity and speed of decision making). Instead, what is needed is to embed the leadership development intervention in the organizational system.

Our latest leadership development research confirms the need for action in this area as three of our top ten key actions were related to embedding leadership development interventions into the broader organization. We found that organizations with successful leadership development interventions were 5.9 times more like to review current formal/informal mechanisms for building leadership skills, prior to building a leadership development intervention than those organizations whose interventions were not successful.

It is critical that organizations adapt formal HR systems to reinforce the leadership model/the desired behaviours (for example, recruiting, performance evaluation, compensation, succession planning), which had a multiple of 5.6 times. From our experience, adaptation of HR results is truly critical. For organizations that had successful leadership development interventions, almost 75 per cent adapted HR systems accordingly, while only 13 per cent did so for unsuccessful organizations.

Organizations should ensure that the top team role-models desired behaviours in the context of leadership programmes (for example, by acting as programme faculty, project sponsors, mentors, or coaches, which had a multiple of 4.9 times). Other important actions outside of the top 10 list were to measure ROI with the same rigour as other initiatives across three dimensions: participant assessment, behavioural change and business performance (3.6×), and to ensure programme objectives, metrics, tracking mechanisms and governance are clearly formulated and in place (3.3×).

Additionally, the focus on the broader organizational context means that the desired leadership behaviours become espoused by not only the leaders who receive the formal training, but also the rest of the organization.

**All leadership development must bring about a change in behaviour across an organization.** The other core principles explain why this is so, and how to achieve it. This principle explains how those changes become part of the life of the organization, and the new way of doing things.

## Integrating the change through the Influence Model

Integrating or embedding the desired leadership behavioural change in the broader organizational system is critical to the success of a leadership development programme. In our view, **the best way to change people's behaviour is by using what we call the Influence Model,** which is a proven model based on sound psychology and years of practice (see Figure 6.1).

In both research and practice, we find that transformations stand the best chance of success when they focus on four key actions to change mindsets and behaviour:

- fostering understanding and conviction
- reinforcing changes through formal mechanisms
- developing talent and skills
- role-modelling

In any transformation or change (and leadership development is a prime instance), these four elements must all be present.[2]

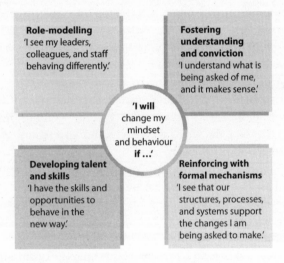

FIGURE 6.1 The Influence Model

The Influence Model is based on an extensive review of more than 130 sources and has stood the test of time. It has been a key enabler of organizational change for more than 10 years and it has informed thousands of client engagements in practice. We know it works. Our research in 2010 sheds light on the degree of difference in transformation success rates for organizations that do or do not deploy the different elements of the Influence Model (see Figure 6.2). It is clear that the results are not trivial.[3]

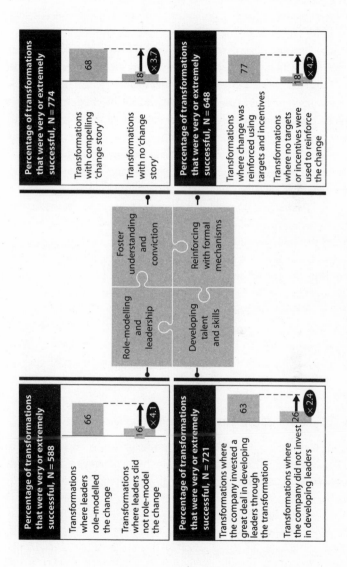

FIGURE 6.2 Transformation rates using the Influence Model

The Influence Model is a cross-cultural phenomenon. Research suggests that much of what is at the core of influence is not geographically or nationally dependent. Basic principles of influence – including reciprocity, scarcity, authority, consistency, liking and consensus – seem to exist in all cultures. As such, the principles in the Influence Model can largely be generalized across cultures. However, cultural differences do impact how to most effectively apply elements of the model. Research indicates that cultural differences can have a bearing on the *relative* effectiveness and application of specific influence strategies. For example, research suggests that group behaviour has even greater influence on how someone behaves in a collectivistic/communal culture (for example, Poland) vs. in a more individualistic culture (for example, United States) – a finding with implications for role-modelling. Conversely, one's own behavioural consistency was shown to matter more in individualistic cultures – a finding with implications for fostering understanding and conviction.[4]

One of the benefits of adopting the Influence Model (and all that it implies about the systematized nature of the leadership development, or any change, effort) is that it prevents the behavioural change from becoming orphaned or disregarded. Instead, it implies a comprehensive change effort that transforms the overarching culture of the organization. This ensures that the desired change effort engages the full organization and not just a select 10 per cent or so of leaders. Below, we provide more details on each of the quadrants, why they are important, and the implications for leadership development.

## Fostering understanding and conviction

The first quadrant is around **fostering understanding and conviction in the organization**. This is critical because human beings strive for congruence in our beliefs and actions. In 1957 the Stanford social psychologist Leon Festinger published his theory of cognitive dissonance, the distressing mental state that arises when people find that their beliefs are inconsistent with their actions. Festinger observed in the subjects of his experimentation a deep-seated need to eliminate cognitive dissonance by changing either their actions or their beliefs.[5]

The implication of this finding for an organization is that if its people believe in its overall purpose, they will be happy to change their individual behaviour to serve that purpose; indeed, they will suffer from cognitive dissonance if they don't. But to feel comfortable about change and to carry it out with enthusiasm, people must understand the role of their actions in the unfolding drama of the organization's fortunes and believe that it is worthwhile for them to play a part.

It isn't enough to tell employees that they will have to do things differently, however. Anyone leading a major change programme must take the time to think through its 'story' – what makes it worth undertaking – and to explain that story to all involved in making change happen, so that their contributions make sense to them as individuals. This is because humans are wired to respond to stories, as stories activate and excite our brains.[6]

When telling this story, it is important to think about how it is framed and presented. Research indicates that how a message is framed affects its persuasive power; we often react differently to the same underlying message based on how it is worded. [7] It is also important to touch on different sources of meaning among employees. We find that people are motivated by different things, with a roughly equal split among the elements of society, company, customer, team and me. Change stories should therefore touch on each of these five sources of meaning. In addition, research has shown that communicating clear goals, especially shared goals, can be a powerful motivator and enhance performance.[8]

There are numerous ways to do this. For example, executives should craft an overarching company change story, fit it to their contexts, and 'cascade' the story to senior leaders in large group sessions where they define what it means for them. This cascade should be repeated until it reaches the front-line. The story should be kept alive through traditional and viral communications (for example, Townhalls, intranet, emails, meetings, celebrations of where it's working). We've also seen examples of organizations establishing 'language markers' (for example, Walmart's '10 foot rule' – when employees are within 10 feet of a customer, they must look him or her in the eye, greet and ask if they can help).

In addition to the content of the story, it is crucial to think through how the story is presented. We often find that executives spend the majority of their time on what to say, and not how to ensure the right level of emotional connection to the people in the organization so that they can truly buy into the case for change. Research shows, however, that the way a message is communicated visually and vocally influences an audience more than the content itself (verbal), with over 50 per cent of the impact coming from the body language of the presenter and visuals, almost 40 per cent coming from the vocals, and less than 10 per cent coming from the content itself.[9]

For leadership development programmes specifically, here are some interventions we have seen work to foster understanding and conviction:

- Developing and disseminating the message that we are only as strong as our people – we will reap many times what we invest in their development
- Publicly committing to developing internal talent
- Promoting voluntary training and development programmes
- Creating and publishing a standard career development profile for each role (for example, training, job rotation, required skills, time to promotion)

## Role-modelling and leadership

The second quadrant of the Influence Model has to do with the **leaders and pivotal influencers in the organization role-modelling or embodying the desired behaviours**, i.e. 'walking the talk'. Humans unconsciously mimic the behaviour and emotions of the people around them. Researchers have shown that we have a tendency to assume the behaviours, expressions, speech patterns, and other mannerisms of our interaction partners without conscious intention,[10] and that even emotions can be contagious.[11]

Leaders have a disproportionate impact on people within the organization, and role-modelling is especially important for those at the top.[12] However, people model their behaviour on 'significant others': those they see in positions of influence. Within a single organization, people in different functions or levels choose different role-models – a founding partner, perhaps, or a trade union representative, or the highest-earning sales rep. In addition, we are also prone to *consciously conforming* to align our own behaviour and thinking with others in order to fit in.[13] Behaviour in organizations is deeply affected not only by role-models but also by the groups with which people identify. So to change behaviour consistently throughout an organization, it isn't enough to ensure that people at the top are in line with the new ways of working; role-models and key influencers at every level must 'walk the talk'.

The way role-models deal with their tasks can vary, but the underlying *values* informing their behaviour must be consistent. In a company that encourages entrepreneurial decision making at low levels, one middle manager might try to coach junior employees to know how to spot a promising new venture; another might leave this up to them. Both, however, would be acting in line with the entrepreneurial principle, whereas a boss who demanded a lengthy business case to justify each $50 expenditure would not be. But organizations trying to change their value systems can't tolerate as much variance in their role-models' behaviour. If, in this case, entrepreneurial decision making were a new value, both of these middle managers might have to act in roughly the same way in order to encourage their subordinates to make bold decisions.

A typical intervention is to align the top team (for example, top 200) on the direction of the change and on their role in making it happen. Often their role will include taking symbolic actions that send a strong, positive message to the rest of the organization. Symbolic actions are actions that the organization will notice, and which are representative of the new leadership model and culture. For example, this might mean regularly 'walking the halls' to ask how employees are doing, working alongside front-line staff once a month, or hosting regular lunches with employees. Other interventions include finding and empowering the key influencers so that they become change leaders; and leaders showing openness by asking for – and acting on – feedback, and at the same time encouraging direct reports to do the same.

For leadership development programmes, we have seen countless examples of executives endorsing a programme for everyone but themselves, believing that their subordinates have much to learn but they themselves do not. Over a quarter of all organizations felt that leadership development programmes do not apply to all levels of their organization. Below are some interventions we have seen work in practice.

- Have the top team be the first cohort of the leadership development intervention – and share the experiences with the rest of the organization
- Leaders in the organization acting as programme faculty, project sponsors and mentors

- Leaders creating a learning plan for each of their direct reports and encouraging them to share that plan with their direct reports as an example

As mentioned in Core Principle 2, we use people analytics to assess more accurately who the organization's top talent really are, at different levels of the organization. People analytics can also be used to identify 'influencers', who may not necessarily be characterized as top talent but who are important to win the support of, and who should act as change agents and role-models.

## Developing talent and skills

The third critical element of the Influence Model is **capability building and leadership development**, which is the focus of this book. As we saw in earlier chapters, it is critical to link the programme to context, engage a critical mass of leaders, and to use the latest adult learning principles in designing and running the leadership development intervention.

In addition to engaging leaders on the programme, however, it is important to ensure that everyone who is expected to behave differently is given the appropriate tools and skills. Many change programmes make the error of exhorting employees to behave differently without teaching them how to adapt general instructions to their individual situation. It is one thing for the leader to tell his sales team to 'be more customer-centric', and it's another thing for the leader to coach each sales rep do so and provide them with the right software and customer insights. The organization may urge its people to be 'customer-centric', and even walk the talk, but if it paid little attention to customers in the past, its sales staff will have no idea how to interpret this principle or won't know what a successful outcome would look like. In order to truly cascade the new leadership behaviours to all employees, below are some interventions we have seen work in practice:

- Developing individual development plans for each employee, driven by their direct managers
- Ensuring leaders provide feedback to and coach employees on the desired behaviours. This should be cascaded from leaders all the way down to the front line
- Providing learning opportunities that are supportive of the

desired behavioural shifts, to all employees. A cost efficient way to do this is to provide eLearning modules to all employees

• Have leaders teach the new behaviours, skills and mindsets to their direct reports, having their direct reports do the same, and in this way cascading the learning interventions to the front line. This has the added benefit that the people teaching will further assimilate the learnings. As the organizational psychologist Chris Argyris showed, people assimilate information more thoroughly if they go on to describe to others how they will apply what they have learned to their own circumstances. The reason, in part, is that human beings use different areas of the brain for learning and for teaching.

## Reinforcing with formal mechanisms

The last piece of the Influence Model is perhaps, together with role-modelling, the most critical. It is also the one with the highest numerical success ratio at 4.2 times. The importance of **reinforcing behavioural change** with formal mechanisms builds on the work of B.F. Skinner, who is best known for his experiments with rats during the late 1920s and the 1930s. He found that he could motivate a rat to complete the boring task of negotiating a maze by providing the right incentive – corn at the maze's centre – and by punishing the rat with an electric shock each time it took a wrong turn.

Skinner's theories of conditioning and positive reinforcement were taken up by psychologists interested in what motivates people in organizations. Organizational designers broadly agree that reporting structures, management and operational processes, and measurement procedures – setting targets, measuring performance, and granting financial and nonfinancial rewards – must be consistent with the behaviour that people are asked to embrace. When an organization's goals for new behaviour are not reinforced, employees are less likely to adopt it consistently; if managers are urged to spend more time coaching junior staff, for instance, but coaching does not figure in the performance scorecards of managers, they are unlikely to bother. While it may not be overly rigid to include quantitative KPIs on coaching (for example, number of sessions conducted), the behaviour can be measured through a 360-degree review, with rewards and consequences based on the behaviours the organization is trying to promote.

Some disciples of Skinner suggest that positive-reinforcement 'loops' have a constant effect: once established, you can leave them be. Over time, however, Skinner's rats became bored with corn and began to ignore the electric shocks. In our experience, a similar phenomenon often prevents organizations from sustaining higher performance: structures and processes that initially reinforce or condition the new behaviour do not guarantee that it will endure. They need to be supported by changes that complement the other three conditions for changing mindsets. [14] Other research has shown that learning and behavioural change often occurs through direct associations (Pavlov's dogs)[15] and vicarious reinforcement (watching others suffer the consequences of their actions).[16]

However, research (and our experience) also shows that organizations often reinforce the wrong things and overlook the right things.[17] Organizations often over-weight financial rewards, when employees in practice often value a broader range of both financial and non-financial rewards. According to the Theory of Needs, employees also value achievement (implying that clear targets and feedback on progress are motivators), power (implying that promotions are motivators), and affiliation (implying that shared recognition and team rewards are motivators).[18] In fact, financial rewards have even been shown to hurt motivation in intrinsically motivated people.[19]

In addition, many other structural elements of an organization influence behaviour. For example, the characteristics of a job and the way the work itself is designed (responsibilities, decision-making rights, team support etc.) impacts employees' motivation.[20] In the same way, the organization structure shapes employees' behaviour. For example, a mechanistic organization model (highly centralized, formalized, hierarchical) leads to very different behaviours and mindsets than an organic/agile organization model (highly dispersed, transparency and free flow of information, autonomous units).[21]

To make the behavioural change stick, key interventions are to ensure roles and responsibilities (including accountability) are clear, to refresh/reinforce standards and procedures, to integrate the desired behavioural change into the individual performance management system (ensuring the right mix of financial and non-financial incentives), and to cascade key performance indicators down through the line and build them into key business processes.

Leadership development programmes stall when the surrounding HR systems remain static in the face of expected behavioural change of leaders. While participants gain increased awareness of themselves and others and learn new skills, they often clash with a misaligned incentive system, leaving them frustrated. As one leader put it, 'they [executives] expect me to collaborate across the group, but my bonus is based on the bottom line of my business unit' – an all too common insight. As a result, participants gravitate to old forms of behaviour, and organizations are thus not able to sustain the impact of a leadership development programme. Here are some the key elements we have seen work in practice:

- Embedding the leadership model into individual performance management, at all levels. This requires breaking the desired behaviours down into clear expectations for the employees (for example, in a performance grid). In addition, business KPIs should also be updated to reflect the desired changes (for example, targeting more innovative leaders requires more risk taking and perhaps a push to more revenue from new sources). Organizations should also ensure that the new performance management metrics are linked to rewards and recognition/ promotion, as well as consequence management.
- Embedding the leadership model into the employee value proposition and consequently into the recruiting process.
- Ensure a robust performance dialog process is used to help employees understand what is expected of them and to give them the right feedback to help them develop.
- Aligning processes and delegations of authority to the desired behaviours (for example, if an organization wants employees to be more empowered, providing more decision-making rights is desirable).
- Succession planning for top levels of organization.

# Measuring impact

Organizations vary in terms of how they measure the impact of their leadership development interventions. At one extreme, some organizations do not measure it at all. The Chief Learning Officer of a multinational company, for example, told us that his organization does not measure the ROI of training, as it is such an integral part of the organization – much in the same way that you typically do not measure the ROI of your finance professionals. Nonetheless, we find that it is generally helpful to **measure the impact of leadership development programmes, at a minimum in order to compare different approaches and improve interventions** along the way. This involves formal measurement of outcomes and outputs – above and beyond the four areas of intervention based on the Influence Model – to properly anchor the impact of the leadership development intervention and properly embed it in the broader system. This is distinct from the individual performance management discussed above, but instead focuses on the intervention as a whole. We frequently find that organizations pay lip service to the importance of quantifying the value of their leadership development investment. When organizations fail to track and measure changes in leadership performance (and the performance of individual leaders) over time, they increase the odds that improvement initiatives won't be taken seriously. Additionally, a failure to measure not only decreases effectiveness of training but also makes it harder to illustrate a business case for additional leadership development initiatives.

Too often, evaluation of leadership development begins and ends with participant feedback; the danger here is that trainers learn to game the system and deliver a syllabus that pleases rather than challenges participants. Our most recent research indicates that only a quarter (27 per cent) of organizations measure participant learning, only a third (37 per cent) measure change in participant behaviour, and fewer than half (44 per cent) actually track one of the key metrics of leadership development, the impact on the overall organization (for example, through financial KPIs or organizational health). A quarter of organizations (26 per cent) state that they don't measure the return on leadership development at all.[22] Yet targets *can* be set and their achievement monitored. Just as in any performance programme, once that assessment is complete, leaders can learn from successes and failures over time and make the necessary adjustments.

We typically measure four main elements, similar to the model laid out by Donald Kirkpatrick, yet tailored to the needs of our clients, and use tools such as the Organizational Health Index.[23] These four elements are:

- reaction of the participants
- degree of learning
- behavioural changes
- organizational impact

We do not typically measure the return on investment of a learning intervention, as it is challenging to accurately isolate the impact of the training (see Chapter 13 FAQ 6 for a discussion on this point). However, we know that leadership is highly correlated with performance – organizations performing in the top-quartile on leadership outperform others by nearly 2 times on EBITDA,[24] and organizations that invest in developing leaders during significant transformations are 2.4 times more likely to hit their performance targets.[25]

- **Participant reaction.** This should cover a wide range of elements – course content, faculty, venue, value of time spent, overall net promoter score, as well as open comments.
- **Assess the degree of learning.** This can be done through tests before and after the training, as well as through feedback from the managers of the participants.
- **Assess the extent of behavioural change.** We recommend developing a customized 360-degree feedback tool that incorporates the leadership model, and embedding the 360-degree feedback tool into the performance management framework of the organization to track the impact of leadership development. Leaders can also use such tools to demonstrate their own commitment to real change for themselves and the organization. One CEO we know commissioned his own 360-degree feedback exercise and published the results (good and bad) for all to see on the company intranet, along with a personal commitment to improve.
- **Measure overall organizational results.** This has potentially many elements to it. At the individual level, one could monitor

the performance of participants vs. non-participants, for example, in terms of revenue growth year-on-year. Another approach is to monitor participants' career development after the training, for example, in terms of the proportion that were appointed to more senior roles one to two years after the programme, as well as the attrition rates of participants vs. non-participants. By analysing recent promotions at a global bank, for example, senior managers showed that candidates who had been through a leadership-development programme were more successful than those who had not.

We also measure the impact of the projects that are carried out by programme participants. Metrics might include cost savings and the number of new-store openings for a retail business, for example, or sales of new products if the programme focused on the skills to build a new-product strategy. The committee evaluating the project (typically made up of senior leaders) often have a good sense of what project quality typically looks like, and whether the participants on the programme have delivered projects that are higher than what would be expected without the learning intervention.

Finally, it is critical to measure overall organizational health. This will show, at an organizational level, the changes in overall health, the leadership outcome, the leadership practices, as well as the specific behaviours in the leadership behavioural report. Some companies include health-related metrics into their management accounting systems, while others monitor health 'in real time' by asking employees one health-related question a day, every day.

For example, American Express quantifies the success of some of its leadership programmes by comparing the average productivity of participants' teams prior to and after a training programme, yielding a simple measure of increased productivity. Similarly, a non-profit we know recently sought to identify the revenue increase attributable to its leadership programme by comparing one group that had received training with another that had not.[26]

## *The link to organizational culture*

We often get asked the question: *Are a leadership model and culture the same thing?* They are not. Marvin Bower, McKinsey's Managing Director from 1950–67, defined culture as 'The way we do things around here', and we find this to be a practical and simple definition.[27] As such, culture fully encompasses leadership behaviours but is even broader. For example, part of a corporate culture is the dress code, meeting etiquette and social events. Many of these elements may not be formalized in a leadership model (and may not be formalized at all), but form an important part of how the organization operates. We often measure culture using the organizational health index, as it is quantitative, actionable, and directly linked to performance; the OHI's underlying management practices, in particular, are a good representation of how people do things in the organization.

However, an *outcome* of a leadership development intervention that encompasses all elements of the Influence Model is a shift in the culture. Leadership development at scale changes the expectation of employees in terms of what behaviours to display in different situations. Through the Influence Model, new leadership behaviours become the practices that the organization does normally – transforming 'the way people do things'. Leadership development done well thus shifts the underlying culture towards a culture of leadership and specific leadership behaviours, in line with the leadership model.

There are two implications for organizations. First is that leadership development interventions should be fully aligned with other cultures or people interventions that the organization may be undertaking. Second is that organizations should think about the aspirational end state of leadership development as creating a more leadership-oriented culture. It is not merely about tweaking the underlying formal and informal mechanisms – these are input drivers – but rather about shifting the underlying way of working of all employees, at all levels.

The end game is thus a transformed organization with a transformed culture. This does not mean that the organization needs to let up on the system embedment – it is critical that each of the four quadrants of the Influence Model continue to work in tandem. But it does mean that the relative effort to sustain (and perpetuate) the change diminishes. New recruits are immediately swept up in the culture and begin adapting their behaviours quickly (or leave if there is not a cultural fit). The leadership culture becomes self-perpetuating – no longer dependent on specific individuals or on top down interventions – but embodied by all employees as the normal way of working.

## Implications for leadership development

**People's behaviours are heavily influenced by their broader context**, and in order to sustainably shift their behaviours, you need to shift the context. When designing a leadership development intervention, the actual capability building journey is only 25 per cent of what is required. In addition, it is critical to ensure leadership role-modelling, conviction and understanding throughout the organization, and adapted and aligned organizational processes and structures.

**Technology plays a key role in enabling the system embedment**. Recently we have embedded a 'digital variation' of the Influence Model, which allows for even more scale, speed and impact. Among other levers, technology enables quicker feedback loops (allowing individuals to see the impact of their actions in real time), personalization (for example, of messages and content, leading to greater relevance for each individual), shorter links (for example, between employees and managers, fostering more transparency) and community building (for example, through sharing of experiences between colleagues). These levers can be applied across all four quadrants of the Influence Model.

In addition, measurement is critical. Setting targets means that organizations have to *put hard numbers on the soft stuff*. They must tie learning objectives not only to participant feedback, but also to specific behavioural changes and overall performance improvements. This is done by base lining the as-is state and conducting regular 'pulse checks' to gauge improvements over time.

Finally, organizations should think about leadership interventions as cultural interventions. Leadership must be carried out not as isolated initiatives, but as fully embedded in the broader organizational culture and context.

# Case study: The power of holistic system change

## Context and challenge

In 2011/12, this consumer electronics organization was in crisis. Since 2000, revenues had declined by one third, profit margin had dropped to 7 per cent, and the stock price had fallen by 60 per cent; the company had under-performed the stock market indices for a decade. It was adrift in a perfect storm: the lighting division had pioneered LED technology and in doing so had moved from a comfortable oligopoly to a highly competitive semiconductor space. The healthcare division experienced a business model disruption as hospitals moved away from capital-intensive investments, forcing a transition to service provision. And the Consumer Lifestyle division (tv/audio) faced fierce competition at scale from Asian competitors. Its leadership realized that the organization had to reinvent itself. This was not only about strategy, processes and organization structures, but also about cultural change.

## Approach

McKinsey began by measuring the top team's attitude across the three fundamentals aspects of leadership: alignment (Does the team share a view on where to lead the organization and how to lead it there?), execution (Is the team effectively designed, and does it have high-quality interactions that drive superior performance?) and renewal (Is the team able to sustain its energy and does it have the capacity and ability to adapt to change?). In May 2011 these scores were some of the lowest McKinsey had seen; by the end of the leadership development programme, they were amongst the highest.

The organization decided to invest in building the leadership capabilities required for the transformation, and established a new practice around leadership by focusing on two critical characteristics: Feedback, and Courageous Conversations. In doing so, a new language of 'learning and protection, elephants in the room, hot buttons' began to emerge. The language itself became a catalyst to help teams move where they had previously been stuck. And a new language helped address the fear inherent in all transformations. The programme was anchored in three behaviours that shaped culture and articulated values. These were specific to the organization at that time: *Team up to excel*; *Eager to win*; *Take ownership*, and were cast as a series of 'from–to' shifts:

- 'Team up to excel' meant a shift *from* valuing relations over results, avoiding conflict and protecting functional interests *to* using tension as a source of learning and renewal, to deepen trust and drive collective performance
- 'Eager to win' meant a shift *from* avoiding risk, valuing insight over action and being complacent *to* taking pride in winning and delivering on commitments, driving operational excellence with passion and constantly raising the bar
- 'Take ownership' meant a shift *from* abdicating responsibilities, explaining non-performance with excuses or blaming others *to* being accountable for performance one could not entirely control by himself/herself

In the wider company context, the new CEO hosted a top 300 leadership summit to present the case for change based on the insight he gained in dialogues with hundreds of customers, investors and employees across the world: '*We had our first collective courageous conversation addressing major elephants in the room. Tough – yet energizing – we built a fact-based case for change and a compelling story, where it became clear what was asked of us. This was the start of our Transformational journey, 'Accelerate!' which we clearly positioned as a marathon, not a sprint.*' At its next leadership summit in 2012, the organization chose a different framing by connecting the transformation to its core values. The company's founder spoke in a 1930s video of the values of entrepreneurship and innovation; and all sectors presented how they were still living these values, showing the latest innovations and customer impact – this organization at its best. It was a turning point where many senior leaders' involvement turned into commitment. From that moment many leaders stepped forward to become part of the 'Accelerate!' journey.

The new challenge was how to get the rest of the organization to this level. To this end, the organization embedded culture as one of the five pillars of the transformation, to ensure it was front and center. It then chose a holistic approach the focused not only on capability building, but also on creating the right external environment to enable the desired behavioural shifts:

- The top 1,200 leaders went through a structured leadership development journey, focusing on the mindsets and skills needed to live the new behaviours. The program, called the Accelerate Leadership Programme (ALP), created a space where natural, cross-functional teams raised their individual and collective awareness on limiting mindsets in facilitated workshops, resulting in clearly defined learning practices that were then embedded in real life with coaching on the job
- The desired behaviours were not only discussed in the workshops, but actively embedded in the organization. Leaders were coached on the importance of role-modelling and the specific symbolic actions they could take to signal the change, which helped ensure that the new behaviours trickled down the organization
- The organization's leaders developed a compelling change story linked to the transformation, which was communicated broadly and cascaded down the organization. Each leader took the 'DNA' of the story, and tailored it to make it their own for their department
- There was a complete change in the incentive system, and incentives became linked to the extent to which employees lived the three desired behaviours

## Impact

The ALP leadership journeys were truly liberating as they offered a space where deep and paralyzing fears blocking the change could be addressed. People found a common language to coach and – most liberating – experienced how conflict could be a place of learning and new ideas, not a place of personal judgment. As such they were 'experiences' that, over time and repetition, created a shift in the beliefs and values of the organization. This is the essence of culture change – the real change is not on the level of behaviors – behaviors are the mere product of underlying beliefs and values. And these only change by consciously creating experiences that shift these beliefs over time. The impact could be measured in two ways: first, the share price which recovered the dip from the preceding years (from a base of 1.0 in 2009, it stood at 1.2 in 2012 and rose to 1.8 in 2014). Second, by the degree to which the organization was living the new culture, and the effectiveness of teams in doing so. While the top team scores were amongst the lowest globally at the beginning of the programme (scores of 49–58), within 3 years they were amongst the highest in our database (scores of 87–93).

## Reflection

While the holistic nature of the programme was a key success factor in itself, there were three other elements worth highlighting. First, the change efforts were anchored in performance transformations. While workshops are often disconnected from business realities, the ALP programme focused heavily on the specific business challenges that leaders were facing, to ground the personal transformation work. In addition, a whole network of internal ALP facilitators and coaches were trained, so they could provide continuous (sometimes tough) feedback to participants during the course of their day to day work, when old habits emerged.

Second, leaders who were part of the programme recognized how a business transformation also meant a personal transformation. The leadership develop culture journeys truly opened people up to change, helped leaders work through their vulnerabilities, and helped take away fear. This upfront investment in the cultural shifts at the beginning laid the foundation for the transformation. In addition, leaders recognized the importance of stepping into the unknown, and avoid 'death by planning'. Leaders were coached to truly transform themselves and their teams, experiment, and learn along the way.

Third, the leadership development programme and broader culture change was managed with the same rigour as the business-related initiatives. The initiatives were measured at multiple levels, including at the organization level, across teams, and for individuals. For example, certain divisions created a fixed quarterly 360-degree feedback loop for all teams, to assess whether they had progressed in terms of embracing the new culture and behavioural shifts. Other behavioural assessments will never be 100% objective, the fact that they triggered a proper feedback discussion ensured that leaders took the initiative seriously.

## Summary

We showed in Chapter 2 that there is no silver bullet to leadership development. Organizations need to do many things right, centred around four key principles:

- Focusing on the critical shifts that drive disproportionate value
- Engaging a critical mass of pivotal influencers across the organization to reach a tipping point
- Architecting programmes that maximize behavioural change based on neuroscience
- Integrating and measuring the programme in the broader organization

These four core principles will embed the new behaviours across the organization, in a sustainable manner (see Figure 2.3 for a reminder of the *Leadership at Scale Diamond*). They form part of an integrated system for leadership development. Our research and experience shows that **all four principles must be present in order to increase the leadership effectiveness across an organization.** Even if three out of four principles are adhered to, the leadership development impact is often severely compromised. In addition, we re-emphasize that the four principles are dynamic and never static. Once an organization has put in place all four principles, it is time to re-visit Core Principle 1. As context shifts, so do the behaviours, skills and mindsets you need to foster, and the cycle continues.

There are many different ways to put a leadership development intervention into practice (for example, the number of forums days, the exact learning modules used, the facilitators deployed, whether it's on-site or at a remote location). Budgets often put a constraint on the solution space available. However, what is key is to incorporate the four principles in the programme. Doing this should greatly enhance the chances that the interventions are successful and that the changes are sustained. In the next part of the book, we display a typical way that we bring the four principles to life.

## PART 2
# Our approach in practice

# 7

# A roadmap for successful leadership development

*Florian Pollner, Johanne Lavoie, Nick Van Dam*

The 4Ds | Diagnose the gap to where you want to go | Design & Develop the interventions | Deliver the programme | Drive Impact | Other considerations for increasing leadership effectiveness

In the previous chapters, we presented our latest research on leadership development success. We outlined our **four core principles of leadership at scale**: *focus on the critical shifts (always linked to context) that drive disproportionate performance; engage a critical mass of leaders through organizational journeys, not cohort-specific episodes; architect the programmes to foster behavioural change and learning transfer by using modern adult learning principles grounded in neuroscience; and integrate and measure the programmes.* If organizations ensure these four criteria are met, they have a great chance of ensuring that the leadership development interventions meet and sustain the desired objectives.

However, we also showed a clear correlation between the number of actions that organizations took and the success of their interventions. Rigour and depth in terms of leadership development actions really matter. For example, when we talk about designing for learning transfer, we could stop at field, forum and coaching. However, to truly ensure success, we can go further and include one-to-one coaching, peer coaching, peer learning groups, and use technology to provide timely reminders. To reach scale, we could roll the programme out to your top 200, or we could further engage change leaders and influencers who are not necessarily high in the organization, use technology to cascade the programme to all employees (including front-line), and embed the intervention into the onboarding programme for all new recruits. This chapter outlines the approach we typically adopt in practice, through each phase of the process. Chapters 8–12 provide additional details on each stage, bringing the approach to life through the lens of an extended (fictitious) case study.

## The 4Ds

So now we get to the approach in more detail. Below we outline our typical approach in terms of the 4Ds:

- **Diagnose** the gap to where you want to go
- **Design** & **Develop** the interventions
- **Deliver** the programme
- **Drive Impact**

After each stage, there are several outputs or results; these make take the form of, for instance, a documented agreement with the CEO and top team or a programme plan agreed with the CHRO. We also give an indicative work plan, to show how a programme might look over time. For each stage, it might be helpful to think in terms of the 'what', 'who' and 'how' (individual and collective), in line with our four core principles. Figure 7.1 below outlines the four stages and the key elements of each.

| **Diagnose** What is the gap to where you want to go? | **Design & Develop** What do you need to get from here to there? | **Deliver** How should you move to action? | **Drive Impact** How do you keep moving forward? |
|---|---|---|---|
| Determine the leadership behaviours required to achieve the strategic aspirations, and prioritise the key shifts; assess where the organization is today in terms of leaders and leadership development | Design & Develop the required interventions for all target groups, and develop programme content; design system integration requirements; identify who should go on the programme; create the business case for delivery | Deliver the programme across all cohorts, using modern adult learning principles; embed in the system Implement structured programme governance and metrics | Rigorously track the impact and adapt programme as needed; develop clear plan for programme graduates; think 'what's next' in terms of the leadership behaviours required |

FIGURE 7.1 The 4Ds

It is worth pointing out that, although we generally (but not slavishly) follow the 4Ds when working on leadership development, there are many ways to make it work. The four stages themselves are not critical. Sometimes there are five stages, and at other times there are three, and sometimes the stages overlap. Of most importance are the actions that take place during the course of the intervention. Furthermore we always tailor the approach to the situation at hand. For example, organizational leadership development needs can vary greatly, as can the maturity of the existing leadership development interventions in place. In addition, **technology is a cross-cutting theme that must be kept in mind throughout**, as it continues to push the boundaries of what is possible in terms of breadth, depth, pace and effectiveness of delivery. Finally, it is worth noting that that the stages are linear in terms of initial implementation, but must be reviewed in an iterative fashion as the programme develops.

## *Diagnose the gap to where you want to go*

**The first step is to identify the leadership aspiration, and diagnose the gap to get there.** This typically leads to four main outputs: a leadership model that is tightly linked to the strategy, and aligned with the top team; the critical three to five 'from–to' shifts (behaviours, skills, mindsets) that the leadership programme will bring about; a quantification of the leadership gap at each level of the organization; and an assessment of the current leadership development initiatives and how these initiatives are embedded (or not) in the broader system.

## The leadership model

One of the most important steps an organization can take is to **align its leadership development effort to its strategy.** A leadership (or competency) model is one way to do this. A leadership model is an actionable description of what the organization wants and expects from its leaders and employees. It is ultimately an enabler of an organization's strategies and priorities, and should therefore be driven by the executive team. Organizations can have competency models and values separately (for example, McKinsey), or values-based competency models that are integrated.

Strategy and context are translated into the required leadership qualities and capabilities through a leadership model and, because all organizations are different, no one model fits all. This process of developing the leadership model takes place at an organizational level. If, for example, the strategy of the organization is to create value in overseas activities through multi-faceted entrepreneurial activity, its leadership model should include elements linked to behaviours of an international and entrepreneurial disposition and to encourage and enhance those skills. Input to the model could be the strategy and other organizational priorities, customer data, focus groups, employee surveys, and the latest fact-based research on the behaviours that really matter for performance – for example the leadership staircase that we presented in Chapter 3. Since strategy and organizational contexts change, a leadership model is typically reviewed (and potentially refreshed) every three to five years.

It is critical that **the model is linked to the performance drivers of an organization's strategy**. In this way, there is a tight link between the operational and strategic priorities, and the leadership model themes and behaviours that employees should undertake on a daily basis. As Tom Peters, a bestselling business author, says:

> You are your calendar … If you say something is a priority, then
> it must be quantitatively reflected obviously, dramatically, and
> unequivocally in the way you spend your time. The calendar never lies.

So the model – often evolved through hard work, numerous diagnostics and thoughtful consultation across an organization – must be respected. What all leadership models have, either explicitly or implicitly, is a set of leadership behaviours that are appropriate for leaders and that are understood (or should be) across the entire organization. They typically have between three and six overarching themes, each broken into two to four specific behaviours. These behaviours can then, in turn, later be broken down into 'performance grids' (for example, numbered 1–5) to incorporate into performance management (more on that later). The specific themes and behaviours can be further tailored by organization level (for example, manager, general manager, executive) and/or by career path (for example, specialist vs. generalist). Some organizations choose to maintain the same themes and behaviours for all levels/career paths and only change the performance grid, some organizations maintain the same themes but change the behaviours, while some organizations change both the themes and the behaviours (essentially creating different leadership models by organizational level/ career path). Regardless of the option an organization chooses, what

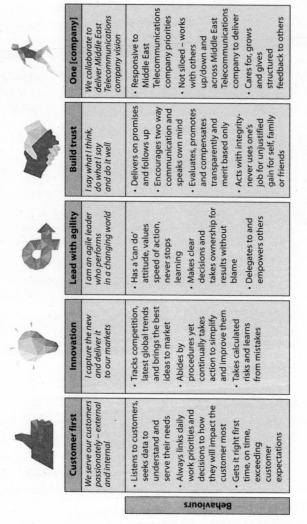

| Customer first | Innovation | Lead with agility | Build trust | One [company] |
|---|---|---|---|---|
| *We serve our customers passionately – external and internal* | *I capture the new and deliver it to our markets* | *I am an agile leader who performs in a changing world* | *I say what I think, do what I say and do it well* | *We collaborate to deliver Middle East Telecommunications company vision* |
| • Listens to customers, seeks data to understand and serve their needs<br>• Always links daily work priorities and decisions to how they will impact the customer most<br>• Gets it right first time, on time, exceeding customer expectations | • Tracks competition, latest global trends and brings the best ideas to market<br>• Abides by procedures yet continually takes action to simplify and improve them<br>• Takes calculated risks and learns from mistakes | • Has a 'can do' attitude, values speed of action, never stops learning<br>• Makes clear decisions and takes ownership for results without blame<br>• Delegates to and empowers others | • Delivers on promises and follows up<br>• Encourages two way communication and speaks own mind<br>• Evaluates, promotes and compensates transparently and merit based only<br>• Acts with integrity-never uses one's job for unjustified gain for self, family or friends | • Responsive to Middle East Telecommunications company priorities<br>• Not siloed – works with others up/down and across Middle East Telecommunications company to deliver<br>• Cares for, grows and gives structured feedback to others |

**Behaviours**

FIGURE 7.2  Sample leadership model: Middle East Telecommunications company

is critical is that the model is memorable, clear and easily understood across the organization. Figure 7.2 shows a sample leadership model.

## Determine the critical shifts

Once the organization has developed the leadership model, it is time to prioritize the critical shifts that will make the biggest difference in the next 12–18 months. As mentioned under Core Principle 1, **organizations should limit their focus to three to five key shifts at a time**. Research and our experience shows that the chances of success are markedly high when doing so. In the telecoms example from Figure 7.2, the first wave of intervention focused only on three critical shifts, which were implemented over a 12-month period before moving onto the next wave of behavioural shifts.

In addition, any behaviour is enabled by the right skills and the right mindsets. As such, organizations should determine the 'from–to' shift in terms of not only behaviours, but also in terms of skills and mindsets. For example, say an organization wants to focus on customer centricity. First, it would map the current and desired behaviours of its sales representatives. The organization could find, for example, that sales reps currently do not cross-sell products, and furthermore apply a one-size-fits-all approach. However, it aspires to have sales reps do proper customer profiling, segmentation-based selling and cross-selling.

Simply adjusting key performance indicators (KPIs) and telling sales reps that they need to be more customer centric will not lead to effective and lasting change. To enable this transition, it is critical to understand the required skill and mindset shifts. Employee surveys, manager surveys, focus groups and deep-structured interviews (DSIs) are some ways to do this. The organization could find, for example, that sales reps have an underlying mindset that 'my job is to give the customer what they want' and 'asking questions is a burden on others and on me'. The mindset shift could be towards something like 'my job is to help the customer understand what they really need' and 'people don't know what they don't know, and I can help'. Likewise, the organization may find that sales reps simply do not have the requisite skills (or software, or data) to conduct proper customer segmentation, or the required product knowledge to cross-sell.

## Quantify the leadership gap

In parallel, there is an analytical element. Here, the organization quantifies its current leadership numbers, strengths and gaps, and assesses these against the leadership model to determine quantity and type of leaders required. This is not merely a matter of counting those in managerial or authority roles; there are many influential leaders throughout an organization who help set the tone and pace of its operations. Not everyone is a leader, of course, but everyone can lead in the right situation. Where a leadership deficit is identified, the root causes (for example, fast growth, inadequate recruiting, retention issues, insufficient leadership programmes) need to be clearly understood in intellectual and practical terms.

We often use advanced analytics to develop a strategic workforce planning model, typically looking three to five years into the future. The model leads to a scenario-based forecast of organizational leadership needs and places these needs (through the link between strategy and leadership development) at the heart of the aspired programme outcomes (for example, faster growth in key markets, improving citizen experience, talent retention).

## Assess current leadership initiatives and their embedment

Finally, it is important to understand the current formal and informal mechanisms for building leadership skills, prior to building a leadership development intervention. We use a technology-enabled assessment called LEED (Learning Efficiency and Effectiveness Diagnostic) to assess leadership programmes, which covers learning efficiency (direct expenditure, time invested, utilization, and learning approach and infrastructure) and effectiveness (business objective relevance, personal relevance, learning path and environment, delivery of programmes and impact tracking). LEED helps organizations' leaders gain transparency into the current state of learning and development (L&D) from multiple angles – utilizing different tools such as a data collection template, perceptions surveys and structured interviews – and aims to give organizations a detailed and in-depth look into where the current strengths as well as areas of opportunities lie. At a major pharmaceutical client, for example, the LEED managed to help identify savings of 13 per cent on L&D direct expenditure. Also, data from the effectiveness module fed a structured gap analysis in measuring the impact of trainings that eventually resulted in a revamp of the learning strategy to address these gaps. See Figure 7.3.

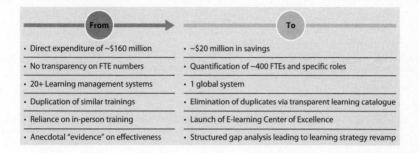

| From | To |
|---|---|
| • Direct expenditure of ~$160 million | • ~$20 million in savings |
| • No transparency on FTE numbers | • Quantification of ~400 FTEs and specific roles |
| • 20+ Learning management systems | • 1 global system |
| • Duplication of similar trainings | • Elimination of duplicates via transparent learning catalogue |
| • Reliance on in-person training | • Launch of E-learning Center of Excellence |
| • Anecdotal "evidence" on effectiveness | • Structured gap analysis leading to learning strategy revamp |

FIGURE 7.3 Learning and development review at a major pharmaceutical client

In addition, the organization should review the congruence and effectiveness of current integration and measurement mechanisms, for example, talent management systems and top team role-modelling. In the cases where there is a current or forecasted leadership gap, the current leadership initiatives and surrounding mechanisms could be key underlying root causes.

This stage cannot happen piecemeal or in isolation. To work well it must have the full commitment of top-management (and prioritization) on the forecasted leadership needs, value to the business and effort required. This high-level intent must be broadcast throughout the organization to ensure that its leadership strategy and leadership model reaches all organizational levels. This stage takes typically four to eight weeks, depending on the starting point.

## Design & Develop the interventions

This is the stage of **design of the leadership development programme, development of all programme content, and preparation for launch.** Here, we take the leadership model and strategic imperatives, prioritised shifts, the data on leadership capacity, and current leadership development mechanisms and pull them together to develop a programme. This stage typically has four main outputs:

- design of leadership development journey by group, including all development of content
- definition of target participants (who, how much, when) and selection of first cohorts
- design of integration mechanisms (change story, symbolic actions, system changes)
- signed-off business case (including target impact, costs, work plan, resourcing required and governance)

## Design the leadership journey and develop programme content

At this stage the organization works with us to ensure that leadership development interventions cover the whole organization. We design programmes in the context of the broader leadership development strategy (for example, in terms of selecting participants for a cohort from all applicable talent pools), and develop the programme content.

The organization then evaluates a holistic set of leadership development interventions and decides which ones best support the desired business outcomes (for example, forums, fieldwork, coaching, mentoring, guest speakers, rotations). It ensures that businesses/'end-users' are part of the content development process to ensure relevance and impartiality (for example, in a healthcare organization, the needs of patients would be addressed at this point).

The way that the programme is delivered is important, too. Organizations are of many different sizes and distributions. It might be prohibitively expensive to bring together in one place many senior people from an international shipping organization, or a long supply chain in a manufacturer. The organization therefore chooses the right form of intervention based on its organizational context (content and delivery) and programmes that truly understand business needs. We design for learning transfer and maximal behavioural change, and typically adopt a holistic set of interventions, including fieldwork (in the form of 'breakthrough projects'), forums and coaching (in the form of group, individual and/or peer coaching) – illustrated in Figure 7.4. We also consider, depending on the programme at hand, including a meaningful kick-off, inspiration and networking events, benchmarking trips (for example, to best practice organizations), expert speakers, mentoring and a graduation event.

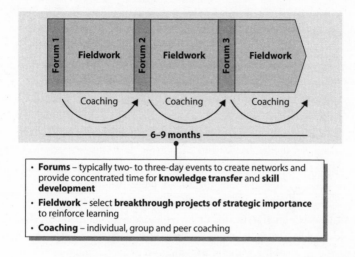

FIGURE 7.4  Field, forum and coaching

The content of the programme (guided by the 'Diagnose' stage) focuses on the most critical leadership behaviours that really matter to performance, based on fact-based research, as well as the underlying mindset and skill shifts required. The research also looks outside the organization for best practices, including latest trends relevant for leadership (for example, technology, macroeconomics). The programme blueprints should be tailored to each organizational grouping (for example, by level), and are often more light-touch for lower levels of the organization, for example, with fewer forum days, smaller breakthrough projects over a shorter duration, and peer coaches instead of executive coaches.

Crucially, at this stage we design the portfolio of interventions and content to maximize learning transfer, to ensure that participants will apply their new learning on the job. It is worth repeating that **the goal of any leadership development intervention is to enhance the on-the-job performance of individuals, in pursuit of the overall organizational performance objectives.** Here we leverage our knowledge of how adults learn and respect the importance of context and depth and pace required to build new skills (a lack of both of these will cause the programme to fail, as we have seen in the previous chapters).

# Define target participants

For individuals, the organization defines detailed and objective selection criteria and identifies candidates to participate in the development programme from a wide range of people (not just top team evaluation or judgment). The key is to engage the pivotal influencers across the organization. Pivotal influencers are able to influence the behaviours and thinking of others in the organization, due to their role, a trusted relationship, or character. They include the CEO and top team, top talent, influencers and pivotal roles (such as branch managers and plant managers), which may not necessarily be high in the organizational hierarchy. Within each cohort, the organization assesses individual needs and tailors the leadership development content to the specific cohort(s) and their context. Finally, the organization ensures that individuals are motivated and ready for the learning journey (for example, through opt-in, management support). Technology through people analytics plays an important role in identifying the top talent across the organization in an efficient and effective manner.

# Design to integrate and measure

Here there are three main mechanisms that should be developed, in addition to the capability building programme. First is fostering understanding and conviction. Here, we work with the CEO and top team to craft a change story, which underlines the reason for the change, paints a vision for the future, and describes what it will mean for each individual, their teams, the customer, the organization and society (the 'five sources of meaning', as outlined in Chapter 6). It is critical that the change story is tailored by each executive to their specific context prior to further cascading. In addition, organizations can share customer or OHI surveys, to underscore the importance of the change.

Second is top team role-modelling. It is, first and foremost, important to align the top team on the direction and their role in 'making it happen' for example, during the course of existing executive meetings or during designated off-sites. We often encourage each executive to make a personal commitment, reflecting on the edict, 'For things to change first I must change', and sharing their commitment to the wider executive team. In addition, we work with the team to develop a list of symbolic actions, and launch the top priorities in terms of impact. Leaders that get this right can really help to propel a leadership development intervention forwards. Experience and research shows that the age-old adage 'actions speak louder than words' holds true across the world. We also identify and mobilize 'influencers', often through technology-enabled social network analysis, so that they become change agents that are empowered to make a difference.

Third is reinforcement in the broader organizational systems. At this stage, we typically start by detailing out the leadership model into performance grids. This is done by taking each behaviour and describing what it means to score below expectations (for example, 1 out of 5), meet expectations (for example, 3 out of 5) and exceed expectations (for example, 5 out of 5). It is important that the behavioural descriptors are objective and observable, to make evaluations based on the grid as fair as possible. For example, the description 'customer centric' is challenging to objectively assess, as it is more to do with traits that a leader may have, as opposed to what the leader *does*. This description could be changed to, for example, 'regularly solicits customer feedback' and 'works with team to ensure customer needs are met on time and at the expected quality' – if these behaviours are indeed what an organization means when it says 'customer centric'. Figure 7.5 provides an example of a performance grid for the leadership model theme of putting the customer first, which includes three specific behaviours, each with underlying descriptions.

In addition to the performance grids, we also ensure that roles and responsibilities are clear down the line, modifying the organization structure, processes and systems as needed. This also includes modifying key performance indicators as required, starting with the employees who are part of the programme.

## Sign off the business case

The final part of this stage is to develop and sign off the business case. Far from being a matter of process, the business case is a critical way to set the leadership development intervention up for short-term and long-run success. The business case should at a minimum include four main elements: target impact, work plan, budget and organizational requirements to deliver the programme.

## Customer First

We serve our customers passionately – external and internal

| Employees | Team leaders to Directors | General Manager and Vice President |
| --- | --- | --- |
| **Listens to customers, seeks data to understand and serve their needs** | | |
| • Proactively asks for and listens to customer feedback<br>• Gathers, understands and distills insights from available customer data<br>• Interacts well with customers | • Sponsors and implements systems, tools and processes to increase data availability and therefore customer understanding<br>• Has a personal relationship with a number of key customers | • Has a broad, forward looking and comprehensive understanding of customers and translates that understanding into strategies and initiatives |
| **Always links daily work priorities and decisions to how they will impact the customer most** | | |
| • Demonstrates ability to effectively prioritize own daily work tasks based on highest customer impact<br>• Is able to clearly articulate how own daily work tasks link to our vision and values<br>• Uses customer insights derived from data to guide daily decision making | • Continually makes and implements decisions based on highest customer impact<br>• Empowers the team for "customer 1st" attitudes and actions | • Powerfully and consciously role models prioritization decisions based on highest customer impact |
| **Gets it right first time, on time, exceeding customer expectations** | | |
| • Fulfills assigned tasks as per the agreed timeline and first time right<br>• Continually strives to exceed customer expectations<br>• Agrees prompt timeline with the customer, ensures the promise is kept and proactively renegotiates the timeline if needed | • Recognizes and celebrates those who regularly exceed customer expectations<br>• Works tirelessly to make it easier for own staff to get it right first time, on time and exceed customer expectations | • Embodies a no compromises attitude in putting the customer first and exceeding their expectations |

FIGURE 7.5 Performance grid for the leadership model theme 'putting the customer first'

First is the *target impact*. The impact in terms of the critical behaviour shifts and leaders reached should already have been discussed during the first stage. However, the business case crystallizes the aspiration – it covers a comprehensive set of measures and ensures they are measurable, time-bound and linked to organizational performance. We discussed in Chapter 6 four types of measurement (participant reaction, learning, behavioural changes and organizational results). In the business case, we typically focus on quantifying behavioural changes (for example, improvements in a 360-degree assessment) and organizational results (for example, increase in leadership outcome in the OHI, increasing in ancillary outcomes in the OHI, business impact from the breakthrough projects, such as increased customer satisfaction, increased revenues from new products, and cost savings).

The second key element of the business case is the *work plan*, including key milestones. In the diagnose and design/development phases, key elements are to conduct interviews and focus groups (and potentially an OHI), conduct top team workshops, design and launch a 360-degree feedback survey for programme participants (built around the leadership model and competency grids), designing the programme content and embedment mechanisms, and selecting programme participants. Key elements during delivery are inauguration of the overall programme (depending on scale), start of each cohort type (signifying that the content is ready), start and finish of each subsequent cohort, governance council meetings, and key communication items. Key milestones during the Develop stage are usually not specified in detail at this moment, save for a date for programme evaluation and assessment, and a decision for the next steps.

The third key element of the business case is the *budget*. The constituents of the budget are the number of participants per cohort, the depth of each journey (for example, the number of forum days and coaching days per cohort), facilitator and coaching costs (whether internal or external), technology costs (software and hardware), venue costs (if offsite), travel, F&B and accommodation for participants and faculty, material and content costs and programme office costs. Organizations should build a dynamic model, with flexible fields for the different programme elements. The programme budget drives what is ultimately included in the programme design and how the programme is run, and should be clarified early. It is important for organizations to consider the leadership development impact it aspires to achieve and required interventions and budget to do so. As we outlined in Core Principle 3, the age of classroom learning is dead, as it is both inefficient and expensive. With creativity, proper tailoring and pragmatism, organizations can design comprehensive and impactful leadership development programmes at competitive costs – for example by using a combination of internal and external faculty, recruiting leaders and alumni as mentors and coaches, setting up peer learning groups and utilizing technology.

The last element is the *organizational requirements to deliver the programme*, (that is, the organizational construct needed). The organizational construct is required to not only roll out the initial programme over the coming two to three years, but also to ensure that the new leadership behaviours and mindsets are maintained and developed in the future. The organizational construct often – but not always – takes the form of a leadership academy. Here, there are a series of design questions and choices that will shape the right decision.

In terms of its objective and purpose, what is the scope of the academy? What programmes does it manage, who is eligible, and how should it relate to the rest of the organization? These three questions define the role and reach of the academy, which can range from top leaders only, to top talent, to the full organization.

In terms of content and delivery, if the academy is part of the continuing leadership development programme, as we think it should be, what are the right competencies that it must develop and where in the organization? This is really a matter of the content of the learning; in leadership terms, this might be straightforward, a result of the development programme, but more broadly, the academy might be responsible for hard skills, in-service training and other soft skills such as negotiation or communication. Another issue is how the academy might customize its learning for different participant groups, and customize the teaching and learning methods as well.

In terms of infrastructure and people, should the academy be physical or virtual? How does it stand in relation to the culture and branding of the organization? What information technology is required and where should it be found and run, internally or externally? How many people are needed? Academies can be run both in-house or be outsourced, as long as there is sufficient control, measurement and management of activities.

In terms of governance, how might the academy sit within an overall structure, how are decisions made, and how is it paid for? These can be vexed questions in larger organizations, where local or regional facilities might want to have control over learning content and budgets.

This is a complex and demanding stage, and typically takes 6–12 weeks, depending on the programme content and the number of cohorts. The business case ultimately ties together the strategy and mandate of the leadership development intervention, and requires top team alignment and sign-off. In addition, it is important to start launching 'quick wins' during this stage, most typically in the form of organization-wide communication, and symbolic actions by the top team. It is also important to build in a buffer for securing the resources and faculty for the launch of the programme.

---

## Best practice: corporate academies

We recently visited a series of best-in-class corporate academies, globally. We found, for example, that an Academy typically has sole ownership for centrally driven programmes and top talent, and is the custodian organizational culture. In some cases, it also delivers functional and technical programmes. Content must be fully aligned with strategic priorities, and anchored in a leadership model. The Academy is staffed with high caliber individuals, and delivery is done through impactful in-person sessions, mobile technology, and on-the-job coaching. The Academy is integrated into key HR functions, but also retains enough independence to remain open to new ideas and to challenge conventional thinking. Impact is closely managed through three main committees (covering the overall programme, business project, and individual learning), and analytics are used to further enhance learning and performance.

# Deliver the programme

At this stage, the organization **launches the delivery of the programme**. This is where the rubber hits the road, and where participants undergo the leadership development journey and we begin to see impact in terms of personal development of individuals, increased leadership effectiveness, and impact on the breakthrough projects. This stage typically has three main outputs: delivery of programme across all cohorts, using modern adult learning principles (field, forum and coaching); implementation of embedment mechanisms (communication, role-modelling, embedding leadership model into all talent processes); and governance and measurement of programme at multiple levels.

## Deliver the core programme

Actual delivery of the programme typically happens in 'waves', covering four main groups. **It starts with the top team**. It is critical to start with the top team not only to ensure that the executives role-model the desired behaviours, but also because the increasing levels of organizational and global complexity require everyone in the organization to continue growing and adapting, including top leaders. Typically there are 8–15 N-1 executives, hence the top team makes up one cohort.

Next, it is important to quickly **engage the immediate next level of the organization** (typically most N-2 and select N-3), as these leaders often play the critical role of bridging the gap between the executives and daily execution. Some organizations characterize all employees in these levels/job grades as 'top talent', while in other organizations (especially larger), the filtering process starts much sooner. These cohorts in 10,000+ person organizations typically amount to 75–150 people (depending on spans and layers, and definition of top talent), equal to approximately between four and eight cohorts.

Next are the top change leaders and pivotal influencers, who are typically 20–100 people, depending on the size of the organization. Finally, the organization rolls out the programme to subsequent cohorts further down the line, in some cases including a graduate programme for top talent, and in some instances even going on to include an induction programme for all new employees. For a 10,000+ person organization and assuming 10 per cent top talent, this amounts to around 1,000 people, equal to up to 40 cohorts. As mentioned above, programmes for top talent lower down in the organization are typically lighter touch, with fewer forum days and less intense on-the-job projects.

The rollout typically starts with a kick-off per cohort, in order to lay out the journey ahead. Each cohort typically goes through a journey lasting between six and nine months (potentially up to 12 months for more senior cohorts, and as little as two or three months for more junior cohorts). The waves are usually staggered, though in steady state, and once the programme delivery capacity has been established, numerous programmes can be run sequentially. Reaching a full organization can be done in two to three years for a large-scale transformation, and in under one year for smaller leadership interventions.

The organization should use the right technology to deliver blended learning (online and classroom), including gamification and daily 'triggers' (for example, mobile-based reminders) to participants. Here, the content is delivered 'just-in-time' and 'on-demand' for participants. Technology also helps build scale in delivery. In addition, it is important to apply an 'open architecture' approach to draw on a broad network of internal and external faculty, coaches, facilitators and experts as needed; this makes the delivery flexible and vibrant. To build scale in terms of facilitation, we regular adopt a 'train the trainer' approach, coupled with a structured facilitator development programme, in order to build a sustainable facilitator capacity in an organization – see Figure 7.6.

This stage is precisely matched to the individual needs of participants, and enables them to take charge of their development, by choosing which modules to focus on and when, and/or by structuring project work independently. It focuses on both mindsets and behaviours to uncover the underlying mindsets and root perspectives that might be getting in the way of learning, and helps people to permanently shift how they act at work. This is also known as helping participants build a foundation of what is often called 'inner mastery'.

## Put in place embedment mechanisms

While the programmes themselves continue, it is vital to place them at the heart of a bigger picture, and enveloped by communication efforts, top team role-modelling, and integration into talent management

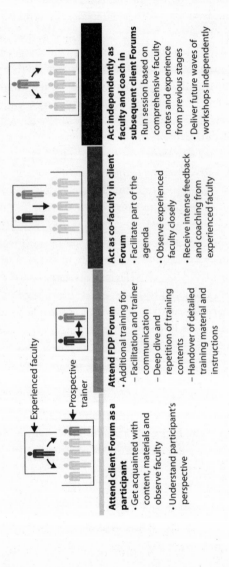

FIGURE 7.6 Facilitator development and train the trainer approach

systems. Communications should be launched, starting with the change story. The change story can be disseminated through a variety of channels and kept alive through traditional and viral communications (town halls, intranet blogs and uploads, celebrating successes/ pointing out 'where it's working', one-on-one meetings, etc.). The leadership model should also be communicated to *all* employees, and technology often plays a big role in embedding the programmes and deepening their impact across the organization.

One organization we know made a big splash by printing the leadership model in a memorable design and leaving a copy on the desk of all employees, in parallel with launching a CEO blog and changing the corporate logo. This sent a strong signal that 'things will be different'. It is also beneficial to celebrate successes and recognizing and rewarding employees who are living the leadership behaviours.

In addition to the leadership programme being rolled out to the top team first, role-modelling and display of symbolic actions by the top team and change agents should also continue. Moreover, we see huge impact when the top team role-models desired behaviours in the context of leadership programmes, for example, by acting as programme faculty, project sponsors, mentors, or coaches.

In the design phase, the leadership model was translated into more detailed performance grids, with observable, objective descriptions for each behaviour. In the implementation phase, the competency model is fed into the talent management system. Four talent processes are especially relevant when rolling out a leadership development intervention:

- **Linking talent strategy to business needs:** this was done during the Diagnose stage, and HR should continue to integrate the leadership model and leadership requirements into strategic workforce planning
- **Recruiting and on-boarding:** The leadership model (and specific behaviours) should be embedded into recruiting, impacting where the organization looks for talent, the methods it uses to assess talent, and the specific skills and competencies it looks for during the process
- **Recognizing and rewarding performance:** The leadership model should be embedded into performance management and individual KPIs, so that employees that truly display the

leadership behaviours are rewarded with financial and non-financial rewards
- **Succession planning:** Building on general performance management of all employees, the leadership model should also be a 'true north' of what is required of future leaders in the organization

## Implement programme governance

In this phase, programme committees (typically covering the overall programme, business project, and individual learning) are formally launched, with clear and separate mandates to ensure the success of different elements of the leadership development intervention. Each committee has a formal meeting rhythm: The people and projects committee typically meet at the beginning, middle and end of the programme, in relation to specific cohorts/journeys, while the programme committee can meet more regularly, on an ongoing basis. The committees track impact along the four different levels of measurement – see Figure 7.7 for typical means of tracking.

| | Description | Typical means |
|---|---|---|
| **Organizational impact** | • Organizational returns (e.g. financial, customer, health) based on training impact, relative to costs incurred | • Financial metrics (e.g. revenue, cost savings) generated from training initiatives/projects<br>• Non-financial metrics (e.g. customer satisfaction, process improvements, organizational health)<br>• Action plan/project completion |
| **Behavioural changes** | • Employee behavioural changes and on-the-job application of learnings | • Direct manager feedback/interviews<br>• 360-degree assessments<br>• On-the-job observations<br>• Performance appraisal |
| **Learning** | • Measurement of knowledge levels before and after training | • Participant self-assessment<br>• Written pre- and post-tests<br>• Direct manager feedback/interviews<br>• On-the-job observations<br>• Role-plays |
| **Reaction** | • Participants' reaction to the training/learning experience | • Participant feedback forms<br>• Participation action plans |

FIGURE 7.7 Typical means of tracking impact

The above measurements serve the dual purpose of not only gauging the impact of the interventions, but also providing a rich baseline around which the programme can be designed and tailored. For individuals, we run individual assessments based on a leadership model to create behavioural baselines; we then tailor delivery to individual learning goals. This allows us to better link development goals to on-the-job learning and group projects, focus on participant strengths (while ensuring minimum baselines across development areas), and more easily find areas to stretch participants outside of their comfort zones.

This is very different from the design and delivery, which are typically more time-bound and can be carried out by a relatively small team. Delivery, however, typically takes six to nine months per cohort and, done over many waves to reach the full organization, it can take one to three years. This stage also begins to see real impact, in as little as the first six months.

## Drive Impact

**This is the final stage, and is open-ended or ongoing**. It starts in parallel with the delivery phase, and has an aspirational end state of truly (and continuously) transforming the organization culture, to constantly enhance performance. It typically has four main outputs: continuous impact monitoring and system embedment of critical behavioural changes; clear plan for graduates (yearly refresh, retention policies etc.); re-assessment of organizational leadership requirements given the context, and decision on next leadership development focus areas; and establishing a culture of self-learning and adaptation.

## Continuously monitor progress and adapt as required

As soon as the first programme is launched, it is important to continuously adapt the programmes, as participant, faculty and manager feedback is gathered. This includes 'micro' adjustments, for example, on the timings and modules within specific forum days or the coaching curriculum, as well as larger adjustments such as project key success factors or even changes to the overall programme blueprint and priorities.

At the end of a specific cohort or programme, it is vital to take a step back and review the impact holistically, and make additional adjustments accordingly. The organization must measure ROI with the same rigour as other (more performance-related) initiatives.

## Develop a clear plan for programme graduates

Programme graduates play an extremely important role for the organization. First of all, as current or future leaders in their own right, it is critical that individualized career path discussions take place with each graduate in order to identify the optimal job opportunities internally and cater to their aspirations. Organizations should also encourage individuals to practice the new behaviours that will contribute to them being more effective leaders – this is especially important in situations where the aspired leadership behaviours are a significant break from the previous ways of working (for example, from hierarchical to inclusive leadership). It goes without saying that performance management should include the leadership model elements and be based on merit, in order to minimize unwanted attrition among top talent. People analytics can also help bolster retention of top talent, by pinpointing and helping to address what is really important to people in the organization. As we saw in Chapter 6, organizations often incentivize the wrong things, habitually neglecting critical non-financial incentives.

From a performance and development point of view, it is recommended that additional capability building opportunities are offered to graduates, to ensure that capabilities are refreshed and further enhanced. This could take the form of yearly networking events (which are also useful to build bridges across different parts of the organization), continued peer coaching in pairs or small groups (what we call 'mini-boards', which bear no additional cost to the organization), mentoring by more senior colleagues, and yearly one-day 'boosters' of content that was covered during the programme. These interventions build on top of on-the-job coaching and feedback from teams, peers and mentors. As we showed in Chapter 4, organizations that truly master the art developing their employees focus the majority of their efforts on instilling a culture of continuous growth and feedback.

In addition, leading talent organizations often use graduates in future leadership development efforts, for example subsequent cohorts in the same programme or for programmes for lower levels of the organization. Graduates can serve as guest speakers, mentors/coaches, and in some cases even faculty during the forums. This serves the dual purpose of increasing learning of graduates, and sending a meaningful and symbolic signal to the organization that leaders take the programme seriously. In terms of increasing learning, research has shown that recall rates of new content after three months are approximately 10 per cent after learning by hearing, 32 per cent after learning by seeing, 65 per cent after learning by doing, and 100 per cent after learning by teaching.[1]

## Re-assess leadership requirements given the context

In Chapter 1 we defined leadership as a set of behaviours that in a given context align an organization, foster execution, and ensure organizational renewal. These behaviours are enabled by relevant skills and mindsets. As such, effective leadership requires alignment, execution and renewal. While the first two components can be implemented with a given performance objective (and leadership model) in mind, renewal is often more challenging as it requires re-defining the target and with that the behaviours, skills and mindsets required to get there. The ability to learn faster than competitors is a critical competitive advantage cited in numerous studies, as well as in the OHI. (The OHI outcome 'innovation and learning' has an $R^2$ of 0.86 with overall health, indicating an extremely strong correlation. Indeed, almost no organizations with fourth or third quartile 'innovation and learning' outcomes are top quartile, only 16 per cent with a second quartile outcome are, while 84 per cent with a top quartile outcome are.)

The same holds true for leadership development: organizations need to continuously modify their leadership development efforts in order to stay up to date on the latest trends and ensure that their employees are displaying the behaviours required to execute the strategy.

A question we often get is *how often should I change my leadership development efforts?* Leadership development is – or should ideally be – linked to context and organizational objectives. In theory, **if and when context changes, so should leadership development**. The context is all-important. Any change in context should provoke a review of the specific leadership behaviours that will be most impactful for performance, and in turn the leadership development efforts.

Strategy has the most influence over an organization's context as the organization reacts to or seeks to shape its operating environment. Strategic thinking derives from military, political, evolutionary and even religious models.[2] For all its necessary relation to a changing external environment, strategy nonetheless often rests on an inside rather than an outside view of the organization; recent McKinsey research shows that this inside view must be weighed against an empirical outside view of a company's position and prospects.[3] In practice, organizations tend to change or refine their strategies every three to five years (think of the 'Five-Year Plan'), and this holds true for government and public as well as commercial organizations. Changes in strategy typically give rise to three types of leadership development change:

- **Adjustments and additions** to existing programme(s) along the way, to stay relevant; this might take the form of an initiative depending on a new technology or new use of an existing one; or it might be occasioned by new research or a new school of thinking (emotional intelligence in the 1990s, neuropsychology in the 2010s).
- **A broader review every three to five years**, to ensure it fits with strategic objectives. This review can be large or small depending on the degree of change in the strategy and organization. Strategic imperatives are the result of strategic analysis and comparative research from other disciplines.[4]
- **A radical rethink:** Some organizations re-invent themselves, sometimes in a bid for survival, sometimes in order to stay ahead of the curve (both common in the technology sector). These large-scale changes with new business models and even organizational structures require new leadership models and therefore leadership development programmes. Sometimes leadership expertise in the form of experience in the sector simply does not exist because the sector itself is so new (common in dotcoms in the 1990s and in new forms of retail in the 2000s); leadership must then be a collective enterprise, as individual leaders learn from each other.

Other changes that are not necessarily time-bound also give rise to new leadership development requirements. Some of the more pertinent are as follows:

- Changes in the corporate structure, for example in the case of merger, acquisition or spin-off
- Technology revolutions, for example during the advent of the personal computer, the internet, and today's shift to big data analytics and digitization
- Demographic shifts, for example from the ongoing retirement wave in many parts of the world due to baby boomers retiring

In short, organizations should continuously modify their leadership development efforts as their contexts change. This becomes increasingly important as the external environment becomes more dynamic. An organization that is able to institutionalize the ability to continuously identify and develop the capabilities required to succeed is often referred to as a 'learning organization'.

The concept of the learning organization is based on the seminal work of Chris Argyris and Peter Senge, among others. Senge, for example, defined a learning organization as a place where people continually expand their capacity to create the results they truly desire, where new and expansive patterns of thinking are nurtured, where collective aspiration is set free, and where people are continually learning how to learn together.[5]

More recently, Kegan and Lahey coined the term 'Deliberately Developmental Organizations', which strive to develop every single person, every day, and where learning is woven into the fabric of daily operations, routines and conversations.[6] Following our four principles – which are a circular process that necessitates a continuous review of Core Principle 1 (the critical shifts required to enable the strategy) – will lead to similar organizational learning and increasing levels of organizational health when implemented effectively. We will illustrate the approach in practice throughout the fictional story in Chapters 8–12.

## *Other considerations for increasing leadership effectiveness*

A leadership development programme is, of course, not the only answer to bringing about corporate change. There are four cross-cutting themes that must be considered at all stages of the leadership development process:

1 **Leadership development is only one way to increase leadership effectiveness and should not be done in a vacuum.** It must be handled holistically from the start. For example, it is unwise to undertake leadership development and only then think about how recruiting fits in, if in fact wholesale recruiting of new people would be more effective. The first two stages, 'Diagnose' and 'Design & Develop', are vital in this process; the first one must indicate a *top-down* intent, and the third must be open to *bottom-up* ideas and interventions. This book focuses on leadership development, and we address other ways to increase leadership effectiveness in the FAQs. In reality, however, you often do these things in parallel.

2 **A cross-cutting theme that must always be addressed is that of team effectiveness.** Individual leadership effectiveness does not necessarily lead to high performing teams, yet high performing teams are a prerequisite for organizational leadership effectiveness. As such, there is enormous value in improving team effectiveness in terms of alignment, execution and renewal, and in embedding the new leadership behaviours in the context of team norms. In our experience, organizations typically also need to explicitly address the 10–20 pivotal teams in the organization as part of a leadership programme, typically covering all N-1 teams as well as other pivotal teams. The interventions are typically minimum one to two days per team, but can also be longer and over multiple sessions, depending on the current effectiveness and criticality of the team. Additional programmes can be offered to other teams in the organization (outside of the top 10–20 teams) on a voluntary, opt-in basis. In addition, individual participants on leadership programmes should practise the new learnings with their extended team.

3 **Leadership transitions are pivotal moments with significant value at stake.** In our experience, what is required is a half-day

session with the leader individually and then a one- or two-day session with the leader and their team, in the context of the transition. Typical modules to cover are identifying high impact opportunities and setting the strategy, assessing organizational dynamics and aligning critical stakeholders, building the team, and developing the critical skills for success in the new role.

4  We have stressed that context matters. However, in addition to the organizational and strategic context (which defines the leadership model and priority areas), **adapting the leadership intervention to contexts within the organization is equally critical**. This involves several dimensions. For example, the organizational level (senior vs. more front line), the leadership development budget available and number of participants have important implications on the programme blueprint. However, the critical success factor is to abide by the four core principles, and we find that this is feasible even with few participants and limited budget. Another organizational consideration is the demographic profile and culture of the participants, both of which can influence content and teaching styles. Age can have a particular impact on teaching methods as, for example, Millennials are in some ways different from their seniors in terms of how they perceive learning and how they like to learn.

## Summary

The success rate of leadership development interventions is depressingly low. Up to 50–90 per cent of leadership development efforts do not achieve and sustain the desired impact. We have identified four core principles that must hold true every time – and doing these four things well will get you far – but we also know that there is no silver bullet. It is about doing many things right. What is positive, however, is that a subset of the organizations we surveyed were consistently able to achieve and sustain their leadership development objectives, through a comprehensive and best practice approach.

As we saw in Chapter 2, leadership development at scale requires a systematic approach that covers four key areas (look back to Figure 2.3 for a reminder of these). In addition, they must ensure *depth of actions* – the chances of success do not rise above 30 per cent until around 24 key actions are taken, and over 40 key actions must be taken to increase chances of success to 80 per cent. The good news is that organizations that covered all 50 actions increased their success rates to almost 100 per cent.

The 50 actions are not a menu to choose from but instead are the detail and discipline of a route map. There are many ways to fail because the pull of doing as few as possible of the 50 actions (usually expressed as a limitation in the resources of time, money and people) is greater than the imperative of getting things done comprehensively. Embarking on a programme of comprehensive change is exceptionally difficult in practice. Organizational behaviour has an entropic tendency; things more readily fall apart (where they can take many forms) than cohere (where there are fewer forms). Great, effective and sustained leadership development requires real resources, time and effort. Organizations must therefore ensure that they dedicate the right resources, and build up the right organizational *construct* to sustain, maintain, and develop the leadership development intervention.

In this chapter, we outlined the typical approach that we use, and the key outputs per stage. Figure 7.8 summarizes the key outputs per stage. It is worth noting that the stages are linear in terms of initial implementation, but must be reviewed in an iterative fashion as the programme develops.

In the next chapters, we illustrate our approach in practice, in much greater detail. We do this through a fictional story, first introducing the story and the main characters, and then dedicating a chapter for each of the 4Ds. We have kept the story in the following five chapters concise, with a focus on the key elements of a leadership development journey and critical outputs at each stage. We also seek, however, to illustrate some of the personal challenges that leaders face during a change programme, and the messy nature of what often takes place behind the scenes to make a leadership development intervention a success.

| ← 4–8 weeks → | ← 6–16 weeks → | ← 12–18 months → | ← Ongoing → |
|---|---|---|---|
| **Diagnose** — What is the gap to where you want to go? | **Design & Develop** — What do you need to get from here to there? | **Deliver** — How should you move to action? | **Drive Impact** — How do you keep moving forward? |
| ☐ Leadership model that is tightly linked to the strategy, and aligned with the top team <br> ☐ Critical 3–5 'from-to' shifts (behaviours, skills, mindsets) that the leadership programme will bring about <br> ☐ Quantification of the leadership gap at each level of the organization <br> ☐ Assessment of current leadership development initiatives and quality of system embedment mechanisms | ☐ Design of leadership development journey by group, including development of all content <br> ☐ Definition of target participants (who, how much, when) and selection of first cohorts <br> ☐ Design of reinforcing mechanisms (change story, symbolic actions, system changes) <br> ☐ Signed-off business case (including target impact, work plan, budget, and organizational requirements to deliver the programme) | ☐ Delivery of programme across all cohorts, using modern adult learning principles (field, forum, and coaching) <br> ☐ Implementation of system embedment (communication, role modelling, reinforcing mechanisms, including embedding leadership model into all talent processes) <br> ☐ Governance and measurement of programme at multiple levels | ☐ Continuous impact monitoring and reinforcement of critical behavioural changes <br> ☐ Clear plan for graduates (yearly refresh, retention policies etc.) <br> ☐ Re-assessment of organizational leadership requirements given the context, and decision on next leadership development focus areas |

FIGURE 7.8 Summary of the key outputs per stage

# 8

# Meet Carolyn Randolph

*Andrew St George, Claudio Feser, Michael Rennie,*
*Nicolai Chen Nielsen*

From Vancouver to Shanghai | Changing times call for changing
organizations | Leadership . . . but how? | The leadership team at
NCL | Carolyn gets the ball rolling

## *From Vancouver to Shanghai*

Carolyn Randolph, the charismatic CEO of New Classic Look clothing
(NCL) was born and raised in Canada. Her fresh, clean style and innate
practicality came straight from the Rockies and her native Vancouver.
Her first job after graduation came from the networks she formed in
college, taking her to Munich as a purchasing assistant at Femme, a mass-
market retailer. She enjoyed the work and learned voraciously. Always
intuitive and self-contained, she found that Femme's corporate environment of dedicated hard work mixed with genuine camaraderie helped
lift her out of her self-protective shell. The company's strong culture and
defined leadership style suited Carolyn's organized, calm approach to
her work and her life. It focused on low costs, optimization and waste
reduction. She eventually worked her way up to purchasing director,
overseeing major strategic purchasing decisions. Carolyn felt like she
was part of a bigger mission, to provide affordable clothing to society,
and she shared that sense of mission with her family and her staff.

Twelve years ago she had received a phone call from the CEO of
NCL, a mid-sized clothes company based in Shanghai. It specialized in
classic fashion, with a modern twist, just Carolyn's style. NCL operated
in 20 countries, and it had aggressive expansion plans. Carolyn was
recruited as deputy Chief Operating Officer. The current COO was
in his late 50s, and the company needed new blood.

Carolyn managed the transition to deputy COO at NCL well.
The employees at NCL liked her and respected her honest views,

problem-solving ability and hands-on approach. She was known to decide carefully and act decisively. After four years at NCL, Carolyn became its COO. She was a perfect fit for the job, and ran the corporation's operations extremely well. Her challenge, as at Femme, was to let go and delegate. As she tended to focus on effectiveness, Carolyn found it difficult to trust her subordinates to do things as effectively as she would herself.

Working with Megan Huntcliff, NCL's CHRO, Carolyn helped NCL's leadership team overcome any obstacles that blocked what she saw as great results. The team found that, although Carolyn rarely showed emotion or gave in to strong reactions, she listened and had a ready sensitivity for their concerns. She was charming, if a bit formal, and she always got to the heart of their problems with a few precise questions.

After five years as COO, the NCL Board promoted Carolyn to CEO. A few other executives jostled for the position, but Carolyn was in pole position. Her results spoke for themselves, and she was well respected at all levels. Her cool ability to surmount bureaucratic politics without ever seeming to think about them helped her win the Board's wholehearted support.

During her first three years as CEO, Carolyn drew on all her strengths: speed, results-orientation, and following up with employees individually to ensure they were on track. The business grew quickly, entering a new market almost monthly. As Carolyn celebrated the start of her fourth year as CEO, NCL was operating in 50 countries, with $6 billion in revenues, 30,000 employees, and a healthy bottom line. Carolyn had led its expansion into lines of clothing for men and children, and had launched a shoes and accessories line, which grew to a third of the size of the clothing business in just a few years.

The shareholders were happy with NCL's progress. The stock price had increased on average more than 10 per cent per year since Carolyn had become CEO, compared to a general industry average of 7 per cent. The higher stock price also shaped shareholders' expectations that the growth would continue, together with margin improvements through automation and efficiency gains. This is the reward for having a fast growth stock: expectations and performance imperatives increase to ever-higher levels. Carolyn was acutely aware of this expectations treadmill.

## Changing times call for changing organizations

NCL's claim to fame was its ability to combine classic design with the latest fashion trends. Yet since its long-time head of design had finally retired, the company had struggled to keep up to date with new trends. Its capable designers could maintain the usual product lines, but needed a boost to freshen their perspective and keep them *à la mode*. To address this issue, after careful searching, NCL acquired a small fashion retail chain called Infinity Fashionista. Through hiring by acquisition, NCL also gained a new top design executive, Fernando Vega, founder of Infinity.

Infinity needed to be integrated into NCL, just as Fernando needed to fit in with the executive team, a challenge that was taking up a large share of Carolyn's time. The initial plan was to put selected Infinity fashion lines and accessories into NCL's stores and, in the longer term, to draw inspiration for fresh, yet still classic designs from Fernando and his staff of edgy designers. The deal made business sense, but Carolyn was unsure of the best way to integrate Infinity.

Drawing on the mergers and acquisitions (M&A) experience of her new Head of Strategy and Business Development, Alice Berman, Carolyn looked for ways to maintain Infinity's strengths while ensuring that NCL continued to have a coherent culture, systems and processes. Part of the integration, Carolyn knew, would be assuring that Fernando – a young, creative entrepreneur who had built Infinity's success in Portugal, Spain and South America – could retain enough control over his products. He was accustomed to running his own show, so she had to make sure his NCL role still gave him sufficient authority. She was even worried about letting him know how much his youthful ideas mattered to NCL, which had to reach Infinity's sleek, up-and-coming audience to remain ahead in this cutthroat industry.

Two other factors compounded Carolyn's challenges. First, NCL faced a wave of middle management and senior team retirements, probably including her invaluable CFO, Peter Cody. The wave would hit in the next three to five years, so it was not an acute threat, but she had only a few obvious successors in place. She had to admit that NCL's leadership pipeline was weak. In addition, most current leaders had been with the company for more than 20 years. While their experience was a key strength, they were also stuck in their existing ways of doing things.

Second, ever since Jamie Winston, the brilliant but difficult Director of Strategy and Business Development, had left the company in a huff, the process of entering new markets with lucrative growth prospects had got harder. The day he stormed out, Carolyn learned what happens when a big company loses a pivotal senior executive – and lacks the right successor. It made her more wary of her hiring choices. She'd recently brought in Alice Berman to replace Jamie, but she wasn't sure Alice was the long-term solution. Alice had talent and excellent experience. She was very likeable and eager, but did she have sufficient executive presence? Compared to Jamie's dramatic assertiveness, Alice's steady assurance seemed a little understated.

Notwithstanding Jamie's sudden departure, Carolyn saw leadership as an organizational issue that could not be allowed to rise or fall with any one individual. She blamed herself for not having a more robust, companywide leadership development process in place. She recalled how she had been hired: NCL had a clear leadership need for a deputy COO, and duly filled it. Hiring her had positioned NCL for the future. Today, its hiring processes were no longer that strong.

Mixed in with all this was a growing sentiment of uncertainty in NCL's market. Carolyn knew that luxury goods and 'nice-to-have' designer clothes were among the first items consumers cut back on during economic uncertainty. NCL was at pivotal point in its existence, and it needed a step-change to promote both growth and stability.

## Leadership … but how?

One Friday morning, Carolyn was reviewing her goals for the week. 'Weekly Top Team Leaders meeting – check. Speech at International Fashion Association – check. Meet with a main supplier's CEO – check. Warehouse quality control visit – check.' Carolyn enjoyed checking things off at the end of the week. She was meticulous in planning and execution, and rarely had tasks left to do by Friday afternoon.

However, the list had one last item: 'Create first draft of five-year strategy.' This was still a work in progress. Carolyn had largely followed the path of the previous CEO. She had refreshed the strategy, of course, but hadn't revamped it. Now, NCL was undertaking a comprehensive strategy review across the business, in order to define a bolder and more aggressive five-year strategy. This was Carolyn's idea. The top team all agreed that it was sorely needed, but now it was her responsibility to get it done. Carolyn was to present the new strategy at the next Board of Directors meeting coming up in two months. The executive committee had time before then to finalize the solid strategy that was emerging, but Carolyn wondered: *would it be good enough?* All eyes would be on her to present the first real NCL revamp since she became CEO.

Carolyn felt that something was still missing. She was running the strategy through her mind as she flipped through different news articles on her phone; then an article caught her eye: 'Leadership is dead. Long live leadership!' She skimmed the article, which asserted, 'Leadership as we know it today is dead. More than a third of organizations say they lack the leadership capacity to execute their strategy, and 50% of organizations do not feel that their initiatives to address the gap are successful.'

Carolyn was intrigued. This article was speaking directly to her: 'To plug this gap, leadership development must change. Companies need a more comprehensive, fact-based, and rigorous approach to ensure business results. A new form of leadership development is arising, and pioneers who fully embrace it will leave their competitors behind.' The article advocated a performance-driven approach to leadership development following a defined four-stage methodology. It stressed the importance of tailoring the design and execution to the specific organization involved.

'That's it!' Carolyn thought. 'We need to take our leadership effectiveness to the next level.' Looking back, this was the moment she decided to shake up NCL's leadership; not necessarily in terms of the people – although she wouldn't rule out making changes if needed – but in terms of how NCL could conceptualize leadership more holistically. Carolyn wanted to increase organizational leadership effectiveness and build a strong succession ladder. She knew this required a fundamentally new approach.

# The leadership team at NCL

Carolyn took some time to consider her colleagues in NCL's Top Team Leadership (TTL) one by one, thinking about their styles and their TTL roles.

- **Megan Huntcliff – CHRO:** Megan knew NCL's business and culture better than anyone else on Carolyn's leadership team. She was the natural person to spearhead a new leadership development initiative, if only Carolyn could bring herself to delegate it.
- **Alice Berman – Head of Strategy and Business Development:** With her excellent track record at a multi-brand retailer in Manhattan, Alice brought an outside perspective to the management team. She had excellent personal relationships, but was also a people pleaser, which made it harder for her to realize her ambitions for shaping NCL's strategy.
- **Peter Cody, Chief Financial Officer (CFO):** Peter's numbers-driven style, focus on work and Irish good humour suited Carolyn well, though sometimes he used humour to stay personally aloof. That was how he kept people at a distance, while still seeming warm. Leadership development was a tricky topic for Peter because he was 66 years old, retirement on the horizon. Nonetheless, he had not yet shown any willingness to develop successors, because he 'loved his job' and saw himself staying put for a number of years.
- **'Bruce' Xi Qing, Chief Operations Officer:** At 48, Bruce was the TTL's youngest member. Born and raised in Shanghai, he knew the local market extremely well. He had succeeded Carolyn as COO and capably managed NCL's operational concerns. Bruce was extremely operationally driven, focused more on the end result rather than the process to get there. Carolyn realized that his approach was one-dimensional, as hers once had been, and she felt she could mentor him to become a more well-rounded leader.
- **Wayne Miller, Chief Sales and Marketing Officer (CSMO):** Born in California, Wayne had been at NCL his whole career, beginning as a young sales assistant. He had

spent most of the past 20 years on the road. As NCL grew, so did his travel agenda, from the U.S. to China, to all of Asia, and now the rest of the globe. His strength was his dedication, but he pushed himself – and his people – too much. Megan overheard one sales VP saying: 'It's okay with me if Wayne never goes home, but I like to see my family now and then.'

- **Fernando Vega, Design Director and former CEO of Infinity Fashionista:** Fernando had founded NCL's newest acquisition, Infinity Fashionista. He'd relocated to China from coastal Portugal as part of the NCL acquisition. He tried to be open-minded about the transition, but he wasn't sure the corporate integration was working. He knew Infinity's main strength was its design expertise, and he worried that NCL's more rigorous processes and systems would trample him and harm the creativity and quality of his designs.

## Carolyn gets the ball rolling

Carolyn knew that drastically improving leadership development was a big task. She decided to engage Megan, her CHRO. She trusted Megan, but Carolyn still hovered. She wanted to be pretty involved for at least the first six months to ensure that the initiative was integrated into strategic planning.

Carolyn emailed the article to Megan, asking Megan to come by her office Monday morning to discuss it. She also sent the article to Hans Lager, her long-time friend and mentor. The advice Hans offered was useful. He agreed that as an organization NCL was strong in strategy and execution, but he felt that it didn't focus enough on the people side, especially leadership development. He suggested that Carolyn should keep in mind that leadership effectiveness, although a critical enabler of performance, would not solve all their challenges. He advised her to define very clearly to Megan what she expected from the leadership development programme, and what she would address through other initiatives.

Hans thought that the structured, success-oriented methodology identified in the article would be effective, but he warned Carolyn keep the big picture in mind. She needed to make sure the programme was tailored for NCL – whether it took four steps or twenty. It was vital that it fitted with the company's strategy, culture and mindset.

He reminded her to involve the whole team – and to keep in mind the goal which was to develop great leaders. She would have to put her trust in her team to handle the full scope of the project, and not try to go it alone. 'Remember, they are already major international corporate executives. Peter is seasoned and knows the financial end. Bruce is coming along as COO, and Wayne is a powerful sales manager. Alice is intimidated, but give her time. If you can't delegate to these folks, you're harbouring the wrong mindset – or you've hired the wrong people. And, we both know how capable Megan is.' If Carolyn could not engage the whole TTL in this initiative, it would fail.

For the next hour, Carolyn and Hans ran through a possible programme, and arranged a follow-up call in the next month. Hans advised on the importance of careful planning: 'Try not to get too far ahead on programme design before you and your team agree on goals. This is a critical first step many organizations overlook. Plan before you act…'

## Summary

Leadership development can take many forms. The specific approach or steps involved are less important than the rigor of the methodology. In addition, it is critical that leadership intervention is tailored to the organization at hand, and that success criteria are clearly defined from the outset.

The programme must start at the top, and be championed by the CEO or highest leader in the organization, together with the broader executive leadership team. Furthermore, the CEO and broader leadership team must be willing to confront personal leadership challenges and grow as leaders. Walking the talk and role-modelling starts from the moment the programme is conceived.

The next stage in the journey focuses on determining the leadership behaviours required to achieve the strategic aspirations and ensuring an aligned top team, prioritizing the key shifts, and assessing where the organization is currently in terms of leaders and leadership development.

# 9

## Setting the leadership aspiration

*Andrew St George, Claudio Feser, Michael Rennie,*
*Nicolai Chen Nielsen*


**Greg prepares the TTL workshop | Thinking holistically about leadership
| The leadership gap | Mapping the 'from–to' shifts | The Leadership
Peak Programme is born | The townhall**


Carolyn went into work early on Monday to think about her approach
to leadership development prior to meeting with Megan. She considered what Hans had said: 'Define very clearly up front what you expect
from the leadership development programme. Align on the desired end
state up front.' Carolyn was not entirely sure what the end state would
look like, but she pictured a high performing leadership team with
clearly defined successors in place. This didn't seem like quite enough,
so she wondered, 'Isn't that what all organizations should have?'

Suddenly she remembered what one of her favourite professors
used to say when they discussed her aspirations. 'Think bigger' he
would repeat like a mantra. She smiled. That's what she needed to do.

'Could leadership become a source of competitive advantage for
NCL?' she thought, jotting down some questions: 'How can we
develop the best leaders? Could leadership excellence become a
recruiting tool to get top talent? How could leadership effectiveness
make us unstoppable? Could we be known as a leadership company?
What type of leaders does NCL need? Should we define an "NCL
Way" of leadership?' Many thoughts were racing through Carolyn's
head when Megan knocked on her door.

'Hi Carolyn, ready for our 10 a.m. meeting?' asked Megan, who
seemed full of energy.

'Sure,' replied Carolyn, 'Come on in.' She began sharing her
thoughts on what leadership could mean for NCL. She talked about
the potential end state – maintaining top performance while becoming

a leadership-driven company, known for having the best leaders in the business. Leadership would become a source of competitive advantage and a recruiting proposition.

It sounded compelling, but Megan wasn't convinced. 'I like the aspiration,' Megan started, 'but I'm not sure focusing on individual leaders is the best way to go. From my experience, we really need to take an organizational view of leadership. Our target is to increase NCL's leadership effectiveness overall. Also, we shouldn't pursue leadership for the sake of leadership. We need to tie it more closely to our performance and our strategy.'

'You're right,' Carolyn said, 'We need to make sure what we do is really tailored to NCL – and that we pursue this across the organization. I've been to so many leadership courses that helped me as an individual leader, but I've had difficulty bringing the new tools back to NCL.'

Discussing the company's next steps, they agreed that they needed more input from the whole executive team – and especially from Alice for strategic alignment – to define their leadership aspirations and determine the key initiatives needed to fulfil them. More concretely, they decided to hold one or two leadership development planning workshops with the top team. Megan volunteered to organize and run the workshops, with the help of Greg Maxwell, a British consultant and leadership coach whom NCL had used in the past.

## Greg prepares the TTL workshop

In the three weeks before the workshop, Greg worked closely with Megan to nail down the agenda. Greg explained that three things had to happen for the workshop to succeed. First, his guiding principle for such workshops was that the executives had to do most – if not all – the talking. His job was to facilitate. He did not want to be the one making leadership development suggestions, since that could take ownership and commitment away from the executives. He urged Megan to carry that spear at the beginning.

Second, the agenda had to be set up to make sure the right discussions took place. As he knew, this wasn't easy to arrange. He planned to collaborate with Alice and Bruce so that the agenda already listed the topics they wanted to raise for strategy and operations. Third and finally, he wanted to maintain high energy levels in the room all day, and to finish on a high note, so that at the end of the meeting the team was energized and committed to making the leadership development campaign happen.

To ensure that the right discussions took place, Greg suggested to Megan that NCL first run the Organizational Health Index (OHI) across the organization. This would provide a baseline picture of NCL's overall health. It also would generate a Leadership Behaviour Report, showing NCL's leadership effectiveness and the specific leadership behaviours and practices that worked best in its context. Megan knew that the exercise would be valuable and it was in her budget, but she wasn't sure whether NCL's employees would start getting anxious about receiving such a survey before any formal announcement of its objectives.

She talked to Carolyn, and they decided that the time had come to announce the leadership development initiative. The next day, Megan sent out a company-wide briefing from Carolyn formally launching The OHI survey.

Greg had also suggested that the preparations should include one-on-one interviews with the top team to assess their views of NCL's vision, mission, strategy, and performance aspirations, and the con-comitant leadership requirements. Greg asked about their perfor-mance goals and gaps. Though the leaders didn't mention it, they were reassured that NCL was maintaining its explicit focus on performance, including in the context of leadership development.

Greg had asked them what leadership behaviours were required to achieve their strategy, and what they saw as NCL's leadership strengths and development needs. He concluded each interview with a brief discussion about what types of change efforts had worked well at NCL in the past and what made them successful.

## Thinking holistically about leadership

Finally, the workshop date arrived. The top team gathered at the Lotus Palace Resort, a classy hotel just outside the city's hustle and bustle. Eight people were present: Carolyn, the six other members of the TTL, and Greg. Carolyn opened the meeting. 'Friends, we have gathered today to take the leadership of NCL to the next level. You have all spoken with Greg during the past few weeks, and we are excited to continue these discussions as a group. NCL has been on a fantastic journey so far, and we have ambitious goals. We are close to finalizing our new five-year strategy, and our shareholders are banking us on to succeed.'

Carolyn continued, to approving nods from around the room. 'While we have had leadership development efforts in the past, we have never thought holistically about the leadership required to help us execute our strategy now and in the future. I mean, leadership is not the only thing we need to be successful, but it is a key element … and I have realized that our leadership development efforts need an overhaul. So today, let's jointly develop our leadership aspirations and lay out the key initiatives we need to undertake to get where we want to go. Greg will get us started …'

Greg began by laying out the agenda. The workshop would have four main parts (Figure 9.1):

**What will we do today?**

| Where are we today? Executive interviews, OHI, and Leadership Behaviour Report | What is a leadership model and why does it matter? | What are the key business drivers, and which ones will make the biggest difference to NCL's performance? | What are the behaviours needed to influence the key business drivers? NCL's leadership model |

FIGURE 9.1 Workshop agenda

Greg recapped the one-on-one discussions he'd had with each of them: 'Everyone is aligned on NCL's vision, mission, high level strategy, and performance aspirations,' Greg started, 'and we are all optimistic about the future.' This pleased Carolyn since she'd spent a lot of time on the recent strategy exercise with the top team. Greg continued: 'You all also have a clear sense of NCL's strengths and challenges. Historically, we have grown very quickly, in large part because of our results-oriented culture. As one of you told me, "People at NCL just get things done". Another strength you all mentioned multiple times is our ability to perform and to problem solve at all levels of the organizations. We have great talent, and we collaborate effectively to make quick, high quality decisions. Furthermore, you all noted our strong corporate culture.'

He paused. 'That's the good news. On the other hand, you cited two areas where NCL could improve. First, some of you feel we have started "playing it safe". While in the past we used to pioneer new styles, channels, and customer experiences, now we often choose conservative or low-risk solutions. Second, we could be more customer-centric. We are very inward looking and focused on execution, which sometimes gets in the way of serving our customers as well as we could.'

'He really understands our business,' Wayne thought. A few other members of the TTL were thinking the same thing.

Greg continued. 'In terms of leadership, we feel that the TTL members function well together. The TTL has the right expertise, and often we work very clearly in the same direction,' he said, reassuring his colleagues before adding a critical caveat. 'However, further down the organization, we all find a lack of leadership, future leadership development, and succession planning. Our employees are great at executing, but few of them seem particularly visionary. We would like to see bolder, more inspirational leadership. Furthermore, we feel that we need better market insight to foresee the latest trends and predict what our customers want, rather than following one step behind.'

For the first time, Fernando smiled. Fashion was about to be front and centre.

## Leadership and health

The discussion moved on to the results of the OHI and the leadership assessment. Greg reported that 76 per cent of NCL's employees had taken the survey, higher than the global average of around 60 per cent, and that over 1,000 free text comments had been gathered. Greg then displayed the OHI results to the team on a slide, which showed that NCL was second quartile overall with a score of 67, and second quartile in terms of the leadership outcome.

Greg gave the executives a few minutes to digest the results. The room was quiet. Clearly, most of them had expected NCL to be in the top quartile, not only overall, but also in leadership. Greg began his debriefing by highlighting the strengths in terms of strategic direction, coordination and control and capabilities, all of which were top quartile. As they had noted earlier, NCL was strong in execution, and its employees were aligned on the overall strategy.

However, there were two outcomes that were third quartile: external orientation, and innovation and learning. Although the team knew that these were challenges, everyone was surprised that they had fallen to the third quartile.

Greg moved onto leadership. He began presenting the Leadership Behaviour Report, a subset of the survey. He introduced the 'situational leadership staircase' (Figure 9.2), explaining that different leadership behaviours are more or less effective depending on the organizational context. He also presented baseline behaviours as an organizational reference point. Again, he let Carolyn's colleagues digest NCL's results before continuing.

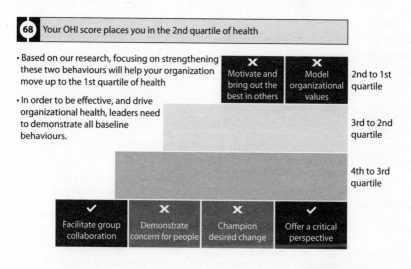

FIGURE 9.2 NCL 'situational leadership staircase'

'This is the technical part,' Greg explained. 'Here is what the scoring means. Our OHI score places us in the second quartile of health. First of all, we need to ensure that we fulfil the baseline leadership behaviours. Currently, our scores on two of the four dimensions fall below what is expected of a second quartile organization. Second, if we want to make the jump to first quartile organizational health, we need to change our leadership style and focus more on bringing out the best in our employees, and on emphasizing NCL's core values – and all without losing any ground in productivity or profitability.'

The team discussed the results in detail, including the possible root causes of weak scores. The TTL members realized that maybe in the past they had focused too much on execution and results, without adequately engaging the rest of the organization in NCL's broader vision and mission.

## Leadership models and values

When the TTL reconvened, Greg introduced the technical concept of a leadership model (Figure 9.3). He offered a quick note on language. 'There are many different, confusing names for what we are trying to do. We are defining the leadership themes, values, or principles that will guide how NCL works. Organizations typically state four to six of these precepts. Some organizations separate their values and leadership themes, while others combine them.' He popped up a slide for the team members to study:

| Terms | What we mean |
|---|---|
| Vision | Where an organization wants to be. Communicates both the purpose and values of the business – focuses on the future |
| Mission | How an organization will get to where it wants to be. Defines the primary objectives of the business – focuses on the present leading to the future |
| Values/Principles/ Leadership themes | Important and lasting beliefs, principles or ideals usually shared by a group of people about what is (and is not) desirable. Values have a major influence on individual attitudes and behaviours and serve as broad guidelines in all situations |
| Competencies/ Behaviours/Mindsets/ Ways of thinking | The way in which one acts or conducts oneself, especially towards others. You know you're 'winning' when you see people living out these behaviours |
| Performance grid/ Assessment grid/ Evaluation framework | Evaluative assessment framework that outlines expected behaviours across difference levels of performance (e.g. 1–5). Behaviours often differentiated by level in the organization |

FIGURE 9.3 Defining NCL's leadership model

Greg continued. 'NCL has a list of values embedded in its performance management system. However, the performance assessment is binary – you either live up to the values or you do not – and they do not really drive employee behaviour.' The executives nodded. 'We are trying to do something different. A leadership model shows what NCL expects of leaders throughout the organization (with the understanding that everyone on any level can be a leader). It focuses on the themes that make the biggest difference, and it supports senior leaders in achieving their strategic and operational goals. It reinforces specific behaviours and ways of thinking – that's mindsets – from senior leadership to the front-line, and it is integrated into core talent processes. This is distinctive to NCL, not just a generic list of qualities.'

'The goal we recommend is to link NCL's leadership model to its vision and mission and to anchor it in observable behaviours shown on a performance grid we can use as the basis for assessing each employee.' (Figure 9.4).

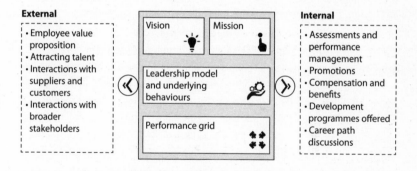

FIGURE 9.4 Vision and mission at NCL

## Leadership behaviours that can really make a difference for NCL

After a brief lunch, the team attacked the question everyone was waiting for: *What should NCL's leadership model look like?* The TTL members had many ideas, but Carolyn wanted them to focus on what really mattered to the business.

'We call this session 'grounding the leadership aspiration in performance',' Greg said. 'It means that we make leadership count right here. Let's review our strategy's critical business drivers, before we get into the leadership required to execute it.'

Megan and Alice had worked hard with Greg to prepare for this session. They knew that organizations encounter a pitfall when they define their leadership model in a vacuum, focusing more on great individual leadership competencies and not on the overall organization's needs.

'Let's get down to what fits our company,' Megan said. 'We want to talk specifically about NCL and the leadership behaviours that fit our long range goals and plans. First, with thanks to Peter for the background data from his team, Greg will present a 'driver tree' that shows the sub-elements of our revenues and costs. Greg…'

'Let's track revenues first,' he said. 'Your revenues came from the number of stores, multiplied by revenue per store, which is made up of the number of customers who walked in, multiplied by the percentage of people who bought something, multiplied by the average purchase size per customer.'

The team discussed each element, breaking the tree into further levels of detail. To the very right of the tree, the team listed specific behaviours that would enable NCL to succeed within each business driver.

The last step of this exercise was to overlay the revenue analysis with NCL's future strategy. The team was already conversant with the five-year strategy – now a work in progress. Carolyn was glad to see Alice step up and not hold back as she facilitated a rich discussion of the specific behaviours that most affected the business. Then Alice turned to Bruce, who covered the operational aspects. It soon became clear that inorganic growth would play a big role in reaching their top-line targets. Furthermore, they saw that NCL inevitably had to embrace digitization fully. Peter explained that this would improve the customer experience and drive down costs.

'Great,' said Carolyn, noticing that her assistant Mai had opened the door and was checking with her. 'Now, I think afternoon tea is ready for us. Let's have a break and then move onto our next step.' Carolyn had wanted to make her team feel special, and to give them time to reflect on what they had heard; time and space were in short supply in day-to-day NCL; and afternoon tea provided both, plus the message that it was OK to have an occasional luxury.

Greg opened the final three-hour session: 'Now we have the information to create our leadership model,' he said. 'We've looked at four sources of input: the executive interviews; the OHI and Leadership Behaviour Report; the leadership model benchmarks; and the business drivers. Can we consolidate them into a set of themes people can remember?'

The team embarked on a lively discussion of NCL's leadership model. Within each common theme that evolved, the team defined two to three critical behaviours that would bring the theme to life. Carolyn kept pushing them. 'Think bigger,' she challenged. 'Will this really get us where we need to be?'

Toward the end of the day, the TTL put the finishing touches on the first draft of NCL's new leadership model. It consisted of five themes that leaders and employees should live: *Is results-oriented, brings out the best in self and others, puts the customer first, fosters bottom up innovation, and is a technology leader.* Each theme was furthermore broken down into two to four specific behaviours. The TTL also prioritized the critical behaviours to focus on first.

Megan summarized the day's results: 'We accomplished our goal of developing a fit-for-purpose leadership model, with five meaningful themes and a total of 15 leadership behaviours. The new model will embed all of our existing values. We cannot do everything at once, so we have decided to emphasize the themes *brings out the best in self and others* and *fosters bottom-up innovation*, which are comprised of five specific behaviours in total.'

Alice added, 'Another way to look at this strategically is through the three OHI dimensions of alignment, execution, and renewal – concepts which define good leadership. Our five leadership themes will ensure that we build on our strengths in alignment and execution, while addressing the gaps we've identified.'

Carolyn wrapped up the meeting: 'The next steps are to finalize the model and behaviours, agree on the specific leadership requirements and aspirations, and discuss how to bring the programme to life, including the TTL's required role. Greg and Megan, please work on this and review it with Alice for strategic alignment, Peter for budget, Bruce for operational fit, Fernando for product concerns, and Wayne for sales and customer impact. We will approve these points during our next TTL meeting.'

## *The leadership gap*

Following the workshop, Megan spent two weeks refining the leadership model and identifying NCL's leadership gaps using focus groups, discussions with managers, and data from the existing talent management system. A day before the TTL meeting, Carolyn blocked out two hours with Megan to review the slightly updated leadership model and discuss the leadership gap.

'The focus groups pretty much confirmed our hypothesis,' Megan began. 'Performance is one of our edges, but it stops there, it's one-dimensional. That means our leadership is not inspirational and is not bringing out the best in others. The focus groups liked the themes we were proposing. They didn't add any new ones, but they tweaked the behaviours slightly.'

'I also analysed our leadership requirements. I worked with the TTL and department heads to refine the numbers, and we landed on a total need for at least 650 leaders, down to N-4 level, given our future growth plans. This includes regional managers, but it doesn't include store or plant managers, though Bruce will want to set something up for them. This chart (Figure 9.5) summarizes what we know and what has to happen:'

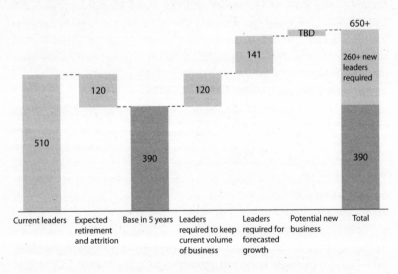

FIGURE 9.5 NCL Leadership requirement over next five years

'That is our total leadership requirement over the next five years?' asked Carolyn.

'Yes,' said Megan. 'This is the aggregate chart, but I also have one for each organizational level. I broke it down by the type of leaders, by function and by geography. We are targeting a growth of around 7 per cent per year, which means an increased leadership need of around 5 per cent per year, depending on how we split geographies.'

'When Alice and I reviewed the planning component, we realized that this doesn't factor in potential extraordinary leadership needs, like for acquisitions or special projects. Bruce cautioned that it doesn't address some operational concerns, like crisis management or extra needs in retail, supply lines, or manufacturing. Wayne wants a contingency for unexpected sales growth and training on new sales management technology, and, of course, Peter wants a detailed budget. With that still to consider, we're looking at a leadership need of more than 260 extra leaders in the next five years, more than 50 per year. Even if we don't grow, we need just under half that number, around 25 a year.'

Carolyn stared at the chart, realizing that pace and scale were as important as content and delivery, and that leadership development had to align with strategy and productivity and performance goals. That was a lot of moving parts. She had a sinking feeling in her stomach that she had let this go wrong on her watch. Had she let down the company and the TTL? She knew NCL wasn't going to look very well managed at the top if she couldn't fill its leadership ranks.

She took a deep breath. 'Can we fill this need? Did you check our pipeline of leaders and our current leadership development initiatives?'

'Yes,' Megan said, 'I reviewed our current leadership development initiatives for effectiveness and efficiency. We are spending about $4m on pure-play leadership development, excluding other L&D. That is below industry benchmarks, and we are spending it the wrong way: 13 per cent is going to travel and accommodation, and 40 per cent goes to third-party courses. We could shift some of that in-house. Furthermore, most training is with live instructors. We could use more virtual instructor-led courses and more web-based self-study, to save money while maintaining or even increasing quality. There is also little focus on on-the-job development.'

Megan continued. 'Our end-user surveys suggested linking leadership development to our strategic objectives. Greg and Alice agree with me. I was struck by one senior executive who said, "Trainings are largely developed independent of overall business goals". Finally, we don't measure the business impact of our leadership development initiatives. Instead, we rely mostly on participant feedback.'

She sighed, 'I know that's a lot of bad news at once, but we've got to discuss it together and with the TTL.'

Thinking about how to institute change on so many levels, Carolyn had a growing sense how much was at stake if she failed.

'Megan,' Carolyn said. 'Take a crack at the high-level design to address the leadership gap. Huddle with Greg and whoever else you need. Then bring that back to me and we'll decide how to proceed. Let's meet in a couple of weeks – while we still have some margin before the Board meeting – and then we'll report to the TTL.'

'Meanwhile, you have my OK to talk to individual TTL members as needed to map out a draft of the high-level design.'

## Mapping the 'from–to' shifts

That week, Megan and Greg conducted one-on-one interviews with selected employees. They focused on the two key themes the TTL had prioritized: *brings out the best in self and others* and *fosters bottom-up innovation*. Megan knew that in order to sustainably shift employee behaviours, the leadership programme had to address underlying mindsets as well.

To uncover employees' mindsets and identify specific necessary shifts, Megan used Deep Structure Interviews (DSIs), which explored hidden levels of individual and organizational behaviour. This reflective process resembled a free-flowing conversation, relying on an open, trusting relationship between interviewer and interviewee. It was useful for exploring firmly held mindsets, assumptions, and basic values. It could help Megan uncover deep-seated anxieties and group or individual mental barriers to change.

Megan and Greg had a series of fruitful conversations. As she got to the bottom of NCL leaders' mindsets, she learned that many employees held deeply felt beliefs that the programme had to address, in order for the new leadership model to succeed. Megan set up a chart for each theme showing the main behavioural shifts, and the required mindset changes. She prepared this summary (Figure 9.6) of the mindset shifts as a reference for Carolyn and the TTL:

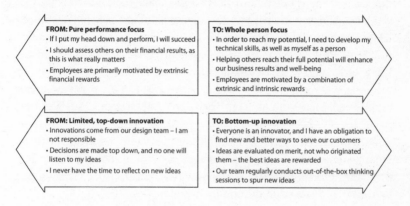

**FROM: Pure performance focus**
- If I put my head down and perform, I will succeed
- I should assess others on their financial results, as this is what really matters
- Employees are primarily motivated by extrinsic financial rewards

**TO: Whole person focus**
- In order to reach my potential, I need to develop my technical skills, as well as myself as a person
- Helping others reach their full potential will enhance our business results and well-being
- Employees are motivated by a combination of extrinsic and intrinsic rewards

**FROM: Limited, top-down innovation**
- Innovations come from our design team – I am not responsible
- Decisions are made top down, and no one will listen to my ideas
- I never have the time to reflect on new ideas

**TO: Bottom-up innovation**
- Everyone is an innovator, and I have an obligation to find new and better ways to serve our customers
- Ideas are evaluated on merit, not who originated them – the best ideas are rewarded
- Our team regularly conducts out-of-the-box thinking sessions to spur new ideas

FIGURE 9.6 Required mindset shifts

## The Leadership Peak Programme is born

The plan Megan presented to Carolyn on the Monday morning two weeks before the Board meeting included the updated leadership model, a synthesized version of the diagnostic results, the focus group output, the required 'from–to' shifts, and a high-level, company-wide action plan. The plan included a blended learning approach, with content anchored in the leadership model. Megan wanted to include on-the-job project work and, at Alice's urging, a mentoring/coaching component, to bind the programme to business results.

Carolyn liked it a lot, but she made one additional push: for the TTL members to go on their own leadership development journey. This was only part of the response Carolyn had crafted over the week in Vancouver, but she wanted to get it underway in light of the focus groups' feedback.

She had realized that if this leadership development challenge was personal to her – if her ideas had been off and she'd made mistakes – it was also personal to the other TTL members. They needed to up their game. She also felt – though she didn't say it – that the TTL members could benefit personally from leadership training, herself included.

When the TTL discussed a name for the initiative, Peter suggested the 'Performance Leadership Programme'. But the TTL realized that was too grounded in the previous ways of thinking. It failed to capitalize on the new leadership aspirations. They finally landed on Leadership Peak Programme (LPP). This epitomized the 'leadership stairway' NCL was erecting as an organization. It also offered a metaphor for reaching one's individual potential, a priority the team felt was strategically aligned with the big focus areas of bringing out the best in others.

Megan felt relieved. With the full team behind her, Carolyn focused 100 per cent on how she would bring this home at the Board meeting, now only a fortnight away. It was now two months since Carolyn had first read the leadership development article.

## The Townhall

At the next quarterly Board meeting, Carolyn presented the five-year strategy, overall OHI results and leadership development plans, in that order. The Board approved the five-year strategy, but it faded out of their minds when they saw the OHI results. They were very absorbed with the findings, but not so happy. The lower quartiles drew plenty of criticism, and Carolyn took a lot of heat before she could get them to focus on the leadership development plan. She explained how it would move NCL onward and upward, and correct the low quartiles. After a lively debate, the Board approved the leadership development proposal, urging Carolyn to move quickly.

The following week, the executive team presented the five-year strategy at an extra-ordinary townhall meeting in the NCL dining room, with a live video broadcast to the rest of the organization, including its plants and stores. Different executives presented their segments of the strategy. While the content was great, the employees felt the executives were presenting 'their bits' of the plan. It didn't seem fully coherent yet. Many of them couldn't see how they fitted in.

Megan presented the leadership development plan as a dramatic finish at the end of the meeting. She was reluctant to share too much yet, but she stated boldly that this initiative would touch all employees, at all levels, one way or another.

The audience members felt cautiously optimistic about the leadership programme. NCL had been through so many performance initiatives and changes, not to mention the takeover of Infinity, that its people felt a measure of change fatigue. Nonetheless, this looked exciting and each person could consider how it might affect his or her career path. Now everyone was engaged or at least knew about the new programme, from the highest level managers to the front-line employees.

As Carolyn drove home that evening, she reflected on the past few eventful weeks. She now had an approved five-year strategy, approved leadership development programme and budget. But she knew this was just the beginning of the journey, and that the next two months would be critical. As Carolyn pulled into her driveway, she decided to keep a closer eye on Megan's progress in the following weeks – just to make sure nothing fell through the cracks.

## Summary

At this stage in the journey, an organization should have created a tailored leadership model (or refreshed the existing model if one exists). The organization should prioritize the critical shifts to focus on, and quantify the leadership gap. In addition, the organization should review current leadership development initiatives, as well as current ways of embedding leadership in the broader system. Finally, it is important to ensure that the entire top team is involved from the beginning and aligned around the leadership development priorities.

| Diagnose<br>What is the gap to where you want to go? | Design & Develop<br>What do you need to get from here to there? | Deliver<br>How should you move to action? | Drive Impact<br>How do you keep moving forward? |
|---|---|---|---|

☑ Leadership model that is tightly linked to the strategy, and aligned with the top team

☑ Critical 3–5 'from-to' shifts (behaviours, skills, mindsets) that the leadership program will bring about

☑ Quantification of the leadership gap at each level of the organization

☑ Assessment of current leadership development initiatives and quality of system embedment mechanisms

The next stage in the journey focuses on designing the required interventions for all target groups (capability building content and system embedment), identifying who should go on the programme, and creating the business case for delivery.

# IO

# Designing the roadmap

*Andrew St George, Claudio Feser, Michael Rennie,*
*Nicolai Chen Nielsen*

Reviewing the critical design choices | Ripples in the pond | 'Building
the plane in flight' | High level blueprint for Leap programme | Developing
the business case | Organizations don't change, people do

Megan was buoyed by the Board's approval of the leadership development programme. Now she needed to take what she had learned in
assessing NCL's leadership need and the leadership gap, and create modules to implement the necessary changes. She and Greg set about shaping
and designing the NCL programme, calling on the TTL and their staff as
necessary. As they considered intellectual, practical, financial and project
imperatives, Greg helped Megan develop an interdisciplinary approach.

They focused on three areas of planning: The first was addressing
critical design choices, including the Leadership Peak Programme
(LPP) scope and mandate. Second, which programmes should they
launch first, and when? Third, they started designing actual programmes, beginning with each module's content, pace, intellectual
level, and range of learning styles.

When Megan and Greg sat down with Carolyn to update her on
their progress, she was pleased, but she threw them a curve ball.

'You're right to start with the VPs and top leaders,' she said, 'but I
want to start higher. I took some time off to think before last quarter's
Board meeting, so I've been considering this for a while. I'm pretty
sure we need a big dose of our own medicine. The TTL should have
leadership training, too.'

Pretending not to notice their stunned looks (she could imagine
what they were thinking: 'What a distraction! Who's going to teach
those executive egos?'), Carolyn continued. 'I'm bringing in Hans
Lager for a couple of months. He'll work with the TTL members.'

Megan had little left to say. 'Sure, Carolyn, sounds good. I would love to kick off my own coaching with Hans sooner rather than later.'

Megan hadn't expected leadership coaching. She might have seen it coming, but, as usual, she was running just to keep up with Carolyn. However, she thought it was a great idea and sorely needed, and she was excited to start her own coaching with Hans in the coming week. Deep inside, however, she was also relieved that Carolyn would tell the TTL the plan, as they would not exactly be thrilled with the news.

## *Reviewing the critical design choices*

The next step was to discuss the programme design with the TTL, which would take place during two half-day workshops in the office. The first session would centre on programme scope, and the second session would focus on selecting the programme participants.

## Workshop 1: Programme scope

Megan opened the workshop by addressing the choices ahead in designing the LPP to really fit NCL. The team set a twofold objective and mission for the LPP:

1 To achieve a top quartile leadership score, on the way to a top quartile overall health score
2 To have the business impact of the programme projects pay back the cost of the programme each year.

'We have a centralized mandate to drive leadership development across the whole organization. Attending the LPP is going to be mandatory for all designated participants company-wide, so we will work with and through the business units.'

Having gone over the numbers with Peter, she told the team that NCL Group HR would bear the costs centrally and then allocate them out in order to allay the fears of business unit budget directors.

By the end of the workshop, they had decided six key elements:

1 Everyone at NCL should go through different LPP programmes at some point
2 Reaching the whole organization quickly would be critical

3 For top talent, the LPP would involve field, forum and coaching programmes, each lasting 9–12 months and tailored to different levels

4 Non-top talent would take a one-day programme each year, tailored by level

5 Everyone – from the C-suite to the factory floor – would participate in Values Day, to shed additional light on NCL's values, and discuss how to embody them as part of the company's meaningful mission

6 These programmes would replace all the current leadership development initiatives company-wide, and would supplement the current technical/skill-building programmes, which would still be open to employees

## Workshop 2: Selecting the programme participants

During the next TTL workshop, Megan focused the discussion on which people NCL should select to participate in the LPP. They discussed selection criteria, and set out how to measure individual performance after LPP participation. Finally, they reached a consensus for the first year, which they called 'Cohort 1'.

During that time, they would base evaluations on existing performance reviews. In subsequent years (what Greg called 'LPP steady state'), selecting participants and appraising LPP 'graduates' would be part of a new performance management system, based on a new 3 × 3 matrix – see Figure 10.1. One axis would be key performance indicators (KPIs), and the other axis would be evaluations of how well an employee exemplified leadership model behaviours. They decided that any leader categorized as 'top talent' would gain access to the LPP.

They planned 360-degree reviews for all employees, except store level, supply line and factory associates. Pending Bruce's input, they sketched a separate leadership development track for those employees, approximately 80 per cent of the workforce. Store and plant managers would be trained and would assess their employees based on the leadership model. NCL would hold Values Days regionally, in stores, factories and warehouses.

At this point, Wayne asked, 'How many people should be in the "top talent" bucket, that upper right hand corner?'

Since Carolyn, Greg and Megan had already done some math on this, Greg answered, 'The top talent bucket varies across organizations; some have more than one list, some are more exclusive than others. It's tailored to the particular company. Some large organizations have "top 700", some have "top 200", and some have as few as "top 40" talent lists.'

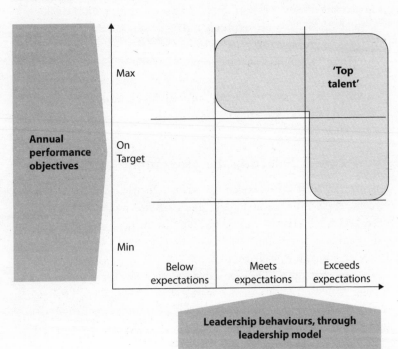

FIGURE 10.1 The 3 × 3 matrix

Megan added, 'Let's be as precise as we can. NCL has 30,000 employees, of which 24,500 are shop level or warehouse and factory based. We assess them on a different system and they'll have access to good training. This leaves 5,500 potential LPP candidates, so, Greg, what's the right weighting?'

'Among any 5,500 employees,' Greg said, 'no more than 15 per cent (approximately 800) should be labeled "top talent", to keep the name and programmes sought after and exclusive. In reality, many organizations struggle to identify true top talent beyond that 15 per cent.'

Sobered by the thought that their leadership bench might not be deep enough, the team looked at what 15 per cent would mean. The 800+ 'top talents' were spread over four organizational levels: the TTL, the VP/director level (all included, by virtue of their level), the general manager level, and the manager level. The 15 per cent rule meant approximately the following split (Figure 10.2), which would later be refined bottom up:

| Org level | No. of employees | Top talent (15%) | No. of cohorts | Participants/ cohort |
|-----------|-----------------|------------------|----------------|---------------------|
| CEO | 1 | 1 | 1 | 7 |
| TTL | 6 | 6 | | |
| VP | 32 | 32 | 3 | 19 |
| Director | 157 | 24 | | |
| GM | 812 | 122 | 7 | 17 |
| Manager | 4501 | 675 | 32 | 21 |
| **Sum** | **5509** | **860** | **43** | **N/A** |

FIGURE 10.2  Splitting the top talent

Megan then explained, 'I do most of our executive onboarding and I track the retention reports from our BUs. Employees tend to stay at each level for five years, so that's approximately 20 per cent of new entrants on each level annually. We have a natural churn of approximately 10 per cent per year, so in steady state there would be approximately 240 new top talents or top talents promoted to a new level overall per year.'

'Here are the totals,' she said. 'That's more or less nine directors and VPs, 36 GMs and some 200 managers, meaning about 14 cohorts per year, in steady state. There would, however, need to be an initial push to get all top talent through the programme upfront.' Applying this data, the team came up with a set of LPP programmes that would match participants three ways: organizational level, work context (specific discipline or specialization), and the number of top talent slots needed.

They set out four tiers:

1 The Top Talent Programmes, tailored to fit four (non-store, non-factory) employee organizational levels, and to reach around 800 people at the company's current size. These programmes would include a programme for the TTL, for VPs and Directors, for General Managers, and for Managers

2 The Core Leadership programme (one day per year), mandatory for all employees, tailored by organizational level

3 Values Day, mandatory for all employees

4 Induction, mandatory for all new employees

## Ripples in the pond

A week later, Megan and Greg reflected on the progress of the design phase. The working outline now included who should participate in the LPP, how many participants they needed, what they should learn, and when – and over what period – they should be learning (linked to both the leadership model and to any extraordinary business-specific skills NCL needed). Yet their decisions – as refined in the team meeting – had wider implications. Megan was feeling the impact of a factor Greg already knew about: a leadership development programme, properly undertaken and pursued, has many ramifications across an organization.

'I feel like I'm tackling an octopus,' she said fretfully to Greg. 'I have to see if all our planning has allowed for the LPP's far-flung impacts. It's like throwing a stone in a pond and watching the ripples spread.'

'That's the usual course,' he confirmed. 'But, knowing that doesn't make it easier.'

'I do know we need to reward the behaviours we want to promote, that makes sense, but can we use the current performance management system?'

'Yes and no,' said Greg. 'Yes, you'll need a performance management system, but no you can't use the current one. You'll have to change the criteria, which means changing what supervisors pay attention to. You'd have to update the performance management system so we assess people on how well they embody the leadership model as well as on business performance, measured through the new 360-degree review.'

'How about the leadership themes?' Megan asked.

'That's up to you and the TTL,' he said, 'but I'd advise keeping the themes uniform across NCL and tailoring specific behaviours by level. Then, your 360-degree evaluations can feed into compensation, promotion, talent management and succession planning.'

'Of course,' Megan agreed. 'So we first have to train our assessors and appraisers.'

'Yes, and that's a great opportunity to amplify the LPP's impact,' said Greg approvingly.

'I reckon it goes well beyond that,' Megan added. 'We should align our recruiting strategy with the leadership model, which also indirectly influences how we interact with our external stakeholders, including suppliers and customers.'

'Spot on,' said Greg, 'but I would push you to think even more broadly. Have you heard of the Influence Model? It's important to touch on all four of its quadrants, to ensure the leadership intervention is sustained.' Greg and Megan continued to work on the design of the programme content, and also developed the plan for embedding the change in the system.

## 'Building the plane in flight'

On each programme element, Megan still required Carolyn's sign off. She had hoped that the programme itself would free Carolyn to delegate rather than micro-manage, but she also appreciated Carolyn's attention and reassurance.

Still, thought Megan, 'Carolyn needs to let go and trust me more … but I'm not sure now is the time to tell her. Maybe I can show her.'

First, Megan walked Carolyn through the four Influence Model elements they needed to incorporate in the LPP to bring the new leadership model to life: fostering understanding and conviction, reinforcing it with formal mechanisms, role-modelling, and developing the talent and skills needed for change.

Megan explained that each element carried a series of imperatives: for example, fostering understanding required an internal communications strategy, internal marketing materials, and a corporate communication campaign.

Carolyn liked it a lot. 'Great, let's get going on the LPP sooner rather than later. The Board, the TTL, some of your team have already been talking about the new leadership programme around the company. I'm also worried that after the townhall meetings, some less than enthusiastic managers might even be pleased to see us fail so that they can promote their own ideas. Timing is really important.'

'We'll stagger the rollout of programmes,' Megan reported. 'From what you say, it seems important to launch quickly, even if we do not have the LPP programme fully designed yet.'

'That's going to be the only way to maintain momentum', Carolyn agreed. 'We have to ensure that people see something tangible after the townhall announcement. We'll learn from the first few programmes and adjust the design of the subsequent programmes accordingly.'

'The pace of the programme is a key factor,' she added. 'The Board wanted us to move along expeditiously when it agreed to the initiative. One director told me, "Do this fast: Markets change rapidly and often become more complex, and so do the requirements to compete. Any leadership development we do – and the resulting increase in leadership effectiveness we think we might get – must exceed that increase in complexity".' She didn't report the strict edge in the director's voice, but Megan picked up on the message.

'Here's our proposal,' she said (see Figure 10.3). In the first year, LPP would launch four initiatives:

1　'360-degree reviews' – for the TTL, directors and VP level leaders
2　The TTL Journey, preliminarily called Elevate – Greg agreed with Carolyn that change had to start at the top to support leadership development of the top team and to show the rest of the company that the TTL took this programme seriously and was walking the talk. This would encourage the rest of the organization to support the initiative and to change their behaviours as well
3　The top talent programme for VPs and Directors, preliminarily called Leap – this programme would start with two cohorts the first year, to cover the current top talent at this level. Then it would run annually to sustain the natural intake of new top talent
4　Values Day – This would roll the new leadership model out to everyone, and show that things are changing, with more emphasis on how to live the leadership model

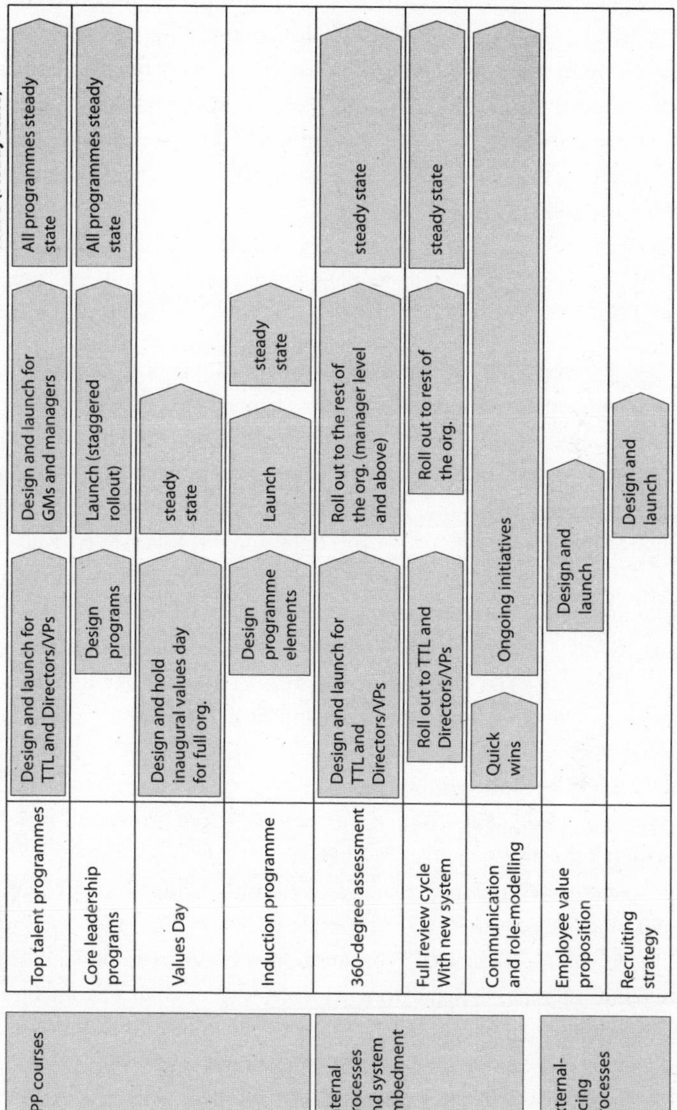

| LPP courses | Activities | Year 1 | Year 2 | Year 3 (steady state) |
|---|---|---|---|---|
| | Top talent programmes | Design and launch for TTL and Directors/VPs | Design and launch for GMs and managers | All programmes steady state |
| | Core leadership programs | Design programs | Launch (staggered rollout) | All programmes steady state |
| | Values Day | Design and hold inaugural values day for full org. | steady state | |
| | Induction programme | Design programme elements | Launch / steady state | |
| Internal processes and system embedment | 360-degree assessment | Design and launch for TTL and Directors/VPs | Roll out to the rest of the org. (manager level and above) | steady state |
| | Full review cycle With new system | Roll out to TTL and Directors/VPs | Roll out to rest of the org. | steady state |
| | Communication and role-modelling | Quick wins / Ongoing initiatives | | |
| External-facing processes | Employee value proposition | Design and launch | | |
| | Recruiting strategy | | Design and launch | |

FIGURE 10.3  LPP proposal

In addition, there will be ongoing role-modelling and communication initiatives.

'We expect steady state to include the rest of the programmes,' Megan told Carolyn, 'but we'll get to that after the successful design and launch of the first two programmes. We have to do them really well, because after that, steady state will roll out the 360-degree reviews to the whole company with the updated performance management system, promotion/consequence management decisions, compensation decisions and succession planning.'

## High-level blueprint for the Leap programme

The following week, Megan and Greg worked on the Leap programme design with her staff, going from the assessment phase – identified gaps and 'from–to' shifts – to actual needs. They identified leadership modules and initiatives they could shape to support the behavioural shift that the leadership model required. For example, to bring out the shift from performance focus to performance and development focus, they realized that they would need to include modules on identifying strengths, coaching others and conducting challenging conversations. This would not be as straight forward as simply telling people to start developing others.

After addressing each element of the model, they sat at the conference table in Megan's department staring at a long list of potential modules and topics.

'This is a lot,' Megan sighed.

'Never fear,' Greg said. 'Sometimes organizations want too much. Let's focus on the shifts that really matter.'

They prioritized topics to address in each leadership area and ensured a clear link to the leadership model.

'Keeping the participants grounded in NCL's context requires ranking some of these critical from-to shifts higher than others,' Greg warned Megan.

She agreed, 'We'll have to give more programme space to those shifts.'

Then they turned to delivery methods. Megan, with the help of her team, had prepared an evaluation, comparing online vs. in person, and self-directed vs. mandatory learning. 'Before we study the chart,' Megan said, 'Let me fill you in on a discussion my team and I had with a neuroscientist about the merit of various interventions. She gave us a list of key measures for our training programmes.'

- Ensure a risk-free environment to stimulate learning and experimentation
- Make the programme exciting and rewarding to keep participants motivated
- Stretch participants outside their comfort zones
- Make it experiential, through action learning, on the job applications, and tailored breakthrough projects that add business value
- Focus on strengths of each participant (while ensuring that all other areas meet a minimum bar)
- Include individualized coaching (360-degree reviews at the beginning, and then individual or group coaching plus mentoring). This is a great way to make the programme meet both organizational needs as well as individual needs. If there are budget constraints, peer coaching pairs can be set up instead
- Address underlying mindsets – this can be done through the choice of modules and facilitated sessions, as well as through individual reflection and coaching
- Include some degree of flexibility in how teams do their project work or online learning in between modules, or the like, to give participants some control
- Measure progress and business impact
- Align surrounding systems to support and enhance participants' behavioural shifts

'We've also reviewed different learning approaches, and mapped out the pros and cons of each one,' Megan continued. 'For example, we looked at in-person classroom training, virtual classroom training, action learning for forums, on-the-job application of new skills, extended breakthrough projects, and job rotations for fieldwork. We also looked at the pros and cons of different types of coaching and mentoring.'

Then, mustering some of the confidence she'd gained from the initial coaching session with Hans, Megan showed Greg her department's working draft of the Leap programme. He had worked on earlier versions, but he was pleased with this new working document (Figure 10.4).

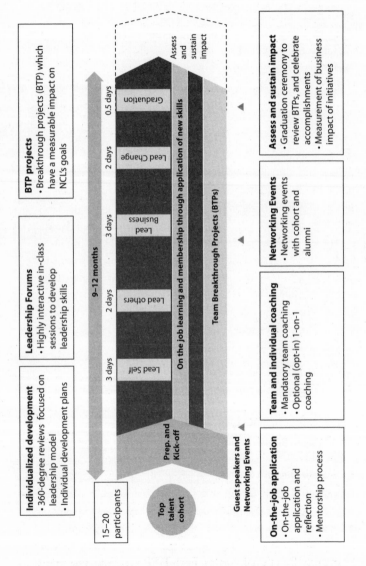

**Individualized development**
• 360-degree reviews focused on leadership model
• Individual development plans

**Leadership Forums**
• Highly interactive in-class sessions to develop leadership skills

**BTP projects**
• Breakthrough projects (BTP) which have a measurable impact on NCL's goals

15–20 participants

Top talent cohort

3 days — Lead Self
2 days — Lead others
3 days — Lead Business
2 days — Lead Change
0.5 days — Graduation

9–12 months

On the job learning and membership through application of new skills

Team Breakthrough Projects (BTPs)

Prep. and Kick-off

Assess and sustain impact

**On-the-job application**
• On-the-job application and reflection
• Mentorship process

Guest speakers and Networking Events

**Team and individual coaching**
• Mandatory team coaching
• Optional (opt-in) 1-on-1 coaching

**Networking Events**
• Networking events with cohort and alumni

**Assess and sustain impact**
• Graduation ceremony to review BTPs, and celebrate accomplishments
• Measurement of business impact of initiatives

FIGURE 10.4  NCL's Leap programme

The next day, Megan and Greg held a conference call with her LPP team, and NCL's senior HR professionals worldwide. Megan walked them through the Leap programme plan. She set up a working group from different HR offices to meet weekly to ensure that the programme content was relevant and reflected best practices. Leap had five main elements:

1 **Individualized development**

- Tailored 360-degree reviews, based on the leadership model
- Individual development plans (IDPs) including strengths, development areas, aspirations in the company, and key actions to pursue. Each participant would develop their IDPs by forum 1, and discuss them with a coach during the programme

2 **Forums**

- Lead self, based on Centred Leadership elements and focusing on helping participants increase their self-awareness and lead from a core of self-mastery
- Lead others, building on Centred Leadership elements but with a focus on interpersonal dynamics, laying the foundation to manage and lead groups of people
- Lead business, which focuses on the participant's role as a leader in the organization, and builds critical business skills (problem solving, strategy, industry dynamics)
- Lead change, focusing on setting performance and health aspiration, developing a change management plan, and implementing the change

3 **Fieldwork**

- On-the-job application of new skills, where participants applied their learnings in their day-to-day jobs, and also kept a journal to reflect on their successes and challenges
- Breakthrough projects (BTPs), which were above and beyond the day-to-day jobs of the participants, carried out in cross-functional groups. Each BTP was linked to strategic priorities for NCL and served a dual purpose of creating business value while helping participants practice new skills

4 **Coaching and mentoring**

- Individual (one-to-one) coaching at the beginning, middle, and end of the programme
- Team coaching to discuss both BTPs as well as individual learning plans and on-the-job application
- Mentors were assigned, to support the application of skills and provide feedback

5 **Inspiration events**

- Guest speakers
- Visiting best practice companies
- Social events

Many useful ideas emerged that improved the Leap programme, either adding to its benefits or avoiding potential pitfalls.

One team member suggested crowdsourcing part of the content, asking NCL's own people through the corporate intranet what they really wanted; this would add cultural and regional input.

As an impartial outsider, Greg cited best practices from other organizations and the latest thinking on leadership development topics. He focused on making NCL a learning organization.

'The ability to learn from every interaction with every stakeholder will prove crucial in the programme's success or failure,' Greg explained, 'and it's a competitive advantage.' Megan made a note to mention that edge to Carolyn.

In terms of governance, the team settled on 'three Ps', covering People, Projects and the Programme. First was what they called the 'Development Council', which would hold participants and faculty accountable for participant learning. The Council would review individual development plans of participants, conduct regular check-ins, and review follow-up 360-degree assessments and other surveys to gauge learning and development. Second was the 'Project Council', which would sign off the initial design of BTPs, conduct regular assessment on progress, provide input and coaching, and conduct the final evaluation. Third was the 'Programme Council', which would evaluate overall progress against targets, budgets and milestones, for example through regular steering committee meetings. They agreed that there could be overlap in the memberships of the different councils; what was important was the 'hats' that the members would wear as they carried out the different mandates. For example, it was important to clearly separate participant learning and project success, in order to balance the trade-offs and ensure both objectives were given sufficient focus.

## Developing the business case

After finalizing the Leap programme, and developing the required content, the team conducted a similar exercise for the other three elements that would launch in year one: the TTL journey, the 360-degree design and execution, and the inaugural Values Day. They also designed the ways NCL could help embed the change in the system, which included three main elements:

1 Crafting a change story and communication plan
2 Drawing up a list of symbolic actions and quick wins that change leaders could do to signal that the change was real
3 Defining the changes that needed to take place in the talent management system, organizational structure, delegation of authority matrix, and key processes in order to enable the new leadership behaviours

They then went on to create the business case, which included four elements. First was the target impact. They reiterated the goal of achieving top quartile OHI results with a top quartile leadership outcome, and also made estimates for what they aspired to achieve in terms of participant feedback, 360-degree assessment improvements, and business results from the BTPs. They noted that the leadership programme could pay for itself through the additional impact of the BTPs.

Second was the implementation timeline, which they structured into three horizons, covering year one, scale-up in years two to three, and then continuous development of the programme in steady state. Third was the budget. The team looked for ways to reduce costs without affecting quality, for example by building up in-house coaches, develop in-house facilitators for the top talent programmes for General Managers and Managers (they decided to continue to use external facilitators for the top talent programmes for the TTL and VPs/Directors), and to leverage alumni as faculty for selected modules in future cohorts.

Finally, the team laid out the organizational requirements to design, launch, scale, and maintain the programme. Megan was adamant that the leadership programme required a high caliber individual to lead it. She did not feel that NCL had the capabilities in-house, and she therefore included in the budget the hiring a new Chief Learning Officer, together with a small team of two people for the first year.

## Organizations don't change, people do

After Megan had finished, Carolyn sat down alone with Hans, who had begun coaching the TTL. Hans already knew the programme's rationale, content, scope, pace, and duration. He was particularly interested in its intent and its effect.

Hans was very positive. He liked the way they had taken a whole-person approach based on NCL's strengths. He also felt the programme was comprehensive.

Carolyn explained that Megan, Greg, and the LLP team were running it, but because they've taken an open approach, some of the participants are already advising and shaping the programme. Hans was delighted. He felt a democratic rather than an autocratic leadership style was exactly what NCL needed. But he advised Carolyn to consider a few other areas: communication would be critical – talking and listening widely. If someone wants to talk to the CEO, only the CEO can listen – that's part of the job, just as it's part of the CEO's job to turn up and speak to NCL employees. Role-modelling, symbolic actions, story-telling, and celebrations are all inordinately important.

Hans also discussed with Carolyn how they could use the leadership development programme to make NCL really fly. They should think ahead about how to integrate it with broader HR systems so that recruiting, performance management, promotion, succession, and compensation are all consistent, transparent, and impartial. It would be a big challenge – but the future won't wait. Organizations need to adapt and change at the right speed.

Hans questioned Carolyn about her personal involvement in the project. 'You know', she answered, 'I've been doing a lot of personal reflection the past few weeks. I realized that I'm still micromanaging people and tasks. I know being a controlling boss is an issue, but I can't risk getting bad results.'

Hans urged Carolyn to address the issue now. 'Operating with a strong results orientation and keeping the team on track are very much 'quartile 2' behaviours. To transition to quartile 1 leadership, you need to maintain these important behaviours, but supplement them with more inspirational leadership that helps others reach their full potential.'

'I want to do that, and I know that intellectually, but not emotionally, not yet,' Carolyn admitted. 'I want to lead through values and vision, and I really want to move NCL up to the top leadership and health quartile.'

'Among other things,' said Hans, 'that requires a renewed personal effort from you.' They discussed her goals, and agreed that Hans would work with her on this particular personal transformation programme.

After their conversation, Carolyn noticed an email with a report from Megan. Her first impulse was to double-check Megan's work. But she stopped herself. She needed to trust Megan and bring out the best in her. And she couldn't do that by micromanaging.

## Summary

At this stage in the journey, an organization should have designed the overall blueprint and developed the content of the leadership development journey by group, defined target participants and timing for cohort rollout, designed the system integration elements (change story, symbolic actions, reinforcing mechanisms), and signed off the business case (including target impact, work plan, budget, and organizational requirements to deliver the programme).

| Diagnose What is the gap to where you want to go? | Design & Develop What do you need to get from here to there? | Deliver How should you move to action? | Drive Impact How do you keep moving forward? |
|---|---|---|---|

- ☑ Leadership model that is tightly linked to the strategy, and aligned with the top team
- ☑ Critical 3–5 'from-to' shifts (behaviours, skills, mindsets) that the leadership program will bring about
- ☑ Quantification of the leadership gap at each level of the organization
- ☑ Assessment of current leadership development initiatives and quality of system embedment mechanisms

- ☑ Design of leadership development journey by group, including development of all content
- ☑ Definition of target participants (who, how much, when) and selection of first cohorts
- ☑ Design of reinforcing mechanisms (change story, symbolic actions, system changes)
- ☑ Signed-off business case (including target impact, work plan, budget, and organizational requirements to deliver the program)

The next stage in the journey delivers the programme across all phases (to reach steady state), implements system embedment elements, and implements governance and measurement of the programme at multiple levels.

# II

# Delivering the Leadership Peak Programme

*Andrew St George, Claudio Feser, Michael Rennie,*
*Nicolai Chen Nielsen*

The TTL journey | Shifting their icebergs | Tom leaps forward | The
broader organization | Behind the scenes

NCL now stood at the start of an intensive leadership development effort.
The Board had clearly communicated the reason for the initiative, and
Carolyn had set out to achieve the desired impact. Carolyn, Megan and
the TTL now had to build and maintain a wide range of support companywide as they launched the first wave of the programme, starting with
Elevate (for the TTL), Leap (for VP/Director top talents), the 360-degree
reviews, and the inaugural Values Day. Thereafter the programme would
scale in years two and three, only increasing the complexity.

Carolyn knew the TTL had to embrace the programme enthusi-
astically and unanimously. Yet she also knew she had to leave room
for dissent, in case some colleagues had different views, and that she
should listen carefully to any clash of values. Above all, Carolyn wanted
change to start at the top. The TTL executives needed to become role-
models of the desired leadership behaviours in their everyday work
and in the context of the Leap programme.

She encouraged them to act as programme faculty, project sponsors, mentors, or coaches. She told Wayne, Peter, Fernando, Bruce, and
Alice what Megan and Greg already knew: she wanted all of the TTL
members to travel personal leadership journeys so they experienced
leadership growth.

Megan had asked Carolyn to arrange for the TTL coaching sessions
with Hans. He saw great potential for Carolyn, for the top team as a
whole, and for NCL in general. Before the launch, he made time to
sit down with Bruce, Alice, Wayne, Peter, and Fernando. He'd already
worked with Megan and Carolyn.

Carolyn knew that each person had numerous strengths, but also areas hindering their full potential as leaders. Bruce was younger than the other TTL members, and he needed to have standing with them as her likely successor, and elevate his thinking to a more company-wide, strategic level. Carolyn had started mentoring Bruce, as he was a potential successor, and she vowed to continue helping Bruce develop as much as she could.

Alice was too quiet to have value in TTL team meetings. She liked Carolyn's work, but she wondered why her new Strategy chief didn't assert herself. If Alice was just a behind-the-scenes strategist and a public yes-woman she wasn't going to be nearly as useful as her credentials, and Carolyn was worried.

Peter was cautious regarding the programme, not only because it was eating into the budget, but also because of his impending retirement. He didn't see a need for personal change, yet he had not yet started any form of succession planning. Carolyn knew that Peter would likely not think about potential successors without an explicit push, and she wondered whether Hans could help re-frame the topic of succession in terms of Peter leaving a legacy.

Wayne was perhaps the most worrying. He was driving himself hard, and constantly on planes. Carolyn knew that this was not sustainable. She believed that Wayne probably knew this as well, yet he was driven by underlying fears of failure – he believed that he *had* to work this hard in order to be successful. Until he could shift this mindset – and understand that delegation could actually enhance the performance of his whole department – he would not change his behaviours. Carolyn made a note to follow Wayne's development more closely, and help in any way she could.

Fernando was a tricky one. His previous results spoke for themselves, and he was extremely confident in his abilities. As such, he doubted that his colleagues or the LPP could teach him anything. While he did, in fact, have extraordinary talent, his reluctance to learn new things was holding him back. Carolyn hoped that Hans could help Fernando to seek more diversity of opinion and be more willing to try new things, which she believed could help him push his creativity and designs to the next level.

## *The TTL journey*

Carolyn and Megan launched the LPP with a TTL workshop so the members could define their aspirations jointly and decide how to approach their top team transformation. To prepare for the workshop, Greg conducted one-on-one interviews with each executive to understand the dynamics of the TTL in more depth. He also ran a top team effectiveness (TTE) survey, to establish a baseline.

After Hans' coaching, Carolyn was conscious of not imposing a programme on the TTL, but rather co-creating it with them. Previously, she would have developed a programme with Hans, listing a certain number of workshops for the TTL, and then presented it to them, top-down. However, Hans made it clear that buy-in through co-creation was critical to spur the TTL to embrace the LPP fully. Now curious, she wanted to see if their solution was better than hers.

Greg started the workshop:'The LPP touches on leadership development at every organizational level plus individual development. To affect the whole company, focusing on creating the desired behaviours at scale really matters. Supplementing it with individual development plans and coaching is also critical – but not sufficient. We also need include team effectiveness. Teams are a critical but often neglected element in scaling up leadership effectiveness. Top teams seldom function as well as they should, and top team effectiveness in developing organizational and individual leadership competencies is critical to NCL's overall leadership.'

The TTL discussed the one-tone feedback that Greg had gathered (anonymously) and also reviewed the results of the TTE survey. The survey looked at four main dimensions: Alignment, Execution, Renewal, and Composition, although the team only focused on the first 3 dimensions – see Figure 11.1.

Then Greg got to use one of his favourite mantras: 'It takes more than a workshop to build a top team. We have gathered the data from the top team effectiveness survey, and today we will start discussing the results. The next step is doing something about those results, so finally we will agree on actions that will improve our effectiveness.'

At the end of the workshop, The TTL agreed to discuss the leadership development programme at the weekly TTL meetings, and to hold follow-up workshops with Greg every two months for a year. Greg's job was to create a safe environment, away from work, and to set up their journey as a team. He would guide them in sharing feedback and helping each other grow. They planned a follow-up TTE survey in six months.

| Alignment | Shared understanding of business | • Shared assumptions regarding the **organization's context**<br>• Alignment on **strategy** and **performance goals**<br>• Understanding **operational implications** of targets |
| | Intersection of personal beliefs | • Shared beliefs on the top team's **purpose**<br>• Shared core of **professional values** governing team behaviour<br>• Balance between **individual and collective** interests |
| Execution | Effective team configuration | • Effective **structure** and **processes** – rights and responsibilities<br>• **Right composition** – mix/level of skills and capabilities<br>• Focus of the top team's **time** and incentives to **work together** |
| | High-quality interaction | • Mutual **respect, understanding** and **trust**<br>• Open communication, **challenge** and **no 'groupthink'**<br>• Constructive **conflict management** and resolution |
| Renewal | Sustainability | • Investment in maintaining **team motivation** and **energy**<br>• **Balance of team attention** across different time horizons<br>• Effective **succession planning** |
| | Adaptability | • **Awareness** of the organization and its wider context<br>• **Openness** to change and learning<br>• **Communication** with organization and external stakeholders |

FIGURE 11.1 Key elements that top teams need to address together

## Shifting their icebergs

As a result of the TTE exercise, the top team members also embarked on a personal development programme. They agreed to several one-on-one coaching sessions with Hans over a period of six months to discover their 'iceberg' – their behaviours, their underlying mindsets, and their deepest assumptions about the world, and shift core beliefs that were holding them back. For some, this change was painful, for others it was joyful, and for all it was challenging. Over time, however, the TTL members found their personal journeys very satisfying.

Growing into his role as COO, Bruce took a broader view of NCL and developed a more personal sense of himself as a leader. Working with Carolyn and Hans, he learned the value of being well-rounded as a leader. His broader perspective made him more effective, not just in overseeing shop and factory operations, but company-wide.

Alice found her footing as an NCL leader. She built her knowledge of the company, made friends, came to enjoy Shanghai, and finally made herself more at home, renting an apartment with a view of Pudong. As her confidence grew, she became a stronger advocate for strategic thinking. When she insisted that the LPP needed a stronger mentoring component, the TTL concurred. Her greater candour made her and Carolyn closer and more productive, and Alice continued to push to make the LPP even more relevant as an enabler of the overall strategy.

Wayne became a more effective leader of and mentor to his regional managers, viewing them with more respect, giving them more authority, and nurturing instead of brow-beating them. Over the course of a year, he found he could maintain great sales — thanks to his strengthened managers — while traveling only two weeks a month, not weekly. He also benefited from the change at home, where he felt much more present and content.

Peter identified a quartet of promising, high-level finance managers in their 40s and 50s and began mentoring them personally. Except for Harish Menon, the Asian regional finance manager, who was based in Shanghai, Peter rotated them in and out of the headquarters. Soon he had trusted VPs in each NCL continental finance office. As he developed warmer relationships with these protégés, his greater openness ignited friendships with his other colleagues. Peter still ran the numbers, but now he rarely hid behind them. As his 67th birthday came and went, he still didn't discuss retirement — but he admitted that he looked forward to one day 'slowing down'.

With Hans' coaching, Fernando sought to use his skills to unite different parts of the company and break down silos. Under his leadership, he brought together Infinity's and NCL's designers, and created a strong, unified team spirit. Furthermore, for the first time in many years, Fernando was able to admit if he did not have the answer. He became more comfortable seeking out different opinions for new design and, as a result, the popularity of the new designs soared.

As Carolyn gave Megan more independence, she embraced it gladly. Megan's frustrations dwindled, and Hans helped her with the stress of her extra leadership duties. And as she came into her own as CHRO, she mentored the top talents in her team to expand their leadership reach. While she found NCL's mission increasingly fulfilling, Megan also took on helping high-potential women throughout the company achieve professional growth through the LPP.

# Tom Leaps forward

Participants for the first cohort of the Leap programme were selected based on the existing performance management system, as the 360-degree review had not yet been implemented for a full cycle. One of them, Tom Zhang, had never participated in leadership development, but he wanted to. He had wondered if he would ever get such training at NCL and had even looked at other corporations with better leadership development prospects. He stopped looking around when he saw the posters about Leap and attended an informative townhall. The presentation implied that his future progress at NCL depended on becoming a better leader.

When his boss, Harish Menon, told him he'd been selected for the programme's first cohort, he readily joined. He knew from reading management literature that leadership was vital and could be learned. In his view he was en route to becoming a better NCL leader.

## Creating his Individual Development Plan

Three weeks before the programme's kick-off, Tom received a 360-degree survey tailored to the behaviours in NCL's leadership model. Tom sent the survey to his boss, supervisors, peers, and team members. He also filled it out himself. This was the first time he'd ever done a comprehensive 360-degree review.

The kick-off set out the journey ahead and allowed the participants to meet each other over a half day and lunch. A week later the Leap participants started their full curriculum and met their leadership coaches. Tom was assigned to Eve Bullard, an experienced coach originally from Kenya, but who had been in Shanghai for the past eight years. Tom completed his Individual Development Plan (IDP) with Eve, who explained that it would guide his personal journey. The plan included his aspirations, strengths, weaknesses and development areas, as measured by the 360-degree review. The 360-degree review did not directly capture his personal goals, which emerged during his planning discussions with Eve. Together they identified the 'One Big Thing' that Tom would work on over the coming four months.

As Eve linked their coaching sessions to NCL's leadership model, Tom saw how the whole effort was integrated. The leadership development work was tailored to cohort groups and to individuals. As Eve explained, the programme was deliberately long-term, coherent, and integrated. It met the leadership needs of the organization and it met his individual needs (as defined through one-on-one coaching at the beginning, middle, and end of the programme). Tom wanted to explore how to become more cheerful and confident, and how to bring more of himself to his work without living only for the numbers. Peter, Harish, and now Eve all stressed that balance to him.

During the programme, Tom used his IDP to guide his personal development plan, apart from the cohort-level programme. With some reticence, he told his finance team about his personal development aspirations, and asked them for feedback. This was uncomfortable for Tom and his direct reports; in fact, the first session was nearly disastrous. After consulting with Eve, Tom was more careful to create a risk-free environment where staffers felt free to speak their minds. Tom kept a journal of his progress and updated his IDP after each meeting with Eve, who helped him select new focus areas in his quest for personal leadership growth.

## Engaging during the forums

The programme's four main forums spanned ten days in total. Each forum was held off-site, away from the NCL offices, to give the participants an opportunity to reflect more deeply and focus on learning. The first forum was called 'lead self' and lasted three days.

Tom and his fellow participants were star struck when the CEO herself, Carolyn Randolph, walked on stage to introduce the first module about how to live the new leadership model more fully. They were energized to hear her speak so warmly about her belief in NCL's future leaders – meaning them.

Tom found the next three days fascinating and engaging. The programme started with a module addressing personal meaning. It went on to discuss strategies for dealing with triggers and managing personal energy. Tom worked with Eve on how to actualize the next module: building a support network. Finally, the forum pushed the cohort to seek deeper engagement at work and at home. The programme focused consistently on how to embody NCL's leadership model.

The forum was different from anything Tom had experienced before, with no classroom presentations or formal lectures. The laid-back atmosphere gave the participants space to think about their authentic identities. It began a process of personal change in Tom.

The remaining forums carried the thread of the first. Each one focused on values; each provided space to reflect, practical tools; and each helped every participant with 'action plans' to become a more well-rounded leader. Experienced facilitators from the company and its consulting network led the sessions. NCL brought in subject matter experts for specific modules. To Tom's surprise, at least one member of the TTL facilitated a module or two at every forum to show the C-level's commitment to the programme. He especially enjoyed Peter Cody's session.

In the 'Lead Others' forum Tom learned some practical interpersonal tools, like how to coach others in a strength-based way and how to create and lead high-performing teams. He role-played coaching situations with Eve. He admired her ability to portray any role convincingly and to guide him to respond correctly. Practising with Eve touched on Leap's core elements of alignment, execution, and renewal, and the facilitators encouraged the participants to use their new tools with their work teams.

During the third forum, 'Lead Business', the focus shifted to more technical skills, linked to the NCL's core strategic themes: customer centricity, innovation, and speed to market. Discussing these topics in a cross-functional setting was extremely powerful. Many of the participants hadn't known each other before Leap, though they all held senior positions. Tom made friends right across NCL.

This forum marked the first time NCL had taken a truly cross-functional approach to problem solving on critical business topics. As a result, the company found new and better ways to serve its customers and meet its business goals. For instance, in the innovation module, Tom's group designed a new process that could radically enhance shop-level customer-centricity by merging and activating customer data from the newsletters, website, and checkout desk.

The last forum, 'Leading Change', brought everything together. After reviewing the overall OHI results for NCL, the participants focused on the subset of results from their specific organizations to make the work relevant and actionable. Each person spent time reflecting on his or her role as a change leader, and learning how to become more effective. Afterwards, Tom felt confident that he could lead his organization towards better performance and health, working from a position of personal mastery and self-awareness while using NCL's values to bring out the best in others.

## The fieldwork and 'breakthrough projects'

In between the forums, Tom carried out two types of fieldwork. First, he was responsible for applying his new skills on the job and practising the 'One Big Thing' he wanted to change. As a result of the 360-degree review, his self-reflection, and discussions with Eve, he targeted becoming a better listener. Working with Eve, he had identified the underlying mindset that made him a poor listener – Tom thought that Mr. Menon, his boss, wanted him to deliver everything quickly, which led him to believe that many tasks were more urgent than they were. As a result, Tom interrupted people or rushed to cover new topics without engaging his employees. To work on his 'One Big Thing', Tom asked his team members to tell him – risk free – if he failed to take time to listen to them. He kept a journal about how well various methods worked and discussed it with Eve. An app on his phone sent regular triggers to remind him of his IDP goals.

Tom's second level of fieldwork involved BTPs carried out in cross-functional groups. The first cohort ran four BTPs, beyond their daily jobs. Their work on strategic issues had a dual purpose: to allow participants to work in groups and practise their new leadership skills, and to push NCL's business agenda forward with tangible results.

Tom's project focused on **improving customer experience**. Given such a broad mandate, the Leap team focused on call-centre operations. They mapped customer touchpoints and designed and implemented improvements, including coaching the call-centre staff. They piloted measurements and presented the data and analysis to the Project Council both mid-way through the programme and at the end.

The results were clear: they had increased first-time caller resolution from 60 per cent to 80 per cent in the pilot areas, reduced time to resolution by 30 per cent, and cut absenteeism in the pilot team by 50 per cent compared to non-pilot areas – likely due to the increased training and more efficient work routines. Furthermore, the team worked through numerous team dynamics issues with call-centre staffers, including coaching, conflict resolution, and leading among peers.

By the end of the programme, the Project Council approved the funding for implementation – this included hiring a full time 'customer experience' team, outfitting each store with new technology, and conducting customer experience training for all front-line colleagues. The team estimated that increased customer satisfaction had led to a 2 per cent increase in sales in the five pilot locations, which for NCL as a whole could potentially mean up to $100 million increase in revenue, on the current base of just over $6 billion. The executive team was clearly very excited about this project.

The first Leap cohort had three other BTPs. The first one focused on **understanding and reaching millennials** through new design offerings. In the past few years, NCL had faced a challenge in reaching younger generations. The Leap team felt they had 'cracked' a big part of the problem by conducting in-depth interviews, focus groups, and research on millennials, and by offering exciting products from the Infinity Fashionista line. The team identified a number of trends and 'white spaces' in the market where NCL could grab a bigger share of the millennials' buying power. The team had estimated that each 5 per cent of the millennials market that NCL could win (in the appropriate geographies), would lead to an increase in revenue of ~1.5 per cent. This was clearly a very attractive opportunity, and the team would continue its work on this project for the next three months to wrap up the launch.

The **process excellence project** had identified the five key processes that really mattered for NCL, mapped each one in detail, identified the sticking points, designed improvements, and piloted each one in three different locations. The results had been extremely encouraging, with double digit increases in efficiency measured across the board. The team encountered some internal resistance to the change, and Carolyn or Bruce had to step in a few times, but the team members were confident that the results would speak for themselves in the future. The Project Council agreed that under the leadership of the members of the existing 'Operations Improvement' team, NCL would roll out the improvement initiatives internally over the next six months. The team estimated that the primary benefit of the improvement initiatives would be to free up the resources of a combined 30 full time colleagues, whom NCL could deploy elsewhere. In addition, they expected a marginal increase the overall quality of the output of the processes.

Finally, the South America market entry team had faced more challenges with its business case. Competition was intense, featuring a number of dominant local players, and successful market entry would require a significant marketing budget. In addition, NCL did not have the required expertise in-house, and it seemed risky to enter the market. The executive team decided to disband this project, and re-visit it in 12 months' time. The time window would to allow the Infinity Fashionista line to make some headway in South America.

## Other programme elements

Tom greatly enjoyed his coaching sessions with Eve, the first time he ever received proper 'executive' coaching. She helped him a great deal. Tom also benefitted from time spent with his mentor and boss, Harish, who was already passing along Peter Cody's legacy – though Peter remained very much in action.

This personal attention from Harish, who had wisdom and a wider view, was a revelation to Tom. Harish also helped Tom's BTP team navigate the organization and opened doors to other senior colleagues where needed. Some teams also opted to establish regular 'peer coaching' for participants to meet regularly to discuss their IDPs and personal development. Tom asked Harish if he also could have phone or Skype coaching sessions with Eve a couple of times a year to follow up.

In addition, participants had access to live webinars with experts on various topics, as well as digital courses on the latest trends, such as analytics, digitization, automation, and Virtual Reality. The courses were mobile enabled, and delivered in bite-sized pieces, much to the delight of participants. Some courses were mandatory and some were optional, although Tom completed the vast majority.

Tom was moved by the Leap programme's occasional 'inspirational events', such as a visit to a best-in-class leadership academy, where the participants saw a mature learning organization in action. NCL also brought in a renowned leadership guru to speak at the Leading Business forum.

A few weeks after the last forum, Carolyn Randolph reappeared to host the first graduation ceremony, designed to consolidate the learning and celebrate the participants' journey. Thinking back on his coaching, team effectiveness work, mentoring, and the meaningful NCL values he had absorbed, Tom felt extremely grateful. He knew he'd made huge strides in becoming the leader he wanted to be. As he walked out of graduation, Harish took him aside. 'You've made great progress, Tom,' his mentor said. 'And I'm proud of you. If you put all you've learned into practice as well as Peter and I think you will, you'll become my Assistant VP in Asian Finance by the end of the year. How does that sound?'

## The broader organization

Over the following months, the LPP became more widely known and valued throughout NCL. Yet, Carolyn heard from some sceptics, and she worried that she might not be able to take the whole company, all 30,000 staff members, with her on this journey. But, she had a great tool in mind.

The TTL's initial planning had included a company-wide Values Day. Carolyn thought a lot about how to make the most of it – to give it a bit of theatre, to draw more attention. She wanted to celebrate the LPP programme and inspire everyone to think about and embrace NCL's values.

Megan had always appreciated organizations that had a strong set of values, which were celebrated regularly. She wanted Values Day to accomplish that. Across 50 countries, the organization came together in regional gatherings linked online to celebrate NCL values. She asked each business unit to adopt a values project to carry out during that day.

The TTL further wove the leadership model into the fabric of NCL in the form of Performance Management – assessing the implementation of the leadership model. The LPP trained assessors and rolled out a new performance management programme. Everyone in the company – except for those in the separate programme for stores, warehouses, and factories – undertook an initial baseline 360-degree review and then, a year later, took a second 360-degree review to assess how well they learned the new leadership model and acted on feedback.

In addition, Bruce had led the creation of an NCL App, which was the one-stop shop for all things related to the organization. It started with simple communication updates, but later expanded to include discussion forums, live polls, and competitions. Bruce was also working with Megan to create or curate learning modules linked to the new leadership behaviours, which would be accessible to all employees.

## Behind the scenes

Carolyn was secretly proud of what she and Megan's LPP team had achieved. She was beginning to see a shift in mindsets and perspectives, which, in turn, produced different behaviours at work. She visited Megan and the small LPP team toward the end of the initial nine months of the programme, right after the first graduation ceremony. She was keen to know what progress Megan could see. Throughout the initiatives, Megan had tracked the KPIs, participant feedback, and more. She spoke to participants and their managers about the difference they saw in those who participated.

Carolyn noticed that the staff's language had changed; now she was hearing of role-modelling and symbolic actions, of storytelling and theatre. The performance edge showed financially that a happier NCL (according to its OHI scores) was also a more profitable NCL.

At the end of the LPP team meeting, Carolyn asked Megan to stay for a cup of coffee. They reflected on the changes that had happened since the TTL's decision to run a leadership development programme. Now, the whole company shared a language of values and leadership, as seen in the constant communication about flourishing leadership changes. Bright posters conveyed new words and phrases in all corners of the company, from boardroom to warehouse, from design atelier to factory floor.

On their way into the building's courtyard, Megan and Carolyn overheard a group of employees (whom they now called 'colleagues' or 'partners') talking in the hallway near the learning area. 'We can really feel the change. I'm excited for this to reach me as well'. Megan smiled: Successful launch; inaugural Values Day; New HR systems in use. But Carolyn also knew that pace was critical. She and Megan needed to reach the rest of the organization, and quickly, to boost leadership and performance and to change the company forever. There were big plans for the following year, to launch the programmes for the GMs and Managers and roll out almost 40 cohorts as part of the initial push to reach all top talent.

## Summary

At this stage in the journey, an organization should have delivered the leadership programme across all cohorts, embedded the desired changes in the broader organization, and implemented the governance and impact tracking at various levels.

| Diagnose What is the gap to where you want to go? | Design & Develop What do you need to get from here to there? | Deliver How should you move to action? | Drive Impact How do you keep moving forward? |
|---|---|---|---|
| ☑ Leadership model that is tightly linked to the strategy, and aligned with the top team<br><br>☑ Critical 3–5 'from-to' shifts (behaviours, skills, mindsets) that the leadership program will bring about<br><br>☑ Quantification of the leadership gap at each level of the organization<br><br>☑ Assessment of current leadership development initiatives and quality of system embedment mechanisms | ☑ Design of leadership development journey by group, including development of all content<br><br>☑ Definition of target participants (who, how much, when) and selection of first cohorts<br><br>☑ Design of reinforcing mechanisms (change story, symbolic actions, system changes)<br><br>☑ Signed-off business case (including target impact, work plan, budget, and organizational requirements to deliver the program) | ☑ Delivery of program across all cohorts, using modern adult learning principles (field, forum, and coaching)<br><br>☑ Implementation of system embedment (communication, role modelling, reinforcing mechanisms, including embedding leadership model into all talent processes)<br><br>☑ Governance and measurement of program at multiple levels | |

The next stage in the journey is about developing the programme, which includes continuous impact monitoring and reinforcement of critical behavioural changes during steady state, creating a clear plan for graduates (yearly refresh, retention policies etc.), and regularly re-assessing the organizational leadership requirements given the context.

# 12

# Driving impact

*Andrew St George, Claudio Feser, Michael Rennie,
Nicolai Chen Nielsen*

The townhall: Part II | Taking stock | Carolyn
reflects | Upwards and onwards | Bedtime story | Summary

## *The Townhall: Part II*

Three years had passed since the launch of the LPP. All programmes
were now up and running, there was a close knit alumni community,
and the new 360-degree review and performance management systems had been rolled out. In addition, Values Day was quickly becoming a part of the fabric of NCL.

Carolyn was about to address the townhall meeting for the European Office. She made her way to the stage and welcomed everyone.
Before the LPP, she would have done most of the talking, but things
were different now. Now she was intent on 'bringing out the best' in
her fellow executives, and called on each member to co-present with
her. Having them speak about their areas at the townhall helped her
project the image she wanted to demonstrate, the sense of an engaged
team in meaningful action.

The new townhalls – now quarterly – were part of a TTL communication initiative. Each meeting was filmed and made available on the
corporate intranet, so all colleagues could follow the latest company
news. Carolyn hoped that colleagues could feel in this latest townhall
that the TTL was more aligned than ever. Certainly they spoke more
cohesively, and there seemed to be a stronger chemistry among them.
Carolyn looked around and felt that things were very different from
when she and Megan had started this journey.

# *Taking stock*

After the townhall, Megan was due to discuss the LPP's progress with Carolyn over coffee. Before the LPP, Megan had dreaded the update meetings with Carolyn, since they typically ended up as 'cross-examinations' where Carolyn would focus more on problems rather than the bigger picture. It had felt as if Megan were executing tasks for Carolyn. Now, however, Megan had felt more freedom to carry out her vision for the initiatives she was running, with Carolyn coaching and supporting her along the way.

Megan decided to include Greg in the discussion, and together they briefed Carolyn on the progress of the LPP, which was now running in steady state.

Megan and Greg started to recap the measurements that had come out of each cohort. Greg had drawn up the findings. Carolyn listened as he explained: 'Well, first of all, participant feedback has been very positive. The programmes averaged more than 6.4 out of 7 in terms of "value compared to the time spent", more than 6.6 out of 7 in terms of overall effectiveness, and had an Net Promoter Score (NPS) of 81, which is extremely high.' Greg continued by breaking the scores down by programme, and by programme element.

Megan continued. 'Here is the anonymous feedback,' she said. 'Have a look.'

Carolyn read:

> This programme has profoundly changed my life. It goes way beyond what I have been exposed to before, and the focus on not only the hard skills of leadership, but also on the softer, personal side has led me to learn many new things about myself and made me happier and more effective both at work and at home.

A second participant wrote:

> This programme reinforces my belief in the future success of NCL, and is a key reason why I am so happy at the company.

And a third:

> This is the best programme I have done for ages; it brings to my work the same kind of meaning that I have in my faith community. I can see a purpose and direction here.

Carolyn smiled.

Megan continued, with a presentation of the 360-degree review scores. 'The average scores across the company increased from 3.8 to 4.4 during the last three years, a 15 per cent jump, implying that employees in the organization are living the NCL leadership model much fully than at the beginning of the programme.' Megan reported that she'd spent a lot of time speaking with employees, and the vast majority noticed a clear, positive shift in the behaviour of their colleagues in line with the leadership model, and they felt that their effectiveness had increased as a result of it. Carolyn was impressed by the large degree of change. But she wondered if it meant that NCL executives were poor leaders before the programme? Either way, the programme and the individual 360-degree review had shed light on some important truths about NCL that – fortunately – they had been able to act on.

Finally, there was the all-important business impact. Attributing business results to a particular leadership development intervention would always be challenging. The OHI offered a way to do this indirectly. NCL had started the programme in the second quartile, both overall and in terms of the leadership outcome. The organization re-ran the OHI yearly, and the results were largely positive. NCL had increased its score an average of 4 percentage points each year, from 67 to 79 overall, and had achieved a top quartile score overall and for the leadership outcome at the end of year two. This was a strong improvement, but there was still room to grow. The next aspiration: to break into the top decile on both dimensions.

In terms of the BTPs, they had delivered concrete value during the past three years. Over two-thirds of the projects across cohorts had gotten the green light for implementation, and the projects from first cohorts had now been fully implemented. Megan estimated that by year three, the projects did indeed pay back the cost of the LPP each year, which was one of the stated goals of the programme.

Going forward, Megan resolved to measure a few additional metrics, besides the ones discussed so far. For example, she wanted to look into the churn rates of graduates vs. their peers, and at NCL's ranking in the annual 'top employers to work for' magazine rankings. Megan had a dream of making it into the top 10.

'What about LPP alumni,' Carolyn asked. 'How has our engagement with them been?'

'I've held individual career discussions with each programme participant to ensure that NCL can make the best use of their talents and take their aspirations into account,' Megan responded. 'In addition, the yearly one-day 'boosters' that we agreed to do have been a great success. The alumni love spending a day with their cohorts, while reinforcing the programme content. We are also continuing to use the programme's alumni (across all levels) as change agents in the organization, and as programme faculty.'

## Carolyn reflects

After the meeting, Carolyn thought about the journeys of each member of the TTL. It became clear that while the TTL had become more effective, not everyone had moved at the same pace. Hans thought this was entirely natural; individuals change, not organizations. It would take time, as Carolyn knew from her own experience.

She then thought about her own journey. She had learned to manage less, delegate more, and trust that others would share her vision. Working with Hans, she had systematically identified her limiting beliefs and begun to shift them. For example, she openly asked other TTL members for feedback. She also felt more confident when addressing the NCL Board, even when the Board disagreed with her recommendations. She now took dissent as a means of learning and did not assume that she – or others – were automatically right or wrong.

She still felt that NCL needed more organization-wide direction. It was critical to continuously link the LPP to the strategic objectives of the company. 'Design the programme with overall organizational objectives in mind,' she was thinking, echoing Hans' words, 'and the programme will enhance performance.'

Individual changes were at the heart of this, aggregated across the whole company. Not everyone changed, but the measurements showed that many did; those who did not would either move on, or realize the need for change, or even – as Carolyn had found – improve the LPP itself by adding a plural voice that was being heard for the first time at NCL. It all came down to people, people like me, she thought. And people like me working together in an organization.

Carolyn reflected on this positive tension of organizational direction and individual change. At the end of the day, this was about people, about all the moments that influence how people think and behave, in a given situation. The sum of how colleagues behave drives the leadership effectiveness of the company, and its overall performance. It seemed so simple, she thought.

## Upwards and onwards

Carolyn's meetings with Hans were becoming less frequent, but she still found it beneficial to speak with him every once in a while. Now that the LPP was in steady state, Carolyn was eager to discuss the next horizon for the programme and for herself. She arranged to meet him for a late lunch on a Friday.

Hans was impressed with the way it was going. But Carolyn had concerns.

'I'm concerned about what's next,' she said. 'The market around is changing quite rapidly, and I don't know if my colleagues are equipped to deal with these changes … I'm not sure if I am either.'

Hans had gone through many leadership programmes before, and he knew that three years was only the beginning of an ongoing journey. 'The complexity around us is increasing,' he said. 'And it will continue to do so in the future. As a result, organizations must evolve. NCL cannot stand still, and neither can the LPP.'

They discussed the next horizon for the LPP. While the strategy was largely the same as when the programme launched, Hans stressed that the programmes had not yet covered all the behaviours in the leadership model. It was important to tweak the LPP's various programmes (top talent programmes, the one-day programme for all employees, Values Day) each year to ensure all 'from-tos' were addressed, as well as the communication and role-modelling initiatives. 'In a further two to three years,' Hans said, 'the LPP will have addressed all 15 behaviours in the NCL Leadership model, and the culture will truly be transformed.' Carolyn nodded. She knew that the ultimate measure of success would be a transformation of the organizational culture, with the leadership behaviours becoming part of NCL's DNA.

They also discussed the skills needed to manage an increasingly complex and volatile operating environment. Carolyn was keen to continue the Centred Leadership elements in the programme to build adaptability, but also ramp up the content around problem solving and design thinking. Hans agreed, and suggested that Carolyn also consider 'raising the digital quotient' of the company, as a cross-cutting theme.

'The LPP must continue to evolve,' Hans concluded. 'An organization that is able to institutionalize the ability to continuously identify and develop the capabilities required to succeed becomes a learning organization. NCL is not there yet, but it is on its way.'

## Bedtime story

Over the following weekend, Carolyn reflected on the programme. She judged it to be a success, not the least because she herself had undergone a personal transformation. It was strange to think about who she had been a year ago, let alone three years go. She felt she was a different person now, wiser and calmer.

That weekend, Carolyn read a bedtime story to her grandchildren, *The Wonderful Wizard of Oz*. She also loved this story as a child, and enjoyed reading it again. One passage, in particular, from Glinda the Good Witch, struck her. It helped her make sense of the past three years that she had just spent implementing the new strategy, working on the leadership programme, and progressing on her own leadership journey: 'You've always had the power my dear, you just had to learn it for yourself.'

## Summary

At this stage in the journey, an organization's leadership development efforts have been rolled out and are likely running in steady state. Programmes' impacts are continuously monitored, and the aspired behavioural changes continue to be embedded in the broader organizational system, so they become part of the culture. In addition, alumni are continuously engaged and their career progression is managed carefully.

However, the programmes do not stand still. They must be reassessed regularly, to ensure that they are delivering the leadership capabilities and behaviours across the organization that are required to execute the strategy. As such, the 4Ds become iterative, and continuously evolve to stay relevant in a changing environment.

| Diagnose — What is the gap to where you want to go? | Design & Develop — What do you need to get from here to there? | Deliver — How should you move to action? | Drive Impact — How do you keep moving forward? |
|---|---|---|---|
| ☑ Leadership model that is tightly linked to the strategy, and aligned with the top team | ☑ Design of leadership development journey by group, including development of all content | ☑ Delivery of program across all cohorts, using modern adult learning principles (field, forum, and coaching) | ☑ Continuous impact monitoring and reinforcement of critical behavioural changes |
| ☑ Critical 3–5 'from-to' shifts (behaviours, skills, mindsets) that the leadership program will bring about | ☑ Definition of target participants (who, how much, when) and selection of first cohorts | ☑ Implementation of system embedment (communication, role modelling, reinforcing mechanisms, including embedding leadership model into all talent processes) | ☑ Clear plan for graduates (yearly refresh, retention policies etc.). |
| ☑ Quantification of the leadership gap at each level of the organization | ☑ Design of reinforcing mechanisms (change story, symbolic actions, system changes) | ☑ Governance and measurement of program at multiple levels | ☑ Re-assessment of organizational leadership requirements given the context, and decision on next leadership development focus areas |
| ☑ Assessment of current leadership development initiatives and quality of system embedment mechanisms | ☑ Signed-off business case (including target impact, work plan, budget, and organizational requirements to deliver the program) | | |

# PART 3
# Frequently Asked Questions

# 13
# FAQs on leadership development

*Cornelius Chang, Faridun Dotiwala, Florian Pollner*

**Q1 How should I prioritize my leadership development spend with a limited budget? For example, broad and shallow or selective and deep?**

The short answer is that you need a bit of both, and it depends on context. But if we had to choose, we would incline toward a top-down approach – focused on what we call *pivotal influencers* – that is selective and deep. This is simply because leadership includes role-modelling, and pivotal influencers have a disproportionate influence on the behaviours of others in the organization, due to their role, a trusted relationship, or character. Pivotal influencers role-model the behaviour they want to encourage in others and the behaviour trickles down. The top 100 (N, N-1, N-2 and pivotal influencers) can reach 100,000. Coupled with a selective leadership development intervention should be a tailored leadership model at all levels, system embedment, and a culture of on-the-job development so that all employees know what good leadership looks like and receive on the job apprenticeship, even if they do not go through a formal leadership development intervention.

In addition to the pivotal influencers, when thinking about *broad vs. deep* interventions, it is worth focusing on the pivotal roles that will deliver the strategy most faithfully. For a consumer-focused strategy in an FMCG organization, for example, those who lead sales, customer-care and marketing might be prominent; in a healthcare provider focused on research, those who lead in innovation, R&D and clinical trials might be more to the fore.

**When in doubt, focus on the hierarchy and the critical roles, with a clear expectation that role-modelling and influence will spread the leadership mindsets and behaviours throughout the organization.** You should be able to answer these three questions:

- **Who is critical?** All leadership development programmes should start with a strategic alignment. Are there certain audiences or segments within the organization that are critical to executing elements of the strategy? Are there gaps in certain segments that are making it difficult to advance the CEO's agenda?
- **What has been done before?** Ask about previous investments in leadership development. Explore whether it makes sense to continue investing in those areas. Do a Start/ Stop/Continue analysis of existing or legacy programmes, and then compare these with new solutions.
- **How does this balance initial investment vs. shelf-life vs. reach over time?** Another way of thinking about *broad vs. deep* is to determine where there is a strong case for a sustainable programme for a critical mass of leaders. It may be that initially a programme will start out as a discreet piece of work with selected leaders, but will in due course evolve into a wider enterprise. One can think of a 2 × 2 matrix, selective vs. broad penetration on one axis, and shallow vs. deep immersion to the programme on another. To adequately shift the organizational context and culture, a critical mass of the leaders need to be reached at a deep level. This implies a move towards the top right hand quadrant of the matrix, towards sufficient depth and breadth.

**Q2 What are the pros and cons of conducting leadership development in mixed cohorts vs. actual teams?**

In reality, this depends on the objective that you want to achieve. There are two imperatives to consider: first, if you intend predominantly to strengthen individual leadership capabilities and collaboration across the organization, then the composition of the cohort matters little. Second, if you want collective changes in behaviour and especially behaviours that rely on a team, then keeping teams intact is better.

Mixed cohorts tend to be oriented towards individual development; they create a safer space for reflection, peer coaching, and sharing. In addition, if the cohort is properly recruited and the programme design appropriate, there can be a positive effect across the organization in terms of breaking down silos and fostering cross-entity networks and collaboration. Cohort members are able to meet others from outside their departments and gain an appreciation of others' work, and there may well be a continuation of this 'cohort effect' long after the programme formally closes. To put it into numbers, a programme with a mixed cohort of 20 participants can help strengthen 380 individual one-to-one connections; with five cohorts (to reach the top 100) this makes 1,900 connections in total. If an organization is able to strengthen the individual connections across all top 100 at the same time (for example, through a 'Top 100' event), the number of unique connections reached is almost ten thousand.

Single-team cohorts tend to be more task- and team- focused, and (as in the instance of a professional sports team) become high-performing units. In a single-team cohort, roles can be clarified and team dynamics explored; team development can take place (the literature of team development is extensive).[1]

In practice, we find that **a combination of both individual and team-based leadership development has the biggest effect**. While we often design programmes with mixed cohorts, we recommend supplementing them with dedicated (shorter) sessions for the top 10-20 teams in the organization.

**Q3 How do I deal with those unwilling or unable to be part of the broad leadership change? Are certain parts of the workforce inevitably left behind?**

Most organizations have a range of what we might call engagement levels among employees. In our experience, there are four main employee groups in terms of engagement during a transformation or leadership development intervention.[2]

- Around 20 per cent are **active and engaged leaders**, with high levels of influence/energy, and high degree of excitement for the change: these people will contribute to the success of the leadership development programme.
- Around 50 per cent are **contented followers**, with low levels of influence/energy, and high degree of excitement for the change: these people understand and support the importance of the programme, but may not have the capacity or facility to contribute.

- Around 20 per cent are **passive observers**, with low levels of influence/energy, and low degree of excitement for the change: these people are unaware of the intent or rationale of the programme or are married to the past, and are essentially disengaged.
- Around 10 per cent are **active antagonists or saboteurs**, with high levels of influence/energy and low degrees of excitement for the change: these people, like mutineers on a ship, are actively antipathetic to the programme, for historical, personal or narrow professional reasons.

How, then, should each group be addressed? The key is to tailor the approach to each group. The first group, the active leaders, can be trusted to take on roles as mentors, sponsors and coaches of participants, and can play a role as faculty in the programmes. They should be assigned pivotal leadership positions and be engaged as initiative leaders; in fact, the more this group is stretched, the better.

The second group, the contented followers, needs to understand the aims of the programme and to be informed and trained (where they are part of it); ideally, they should have the skills necessary to work on relevant initiatives with the first group, and a portion of this group could also go on a leadership development journey.

The third group, the passive observers, simply needs to be informed. This includes communicating aspirations and success stories of the intervention, and ensuring linkages to the teams/leaders driving the change.

The fourth group, the antagonists, needs to be swiftly confronted and converted to a supporter; if that doesn't work, the antagonists should be re-deployed within the organization to minimize negative impact, or fired. Our research shows that the number one regret of change leaders is not moving faster to neutralize people resistant to change. We find, however, that about 50 per cent of antagonists can be converted, and they can become some of the most powerful symbols of positive change in the organization due to their high degree of influence. Organizations must carefully monitor potential *converts* from the very beginning, and continue to involve them as thought leaders and change agents once they are converted.

We often ask CEOs how many people they think will not make – or may even resist – the required change during a transformation, and the response is typically around 30 per cent. In our experience, however, this number can be reduced to five to ten per cent if the change programme is managed well.

In essence, parts of the organization will often be left behind. In fact, organizations with strong cultures find that employee fit becomes increasingly binary.[3] What is key during a leadership development intervention is that organizations map out the different groupings and tailor interventions to each one.

### Q4 Is leadership development just for large organizations? What about SMEs?

Leadership is a phenomenon that we observe in all species that have some form of a brain and social activity. For instance, bees – an eighteenth-century model for social interaction[4] – have a queen bee; anthropological studies of primates, from Robert Yerkes in the 1930s through Jane Goodall in the 1970s to Robin Dunbar in the 2000s, show that primate groups have alpha leaders and optimal sizes.

More specifically for organizations, whenever and wherever groups gather to achieve an aim (by means of a commercial, governmental, charitable or voluntary entity), those groups need to be led. And some groups performing the same task will do better than others (faster, more efficient, more thorough etc.). All performance can be enhanced through improved leadership, irrespective of the size of the group or organization.

In small and medium-sized enterprises (SMEs), leadership development tends to match the growth of the organization itself. As it grows, so too do its requirements for leadership; in a seminal article, Larry Greiner mapped out five phases of company lifecycle, each of which require different types of leadership behaviours for success (these were amended to six phases of the 'Greiner Growth Curve' in 1998).[5]

SMEs should thus also focus on developing their leaders, and not fall into the trap of delaying leadership development until reaching a certain size. This is particularly true in phases of rapid growth, when demands on leaders not only change but multiply as more staff need to be lead and managed.

As we discussed in Core Principle 1, we find that organizational health is often a useful primary lens (in conjunction with secondary, organization-specific lenses) when identifying the key leadership behaviours for an organization. We work with numerous multi-asset organizations and family owned businesses, where individual entities sometimes have as little as a few hundred employees. For these smaller entities, health continues to be relevant and the four core principles of leadership development remain the same as for larger organizations, even when budgets are more restrictive (see also next FAQ).

**Q5 How does leadership development typically differ by organizational level?**

We discussed in Question 1 that it is typically advisable to concentrate leadership develop spend higher up, if forced to prioritize. In reality, too, we often also see leadership development budgets per employee decline the lower you go in an organization. Leadership development interventions at lower levels of the organization must therefore fit into these boundary conditions. What is key is that the four core principles are adhered to – something which can be achieved through pragmatic and crafty design and rollout, despite budgetary constraints.

**Core Principle 1** continues to be highly relevant at all organizational levels. Leadership development interventions should always focus on the critical shifts that are most important to the performance objectives of the organizational entity at hand, regardless of whether this is a business unit or an individual team. Leaders with a limited training budget can draw on the research and methodology presented in this book to pinpoint the behaviours, skills, and mindsets to develop.

On the contrary, it is not advisable to give employees a 'training catalogue' and budget to pick courses, unless these courses reflect organizational performance priorities. With regard to content, what we often see lower down in the organization is that leadership development begins to include more and more functional and technical skills, in addition to leadership skills, as these are often required to help individuals be better at their day-to-day jobs.

**Core Principle 2** states that a critical mass of leaders must be engaged in order to reach a tipping point in the organization towards behavioural change. At lower levels in the organization, the same rule applies. A more limited budget can mean a greater emphasis on technology, internal facilitators, and even managers and peers playing the role of coach/facilitator in order to reach sufficient scale. Massive Open Online Courses (MOOCs), for example, are an effective way to do leadership development at scale. Similarly, some organizations invest in development of tailored online learning courses, which can then be utilized at a marginal cost of close to zero. The advantage of rolling leadership development interventions lower down in the organization is that the efforts are often more intimate and it is easier to assemble colleagues for shorter on-site sessions. In some instances where a middle manager wants to roll out leadership development for their team, everyone could end up gaining access to the programme, which then has more impact than if the programme was only for 5–15 per cent.

**Core Principle 3** emphasizes the need for a holistic approach to leadership development grounded in neuroscience. It posits a field, forum and coaching approach, as well as the principles of ensuring there is a positive context, a focus is on further developing strengths, stretch, and self-directed learning. These principles should continue to be adhered to at all levels of the organization. For example, a front-line leadership development programme administered by a team leader should include structured forums (for example, by organizational leaders or peer knowledge sharing sessions), on the job apprenticeship, and coaching and mentoring. In addition, each individual should take charge of their own development journeys, develop individual development plans that focus on their strengths and stretch them.

**Core Principle 4** posits that the leadership development effort should be embedded in the broader system to support and perpetuate the desired behaviours. For lower levels of the organization, this is equally important. For example, individual employees need to see their managers role-modelling the desired behaviours, they must have the conviction to change, the HR systems should incentivize them to make the shift, and the organization structure, processes and authority rights should support them. Some of these elements can perhaps be more challenging for an individual manager to influence, but it remains key to ensure that there is alignment regarding the leadership effort further up in the organization, and that it is not conducted in a vacuum, away from other organization culture and leadership efforts.

A general entry-level programme at level 3 might be inexpensive to run using a digital platform or online learning. A large European healthcare organization delivered online level 3 leadership training for 30,000 staff (and all new staff) but at the same time had only 100 level 1 Graduate Management Trainees. Military organizations spend heavily on initial training and initial officer training to ensure basic minimum standards; commercial organizations tend to spend more heavily on staff in mid and later career to ensure best practice.

## Q6 How does leadership development differ by industry? Is it different for the public or social sectors?

Industry context is always important: different sectors will entail certain strategic goals that will, in turn, produce specific leadership models. For example, a telecoms organization could differ from a utilities or a professional services organization. Equally the governmental (or public-service) versions of those sector organizations will differ again: utilities regulators of professional services bodies run by governments will each have something of their sector and something of their origins in their strategic plan.

We stated in Core Principle 1 that we often adopt health as the primary lens when examining and developing an organization's leadership, as we find that health cuts across industries, geographies, and organizational size. However, we also mentioned that the organizational health index has four 'recipes', made up of a coherent set of management practices that complement one another.

Organizations that strongly align to one of the four organizational health recipes are five times more likely to have top quartile health than organizations that only have weak alignment.[6] There are dominant recipes in every industry, so organizations have a strong starting point about where to focus their energy if we apply a 'recipe lens' to mirror the industry context. For example, B2C and consumer companies often follow a 'Market Shaper Recipe', where they gain a competitive advantage by innovating at all levels and executing quickly based on deep understanding of both customers and competitors. Some of the top practices they should focus on are capturing external ideas, customer focus, competitive insights, top down innovation, role clarity, and business partnerships.

Organizations should see their industry and strategy in terms of the health and Market Shaper Recipe. A multi-perspective approach will then lead to a more tailored leadership model which is better linked to the organization's performance objectives. For example, a national healthcare provider in Europe has at its heart a commitment to continuous improvement in care for patients, population and health, and also to value for money. Here, the need is for leaders equipped to develop healthcare systems in local partnerships, for compassionate, inclusive and effective leaders at all levels, for a knowledge of how to improve, for learning, and for enabling regulation and oversight.[7]

In addition to industry-specific and organization-specific leadership behaviours, there are also certain leadership behaviours which should always be considered. Our research pinpointed 4 'baseline behaviours' which should always be present. In addition, we stressed the importance of building adaptability to help leaders transition between changing contexts.

### Q7 What is the return on leadership development?

In Chapter 5, we discussed the importance of measuring the impact of a leadership development intervention. We typically measure four elements:

- reaction of the participants
- degree of learning
- behavioural changes
- organizational results

We do not typically measure the return on investment of a learning intervention, as it is challenging to accurately isolate the impact of the training.

However, there are ways to think through what the returns actually are, and they all point in the same direction: the return is big. First, one can quantify the financial impact of the BTPs related to the leadership development programme, which participants undertake above and beyond their daily jobs. The impact of these projects could be enhanced revenue (for example, new products or growth markets), reduced costs (for example, through procurement savings programmes), or improved processes and ways of working (which could enable quicker speed to market and higher efficiency per employee).

In our experience the impact of the BTPs often pay back the cost of the leadership development programme.

Second, we always recommend measuring the impact on organizational health and on the leadership development health outcome in particular. However, organizations could take this one step further and approximate the impact that the leadership development programme specifically (separate from other health-related interventions) will have on the overall health, and then use benchmarks to approximate the financial impact of the health increase. Our research tracked companies over a 12-month period, and showed that organizations that worked on both performance and health improved health by four to six percentage points in 12 months, and grew EBITDA by 18 per cent (compared to 11 per cent for the S&P 500 in the same period).

Third, organizations can calculate the breakeven in terms of performance change required for a leadership development programme to pay itself back. Typically this breakeven point is very small. For example, assume an organization-wide leadership development programme costing $5m. If you look at the financial performance that can be improved through leadership (for example, sales per employee, throughput per employee, performance of assets), how much would the performance have to improve for the average employee (middle 50 per cent) in order for the leadership development programme to pay itself back? Typically this number is very small, with the absolute performance needed still lower than the top 25 per cent of employees in terms of performance; in other words, there is room for even further improvement through better leadership.

In essence, the different approaches all point in the same direction: **the return on leadership development is big, and pays back the direct costs associated with the effort many times over.** In addition, as mentioned earlier, organizations typically have learning and development budgets available – the money is there. The imperative is thus to spend this budget more effectively, and not necessarily to earmark new funds for leadership development.

**Q8 What are some of the other HR levers that organizations can use to increase leadership effectiveness?**

The focus of this book was on enhancing leadership effectiveness at an organizational level primarily through leadership development interventions. Here, we review other levers that organizations can consider to enhance leadership effectiveness. We differentiate between two main ways to do this:

- **Change the context of the organization**: that means its structure, the leadership roles and tasks that its people take on, and how it organizes and motivates them
- **Change the people**: this means altering how people behave

## CHANGING THE CONTEXT

**Organizational structure:** Our definition of leadership posits that 'leadership is a set of behaviours … these behaviours are supported by the relevant skills and mindsets'. Some organizational structures will be more or less conducive to particular behaviours. For example, if you want your leaders to collaborate more, it may be harder to achieve in an organization with strong, vertical departmental structures (these are sometimes called silo organizations, geographical or product-based departments or functions). An alternative to the silo organization is the matrix organization, where members are part of many teams; over four-fifths of employees in the US experience this kind of working.[8] The efficacy of the matrix organization is ambiguous; the clarity of authority and responsibility – and the leadership behaviours that they call out – can all to easily become compromised. However, more agile working practices, where organizations combine both speed and stability, make fertile ground for changes in behaviour and mindset.

**Organizational processes and where decision-making authority resides:** For example, if you want to foster quicker decision-making but employees require numerous sign-offs, the behaviours of speed and decisiveness will not be matched (or served) by the structure around them. Or if you want more delegation, but all authority (or compliance or governance) sits with one person, then the authority rights need to change.

**Employee motivation, especially leaders and top talent:** Changing the HR processes that motivate and retain people across the organization can have a profound and lasting effect on behaviour and on leadership effectiveness. Here, knowing and measuring are of the utmost importance. The field of data analytics has much to offer the HR field.[9] Predictive talent models can rapidly identify, recruit, develop, and retain the right people. Mapping HR data helps organizations identify current pain points and devise improvement actions. Surprisingly, however, the data do not always point in the direction that more seasoned HR officers might expect.[10]

## Changing the people

**Strategic workforce planning:** Already covered in the story, but what is new is how advanced analytics are going into strategic workforce planning. With the help of advanced analytics, we can aggregate vast amounts of data on both talent demand (linked to strategy) and talent supply (looking at the external market), breaking it down by geography, business unit, level, and specific skill type needed. Algorithms can furthermore predict future changes, for example, the impact of change in growth, new product line launches, and model risks of, for example, higher attrition by level. Analytics helps us move from backward looking data to predictive insights, from judgements to fact-based decisions, and from tactical decisions to strategic planning.

**Succession planning:** Two-thirds of US public and private companies have no formal CEO succession plan, according to a survey conducted by the National Association of Corporate Directors in 2014. And only one-third of the executives who told headhunter Korn Ferry in 2015 that their companies do have such a programme were satisfied with the outcome.[11] So, succession planning is underused and imperfect. A good succession plan links to leadership development in three ways: over time, in terms of leadership criteria, and in terms of choice.

First, succession planning should be a multi-year structured process tied to leadership development. The CEO succession then becomes the result of initiatives that actively develop potential candidates. For instance, the chairman of one Asian company appointed three potential CEOs to the position of co-chief operating officer, rotating them over a two-year period through key leadership roles in sales, operations, and R&D. One of the three subsequently dropped out, leaving two in competition for the top post.

Second, a trio of criteria can help companies evaluate potential candidates: know-how, such as technical knowledge and industry experience; leadership skills, such as the ability to execute strategies, manage change, or inspire others; and personal attributes, such as personality traits and values. These criteria should fit the strategic, industry, and organizational requirements of the business on, say, a five- to eight-year view.

Third, CEO-succession planning can attract biased thinking, and its outcome is the appointment of a specific individual. As we know, decision making is biased; but three biases seem most prevalent in the context of CEO succession. CEOs afflicted by the *MOM* ('more of me') *bias* look for or try to develop a copy of themselves; incumbents under the influence of *the sabotage bias* consciously or unconsciously undermine the process by promoting a candidate who may not be ready for the top job (or is otherwise weak) and therefore seems likely to prolong the current CEO's reign. The *herding bias* comes into play when the committee in charge of the process consciously or unconsciously adjusts its views to those of the incumbent CEO or the chairman of the board.

Recruitment strategy can be hugely influential over time, and must be linked to the leadership model. Some recruiting can be seen as an extension of the organization's values (as in values-based recruiting) where it uses its brand or its perceived values to attract like-minded applicants. Equally, there may well be a need – in order to overcome the bias towards conformity – to seek out potential employees who may well have values that challenge the organization's received wisdom. People Analytics can now be used to improve recruiting results and eliminate biases (for example, in terms of diversity, see Question 3 in Chapter 14).

# 14
# FAQs on trends relevant to leadership

*Emily Yueh, Mary Andrade, Nick Van Dam*

Automation, digital platforms, and other innovations are changing the fundamental nature of work. McKinsey Global Institute recently found that about 60 per cent of all occupations have at least 30 per cent of activities that are technically automatable, based on currently demonstrated technologies.[1] This means that most occupations will change, and more people will have to work with technology. This will have an impact in developed and developing economies alike, and the requirements of leaders – and therefore leadership development – will have to adapt accordingly. In this chapter, we discuss the direction of the work in future and the implications this will have for leadership. In addition, we review the latest technology trends impacting learning.

### Q1 How is the 'world of work' changing?

The world of work is changing, probably faster than at any point in recent history. We highlighted six important trends for leadership in Chapter 3. These sit within a broader context; and that context is a challenging one: some argue that we are experiencing a Fourth Industrial Revolution.[2]

The first industrial revolution (1760–1840) brought mechanization and steam power; the second (1870–1914), chemicals, electrification and mass production; the third (1960–1990), electronics and digital communication; and we are now entering a new Revolution.[3] This transformation will be well on its way by 2020, and is characterized by developments in previously disjointed fields such as artificial intelligence and machine-learning, robotics, nanotechnology, 3D printing, and genetics and biotechnology.[4]

This Fourth Industrial Revolution will transform both the way we live and the way we work. In terms of work, many existing jobs will disappear, while others that do not even exist today will grow rapidly.

Writing for the World Economic Forum, Klaus Schwab (2016) identified three ways the Fourth Industrial Revolution differs from the Third:

- **Velocity:** This revolution is exponential rather than linear.
- **Breadth and depth:** It builds on the new industrial revolution, and combines multiple technologies; this new pattern of combination promises unprecedented paradigm shifts in the economy, business and society.
- **System impact:** It involves the transformation of entire systems, across and within countries, companies, industries and society as a whole.[5]

Its effects are radical. A 2013 study from Oxford University concluded that developed nations could see job loss rates of up to 47 per cent within the next two decades due to technology and automation, across both blue- and white-collar jobs.[6] This trend is consistent across developed nations.[7] Traditional manufacturing industries have long been moving in this direction – for example, automotive companies now operate almost fully automated plants. Many labour-intensive service industries are moving in this direction, for example Amazon's state-of-the-art automated warehouses (and experiments with drone delivery units), as well as the first fully automated restaurants opening up (including order-taking, delivery, and in some instances even parts of the actual cooking).

Next in line, however, is a wider range of middle-income workers: accountants, lawyers, bureaucrats, and financial analysts. For these workers, computers will become increasingly efficient and effective in analysing large quantities of data and devising insights and solutions from them. As mentioned in the introduction, our latest research finds that existing technologies could have significant effects on more than 60 per cent of jobs. On a global scale, we calculate that the adaptation of currently demonstrated automation technologies could affect 50 per cent of the world economy.[8] However, if current technology continues its exponential development, this number could rise even further.

A related trend is that of *dis-intermediation*. Blockbuster, a video rental chain that at its peak owned over 9,000 stores globally, went bankrupt in 2010.[9] Blockbuster, and the video rental business in general, was disrupted by online providers such as Netflix, which cut out the (physical) intermediary in the video rental business, allowing customers to browse, rent, and pay for films online. In addition, algorithms can recommend films based on user preferences, reviews, and previous rental history. Other industries (including retail, health and education) are beginning to feel the effect of dis-intermediation.[10]

While jobs will disappear, others will be created. One report estimates that 65 per cent of children entering primary school today will end up working in new job types that do not yet exist.[11] Examples of future jobs illustrate just how different the world will look in 10–15 years: drone pilot, 3D printing designer, remote health care specialist, smart home handyperson, data visualization analyst, avatar manager, virtual reality experience farmer, vertical farmer, social networking officer, and professional triber.[12]

Skills and knowledge will erode and evolve ever faster. A significant portion of knowledge obtained during the first year of a four-year technical degree programme is likely to be outdated by the time of graduation. Beyond technical skills or hard skills, employers are equally concerned about work-related practical skills like content creation or judging the relevance and purpose of information, which are also likely to be subject to significant change in the coming years.[13]

**Q2 What are the implications of the changing world of work on the skills employees will require in the next 10 years?**
What, then, do these trends mean for the skillsets employees and organizations must develop to thrive? One comprehensive overview of the skills needed comes from the World Economic Forum's Future of Jobs Report, which looks at the most important skills needed in the workplace in 2020:[14]

1 Complex problem solving
2 Critical thinking
3 Creativity
4 People management
5 Coordinating with others
6 Emotional intelligence
7 Judgement and decision making
8 Service orientation
9 Negotiation
10 Cognitive flexibility

Worth highlighting is the importance of complex problem solving and critical thinking (solving adaptive rather than technical challenges), creativity to ensure continuous innovation, and people-related skills. Especially the demand for creativity is growing quickly, as this is unique to humans and not disposed to automation.

Another report, consistent with the above skills, found that it is the ability to *combine* both cognitive and social skills which will be most important in the future.[15] The report argues that technological advances are making social skills more, not less, important. The research has a strong correlation with our own McKinsey research, including the importance of centred leadership – grounded in a strong degree of self-awareness – which builds an ability to adapt more readily to changing contexts.

In addition to the above cross-cutting skills, we also believe there is a trend towards much more specialized expertise. In line with the general pace of business, the velocity of knowledge acquisition is increasing. It is argued that the age of the *shallow generalist* is over, in a world with Wikipedia at your fingertips.[16] This is already reflected in many parts of the world, where the percentage of managers with generalist degrees is declining. We argue that the traditional 'T-profile' of a knowledge worker is no longer enough, and that workers must keep learning throughout their lives, reflecting a new 'M-profile' (see Figure 14.1).[17] The 21st century depends on people's ability to build intellectual capital as this will be the foundation for value. People need to master multiple domains over the lifespan of their careers and become serial masters.

Finally, it is worth singling out technology. It is ubiquitous; it underpins many changes in jobs and the corresponding changes in skills required in the future. In 2015, almost half (44.5 per cent) of the EU population aged 16–74 had insufficient digital skills to participate in society and the economy. [18] Figure 14.2 shows a view of how digital competency framework might look.

## Q3 What does the changing world of work mean for leaders and for leadership development?

First of all, leaders must have the skills we mentioned in question 2:

- The ability to solve adaptive problems and innovate
- People management
- Centredness
- Capacity for lifelong learning (to develop 'M-profiles')
- Technological know-how

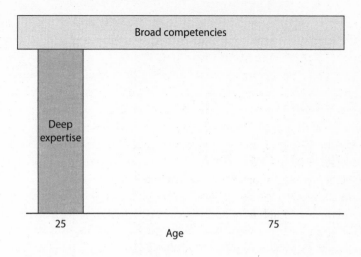

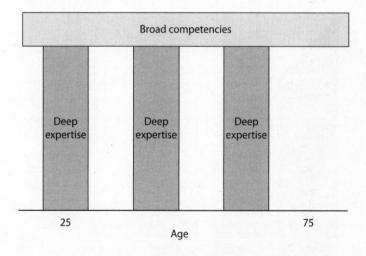

FIGURE 14.1 From T to M: The new profile of the knowledge worker

However, we find that there are four additional requirements for leaders worth mentioning. This is by no means a comprehensive list, and the below skills are related to the skills mentioned above. Nonetheless, we find them to be key for leaders of the future and worth highlighting.

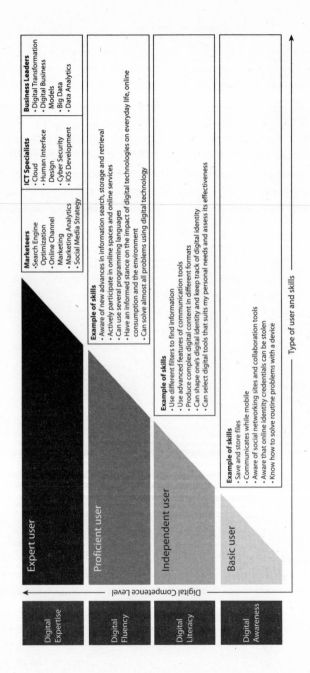

FIGURE 14.2 Digital Competency Framework[19]

The first three requirements for leaders cover three different levels: organizational ecosystems, organizations themselves, and individuals. First is the ability to manage increasingly complex ecosystems. Historically, value chains were linear and built around specific end products and services. However, in the past few years we have seen the emergence of distributed work places and the gig economy. By 2020, 50 per cent of the US workforce could be freelancers (part time and full-time).[20] Many organizations outsource increasingly significant chunks of their work to third parties. For example, many pharmaceuticals no longer do large parts of R&D in-house but work with a sophisticated ecosystem of partners. Growing amounts of data are in 'the cloud' with software used as a service. Large organizations do not necessarily have significant physical assets on their books. These 'any-to-any ecosystems' are built around value-creating interactions that quickly adapt to new needs and ideas – very much driven by the more VUCA world we operate in (and which we highlighted in Chapter 3). As such, leaders must learn how to navigate these ecosystems, collaborate in an agile way, and adapt regularly and quickly. They will need to master strategies and execute at a systems level, and be able to inspire and influence the ecosystem they operate in – often with remote counterparties that they may never see face to face.

Second, leaders will have to manage more agile organizations. A more VUCA world not only impacts organizational ecosystems, but also organizations themselves. We find in our research that the organizations that are best able to navigate a more complex operating environment are those that combine stable operating processes and structure with a dynamic capability (fluidity and speed). Enabling this dynamic element requires more fluid goal-setting, structures, processes, and individual role descriptions. In addition, as technology takes over increasing amounts of the daily operational work through automation and digitization, it further increases the amount of project-based knowledge work. The implications are a new paradigm on organizations, built around cross-functional 'cells' with end to end accountability and with the ability to rapidly shift priorities and reconfigure as needed. Some argue that this essentially 'blows up' the middle manager, as the role of the boss becomes distributed across different positions. In practice, this could, for example, mean a team leader who coaches the team members, a more senior 'work prioritizer' who provides guidance on daily and weekly priorities, and people developers who ensure that individuals are learning and have the requisite coaching and tools to do their jobs.[21] This is in sharp contrast to a hierarchical manager who plays all these roles. As organizations move towards more agile ways of working, leaders must understand their role and how they can maximize the input of all employees.

Third, leaders will have to manage an increasing number of people with more expertise than themselves. While the leadership advice to 'surround yourself with people who are smarter than you' has been around for a while, the adage will become even more important for a number of reasons. First, the bar for knowledge is being raised even further. The rate of knowledge generation is increasing quicker than our ability of any individual to grasp it completely (indeed, it has even been said that as a result, humans are becoming dumber every day), and hence the need for a web of experts to collaborate to solve complex problems. Second, employees are becoming more educated. And third, increasingly distributed economies, agile organizations, and automation will lead to flatter organizations with higher knowledge worker per leader ratios.

While leaders need to acquire more and more expertise and insights from many different disciplines (for themselves), simply in order to make connections, they also need to be able to manage swathes of people smarter than themselves. This requires leaders to be able to lead with questions and rapidly synthesize new information.

For example, at McKinsey, we focus on developing engagement managers (project managers) who are comfortable not knowing everything themselves. Instead, they need to be able ask the right questions and bring a broad array of insights together into meaningful recommendations. Today, during the course of an 8 week engagement, an engagement manager could lead research analysts who are deep content experts, implementation specialists who have more than 10 years of industry experience, colleagues with digital backgrounds, as well as remote solutions experts who are product specialists (for example, regarding people analytics, customer-centric design, or financial analysis). This requires a new skillset (asking the right questions and synthesize), and it also requires a new mindset (for example, openness, humility).

In additional, leaders must be able to foster accountability and true empowerment of employees, and to inspire and make work meaningful for individuals. Linked to the last point, the notion of 'control' in terms of rules is dying out. While rules will never fully disappear, leaders must increasingly use meaningful values to guide the behaviours of employees, who will have much more discretion, freedom, and accountability. As we saw in the leadership staircase, leaders in top quartile organizations emphasize values and role-modelling, and all organizations will eventually move 'up the ladder' and require this form of leadership.

Finally, leaders must be able to lead their organizations through a digital transformation. We discussed that understanding technology is one of the core skills for knowledge workers of the future. However, the leadership imperative goes beyond this – one of the biggest challenges organizations will face in the next decade is to develop at scale a massive number of leaders who can navigate a digital transformation – touching on almost all areas of business at a scale not seen before. All organizations are in the technology firing line, whether they like it or not.

The digital imperative for organizations is completely different than a decade ago – the meaning of a 'digital transformation' has evolved from creating a mobile presence, data mining, and virtual collaboration, towards artificial intelligence, automation, machine learning, and the Internet of Things. However, only about 50 per cent of executives rate their Digital IQ as strong.[23] This presents a huge challenge. **Organizations will need to build leaders that understand the implications of technology and can transform their organizations.** Not just playing along but aggressively getting ahead of the technology curve. Combined with this, leaders will need empathy for employees going through this transformation, who will likely feel anxious from the increasing automation and the new skills required of them.

**Q4 How will the 'future of work' impact how organizations undertake learning and development in general?**

We saw in the previous questions that the world of work, jobs and skills required are changing rapidly. Couple this with the fact that employees are living longer (see Figure 14.3), and there is a strong impetus for lifelong learning for both individual employees and organizations as a whole. There is no way around it. This has to do with both leadership development but also learning and development more broadly.

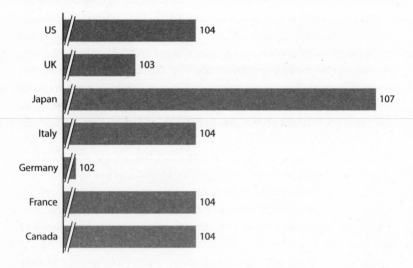

US 104
UK 103
Japan 107
Italy 104
Germany 102
France 104
Canada 104

FIGURE 14.3   Oldest age at which 50 per cent of babies born in 2007 are predicted to be alive[24]

As we saw in Chapter 6, leadership development and culture are intimately intertwined, and an outcome of leadership development (when done correctly) is a shift in the organizational culture. The same holds true for learning and development in general – the outcome of an effective learning strategy that promotes continuous learning is culture geared towards learning.

We argue that all organizations must become *learning organizations*. This is not a new concept, but its importance is increasing, and the role of learning and development will become more, not less, critical in the future. The learning organization is a term given to a company that facilitates learning, continuously transforms itself and becomes a place that employees feel a commitment to. According to Peter Senge, for example, a learning organization exhibits five characteristics: systems thinking; personal master; mental models; a shared vision; and team learning. The concept has gained broad acceptance and a number of companies are implementing these approaches.[25] In 2003, Marsick and Watkins developed a questionnaire called *dimensions of the learning organization*, which can help organizations to diagnose their current status and guide change in areas such as learning opportunities, dialogue and inquiry, collaboration and team learning, and knowledge performance.[26]

More recently, Harvard researchers Kegan & Lahey have suggested the idea of *Deliberately Development Organizations* (DDOs). They believe that organizations will thrive when they deliberately develop every single person, simply because this effort aligns with people's strongest motive, which is to grow. This means that organizations should embrace a culture in which support of learning is woven into the fabric of working life, the company's regular operations, daily routines and conversations. Every meeting and encounter is an opportunity to work on learning goals, and DDOs relentlessly pursue business excellence and the growth of people into more capable versions of themselves simultaneously.[27]

The future of work thus not only places new requirements on leadership development, but also on learning and development more broadly. The imperative is for organizations to become true learning organizations in order to better adapt to the changing environment. Creating a learning organization requires a shift not only in structures and processes but also in the underlying culture of the organization. Organizations that master this shift and are able to 'learn quicker' than the competition will gain a valuable competitive advantage. At the individual level, it is critical that people become aware of the need to continue learning and grow in order to stay relevant for the workforce. They need to embrace mindsets for lifelong learnings.[28]

### Q5. Should organizations change their talent and leadership development system for Millennials? How do they differ?

Older generations often see differences between themselves and up-and-coming ones. And we see that pattern play out today: a barrage of articles and commentators have stamped today's youth as 'Millennials' – workers who are said to be difficult to manage, likely to quit at a moment's notice, raised to think they are exceptional, and prone to make needless mistakes as they forge ahead blindly without permission. The research we have conducted suggests a more complex reality.

Millennials have grown up in a VUCA (volatile, uncertain, complex and ambiguous) world, with the fall of the Berlin Wall, September 11 attacks, financial crisis in 2008, Iraq War, Arab Spring, and Occupy Wall Street Movement as some of the notable highlights. In the same period, the world wide web was created, internet became ubiquitous, and smartphone penetration exploded. Millennials tend to bring an energy and desire for change, a spirit of questioning everything, creativity and ideas, a tendency towards testing ideas in action, and a willingness to speak up.[29] Above all else, Millennials express a desire – much more widely felt by all workers – for meaning in work and life, flexibility and autonomy, more feedback and mentoring, fast advancements, and stretch-assignments and variety – see Figure 14.4.

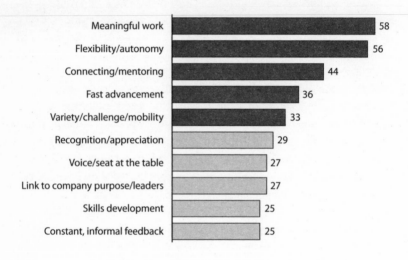

FIGURE 14.4  Number of interview mentions[30]

How, then, might thinking about Millennials provide an opportunity to rethink the workplace? Our research pinpoints a number of best practices, which include ideas on learning and development for Millennials. Collectively, they represent a new workplace dynamic for many organizations, spurred by the high expectations of young employees but meeting a larger need for more thoughtful relations between all workers and employers.[31]

- **Invest in internships programmes:** Launching or continuing internship programmes could be beneficial, assuring that interns do real work and receive genuine exposure. A large number of the Millennials we interviewed were introduced to work this way, and they appreciated the investment from their employers and affirmed loyalty in return.

- **Increase exposure and choice through rotational programmes:** For many Millennials, rotation programmes are a career high point. The best programmes give participating Millennials some choice so that they are matched with rotations of interest to them.

- **Adapt feedback process to increase regularity with development focus:** Many organizations are revamping feedback processes in favour of forward-looking counsel delivered on a regular basis in a way that reduces judgment in favour of growth. Young leaders report that they would rather know their development needs right away than wait for review time.

- **Increase movement and entrepreneurial opportunity:** Millennials want to be challenged with growth/movement opportunities every 12–18 months. While moving all employees this regularly would likely not be possible, organizations can revamp the end-to-end process of posting, selecting, and moving people to make the process more fluid, offer regular moves to high performers specifically, reframe advancement as movement, and regularly put young leaders in charge of critical cross-functional initiatives.

- **Create a culture of mentorship:** Many organizations have experience with mentorship programmes, yet results of these programmes have been mixed. In many cases, what is needed is to make mentorship a more core part of the organizational culture and DNA. One organization we know connects every new employee to someone who has been there for a few years. Another organization uses on the job shadowing systematically: in weekly all-staff meetings, young professionals attend and interact with senior leaders on key decisions.

- **Introduce or enrich flexibility:** It is becoming increasingly important for organizations to offer more choice and flexibility. While there will always be certain constraints, organizations that delay this create a disadvantage in a world where people believe work is part of life, not separate from it. A good example we've seen is a media-tech company that makes flexibility a personal contract between manager and employee. In consequence, every form of flexibility is acceptable for good performers. Another company has created a core time block when all employees must be in the office unless on the road. That allows leaders to call impromptu meetings while offering each employee the freedom to determine the rest. We have also see examples of organizations setting up new policies for extended parental leaves – a valued benefit for the increasing numbers of young leaders who put a real priority on family.

- **Provide two-way channels for speaking up and feedback**: Millennials want to be heard. Many organizations benefit from holding regular townhalls that are small enough for anyone to speak up – with a process to close the loop. In another company, senior leaders join its young leaders' Business Resource Group to listen and respond. We have also found examples of new upward feedback processes so that young leaders can contribute to the reviews of their bosses; Millennials are used to these from rating their college professors.
- **Self-organize an early careers resource group:** Some organizations offer young leaders the option to self-organize, with budgets for professional development, budgets and mandates for initiatives with business impact, and senior leader access and support.
- **Use research/data mining to shift hearts and minds**: Getting the facts is crucial today. Some companies have become leaders at it, engaging their consumer marketing functions to complete original consumer research that helps the business and is shared broadly internally. One company designed training that brings together leaders across generations to shift mindsets. At the very least, mining the employee engagement survey by generation and soliciting Millennials input may start a valuable discussion.

In addition, we have found great examples of additional tools or processes. Some companies offer specialized training and development for Millennials that they value (part and parcel of their development focus). Others offer curriculums tailored for Millennials (to help them choose their own learning path given the dozens of training courses offered). Many companies have revamped narratives for recruiting university grads via website, marketing materials, and one-on-one interactions. These actions fit on a larger canvas depicting what companies can and should do for Millennials (Figure 14.5):

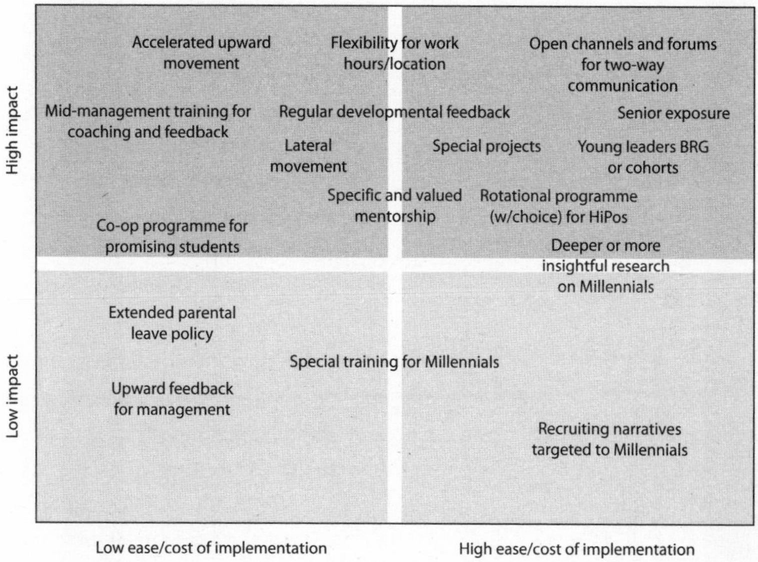

FIGURE 14.5 Relative impact of actions[32]

Implementing the full list of recommendations will be challenging. They change the nature of work by establishing a new standard for the way leaders, managers, and employees interact. But if they do make progress, organizations will not only retain young professionals (who may eventually become their leaders) but also unlock their potential, while increasing the engagement of all employees across the organization.

### Q6 How is technology impacting the delivery of learning interventions?

Profound impacts of technology are to be found in the field of modern adult learning across almost all types of learning. Figure 14.6 shows an overview of the main types of learning, showing two main

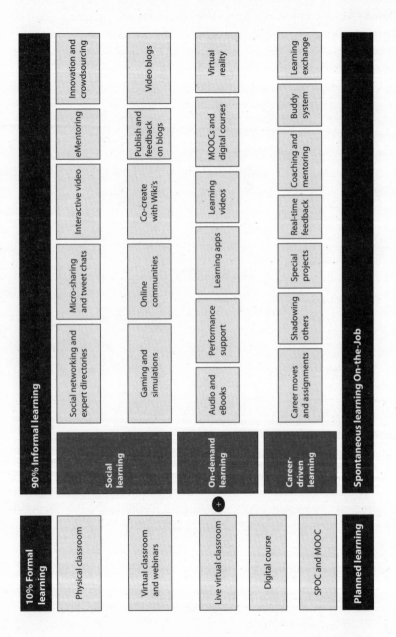

FIGURE 14.6 Formal and informal learning[33]

kinds: formal (including planned learning in classrooms or online) and informal learning (which includes career learning, on-demand learning and social learning). At a macro level, technology is affecting both areas with increased digitization, in order to better equip employees for their jobs.

**Formal learning** constitutes about 10 per cent of learning and is structured and shaped by the organization which determines what kind of learning needs to be completed by people over a specific time in order to develop identified competencies. Formal learning plays a limited but crucial role in building people capabilities in organizations and reinforcing cultural norms. Organizations that take people development seriously provide more time for formal learning. According to the ATD 2016 Global State of the Industry Report, the average number of formal learning content hours delivered per employee in 2015 was 33.5, while the best organizations delivered 42.7 hours of learning per employee in 2015.[34]

Formal learning can be delivered in a classroom (physical or virtual), through self-paced, digital learning programmes (for example, online training, MOOCs or SPOCs (Massive Open Online Course and Specific Private Online Course), webinars, and learning apps), and by providing people with access to online diagnostics and assessment tools such as emotional intelligence and the Myers-Briggs Type Indicator, among others. Under 50 per cent of formal learning hours were delivered in person in 2015, compared to 60 per cent in 2010. This trends towards the growing use of technology in delivering formal learning.[35] There were more than 50 million subscribers to MOOCs in 2016, and while not all courses are completed, it points towards a huge appetite for digitally-enabled learning. As MOOCs become more formally acknowledged (for example, through credible certificates of achievement), they will support a large-scale and rapid upskilling and reskilling of the workforce.

**Informal learning** represents about 90 per cent of learning and can be defined as semi-structured or unstructured learning. It is driven by the daily developmental needs of employees, and occurs often spontaneously on-the-job through problem-solving, interaction with colleagues, and use of digital learning solutions. There are three different categories of informal learning, as shown in the framework above:

Career-driven learning, On-demand learning, and Social learning. Technology is affecting each one.

1 **Social learning**. Social learning refers to Albert Bandura's theory that indicates that people learn most effectively when they interact with others about a given topic. Technology can enhance this process through online communities, crowd-sourced knowledge, gamification, badges and rewards, and interactive videos.

2 **On-demand learning**. We tend to look for the knowledge and information that will help us work better, smarter and deeper. The Internet, search engines, electronic performance support systems and the growth of mobile computing provide easy access to rich content to fill knowledge gaps. Technology plays a key role in making the right information available at the right time, for example, through apps, audio and eBooks, learning videos and virtual reality applications. A major challenge for many people is information overload and the fact that it is difficult to find what is needed. As a result, people can waste time searching and surfing various internal portals. Therefore, L&D functions need to design learning platforms that provide a personalized view of learning and are supported by social media features (for example, rated, recommended and relevant content). Technology can also enhance this process by learning about user preferences and predicting what types of content are needed when, and through what channel.

3 **Career-driven learning**. Significant learning takes place when employees move into different roles or work on new projects that challenge them to work with new teams in a different context and with different goals. It is effective if these experiences are supported by on-the-job coaching and mentoring, and supplemented by formal classroom and digital learning programs. Technology can enhance preparation for a new role through simulations (for example, when moving into new cultural context) and also through nudges

and real-time feedback, which is especially useful when new behaviours are required (for example, more delegation, inspirational leadership).

Across both formal and informal learning channels, it is clear that technology is making inroads and digitization is increasing. In parallel, there are a number of more specific technology trends. By no means comprehensive (nor fully mutually exclusive), below is a summary of 10 major shifts we see in digital learning. Some are here today, while some are more 'next practice' and not yet fully seen in the market.

- **Micro-learning:** In the 2000s L&D tended to use a limited range of delivery, for example, live learning, webinars and eLearning. People today, however, are consuming information in smaller doses. Content has to be delivered in much more flexible ways, and allow consumers to digest them in shorter cycles. As a result, learning has sped up to account for end-user lifestyles and preferences, with shorter one to five minute modules, snack-bites about hot topics, and not just in the form of documents but through a variety of media.
- **Personalization:** Consumers expect increasing levels of personalization across product and services – for example customized coffee orders, tailored clothes bought online, and recommended music playlists based on one's search history. In the same way, learning is becoming increasingly personalized and adaptive ('classroom of one'). Users can pick their own learning curriculum as needed, and can advance at their own pace. In addition, learning is becoming intelligent and 'adaptive'. Adaptive learning is being explored in academia (in fact, it calls back to a time of personal tutors and highly personalized learning conversations in elite universities). It places the individual at the heart of the learning exchange. It is based on how each individual is doing in any learning environment; the system adjusts to the individual – including tailored feedback on and suggest remedies for problem areas, tailoring delivery method based on what you prefer, and content curation. At McKinsey, for example, we use adaptive learning in our online simulations for engagement managers

that seek to replicate real cases. Users are confronted with a 'real-life' situation and are prompted to make decisions from a complex set of interdependent choices, at key points on a project. We pull data from the simulation and offer the individual targeted feedback and learning suggestions, to work on their specific areas for improvement. At its extreme, you could image a 'personal assistant' that is linked to your calendar, and which offers tailored learning 'bites' throughout the day based on your specific needs (for example, a short video about industry trends, prior to your meeting with a CEO, or techniques for inspirational leadership, prior to a team meeting where you are presenting the new strategy). This will lead to an even tighter link between learning and the work you do every day.

- **Evidence-based learning and use of big data:** Data and artificial intelligence is linked to most of the trends on this list. Here, we mean data used to enhance the learning process. This includes both what is taught (looking at correlation between course completion and success on the job, for example), and delivery channels (what channels result in highest degree of learning). In addition, within specific courses, data can help understand at what specific points users get bored, drop off, or skip (for example, by tracking usage at a micro level).

- **Artificial intelligence and increased interactivity:** More sophisticated chat bots are emerging, which can enhance learning through simulated conversations that begin to feel like a real dialogue. One professor at Georgia Tech used a virtual teaching assistant to chat with students, with some students not even realizing that the assistant was a machine.

- **Gamification.** Gamification (the application of game principles in non-game environments) is not new within learning, but it is becoming more sophisticated. At its best, gamifying a learning experience can be fun, challenging, and bring out the competitive nature of individuals (for example, through leader boards), which increases user engagement and learning. There is also a trend towards group-based games, where users collaborate and help one another.

- **Micro-credentialing and external recognition:** In addition, the 'credentials, that one can earn from completing certain courses or publishing knowledge can become stamps of credibility, for example, by showing up on employees' intranet pages (or even externally on, for example, LinkedIn). Employees are able to chart their own development paths and define more clearly what they want to be known for from a skills point of view. This supports the broader trend at work of having multiple careers across different organizations. In order to stay relevant in the workforce, employees must continuously acquire new skills, and micro-credentialing helps increase the incentive to do so by clearly signalling the profile one has built up.
- **Social learning.** Imagine Facebook as it is today, with all the content showing up on your wall, but where you are not able to like or comment on anything. This would likely dramatically reduce your user experience. The reverse is also true for digital learning experiences – including the ability for users to interact greatly enhances engagement and peer-based learning.
- **Mobile and multi-channel integration:** People are spending on average between three and five hours on their smartphones per day, and the number has been growing over 20 per cent per year the past few years. Studies have also found that around 70 per cent of people learn on their mobile devices, and over 50 per cent of people learn at their point of need (i.e. 'just in time') – and both of these numbers are expected to increase further in the future.[36] Coupled with this is a move towards seamless integration across devices (for example, smartphone, tablet, desktop) – enabling users to 'pick up where they left off' at any time or location.
- **VR and AR:** Virtual and augmented reality are beginning to make bigger inroads into learning. A virtual reality headset, for example, allows you participate in a classroom with your classmates, or engage in a factory tour with experts – all from the comfort of your living room or office. Far from

just being about new ways of delivery, VR and AR are also pushing the boundaries of the content and experiences we can create. For example, the Stanford Virtual Human Interaction Lab uses VR to build empathy and combat racism by enabling users to experience reality through the body of someone else.

- **Wearable tech:** The functionalities of wearable tech are growing, and currently include fitness and health tracking, communication, calendaring, navigation, and medical treatment (for example, for voice or hearing disorders). There is a lot of potential to leverage wearable tech in learning, however, to support specific learning objectives. For example, the technology could pick up on voices and intonation, and play back the amount of time a person is talking (vs. listening) and the intonation they are using. This could help people who wish to listen more, manage their tempers, or adopt a more energetic presentation style. Feedback is a critical enabler of learning, and wearable tech can provide facts on a growing number of dimensions.

# Conclusion: Our letter to a CEO

*Andrew St George, Claudio Feser, Michael Rennie,*
*Nicolai Chen Nielsen*

Dear CEO,

We hope you have enjoyed this book. Before you put it down, and perhaps back on your shelf, we would like to wrap up with three questions that we hope will offer reflection and motivation for action: What is the essence of leadership at scale? Why is it important? What next?

## What is the essence of leadership at scale?

We have just set out our view that leadership affects both health and performance in your organization. The news is that health can be measured and it can be improved by developing leaders. The converse is also true – it is virtually impossible to achieve top quartile health with non-top quartile leadership. Leadership also directly improves performance. Here, we make the same assertion as with health: achieving your performance aspirations without a critical mass of leaders demonstrating the required behaviours across your organization is virtually impossible.

We have showed how you can improve your organization's performance and health through leadership, and why it is essential to do so. We used our research and practice to define the Leadership At Scale Diamond, consisting of four core principles: i) focusing on the critical shifts linked to context, ii) engaging a critical mass of leaders through breadth, depth, and pace, iii) architecting programmes to maximize behavioural change by using modern adult learning principles grounded in neuroscience, and iv) integrating and measuring the programme in the broader organizational system.

We gave an outline of our typical approach (Diagnose, Design & Develop, Deliver and Drive Impact) and the results at each stage. And in our story we showed how a leadership development programme looks from the outside and feels from the inside. Finally we highlighted some of the issues that might arise from our approach to whole-system development, and how to address them.

# Why is it important?

Great leaders in your organization drive organizational health and performance, and therefore create shareholder value. You know how a well-led organization looks and feels, and how its people get things done. That is the ideal.

However, almost half of all organizations – maybe yours is one of them – face some kind of leadership gap that they are not able to fill. And even if you do take action, you have to overcome the fact that most of today's leadership development approaches do not work for organizations as a whole: in essence, almost half of organizations feel that their leadership development efforts do not yield and sustain the intended results.

You may share our frustration that leadership is widely seen and mostly written about as a soft discipline, often with limited hard data. A lot of practice is also based on anecdotal evidence. We like to bring knowledge to bear on practical issues. We have combined data from over 375,000 employees in over 165 organizations – just like yours – and added years of practical experience, as well as our own internal approach to developing our people, to crack the code for developing leadership (and leadership programmes) that really drives organizational health and performance.

Done well, leadership development at scale pays for itself many times over, both directly through the project work that is undertaken as part of the programme, and indirectly through the multitude of positive behavioural changes that ripple throughout the organization. In addition, we showed that organizations typically have learning and development budgets available – the imperative is thus to spend this budget more effectively, and not necessarily to earmark new funds for leadership development.

Yet leadership development is not the medicine for all ills. There are always limitations of time, money, culture, organizational will, capacity and situation. And leadership development is often not the first that comes to mind: strategic change, innovation, customer focus, agile or lean operations might be foremost; but we have found that leadership development is germane to all these sooner or later, and much better sooner and faster.

Other approaches, such as talent acquisition and succession planning, are equally important and often done in parallel with leadership development efforts as part of broader initiative. With this knowledge, you can take a comprehensive approach to increasing the leadership effectiveness in your organization. Leadership covers many disciplines, so we included the latest cross-cutting themes relevant to leadership development, including technology and neuroscience.

We do know, however, that leadership development is one of the top three things you can do to bring about change in your organization.

## What next?

So, the big question, and one which all leaders have to answer every day, short or long term: what to do next?

We live, as you know, in interesting times. Since the first industrial revolution until the end of the nineteenth century, organizations prospered from the efforts, broadly, of remarkable individuals (pioneers like Brunel, Maybach, Carnegie, Ford); the twentieth century saw two more industrial revolutions – the electro-chemical revolution and the electronic-information revolution – as we gathered in ever larger groups to make and do at scale. Here, management ruled; the twentieth century was the management century.

Now in the Fourth Industrial Revolution, which is changing work and lives more rapidly than before (by means of technological change and systemic impact), we need leadership at scale.

Here is why. Management is necessary but not sufficient. Leadership now means fast decisions based on imperfect information in rapidly changing environments. It becomes ever more difficult for you and your people to align others, execute your strategy and renew your organization, especially during an organizational transformation.

Looking to the future, we hold the following three imperatives to be true, based on what we have found, what we know collectively as an organization, and what the hundreds of colleagues and friends from McKinsey Academy and beyond tell us.

- **Learn everywhere:** Leadership development is the quintessence of the learning organization; if you are not committed to learning, you will likely not be committed to developing the leaders you need. The future belongs to those organizations that are ready to learn and create conditions for learning, faster than their competition – in other words, those that have learned how to learn.

- **Embrace challenges fast:** The large-scale organizational challenges implied by deep global trends will require swift reaction and response at scale. You get ready for this perpetual change by readying your leaders. Playing catch-up is no longer an option.

- **Go beyond organizations:** As organizations change shape, and do so more frequently and profoundly as opportunities and disruptive forces shape them, leadership itself flows beyond the single organization into the societies around our organizations. The leadership in your organization can affect your society for the better, and it is your duty to shape the right behaviours, skills and mindsets broadly.

And finally …

We hope you share our view of how much can be achieved by developing leaders in your organization, and the risks of not doing so. We know that thinking needs to change with new evidence, and hope that, knowing what we know, you now see what we see and therefore feel as we do about leadership.

We'd also like to share our broader view. We have reached a crucial stage in the evolution of all our organizations and institutions, be they commercial, governmental, charitable, social or national. How we lead our organizations and institutions, ourselves, and each other, will determine our collective future as we tackle the big environmental, population and political challenges.

We have reached the point in human development where the pace of technological and social change is outstripping the capacity of our organizations and institutions. This has happened before, in the first industrial revolution. The difference now is the extreme speed of change.

Companies, industries, governments and whole societies are transforming with such rapidity that old ways of seeing and doing are no longer enough. In times of such rapid change, we need great leadership and great leaders in all that we do. The imperative is to create better leadership inside your organization and beyond to shape our world for the better. That is what we ask of you.

# Appendix 1: Situational leadership – a note on method

McKinsey's research into situational leadership behaviours set out to explore whether different leadership behaviours are more effective in different contexts. We surveyed over 375,000 people from 165 organizations across multiple industries and geographies, covering organizations across all four health quartiles. Drawing both from our own work experience and from evolving academic research, we tested a combination of 20 leadership behaviours (provided by McKinsey's Leadership Development practice)[1] together with the four leadership styles (authoritative, consultative, supportive and challenging) included in McKinsey's Organizational Health Index (OHI). All 24 behaviours were researched together.

Target participants received an experimental survey module whose questions included the 20 new leadership behaviours, as well as the standard questions regarding the four leadership styles usually assessed by our OHI studies. More than 80 per cent of the organizations contacted opted in to the survey; we accumulated surveys from 165 unique organizations, yielding a total data set of more than 375,000 individual respondents – the largest database of its kind.

## The approach

As a first step, to better understand what leaders do that matters to an organization's health, we decided to ignore the distinction between leadership style and leadership behaviours, giving us a total of 24 leadership criteria. We then standardized all scores to minimize the risk of false conclusions – a statistical necessity. (Practices such as 'Financial incentives' always score low while others, like 'Customer focus', are perennial high scorers. And cultural variations mean that some organizations emphasize particular practices differently than others do.)

Our analytical approach called for standardizing question scores for the 24 leadership items, separating them into respective quartiles of organizational health, ranking behaviours within each quartile in order of descending standard mean (z-scores of the item means) and then comparing the respective rank order of adjacent quartiles of behaviours. This resulted in three pairs of comparisons.

First, the rank order of behaviours in the fourth quartile (the bottom quartile) was compared to the rank order of behaviours in the third quartile to identify large rank gaps, specifically differences equal to or greater than eight positions in rank (of 24 possible ranks). Rank order of behaviours rather than segment mean was used for two reasons. First, because leadership behaviours are correlated with OHI, the mean of every behaviour in a given quartile was higher than even the highest behaviour mean of the lower quartile. In other words, as organizations move up a health quartile, we found that they display all 24 leadership elements to a higher degree than organizations in lower quartiles. Second, we were interested in the degree of relative emphasis within situations as we defined them, hence quartiles. In addition to rank, we added two more filters to ensure robustness: behaviours had to have a z-score delta higher than 0.50, and the placement of the behaviour had to be in the upper third (number 8 or higher) in the rank ordered stack on OHI.

Behaviours that passed these tests were placed into the candidate pool for positive differentiators. For example, a focus on 'problem solving' was ranked 18th within the fourth quartile health segment, but among the third quartile segment it was ranked 7th. The behaviour passed all three filters: the rank difference of 11 rank positions cleared our criterion of at least eight positions, the z-score delta was 1.03, exceeding the 0.50 threshold, and it was in the upper third in the rank ordered stack of the healthier quartile of the pair. (Respective mean z-scores were −0.95 and −0.08. The mean difference 1.03 was statistically significant, $p < 0.01$. Similar effect sizes apply to all behaviours selected for the final model.) 'Problem solving' therefore became a candidate for adoption into the ultimate model. Then we shifted focus to comparisons of the third quartile behaviours vs. second quartile, then second quartile to first quartile. We saw that the differentiators themselves differed depending on which two quartiles were being compared. For example, the practices that set apart the third quartile from fourth quartile were not the same as those that separated second quartile from third or first quartile from second. That is what gives our model its 'situational' aspect. So the analysis led to three distinct sets of behaviours that differentiate organizational health, depending on health quartile.

Second, we explored whether any behaviours that might not differentiate by quartile but, if ranked too low, would be diagnostic of a broken (fourth quartile) company. In a sense, these behaviours, if found, would be structurally similar to the 'hygiene factor' of Herzberg's 2-Factor model of job satisfaction. Behaviours so identified would be placed into the candidate pool for ultimate adoption into a hybrid model of leadership with baseline and situational behaviours.

Finally, we repeated the same analysis but looking at negative differentiators, i.e. behaviours that organizations in a given health quartile emphasize significantly less than organizations in the health quartile below them. The same rules applied, though inversely: in order to make the list, behaviours had to be a negative differentiator for health (ranked at least eight positions higher in the weaker OHI quartile and have a z-score delta of at least 0.50), be a negative differentiator for leadership effectiveness, and be placed in the top third (number 8 or higher) in the rank ordered stack of the less healthy quartile of any pair being compared.

To be sure that we weren't optimizing health at the expense of leadership effectiveness, we repeated the entire analysis, but with one difference. We segmented the 165 responding organizations by their relative quartile in leadership effectiveness, as assessed by 'Leadership outcome' — one of the nine components of McKinsey's OHI. The purpose was to rule out the possibility that we were picking up behaviours by companies that were otherwise healthy, but had poor leadership effectiveness nevertheless. The two sets were largely similar, but had some differences. To reconcile differences between the first analysis and the 'repeat' one, we screened every behaviour so that it had to be either a differentiator or a normative behaviour in both analyses. We retained only those behaviours that met both hurdles. In effect, the 15 behaviours in our final model passed a double acid test: they are not only differentiators of health, but of health and leadership effectiveness.

# The results

Our second research question *Is there 'one right way'?, or is leadership situational for organizations?* was answered clearly from our analysis. The analysis yielded what we call a leadership staircase – a pyramid of behaviour analogous to Maslow's hierarchy of needs.[2] In our hierarchy, like similar ones, some kinds of behaviour are always essential. We found four of these, and call them 'baseline behaviours'. These behaviours are similar to the 'hygiene factor' of Herzberg's 2-Factor Hygiene-Motivator model of job satisfaction: when the behaviour is absent, there is dysfunction (bottom quartile organizational health including low leadership effectiveness), but increased emphasis beyond a minimum threshold does not differentiate further.[3]

As organizational health improves, quartile to quartile, additional behaviours become apparent. We call these 'situational behaviours'. More tellingly, some appear to be positive differentiators: emphasizing them in different situations can lift the organizational health of a fourth-quartile company to the third quartile, a third-quartile company to the second quartile, and so on. We found 11 of these behaviours in total. Hence, of the 24 elements we tested, only 15 made a difference. This staircase model aligns squarely with our own real-world observations.

In addition, we identified certain 'negative differentiators'. Organizations in higher health quartiles emphasize these behaviours less than the organizations in health quartiles below them, from a ranking point of view (the absolute numbers were still higher). When applying these findings, we always counsel organizations to work on all 24 leadership elements –what the ranking does is help prioritize within those.[4]

# Appendix 2: The critical enablers – skills and mindsets

In Chapter 3, we outlined the importance of focusing on the underlying skills and mindsets to enable desired behavioural shifts. Here we illustrate what a link between behaviours, skills and mindsets could look like in practice. It includes the behaviours on the leadership staircase – covering both baseline behaviours and situational skills – as well as behaviours that promote adaptability.

It should be noted, however, that the examples we give here are illustrative and not definitive. They are based on our experience and typical observations, and should be taken as a starting point to build upon. We do not claim to be comprehensive, and acknowledge that a great deal of additional research and tools exist for essentially all the behaviours that we discuss. In practice, a great deal of additional design and tailoring takes place when we embed skill-building elements and mindset shifts into a leadership development programme, drawing from a broad range of sources.

## Establishing the baseline

When an organization does not have the baseline behaviours in place, the first priority is to address this. The overriding mindset required for leaders in this situation could be summarized as follows:

> I need to fix the basics, because they are not there and it's hurting the organization. I need to ensure people are working together effectively, and my role is to lead from the front and offer the right support, coupled with the right degree of challenge.

In practice, this means fostering four baseline leadership behaviours, which are important regardless of organizational health. These are:

- facilitating group collaboration effectively
- demonstrating a concern for people
- championing the desired change
- offering a critical perspective

# Facilitating group collaboration effectively

This is one of the most fundamental leadership behaviours, and its importance is most evident in its absence. It could require a number of key mindsets:

- 'Teamwork leads to better outcomes than the sum of individuals working in isolation.'
- 'We need to have a common direction and be able to rely on one another to achieve it.'
- 'People have different preferences and working styles (each of which are equally valid), and not everyone is like me.'
- 'Meeting preparation is important but not enough – I also need to ensure collaboration and creativity in the context of the meeting itself, as well as rigorous follow-up.'

Coupled with this are a number of skills.

1 **Group collaboration and team formation**. Leaders may not always have the luxury of choosing their teams, but it is critical nonetheless to understand the skills required for the task at hand and whether the current team members have them.
2 **The ability to create joint accountability and commitment.**
3 **An understanding of team dynamics**, and how to make different working preferences gel into a high performing teams.
4 **A culture where honest dialogue is possible**, and where conflicts are resolved quickly and effectively.
5 **Fair (and ideally win-win) outcomes**.
6 **Practical skills in running meetings effectively** that can support a leader in facilitating group collaboration.

# Demonstrating a concern for people

First and foremost, leaders need to genuinely care about their colleagues. Coupled with this, it is important to have the mindset that people can only perform at their best if they can be themselves at work, and that one-to-one coaching with direct reports is *necessary* to bring out the best in people (often the latter 'process' point is not present in leaders' minds and, as such, coaching simply does not happen).

Key skills that we often teach in leadership development programmes are the ability to pick up on signals of individuals (for example, through body language, facial expressions, tone of voice, and other behaviour), structured coaching and feedback, and trustworthiness. A common framework for coaching is the GROW model, which consists of setting the Goal (where do you want to go), establishing the current Reality (where are you now), defining Options and in some instances potential Obstacles (what are different paths to get there and what could get in the way), and finally the Way Forward (what are the next steps).[5] A simple framework for establishing trust is that Trust = (credibility + reliability + intimacy), divided by self-orientation.[6]

## Championing the desired change

This may require an understanding from leaders that they must create stories to foster understanding and followership, and a deep conviction that they need to not only 'walk the talk', but proactively and visibly demonstrate their commitment to the change effort. Most leaders understand the need for championing change, but often over-estimate the impact of their efforts to communicate and role-model symbolic actions.

Key skills that could help support this behaviour are an ability to create compelling stories, effective and structured communication, an ability to influence others, the ability to understand the effects of one's emotions and to regulate them accordingly, and energy management. Pyramid Principles are a common way to structure written and verbal communication.[7] Additionally, it is worth pointing out the importance of pivotal moments. Pivotal moments can be both symbolic or substantive, but in both cases they provide an important opportunity for the leader to champion the change. Leaders must be able to anticipate (and in some cases plan ahead for) pivotal moments, and seize them as they arise.

## Offering a critical perspective

This may require the mindset that looking at a problem from different angles improves the solution, and that the leader has an obligation as a leader to ask the right questions and challenge the prevailing thinking.

| | Key skills | Key mindsets |
|---|---|---|
| **Facilitate group collaboration effectively** | • Team formation<br>• The ability to create joint accountability and commitment<br>• Understanding of personality types and team dynamics (e.g. MBTI, Big Five)<br>• Fostering open conversations and resolving conflicts<br>• Negotiation (getting to yes)<br>• Meeting preparation, meeting facilitation, and follow-up | • 'Teamwork leads to better outcomes than the sum of individuals working in isolation'<br>• 'We need to have a common direction and be able to rely on one another to achieve it'<br>• 'People have different preferences and working styles (each of which are equally valid), and not everyone is like me'<br>• 'Meeting preparation is important but not enough – I also need to ensure collaboration and creativity in the context of the meeting itself, as well as rigorous follow-up' |
| **Demonstrate concern for people** | • Ability to pick up on signals of other individuals and anticipate concerns and needs<br>• Structured coaching and feedback (e.g. GROW model)<br>• Trustworthiness (e.g. trust equation) | • 'I care about my colleagues'<br>• 'People matter and perform best if they can be themselves at work (instead of shielding their emotions)'<br>• 'It is necessary to have structured, one-to-one coaching and feedback sessions with all my direct reports' |
| **Champion desired change** | • Storytelling<br>• Effective oral and written communication (e.g. pyramid principles)<br>• Ability to influence others<br>• Ability to recognize your own emotions, understand their effects, and self-regulate as needed<br>• Energy management<br>• Ability to anticipate and seize pivotal moments | • 'Stories are powerful ways to foster understanding and followership'<br>• 'I need to walk the talk and visibly demonstrate my commitment to the change' |
| **Offer a critical perspective** | • A strong sense of what great looks like (e.g. from having an external orientation and broad experience)<br>• Critical thinking (e.g. De Bono's six thinking hats)<br>• Effective questioning<br>• Mastering challenging conversations | • 'Looking at a problem from different angles improves the solution'<br>• 'I have an obligation to ask the right questions and challenge the prevailing thinking' |

FIGURE A.1   Key skills and mindsets for baseline behaviours

We find that many leaders struggle on one or both of these elements. Experiential learning often helps with the first mindset shift ('seeing is believing'), while peer or subordinate feedback helps on the second, which is often driven by a fear of ruining a relationship with a colleague or making colleagues 'look bad'.

An important skill to support this behaviour is often having a strong sense of what great looks like (for example, from having an external orientation and broad experience). Other key skills may be critical thinking, effective questioning, and mastering challenging conversations. De Bono's six thinking hats is a simple yet powerful tool to foster critical thinking and a diversity of perspectives.[8]

All these skills are often key components of our leadership programme curriculum. From our experience, participants often find concrete tools and practising to 'master challenging conversations' particularly useful.

Figure A.1 summarizes the key skills and mindsets that may be relevant for each of the baseline behaviours.

## *Digging out: from fourth quartile to third quartile*

Fourth-quartile organizations tend to be reactive, lacking in clear answers, gloomy, and have a culture of fear and mistrust. Leaders need to reverse all of these, and have an overriding mindset that could be summarized as follows:

The organization is struggling. I need to start developing solutions based on facts, move forward quickly without waiting for a perfect answer, maintain a positive outlook, and maintain my composure during this difficult time.

As such, there are four leadership behaviours which are most effective in increasing the chances of survival and moving into the third quartile. These are:

- solving problems effectively
- making fact-based decisions
- focusing positively and recovering from failures
- remaining composed and confident under uncertainty

# Solving problems effectively

In our early research on decoding leadership, we found that problem solving was the number one component for effective leadership.[9] Problem solving includes both conceptual and analytic problem solving, with both quantitative and qualitative inputs. It is deceptively difficult to get right, yet it is a key input into decision making for major issues (such as M&A) as well as daily ones (such as how to handle a team dispute). For fourth quartile organizations, there could be three key mindsets to enable effective problem solving. First, that 'prioritization and focus are critical, to avoid initiative overload'. Second, a conviction that 'a disciplined problem solving methodology exists, which can enhance the answer'. And third, that 'perfect can be the enemy of good enough, and a bias for action is needed in order to turn the organization around'. A number of skills could help foster these mindsets, for example an ability to frame the key issues/decisions required, applying a structured process to break down a problem, identify pros and cons, and synthesize the insights, ensuring efficient decision-making process, and ability to execute quickly and follow up rigorously.

# Making fact-based decisions

This may require that the leader has the mindsets that 'rigorous facts and objectivity matter', 'I must be a stickler for good logic', and an understanding that 'everyone has biases, including leaders themselves'. While these mindsets may seem extremely simple, at times we see organizations making decisions based on incomplete analyses and facts, and with a low bar for quality of work – implying that rigorous facts and logic do not, in practice, matter. As we discussed in Chapter 2, this mindset is likely one of the reasons that the organization is in the fourth quartile in the first place. There are two key skills that may be helpful. First is an ability to exercise good judgment by making quality and informed decisions based on facts, data and analytics. This is increasingly requiring the ability to collect, manage and interpret big data. Second is the ability to understand and mitigate implicit biases. This includes having an awareness of one's own biases and an ability to improve organizational processes to reduce biases. (Common ways to decrease biases at an organizational level are conducting pre-mortems, creating more diverse teams, assigning a devil's advocate, and including stage gates.) It is important to note that the first two behaviours – solving problems effectively (and moving quickly) and making fact-based decisions are not trade-offs, but are complementary. It is up to leaders in fourth-quartile organizations to understand and balance both elements.

## Focusing positively on recovery from failures

This may require an overarching understanding that 'how one frames a situation has a big impact on the ability to recover from it', and the mindset that 'a challenging situation is an opportunity to learn and grow'. Significant research illustrates this point, for example the notion of having a 'growth' rather than 'fixed' mindset, and the importance of grit, defined as 'perseverance and passion for long-term goals'.

Four key skills may help enable positive recovery:

1 The ability to frame and re-frame a situation (which often in itself leads to a mindset shift in the leader and the broader team).
2 Learned optimism helps a leader move from a situation being Personal, Pervasive and Permanent, to it being Situational, Specific and Short-lived.[10]
3 Solution-focused questioning is a technique that can help explore strengths, resources and opportunities rather than concentrate problems, deficits and challenges.
4 Appreciative enquiry takes a constructionist view that organizations are created, maintained and changed by conversations, and changing the conversation can thus change organizations. Appreciative inquiry has a strong focus on positivity, and encompasses techniques that, for example, moves from root cause problem solving to 'envisioning what might be'.

## Remaining composed and confident in uncertainty

The fourth key behaviour for fourth-quartile companies is remaining composed and confident in uncertainty. This may require an overarching mindset that 'an honest assessment of the situation will help me

| | Key skills | Key mindsets |
|---|---|---|
| **Solve problems effectively** | • Ability to frame the key issues/decisions required<br>• Applying structured process to break down a problem, identify pros and cons, and synthesize the insights<br>• Ensuring efficient decision-making process<br>• Fast execution and rigorous follow-up | • 'Prioritization and focus are critical, to avoid initiative overload'<br>• 'A disciplined problem solving methodology exists, which can enhance my answer'<br>• 'Perfect can be the enemy of good enough, and we need to ensure a bias for action in order to turn this ship around' |
| **Make fact-based decisions** | • Ability to exercise good judgment by making quality and informed decisions based on facts, data, and analytics<br>• Ability to understand and mitigate implicit biases | • 'Rigorous facts and objectivity matter'<br>• 'Good logic is critical'<br>• 'Everyone has biases, including myself' |
| **Focus positively on recovery from failures** | • Framing and re-framing<br>• Optimism and cheerfulness<br>• Growth mindset<br>• Appreciative enquiry | • 'How I frame a situation has a big impact on our ability to recover from it'<br>• 'A challenging situation is an opportunity to learn and grow' |
| **Remain composed and confident in uncertainty** | • Ability to see the world as it is and acknowledge where things are going badly<br>• Ability to recognize your own emotions, understand their effects, and self-regulate as needed<br>• Self-confidence and an understanding of own strengths<br>• Personal resilience | • 'An honest assessment of the situation will help me deal with it better'<br>• 'I cast a shadow 'as a leader and therefore need to maintain my composure even in challenging situations'<br>• 'I have what it takes to make things better' |

FIGURE A.2   Key skills and mindsets to move from fourth quartile to third quartile

deal with it better', understanding that 'I "cast a shadow" as a leader and therefore need to maintain my composure even in challenging situations', and a belief that 'I have what it takes to make things better'. Key skills to enable this are the ability to see the world as it is and acknowledge where things are going badly, the ability to sense and regulate one's own emotions (similar to what is needed to champion a change), self-confidence and an understanding of own strengths (for example, through strengths finder and strengths-based coaching), and personal resilience (for example, through positive psychology).

Figure A.2 summarizes the key skills and mindsets that may be relevant for each behaviour to move from the fourth quartile and into the third.

## Moving up: from third quartile to second quartile

As organizations get things under control and transition to the third quartile, the sense of urgency has typically gone down. However, moving up into the upper half of the OHI rankings and into the second quartile still requires real focus. The overriding mindset required for leaders in this situation could be summarized as follows:

> We have the basics in place, especially around the critical skill of effective problem solving. However, I am still involved in most decisions and spend a lot of energy on keeping the ship on steady ground. It is time to start delegating more, focusing on the development of employees, and building in organizational agility.

There are five leadership behaviours that can help organizations transition into the second quartile:

- having a strong results orientation
- clarifying objectives and consequences
- keeping groups on task
- seeking different perspectives
- being fast and agile

The first three behaviours are broadly around execution and people performance processes, and should be mastered first. The last two have to do with innovation and speed, and are typically the focus of organizations climbing the ranks within the second health quartile itself.

## Having a strong results orientation

An overarching mindset could be that 'honouring commitments to stakeholders (colleagues, customer, market, community) is vital to organizational success'. This is different from bottom-quartile behaviours as it is about embedding the mindset of honouring commitments in a broader sense of organizational culture, not because someone is telling you to do it. Task prioritization, disciplined delivery with quality control, and performance reporting and follow-up are skills which could help enable this. In practice, this means that the overall organizational efficiency and productivity improves, and discipline becomes embedded into the daily work.

## Clarifying objectives and consequences

This has to do with linking the organizational mission with individual tasks, and putting structured people review processes in place. Four key mindsets could support this transition: 'Everyone should understand how their work contributes to the overall organizational mission', 'Clarity enhances performance', 'People deserve to know how they are performing (good and bad) … and it is my job to help them improve', and 'Rewards and consequences should be based on merit'. Four key skills could help here: the ability to translate organizational vision into strategic goals and milestones, and cascading them into individual KPIs; effective performance management discussions (both strengths and development areas); and an ability to link performance with promotion, pay and dismissals.

## Keeping groups on task

This is both at an overall organizational level and at a team level. Leaders need to understand the criticality of the organization keeping its eye on the ball at all times, and have the mindset that 'task alignment across the organization reduces wastage and multiplies speed and productivity'. This could require three skills: project management, workplanning, and RACIs; check-ins and visual management; and effective delegation. We have seen instances where the group is on task but working in the wrong direction, and the key differentiator

from bottom-quartile organizations is that it is no longer about survival and firefighting, but about achieving the overall organizational
vision, with *everyone* working in the same direction to do this.

## Seeking different perspectives

This can be summarized in the mindset that 'diversity of views matter — and I don't always have the answer'. This requires genuine
humility and a degree of curiosity. While this may seem simple, at
times we see leaders make decisions with the mindset that 'I know
best', implying that a diversity of views do not, in practice, matter.
Four key skills could help enable this behaviour.

1 The ability to tap into a broad array of stakeholders, including
   external ones. An example of this could be the leader actively
   forging ties with and setting meetings to solicit input from
   different stakeholders.
2 Creating an open and trusting environment. Employees
   need to feel secure enough to raise issues and state their
   opinions to each other and to leaders. Without such an
   environment, a leader may seek different opinions without
   getting them. At McKinsey, one of our core values is the
   'obligation to dissent', which goes beyond merely a right.
   We expect colleagues of all levels to exercise this obligation,
   and we value the quality of the thinking, not hierarchy.
3 The ability to ask the right question. While providing employees with answers may be quicker in terms of getting things
   done, they limit the potential to get a better answer by incorporating different points of view. They also limit the amount of
   learning and motivation for the employee. Open-ended questions can be used to stimulate new thinking and ideas, while
   more close-ended or targeted questions can help channel the
   discussion in a certain direction. See, for example, the article
   'Relearning the art of asking questions' by Tom Pohlmann
   and Neeti Mary Thomas in *Harvard Business Review*, which
   outlines four types of questions depending on the view of
   the problem (wide vs. narrow) and the intent of the question
   (affirming what we know or discovering something new).[11]

4 Listening. Many people are not inherently good listeners; it is said that most people do not listen with the intent of listening; they listen with the intent to reply.[12] However, listening is a skill that can be acquired by becoming more aware of one's actions and practising new behaviours – for example, maintaining eye contact, listening intently to understand (not to answer), paraphrasing to enhance understanding, and resisting the urge to interrupt.

## Being fast and agile

Finally, it is critical for third-quartile organizations (or organizations at the bottom of the second quartile) to be fast and agile. Our recent research shows that organizations that are able to combine a stability with speed and nimbleness are three to four times more likely to have

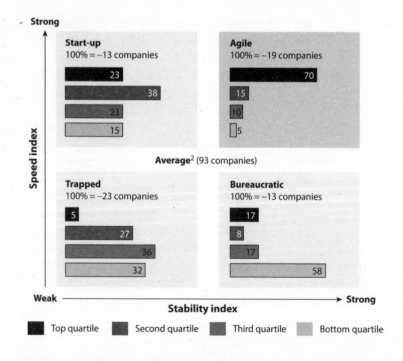

FIGURE A.3 Percentage of organizations within each category, by quartile, for Organizational Health Index (OHI) scores (n = 161)[14]

top quartile health than organizations who lack one of the two elements.[13] Figure A.3 outlines this.

The first three behaviours for the transition between the third quartile the second covered the elements of building 'stability', while the behaviour outlined here helps build 'speed and nimbleness'. Three mindsets could help enable speed and nimbleness: 'Speed matters to competitiveness', 'You can't stand still – we need to keep experimenting and scaling', and 'A certain degree of ambiguity and experimentation is necessary for agility'. These mindsets may be supported by four skills: the ability to collect and act on customer/market insights, disciplined idea generation and ability to scale, rapid learning from experimentation, and inter-disciplinary team effectiveness. In practice, agility is very difficult to get right, and only 12 per cent of the organizations in our sample were agile.[15] As such, in our experience, becoming an agile organization helps not only in the transition to the second quartile but oftentimes also in the transition to the top quartile.

Figure A.4 summarizes the key skills and mindsets for each behaviour to move from the third quartile and into the second.

## To the top: from second quartile to first quartile

As organizations begin to focus on moving up to the top health quartile, it is important to remember that the different levels of the situational leadership staircases are additive. In other words, despite shifting the relative focus in behaviours as organizations transition from one quartile to the next, they must still be sure to continue the behaviours from the quartiles below them, including the baseline behaviours. Top quartile companies should in fact focus on all 15 leadership behaviours, and this is also what we see in practice – top quartile companies do, in fact, do more of all 15 behaviours than second quartile companies, which in turn do them more than third quartile companies, who do them more than bottom quartile companies.

Moving into the top quartile requires a marked shift in mindsets, skills and behaviours of leaders. Success becomes increasingly about enabling the organization to reach its full potential, and the overriding mindset required for leaders in this situation could be summarized as follows:

| | Key skills | Key mindsets |
|---|---|---|
| **Strong results orientation** | • Task prioritization<br>• Disciplined delivery with quality control<br>• Performance reporting and follow-up | • 'Honoring commitments to our stakeholders (colleagues, customer, market, community) is vital to organizational success' |
| **Clarify objectives and consequences** | • Translating organizational vision into strategic goals and milestones, and cascading them into individual KPIs<br>• Effective performance management discussions (both strengths and development areas)<br>• Ability to link performance with promotion, pay, and dismissals | • 'Everyone should understand how their work contributes to the overall organizational mission'<br>• 'Clarity enhances performance'<br>• 'People deserve to know how they are performing (good and bad) ... and it is my job to help them improve'<br>• 'Rewards and consequences should be based on merit' |
| **Keep group on task** | • Project management, workplanning, and RACI<br>• Check-ins and visual management<br>• Effective delegation | • 'We need to keep our eyes on the prize at all times'<br>• 'Task alignment reduces wastage and multiplies speed and productivity' |
| **Seek different perspectives** | • Tapping into broad array of stakeholders, including external ones<br>• Creating an open and trusting environment<br>• Asking the right questions<br>• Listening | • 'Diversity of views matter – and I don't always have the answer' |
| **Be fast and agile** | • Ability to collect and act on customer/market insights<br>• Disciplined idea generation and ability to scale<br>• Rapid learning from experimentation<br>• Inter-disciplinary team effectiveness | • 'Speed matters to competitiveness'<br>• 'You can't stand still – we need to keep experimenting and scaling'<br>• 'A certain degree of ambiguity and experimentation is necessary for agility' |

FIGURE A.4 Key skills and mindsets to move from third quartile to second

> We're doing great, but what I need to do to get to the next level is to appeal to some of the most talented people in the world and get them to realize that what is important for the organization is important for them, and help them unleash their performance.

There are two leadership behaviours that can help organizations transition into the first quartile:

- motivating and bringing out the best in others
- modelling organizational values

## Motivating and bringing out the best in others

This may require overarching mindsets that 'intrinsic motivation is more powerful than extrinsic motivation – people perform better when they are engaged and find meaning in their work, feel ownership, and are empowered' and 'I need to let a thousand flowers bloom'. Contrary to the earlier quartiles, where leadership is typically more top down and the focus is often on avoiding initiative overload, becoming a top quartile company often requires leaders to be comfortable with ambiguity, bottom-up innovation, and letting the organization experiment. It can also be helpful to think of a transition 'from boss to coach'. Bringing out the best in others is no easy feat, and relies on a careful combination of psychology, coaching, and even philosophy.

Six other key skills are helpful in this area:

1 The ability to set and communicate a powerful and exciting vision.
2 The ability to create/recreate meaning for self and others. The key here is to appeal to different 'sources of meaning' in people – when we ask people to rate their number one source of meaning from a list consisting of 'personal development', 'internal relationships/team', 'customers', 'company/performance', and 'society', we see a fairly even split of responses across the five choices. (In reality, people are often motivated by all five elements at the same time, to varying degrees, but the exercise forces people to choose their number one source of meaning.)

3 The ability to inspire and energize others. This brings us back to the energy management, which we also discussed as being helpful for the baseline behaviour of 'championing the desired change'. The difference here is the direction of the energy – rather than channelling it to lead from the front, here it is more about motivating people to take charge and reaching beyond what they think is possible for themselves.

4 Positive psychology.

5 Strengths-based and peak performance coaching – both of which are intricately linked to the first three skills.

6 Empowerment, which is often challenging at lower health quartiles as the supporting systems, processes, capabilities and cultures are not in place. It requires the leader to balance the giving of independence while still providing timely guidance and holding people accountable.

## Modelling organizational values

The second group of leadership behaviours that can help organizations transition into the top quartile is to model organizational values. Here, the key mindsets could be 'I am a role-model for the organization' and 'people want to work for an organization they believe in'. We find that five key skills could help leaders display this behaviour.

1 Self-confidence to make decisions based on a clear set of values.

2 Judgement – which is especially important when dealing with 'grey zones' and using organizational values to guide one's behaviour.

3 The ability to link organizational values to the day-to-day tasks of individuals, and to appeal to their values emotions.

4 Storytelling and the ability to bring values to life.

5 The ability to establish rituals and symbolic actions, based on an understanding of what will have the biggest impact on employees.

6 Integrity, which one could argue is not a skill but rather a trait, but which we nonetheless include as we believe that increased self-awareness can indeed help leaders act with more integrity.

Figure A.5 summarizes the key skills and mindsets for each behaviour to move from the second quartile into the first quartile.

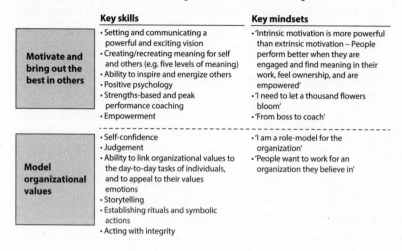

| | Key skills | Key mindsets |
|---|---|---|
| **Motivate and bring out the best in others** | • Setting and communicating a powerful and exciting vision<br>• Creating/recreating meaning for self and others (e.g. five levels of meaning)<br>• Ability to inspire and energize others<br>• Positive psychology<br>• Strengths-based and peak performance coaching<br>• Empowerment | • 'Intrinsic motivation is more powerful than extrinsic motivation – People perform better when they are engaged and find meaning in their work, feel ownership, and are empowered'<br>• 'I need to let a thousand flowers bloom'<br>• 'From boss to coach' |
| **Model organizational values** | • Self-confidence<br>• Judgement<br>• Ability to link organizational values to the day-to-day tasks of individuals, and to appeal to their values emotions<br>• Storytelling<br>• Establishing rituals and symbolic actions<br>• Acting with integrity | • 'I am a role-model for the organization'<br>• 'People want to work for an organization they believe in' |

FIGURE A.5  Key skills and mindsets to move from second quartile to first

## Adaptive leadership

There are two mindsets that could help foster adaptive leadership. First is the mindset 'what got me here won't get me there', alternatively put as 'the world is changing and I need to change with it'. Leaders must maintain the imperative to keep learning and adapting in order to move forward; they do not have all the answers. This dual outlook requires humility, curiosity and being in 'learning' rather than 'protection' mode. The second mindset underpinning adaptive leadership is acknowledging that feedback is important to increase one's self-awareness and development. This mindset goes beyond just being open to feedback, and entails proactively seeking out feedback, reflecting on it, and being prepared to act on it.

A learning mindset could be defined as having a beginner's mindset, interest in other perspectives, desire to learn more about ourselves and our situation, emotional availability, interest in discovery, a focus on the future, and ownership of problems and seeking of solutions in ourselves.

A protection mindset could be defined as having an expert mindset, holding on to own opinions and assumptions, hiding/denying own shortcomings, holding on to the questions and answers we know, emotional unavailability, being uptight and closed, a focus on the past, and a perception that problems are caused by others. In McKinsey's leadership development programmes, we find that helping participants move into a 'learning mindset' is a critical success factor for the learning journeys.

We find that the key skills and tools related to adaptability have to do with increasing one's self-awareness – especially around behaviour or knowledge gaps – and acting on these insights. This requires a certain level of meta-cognition, or 'thinking about thinking', in order to 'know what you know' and 'know what you don't know'. A helpful tool here is the 'four stages of growth' framework. For any skill or behaviour, people can be Unconsciously Unskilled ('I don't know what I don't know'), Consciously Unskilled ('I am aware of what I have to learn, but don't know how to do it'), Consciously Skilled ('I can do it but I need to think about it'), and Unconsciously Skilled ('I can do it naturally, without thinking'). Moving from UU to CU requires increased aware or a new insight (i.e. 'structural awareness'). Moving from CU to CS requires a choice. You have to choose to do things differently. For example, you could put a reminder before meetings to 'speak less, and listen more', and then be conscious about this choice as the meeting progresses. This builds on 'in the moment awareness', but adds in self-regulation, and leads to a change in behaviour as well. Moving from CS to US requires deliberate practice. By continuing to make a choice, your brain builds new neural pathways to help make the practice sustainable. With sufficient practice, the new skill or behaviour becomes natural and effortless.

Realizing that you don't know something or having a similar 'aha' moment is often the first step in adapting to new situation. We call this structural awareness, and it can be triggered by for example, an event, an upset, or self-reflection (for example, during a leadership development forum with a facilitated exercise). For example, a leader could receive a 360-degree feedback report, and realize that they tend to dominate meetings, without giving colleagues a chance to speak.

The next step requires the leader to make a choice to improve in that particular area, followed by deliberate practice in order to do so. This includes fostering 'in-the-moment' awareness, i.e. the ability to catch oneself in the moment and adapt one's behaviour accordingly.

In the example above, the leader would need to become aware of their behaviour during subsequent meetings, for example by giving themselves a reminder to monitor their behaviour, and then choose a different set of actions than they would normally do. In-the-moment awareness can be enhanced through mindfulness meditation, which trains the brain to bring its attention back to the present, building attention density and increased mental clarity.[16]

Our Centred Leadership approach helps to build adaptability by providing practical tools to increase one's self-awareness across the five dimensions of Meaning, Framing, Connecting, Engaging and Energizing. It also helps build resilience to withstand complex and changing environments, as Centred Leaders are able to lead from an inner core of self-mastery. Figure A.6 summarizes the key skills and mindsets for adaptive leadership.

| | Key skills | Key mindsets |
|---|---|---|
| **Ability to learn and adapt to a dynamic context** | • Four stages of growth<br>  – Self-awareness (both structural and in the moment)<br>  – Self-regulation and ability to choose<br>  – Deliberate practice<br>• Centered Leadership practices around Meaning, Framing, Connecting, Engaging and Energizing | • 'What got me here won't get me there' humility/beginner's mind<br>• 'Feedback is important for me to increase my self-awareness and improve' |

FIGURE A.6  Key skills and mindsets for adaptive leadership

As with the situational behaviours, these are guide rails against which we design leadership programmes to bring about a desired change in behaviour, and not a manual that should be adhered to strictly. Furthermore, the guide rails are not comprehensive. There are surely many other ways to bring about the desired behaviours, but we offer a robust starting point.

These tables should not be seen as a manual, however. Rather, they offer examples of skills and mindsets that we have seen work in practice, and which we would consider as a starting point, or 'primary lens', when designing leadership development programmes. However, each context requires adaptation. We often overlay 'secondary' lenses as required – for example an organization's industry context and 'recipe', its stage of growth, or its aspirations and strategy – in order to tailor the programme as required.

# Appendix 3: Boosting individual learning and performance

Here we expand on the five elements we highlighted in Core Principle 3, which can help boost both learning and performance in general:

- single-tasking
- growth mindsets and awareness of stereotype threats
- elimination of biases
- maintaining a healthy lifestyle
- meditation and mindfulness

We do not categorize them as 'adult learning principles', but organizations would undoubtedly benefit from taking them into account, as they enhance learning transfer but also general performance. Especially the areas of maintaining a healthy lifestyle and meditation and mindfulness are making inroads into organizations, and for good reason, as we outline below.

## Single-tasking: the 'idle brain space' neuromyth

Despite the speculation on whether it would be evolutionary useful that 90 per cent of an organ which represents only 2 per cent of body weight and yet consumes 20 per cent of energy, should be idle, the myth that we only use a very small fraction of our brain has prevailed. This neuromyth serves as the basis for several novels and science-fiction movies. It has been further supported by the premature interpretation of activation hotspots obtained by imaging studies. When interpreting the lack of signal in the rest of the brain during these studies, it was forgotten that most functional imaging contrasts two conditions (i.e. the activation might have simply been cancelled out in the comparison) and that a statistical threshold is underlying the results (i.e. having no signal with the chosen statistical threshold does not mean having 'no activation at all').[17]

By now, more carefully interpreted functional brain scans have shown that, irrespective of what a person is doing, generally the entire brain is active and, depending on the task, some areas are more active than others. People learn new ideas and new skills, not by tapping into an unused part of the brain, but by forming new or stronger connections between nerve cells. Doing this requires *attention*, which is the cognitive process of selectively concentrating on one aspect of the environment while ignoring others. Attention is essential not only to learn, but also to carry out tasks in general and succeed at work, in relationships, and for self-awareness.

This insight has important implications for our effectiveness on the job and for learning. Everybody knows the habit of quickly checking e-mails or planning for the next meeting in the middle of a meeting or training session. Today's life and working environment – with smartphones and 'always on' culture – pose serious challenges to our ability to 'single-task'. The problem is that multi-tasking engages large parts of the brain's working memory; this diverts attention away from our initial (primary) focus. In other words, the brain is not able to multi-task because multi-tasking requires us to switch between concurrent tasks[18] (all of which require attention); this in turn commits large parts of the working memory's capacity, diminishing our overall ability to carry out tasks and to learn.[19]

## Growth mindsets and awareness of stereotype threats

There is intriguing work demonstrating that the mindset of a person has a clear impact on the outcome of learning and performance. As an example of this influence, take the following experiment: Female Asian students reminded of their Asian heritage performed much better in a subsequent math exam compared to a group which was reminded of the stereotype that 'maths is hard for girls'.[20] The 'stereotype threat' leads to a negative perception and mindset on your own performance and learning in general significantly deteriorates performance and learning outcomes.[21]

A growth mindset, on the other hand, with a positive attitude towards oneself and learning, improves one's ability to overcome challenges and learn. People with a 'growth mindset', in contrast to those with a 'fixed mindset', love challenges, enjoy effort, strive to learn, value and believe in their improvement and consistently see potential to develop new skills.[22] Studies show that learning interventions in which a growth mindset was instilled in high school students by, for example, describing the brain as a muscle that can become stronger the more it is used, helped to trigger significant improvement in grades and study habits[23]. Organizations must thus cultivate an atmosphere and culture of learning, to help overcome stereotype threats and fixed mindsets. This boosts not only learning but also performance in general.

## Elimination of biases

There is increasing work on the ingrained biases that humans have, popularized by, among others, Daniel Kahneman. For example, people have a 'confirmation bias' (tendency to seek confirming evidence), 'availability bias' (focusing on the most easily recalled information or vivid events), and an 'overconfidence bias' (overstating one's abilities).

The challenge is two-fold: first, people are often unaware of their biases. Second, even if people are aware, they are still as susceptible to making the cognitive errors as others, if pushed to make a quick decision and not using the 'thinking slow' system of Kahneman.[24] We will not go into an in-depth review (for that, please refer to the references). Instead we will draw the implications for learning interventions.

Biases reduce working effectiveness and the readiness of the brain to learning. In terms of general performance, they can lead to employees taking the wrong decision, based on incomplete data (for example, an investment decision). In a learning context, some might think that they have 'less to learn' than others, or approach learning with a mindset of confirming what they already know instead of seeking new insights; both could inhibit the learning process.

The reason to find and counter biases is to help individuals (and for that matter whole organizations and even societies) understand how they make decisions and make better ones. Learning interventions should build in time for self-reflection and explicit discussions about biases. At an organizational level, it is important to build in the right structures and processes to improve decision-making.

## Maintaining a healthy lifestyle

If we are tired, our mind wants to go to sleep. If we do not exercise, the mind becomes restless and less energized. If we are hungry, our mind is thinking of food. If we are overly stressed, we may become anxious and even depressed. These are the basic hygiene factors that need to be in place to enhance our performance and our experience of learning. However, as we show below, these elements are more than hygiene factors. Sleep, physical activity, nutrition, and stress management are essential for both physical energy as well as mental clarity. Getting these factors right is not just a 'nice to have', it should be regarded as a 'must have', in order to enhance employee performance and learning. (These elements are not meant to be comprehensive – they do not cover, for example, interventions based on positive psychology or spirituality – however, they offer the key building blocks to maintaining a healthy lifestyle.)

That sleep, exercise, nutrition, and stress management are important is not new information for anyone reading this book. *Mens sana in corpore sano* ('a healthy mind in a healthy body' interpreted to mean that physical exercise and bodily health are essential parts of mental and psychological well-being) was said almost two thousand years ago by the Roman poet Juvenal. What is different now, with the advent of more advanced fMRI techniques, is our ability to measure the magnitude of the impact of a healthy lifestyle on our ability to carry out cognitive tasks and learn new ones. And that impact is big. Below we review the impact of sleep, exercise, nutrition, and stress management on your ability to focus on tasks and learn new skills. The reviews are brief, and we refer the interested reader to the original references.

### THE USES OF SLEEP

When we speak of learning, we're speaking about three distinct phases:

1 Encoding phase in which we take in new information.
2 The consolidation phase, when the brain forms new connections, through which we ensure the new memory trace will be consolidated to long-term memory.
3 The retrieval stage in which we retrieve the relevant information from long-term memory.

A wealth of scientific studies have highlighted the impact of sleep on all three stages of the learning process. This is true regardless of the specific type of memory involved (for example whether you are learning a new language or a new motor skill).[25]

In addition, sleep deficiencies impair the performance of leaders by undermining important forms of leadership behaviours. Sleep-deprived brains struggle to carry out higher order executive functions involving the neocortex: these are functions such as problem solving, reasoning, organizing, inhibition, planning, and executing plans.[26] To give just a few examples, research shows that after roughly 17 to 19 hours of wakefulness (let's say at 11 p.m. or 1 a.m. for someone who got up at 6 a.m.), individual performance on a range of tasks is equivalent to that of a person with a blood-alcohol level of 0.05 per cent. That's the legal drinking/driving limit in many countries. After roughly 20 hours of wakefulness (2 a.m.), this same person's performance equals that of someone with a blood-alcohol level of 0.1 per cent, which meets the legal definition of drunkenness in the United States.[27]

Another study found that lack of sleep can severely alter emotional intelligence. In a sleep-deprived state, the brain is more likely to misinterpret emotional cues from others and to overreact to emotional events,[28] and you tend to express your feelings in a more negative manner and tone of voice.[29] Recent studies have shown that people who have not had enough sleep are less likely to fully trust someone else, and another experiment has demonstrated that employees feel less engaged with their work when their leaders have had a bad night of sleep.[30] Additionally, it is also well known that lack of sleep has a profound effect on our physical health through its effects on our immune system, metabolism, cell renewal and cardiovascular health. It can also lead to accelerated cognitive decline (brain aging) and early death. The main takeaway: for most people, this means ensuring at least seven to nine hours of quality sleep per night.[31] Key factors that typically affect sleep quality are stress, caffeine, alcohol in excess of one glass of wine (or equivalent), and a non-conducive sleep environment (for example, noisy, light, too hot/cold, uncomfortable pillow, blanket or mattress). In addition, it can be helpful to maintain a fairly consistent sleep schedule, and avoiding long naps during the day.

The issue is that a large number of executives do not get enough sleep, and remain in denial about the facts.[32] Almost half (46 per cent) believe that lack of sleep has little impact on leadership performance. Four out of ten (43 per cent) say they do not get enough sleep at least four nights a week (and nearly six out of ten that they do not sleep enough at least three nights a week). 66 per cent said they were generally dissatisfied with how much sleep they get, and 55 per cent were dissatisfied with the quality of sleep. Almost half (47 per cent) of the leaders in our survey felt that their organizations expect them to be 'on' too long and too responsive to emails and phone calls. And 83 per cent of the leaders said their organizations did not spend enough effort educating leaders about the importance of sleep.

## EXERCISE

Recent studies have shown clearly that the cognitive abilities of someone in good physical condition are different (better) than those of someone in poor physical condition. And that someone in poor physical condition can improve cognitive functions by getting into shape. The majority of studies reviewing the link between exercise and cognitive function have centred on the elderly and show that a healthy lifestyle correlates highly with cognitive performance, on measures such as long-term memory, reasoning, attention, problem-solving, abstract thinking and improvization. Exercise has also been shown to promote brain elasticity and thus improve the ability to learn.[33]

While less conclusive, other studies show that the benefits of exercise are not limited to the elderly, but benefit all adults[34] as well as children in school.[35] One study, for example, looked at more than 10,000 British civil servants aged between 35 and 55, and showed that employees with low levels of physical activity were more likely to have lower levels of cognitive performance, especially related to fluid intelligence (requiring improvisatory problem solving).[36] Studies have also shown that it is in fact exercise itself that increases cognitive function (and not that smarter people are more likely to exercise in the first place).[37]

There are also strong indications that exercise can help enhance creativity,[38] improve mood and confidence (in part due to the release of serotonin),[39] reduce stress (in part due to the release of endorphins),[40] and improve productivity and energy levels (through the release of dopamine).[41] Finally, though not elaborated on here, it is worth mentioning that exercise helps slow aging, prevent age-related mental illnesses (for example, dementia, Alzheimers), improve mood in general, decrease depression, and boost the immune system.[42]

It is important to note that not all cognitive activities are affected by exercise – short term memory and certain reaction times, for example, seem uncorrelated to exercise. In addition, there is a high degree of variance between how much individuals benefit from it. The vast majority of people do indeed typically show improvements, but some show none. Nonetheless, the evidence points towards an important role of exercise in learning and general employee performance.

The next question, then, is how much exercise is enough? The gold standard is that we should do a minimum of three weekly sessions of aerobic exercise (for example, jogging, biking, swimming), at around 30 minutes each time. However, there are many ways to achieve the equivalent of 3 × 30 mins per week more efficiently, which can be especially helpful when busy. Examples include high intensity interval training (HIIT), and shorter high intensity circuit training (HICT) workouts done daily (for example, Tabata four-minute circuits and 'the seven-minute workout'). Adding in anaerobic exercise (strength training) once or twice a week can furthermore enhance physical and mental results. Strength training is especially important during weight loss programmes, as it helps maintain (or even build) muscle mass. It is generally considered safe (and even beneficial) to exercise up to six days per week, at 30–60 minutes per session.[43] However, some studies have shown that over-training can begin to reverse the mental health benefits of training.[44] Individual results will vary, and it is always best to consult a physician prior to changing an exercise regime.

In addition, it is important to consider the effects of one's lifestyle in general. Even when exercising the recommended amount, there could still be health implications from an overly sedentary lifestyle. The majority of the calories we are burn are from 'non-exercise activity thermogenesis' (NEAT), i.e. the energy expended for everything we do that is not sleeping, eating or sports-like exercise, such as walking, typing, performing yard work, and fidgeting. Even trivial physical activities increase metabolic rate substantially and it is the cumulative impact of these activities that culminate in an individual's daily NEAT.[45] The implications? It is important to couple a regular exercise regime with a more active lifestyle. This includes walking more (and measuring this using a pedometer), cycling to work, taking up physical hobbies (for example, gardening, trekking, dancing) taking the stairs, and using standing work stations.

## NUTRITION

Like exercise, the important role of a varied and healthy diet in regards to general health and to cognitive function is not new. Studies have shown, for example, that specific nutrients have important effects on the brain's ability to function and learn. Some of the beneficial nutrients highlighted in a comprehensive study are omega-3 fatty acids, curcumin, flavonoids, saturated fat, vitamins B, C, D, E, choline, carotene, calcium, zinc, selenium, copper and iron.[46]

Other studies have highlighted the role of blood sugar (glucose) levels and insulin on brain function. The brain requires a steady supply of glucose to function properly. Insulin aids this process by helping to move glucose into the cells in the body. If blood sugar levels drop too low, the brain is unable to concentrate and we may even experience dizziness or drowsiness. If, on the other hand, we consume too much sugar (and cause a spike in blood sugar levels) our body produces extra insulin to help drive the extra glucose into the cells. This insulin spike can deplete our normal glucose levels more rapidly than usual, causing blood sugar levels to fall below normal levels one or two hours after the 'sugar rush'. This can lead to impaired cognitive functions (for example, inability to concentrate), mood swings (for example, irritability); it also depresses the immune system and promotes fat storage.[47]

More progressive research has focused on the interaction between microbiomes in the gut and the brain. There is increasing evidence that intestinal microbiota influence brain development and behaviour. Studies on humans have been limited (most are on animals), but researchers have drawn links between alterations in the gut microbiome (for example, from different types of food intakes) and neurological conditions, including autism spectrum disorder, anxiety, depression and chronic pain. One experiment found, for example, that eating yoghurt twice a day, for four weeks, made (human) subjects react more calmly than a control group to a series of images of facial expressions depicting emotions such as happiness, sadness and anger. It is posited that bacteria in the yogurt changed the makeup of the subjects' gut microbes, and that this led to the production of compounds that modified brain chemistry.[48]

Finally, it is worth mentioning the importance of proper hydration. Even mild dehydration, defined as a one to two per cent loss in normal water volume in the body, has been shown to influence mood, energy levels and the ability to think clearly. Mild dehydration can happen in as little as four hours without drinking.[49]

The sum of the above studies reinforce the importance of nutrition in peak cognitive performance. The typical guidelines for managing nutrition are to eat a varied diet with a good mix of proteins, healthy fats, fibre, and complex carbohydrates, avoiding processed/low nutrient foods and sugars, and ideally dividing one's required calorie intake into four to five small meals spread throughout the day to maintain blood sugar and brain glucose levels. In addition, it is important to stay properly hydrated and drink eight glasses of water per day, while avoiding excessive caffeine and alcohol. We also recommend learning the basics of calories and nutrition, in order to be able to understand nutrition labels on food and drink products, and manage one's calorie intake. Important measures to track are one's weight, body fat percentage and waistline. According to numerous studies, the waistline is one of the best predictors of future health, and a large waist circumference is linked to numerous diseases including cancer, Alzheimers and diabetes.

## STRESS MANAGEMENT AND RECOVERY

Stress, in itself, is not bad – as we saw in Core Principle 3, stretching people outside of their comfort zones is an important element of enhancing learning and performance. The issue arises when the stress is too severe or continues for an extended period of time, which can lead to regular bouts of acute stress or chronic stress. Stress has increased in many parts of the world over the past 30 years. Today, over 50 per cent of employees in major economies globally feel that stress negatively impacts work productivity, and six out of ten people feel that their stress levels are rising.[50] Stress has been dubbed 'the silent killer' as well as the 'health epidemic of the 21st century' by the World Health Organization. It affects more areas than people are typically aware of, and can lead to a weakened immune system, fertility problems, higher blood pressure, heart disease, anxiety, depression, insomnia, obesity and muscle pain.

As such, it is critical to understand the symptoms of stress and how to recover. Some common symptoms include headaches, feeling over-whelmed, feeling nervous or anxious, muscle aches, chest pain and rapid heartbeat, insomnia, frequent colds and infections, low energy, and feeling depressed or sad. Research shows that symptoms are recognized by most people (i.e. people know that they are stressed), yet far from everyone deals with stress in an optimal way. A large portion of people do not discuss the symptoms with their physicians even after feeling them for an extended period of time, and many resort to unhealthy coping mechanisms (for example, smoking, drinking, eating junk food, drugs, and withdrawal from friends and family). Additionally, stress can be formally measured in a number of ways, including HRV tests or through questionnaires.

While there are a large number of stress management tech-niques – including prioritization, time management, cognitive therapy, and good old stress balls – our focus here is on the broad concept of recovery. Recovery is an energy management concept that is well known and scientifically adopted in the training plans of professional athletes: Roger Federer and Usain Bolt typically sleep over 10 hours a day and – to perform at their peak during competitions – their training plans foresee periods of total rest to recharge their batteries. Recovery is a stress management technique (for both physical and mental stress) that has to do with understanding one's thresholds and ensuring adequate recovery when the thresholds are breached.

The growing 'always-on' culture that many people (especially lead-ers) experience in many cases hinders effective recovery, often result-ing in increased stress and decreased energy levels and performance. For people to perform at their peak, they need recovery. Recovery can take many forms, but in general it requires elements of the following:

- Daily 'downtime' where you are not checking work emails or 'on call', for example, in the evening and first thing in the morning
- Spending at least 40 minutes a day on an activity you love and that sets your mind free from work preoccupations. This can be as simple as spending time with the family, exercising, cooking, gardening etc.
- Weekly 'downtime' – at least one day a week with no work commitments and where you do not check work emails

- After longer periods of intense work, taking sufficient time off to fully recover. Depending on the type of work you do, this could be, for example, a yearly three-week vacation
- Techniques such as meditation and mindfulness, breathing exercises, relaxation treatments and sound therapy may also help with stress management and recovery

In sum, it is important to view stress management and recovery in the same light as proper sleep, exercise, and nutrition. The four elements are interlinked and must all be in place in order to have a healthy lifestyle. If even just one of them is not there, your health will likely be compromised.

## MEDITATION AND MINDFULNESS

We discussed above that meditation and mindfulness can help with stress management and recovery. However, meditation and mindfulness has benefits in its own right. It is well established that attention is a crucial pre-requisite for learning. There are promising results showing that regular meditation and mindfulness exercises can enhance attention capabilities and therefore improve the general learning process.[51] Moreover, meditation sessions have shown to improve cognitive functions like mental spatial capabilities[52] and the ability to make fine visual discrimination.[53]

Psychologists have been studying the ancient contemplative practice of mindful meditation since the 1970s, and scientific interest in mindfulness has grown rapidly in the past decade. Now, a large number of peer-reviewed studies have carefully described the many physical and mental health benefits of the practice of mindful meditation. These benefits include – besides the above mentioned effects on attention and visual discrimination – reduced stress, relief from symptoms of anxiety and depression, improved sleep quality and emotional well-being[54] and boosts in the immune system. In addition, meditation can help people build more self-awareness, clarity and centredness.[55]

Even simple meditation techniques such as concentrated breathing have been shown to increase grey matter in parts of the brain associated with learning and memory, controlling emotions and compassion. For example, a team led by Harvard scientists has shown that just eight weeks of mindful meditation can produce structural brain changes significant enough to be picked up by MRI scanners.[56]

For these reasons, an increasingly prominent cadre of organizations are giving their employees opportunities to benefit from mindfulness and meditation.[57] Most such programmes have garnered enthusiastic support from employees, who often see a marked improvement in their mindsets and job performance.

For example, employees at the health insurer Aetna who have participated in the company's free yoga and meditation classes report, on average, a 28 per cent decrease in their levels of stress and a productivity increase of 62 minutes a week – an added value of approximately $3,000 per employee a year. CEO Mark Bertolini, who started the programme a few years ago, marvels at the level of interest generated across the company; to date, more than a quarter of Aetna's 50,000 employees have taken at least one class. Leaders like Bertolini understand that providing them with the tools to become more focused and mindful can foster a better working environment conducive to development and high performance.[58]

# About the Authors

**Claudio Feser** is a Senior Partner and one of the founders of McKinsey's Leadership Development practice. Claudio has been in the Firm for 25 years and has published several leadership books, including *Serial Innovators* and *When Execution Isn't Enough*.

**Michael Rennie** is a former Senior Partner and Global Head of McKinsey's Organization Practice. Michael was at the Firm for over 30 years and pioneered McKinsey's approach to culture change more than 20 years ago. He has published *The Performance Culture Imperative*.

**Nicolai Chen Nielsen** is an Associate Partner with McKinsey, and has been with the Firm for 7 years. Nicolai leads McKinsey's latest research on leadership development at scale, and has designed and delivered leadership development programs in the public and private sectors globally.

# Contributor biographies

**André Dua** is a Senior Partner in McKinsey's New York office. He is a founder of McKinsey Academy, the founder of McKinsey's Higher Education Practice, and the founder of McKinsey's State and Local Government Practice. He works on capability building transformations for leading global institutions, public sector transformation at the federal, state, and city level, and works extensively on the future of higher education. Andre has published articles and books on higher education, government performance, citizen experience, and trade and environmental practices, including *Sustaining the Asia Pacific Miracle: Economic Integration and Environmental Protection* (Petersen Institute for International Economics). Andre was a Research Fellow at the Yale Center for Environmental Law and Policy and holds an LLM from Yale University, and a BEc and LLB (both highest honours) from the University of Sydney.

**Andrew St George** advises McKinsey on leadership and organizational development. He has written ten books in linguistics, communications and management, including *Royal Navy Way of Leadership* for UK Naval Command. He works with commercial organizations (finance, retail) public services (NHS, international military, police, fire) and governments. He is a certified Marshall Goldsmith (ICF) executive and team coach. Andrew was educated at Cambridge (BA), Harvard (Kennedy Fellow) and Oxford (DPhil & Research Fellow); he has held faculty appointments at Harvard, Columbia and Oxford (now Associate Fellow, Said Business School); he serves on two charity boards, is a Fellow of the Royal Society of Arts and Royal Geographical Society and an Honorary RN Submariner. Andrew lives with his wife and their three daughters in Oxfordshire and the beautiful Wye valley in Wales; he loves mountaineering, cycling and fly-fishing.

**Arne Gast** leads the Organization Practice across Asia–Pacific, based in McKinsey's Kuala Lumpur Office. His work focuses on operating model design, transformational change, and leadership development – and often includes renewing HR organizations. He works across industries, serving clients in banking, med-tech, electricity, telecom, oil and gas and paper. Arne is the co-founder of Aberkyn, McKinsey's special 'home' for change facilitation that grew into eight global hubs over recent years. He is one of the lead facilitators of Change Leader Forums across the world. He has contributed to many McKinsey Quarterly Articles, and to books (*Blue Ocean Strategy*, *Beyond Performance*, *Mobilizing Minds* and *ReOrg*). Arne holds an MSc in Economics from Erasmus University in Rotterdam and an MBA from INSEAD in Fontainebleau. Arne is passionate about education, having worked with multiple universities, establishing ISB, and leading the Leerkracht Foundation in the Netherlands. In his free time he is a passionate Leica photographer, and tries to keep up his field hockey game. Arne lives with his wife and their four children in Kuala Lumpur.

**Bill Schaninger** is a Senior Partner in McKinsey's Philadelphia office. He is Chairman of Integrated Org Solutions, and leader of Global Talent Management Practice, working with a globally diverse client portfolio (including institutions in Energy, Oil and Gas, Basic Materials, Banking and Insurance). Bill applies analytical rigor and the principles of organizational psychology to the largest and most complicated client settings. He holds PhD in Management and an MS in Human Resources from Auburn University, and an MBA and a BA from Moravian College.

**Charlotte Relyea** is a Partner in McKinsey's New York office and leader of McKinsey Academy. Prior to leading McKinsey Academy, Charlotte was a co-leader of McKinsey's Client Capability Building initiative; and a leader in McKinsey's Tech, Media, Telecom and Marketing and Sales practices. She served media, information, high-tech and financial services companies on topics including sales and marketing effectiveness, front-line capability building, go-to-market strategy and new digital business building. Charlotte holds a BA in English from Princeton University and an MBA with high distinction from Harvard Business School, where she was a Baker, Siebel and Henry Ford II Scholar.

**Chris Gagnon** is a Senior Partner in McKinsey's Dallas office. Chris co-leads the Organization Practice globally, and is head of McKinsey's OrgSolutions group. He helps clients organize in an integrated way, applying analytics methodologies and tools to improve, culture, talent, change management, agility and leadership. Some of the tools Chris and the OrgSolutions group have developed include the Organizational Health Index (OHI), OrgLab, and People Analytics; these tools remove instinct and personal bias from critical organizational decisions. He has published articles in the *Harvard Business Review* and the *McKinsey Quarterly* on topics such as analytics, leadership, organizational health and agility. He has worked in several sectors - private equity, hospitality and leisure (including hotels, casinos, and the fitness industry). Chris holds a BA from Dartmouth College and an MBA from Amos Tuck School of Business Administration.

**Cornelius Chang** is an Associate Partner based in Singapore, leading McKinsey Academy for Asia. Cornelius has extensive experience in Europe, Asia and Australia where he has supported numerous leadership, talent, culture and change engagements across industries (Telecommunications, Agriculture, Energy, Oil and Gas, and Technology). He graduated Magna Cum Laude from the Singapore Management University in Economics and Business. Prior to university, he was a lieutenant with the Singapore Armed Forces having graduated at the top of his cohort. In between serving clients globally, Cornelius can be found roaming food halls and simple restaurants with his wife, stealing inspiration for weekend home-cooking.

**David Speiser** is a Partner in McKinsey's Zurich Office and a leader of McKinsey Academy. He serves leading companies in multiple industries on strategy, organization, and mergers and acquisitions, resource allocation and leadership development. He leads McKinsey Academy's 'Executive Programs', a group of multi-client leadership development programmes for executives in different stages of their careers. Before joining McKinsey, David started, grew and sold a business in the entertainment industry. He holds an MA in Quantitative Economics and Finance and a BA in Economics from University of St Gallen.

**Emily Yueh** is a Partner based in McKinsey's New York office and helps lead McKinsey Academy. She focuses on organizational, executive leadership development and performance transformation work for leading financial institutions, pharmaceuticals and educational institutions on a wide range of topics including organizational transformations, capability building and organizational design. She has conducted global transformations for clients in banking, and has worked with top teams in US retail and wholesale banking. Emily, an Andrew Mellon Fellow, holds a BA in Political Science and Economics from Carleton College and an MBA from University of Chicago Booth School of Business.

**Faridun Dotiwala** is a Partner who leads McKinsey's Human Capital practice in Asia, based in McKinsey's Mumbai office. His work is in the area of leadership development, establishing corporate academies, CEO and top team development and alignment and shaping large scale culture shifts in organizations. He has served multiple clients across the world on these topics, and has been a formal coach and counselor to many senior executives. As a facilitator of transformation, Faridun gets his energy from working hands on with senior teams on helping them work through their most complex leadership and organizational issues – over the past few years, he has interacted with over 200 teams covering several thousand senior leaders. Faridun holds a Bachelor's degree in Engineering from Mumbai University, a Master's degree in Structural Engineering from the University of Wisconsin, Madison, and an MBA from The London Business School. He is a Certified Ontological Coach from the Newfield Institute and holds many other learning certifications. Faridun lives with his wife and son in Mumbai.

**Filippo Rossi** is a Senior Partner in McKinsey's Paris Office, and has over 20 years of consulting experience relating to lean methodologies, primarily within the heavy industries. Filippo leads McKinsey's Healthy Lifestyle initiative, covering the four main pillars of nutrition, exercise, sleep and stress management. The initiative focuses on pinpointing and applying the latest approaches to maintain a healthy lifestyle, with the ultimate aim of improving productivity, optimism and personal satisfaction of participant. It targets both McKinsey employees as well clients, through training programmes, awareness campaigns, and policy changes. Filippo graduated with honours in Civil Engineering at the Politecnico of Milan, and holds an MBA from INSEAD, Fontainebleau.

**Florian Pollner** is an Expert Partner in McKinsey's Zurich Office. Florian leads McKinsey's Leadership and Learning client service across EMEA, and is co-founder and EMEA lead of McKinsey Academy, McKinsey's dedicated Leadership Development entity. Previously, he co-founded the McKinsey Center for Asian Leadership. His core expertise lies in designing and delivering leadership development acceleration, enhancing top team effectiveness, building leadership academies and driving large-scale, often global change and transformations. Florian has deep experience in working with leading global organizations across over 30 countries, with a focus on Europe and Asia. Florian primarily serves financial institutions, combining McKinsey's insights from the Banking and Organization Practices. He holds an MSc in Communication Systems (Swiss Federal Institute of Technology, EPFL) and an MBA from the Rotterdam School of Management (RSM), Erasmus University. Florian is a water sports fan, avid skier and ambitious hobby chef. He lives in Zurich with his wife and two children, and despite intense professional travel he and his family truly enjoy exploring the world in their free time.

**Gautam Kumra** is Managing Partner of McKinsey's India office, based in New Delhi. He led the Firm's Organization Practice in Asia and was one of the leading thinkers behind the Firm's research and insights on transformational change. He is also the leader of McKinsey's Asia Center (a special McKinsey initiative on globalization) and has contributed in shaping the thinking on globalization of Indian companies. His work covers organization, leadership development, operations excellence, transformational change, strategy, and governance in healthcare, industrials, hi-tech/IT and infrastructure. He founded the McKinsey Leadership Institute and convenes the CEO Bower Forum in Asia, providing learning amongst CEOs encompassing leading self, others and leading business and change. Gautam co-founded PHFI – an innovative public-private initiative to strengthen India's public health system by shaping public policy. He has an MBA from the Indian Institute of Management, Ahmedabad and a Bachelor of Technology (Chemical Engineering) from the Indian Institute of Technology, New Delhi.

**Gemma D'Auria** is a Partner in McKinsey's Middle East Office, where she leads the Organization Practice. Her area of focus and passion is organizational transformation and how to drive systemic change at the institutional level, while developing top and emerging leaders. Gemma focuses on a broad range of organization topics, linked to transformation - including shifts in operating model, HR 3.0, leadership development, corporate agility and culture change. She has designed and helped launch multiple large-scale leadership development efforts and corporate academies in the region, across both the public and private sectors, reaching thousands of leaders. Gemma holds a MBA from the Stanford Graduate School of Business and a

Bachelor of Science degree in Government and Economics from the London School of Economics. She has four kids, and loves traveling and adventure – this is what took her to the Middle East from our New York office ten years ago!

**Haimeng Zhang** is Senior Partner in McKinsey's Hong Kong office, and leads the Asia-Pacific Organization Practice. He works with clients in real estate, technology, pharmaceuticals and electronics, in the areas of strategic planning, organization design, agile organization transformation, post-merger management, new business scale up, digital strategy and special initiatives (overseas market opportunity scanning, sustainability, and leadership/capability development). He supports multinational clients on organization topics including top team effectiveness and leadership development program design and HR transformation. Haimeng received his MBA from the University of Chicago, Graduate School of Business and holds a BS in Economics from Shanghai Jiao Tong University.

**Johanne Lavoie** is a Partner in McKinsey's Canadian practice and Master Expert in leadership. She recently authored Quarterly articles on Inner Agility and artificial intelligence, the book *Centered Leadership: leading with clarity, purpose and impact* and a TEDx on integrating movement & stillness in disruptive times. She works across cultures and sectors with a focus on senior executive and team coaching, developing leadership in action, and advising on culture change to help clients and individuals transform their leadership and – through that – their performance. Johanne mixes 25 years of business consulting with extensive studies in developmental and leadership theories. She has an ICF-PCC certification in presence-based coaching, an MBA from Harvard and a degree in Electrical Engineering from McGill. At home, Johanne draws her inspiration from nature adventures in the Canadian Rockies where she lives with her husband and their two daughters, or at sea on their sailboat.

**Julia Sperling** is a Partner in McKinsey's Frankfurt Office, where she focuses on organizational topics across industries. Before joining McKinsey, Julia wrote her dissertation in Cognitive Neurosciences with summa cum laude at the Max-Planck-Institute for Brain Research and received her MD from the Goethe University Frankfurt with research fellowships and electives at Harvard Medical School, Queen Square (London), and the WHO. As an MD and neuroscientist,

Julia leads McKinsey's work on applying modern adult learning techniques grounded in neuroscience in leadership development programmes. Julia has also pioneered McKinsey's research on behavioural science and applying 'nudges' to generate positive behavioural change, and currently leads the Firm's global knowledge priorities in this area. When based in the Middle East, Julia was a founding member and the leader of McKinsey's healthcare practice in the region. She has also overseen for a decade McKinsey's work on women in leadership in Saudi Arabia. With her return to Europe in 2017, she took over the initiative 'Chefsache', which aims to help women reach and thrive in leadership positions in Germany. Julia lives with her husband and son in Frankfurt.

**Mary Andrade** is the Director of the Learning Design and Development Center of Excellence at McKinsey, and is based in Los Angeles. She is pioneering 21st century learning methodologies, approaches, and design for McKinsey and the learning industry. She is an authored, experienced learning professional with a twenty-year track record of success in creating learning curricula, applying innovative design and development techniques, and delivering solutions to large organizations deploying at scale. Her experience in learning modalities spans from live multi-factorial simulations to micro-learning digital solutions. Mary holds a BS with a double major in International Business and Marketing from the University of Colorado Boulder, and an MBA with an emphasis in Information Systems Management from the University of Texas at Austin. Mary and her husband are wine and food enthusiasts who enjoy cooking something different every day and rarely make the same meal twice. To balance this passion for food, they explore America's natural treasures in hiking boots with a camera at the ready.

**Michael Bazigos** was formerly Vice President of McKinsey's Org-Solutions, and co-led the Organizational Science Initiative (a collaboration between McKinsey and Gallup). Michael helps organizations perform through evidence-based approaches to their most pressing issues in talent and organization. Earlier leadership roles spanned both industry and consulting sectors at KPMG, IBM, and PwC's legacy management consulting unit, and a ten-year stint as Adjunct Professor in the graduate programme in Organization and Leadership at Columbia University. Michael earned his PhD in Organizational Psychology from Columbia University. He's published widely in professional and business journals including *McKinsey Quarterly* and *Journal of Leadership Studies*, and serves on the HR People and Strategy's Advisory Board.

**Mike Carson** is a Partner in McKinsey, and a founder of Aberkyn, leading the growth of Aberkyn's global network of local hubs; he is based in London and Amsterdam. His work focuses on transformational facilitation, executive leadership coaching, team leadership and large scale change within healthcare, financial services, defence and professional sport. He helps leaders develop personal insights that transform their own lives and work by creativity, insight and language, working through improvisation, film, drama, storytelling, poetry, literature, reflection and conversation. He is deeply passionate about sport – especially football, and its potential to transform society. He interviewed 30 Premier League (UK) managers about their leadership, to write *The Manager – Inside the Minds of Football's Leaders* (2013). Mike is a former Royal Navy Operations Officer (serving in war zones across the world), holds a BSc in mathematics from the University of Manchester and an MBA from INSEAD. He lives in Winchester with his wife and their four children, and is a lay pastor in the Church of England.

**Michiel Kruyt** is a Partner and one of the leaders of the Organization Practice of McKinsey, specializing in performance transformation, behavioural change and leadership development in top teams and their organizations. He uses organizational psychology and adult learning approaches as well as his international business experience in his work with clients in different industries. Michiel is a co-founder of Aberkyn, McKinsey's 'home' for change leaders, and currently co-leads it. He lives with his wife and three children on the outskirts of Amsterdam.

**Nick van Dam** is a Partner and Global Chief Learning Officer at McKinsey. He has a passion for people development and helping individuals to reach their full potential, and applies his expertise to both McKinsey employees as well as on client engagements. He is an internationally recognized advisor, author, speaker, and thought leader on Corporate Learning and Development. He is a Professor of Corporate Learning and Leadership Development at Nyenrode Business Universiteit and the University of Pennsylvania. He is board member of ICEDR, the world's premier network in global talent management, leadership development and strategic change. Additionally, he is on the Corporate Advisory Board of edX, a nonprofit founded by Harvard and MIT to bridge the gap between education and employment. Nick is the founder of the e-Learning for Kids Foundation which has provided over 20 million elementary school aged children with free digital lessons. He has authored and co-authored over 25 books including *YOU! The Positive Force in Change.* He has a PhD in Human Capital Development from Nyenrode Business University, a MA from the University of Amsterdam and holds a Bachelor degree in Education, Economics and Business Economics from the Vrije University Amsterdam. Nick lives in Amsterdam with his wife, and has a son at university in Spain.

**Ramesh Srinivasan** is a Senior Partner in the New York Office of McKinsey. Ramesh leads McKinsey Academy. He has extensive experience working on a broad range of organizational change – related topics in a variety of industries including high-tech, healthcare, banking, and industrial companies. He has expertise in merger management, organizational design, talent and leadership development, performance management, and capability building. In addition to serving clients on this topic, Ramesh is one of the global leaders of McKinsey's internal leadership and professional development programmes, and is Dean of the Bower Forum, McKinsey's program for CEO learning. Ramesh has a Business Technology degree in Computer Science from IIT Madras, and an MBA from the Indian Institute of Management, where he was awarded a gold medal for academic excellence. Ramesh is on the Board of Overseers at NYU Tandon School of Education. Ramesh's wife is a teacher at a NYC public school.

# References

Note: MID (McKinsey Internal Docment): used for McKinsey internal purposes and derives from proprietary methodology, survey, or anonymised client data.

## Introduction

1 World Economic Forum, Global Agenda Councils, *Outlook on the Global Agenda 2015*, available from http://reports.weforum.org/outlook-global-agenda-2015/ (accessed March 2018)

2 The State of Human Capital 2012 – False Summit: Why the Human Capital Function Still Has Far to Go, a joint report from the Conference Board and McKinsey, October 2012, available from https://www.mckinsey.com/~/media/mckinsey/dotcom/client_service/organization/pdfs/state_of_human_capital_2012.ashx (accessed March 2018)

3 McKinsey Org Solutions, Relationship between Leadership and average TRS, December 2015 (MID)

4 McKinsey Quarterly Transformational Change survey, January 2010 (MID); McKinsey Global Survey Results June 2009 (MID)

5 Meindl, J.R. and Ehrlich, S.B. (1987) 'The romance of leadership and the evaluation of organizational performance', *Academy of Management Journal*, 30(1), 91–109

6 Bligh, M.C., Kohles, J.C. and Pillai, R. (2011) 'Romancing leadership: past, present, and future' *The Leadership Quarterly* 22, 1058–1077

7 McKinsey Leadership Development survey, 2016 (MID)

8 *Ibid.*

9 Beer, M., Finnström, M. and Schrader D. (2016) 'Why leadership training fails – and what to do about it', *Harvard Business Review*, October

10 Gitsham, M. (2009) 'Developing the global leader of tomorrow', Ashridge Business School

11 Trainingindustry.com (2017) 'Training industry report', available from: https://trainingmag.com/trgmag-article/2017-training-industry-report (accessed March 2018)

12 Kellerman, B. (2012) *The End of Leadership*, HarperCollins

13 2014 MCB global executive survey on capability building (MID)

14 *Ibid.*

15 Pfeffer, J. (2015) *Leadership BS*, HarperCollins

16 Within the leadership field there is a large literature on contingency theories and studies on effective leadership behaviours. A search on Google Scholar (April 2017) for example using the terms 'contingency theories of leadership' results in 165,000 hits.

## *Chapter 1*

1 McKinsey Org Solutions, Relationship between Leadership and average TRS, December 2015 (MID)

2 Organizational Health Index database (n = 60,000); 'Return on Leadership – Competencies that Generate Growth' report by Egon Zehnder International and McKinsey, available from: https://www.egonzehnder.com/files/return_on_leadership.pdf (accessed March 2018)

3 McKinsey Quarterly Transformational Change survey, January 2010 (MID); June 2009 McKinsey Global survey results, available from https://www.mckinsey.com/featured-insights/leadership/the-value-of-centered-leadership-mckinsey-global-survey-results (accessed March 2018)

4 Barsh, J., Mogelof, J. and Webb, C. (2010) 'How centered leaders achieve extraordinary results' *McKinsey Quarterly*, October.

5 www.amazon.com (September 2016): search term "Leadership", filtered by search category "books"

6 Factiva search, December 2016

7 See for example, https://www.kenblanchard.com/Products-Services/Situational-Leadership-II

8 See in the work of Belbin, Tuckman and Wheelan.

9 See *Developing Leaders, A British Army Guide* (RMAS, 2014) and Cavanagh, R., Hesselbein, F. and Shinseki, E.K. (2004) *Be-Know-Do: Leadership the Army Way*, Jossey-Bass. Adapted from the US Army's leadership thinking.

10 Yukl, G. (2012, 8th edition), *Leadership in Organizations*, Pearson Education.

11 See Bazigos, M., De Smet, A. and Gagnon, C. (2015), 'Why agility pays', *McKinsey Quarterly*, December; Aghina, W., De Smet, A. and Weerda, K. (2015) 'Agility: it rhymes with stability', *McKinsey Quarterly*

12 Return on Leadership - Competencies that Generate Growth' report by Egon Zehnder International and McKinsey, available from: https://www.egonzehnder.com/files/return_on_leadership.pdf (Accessed March 2018)

13 Stogdill, R.M. (1948) 'Personal factors associated with leadership: A survey of the literature', *Journal of Psychology*, 25, 35–71

14 Keeping the focus on economics, VoT 3 (2009)

15 Mintzberg, H. (1973) *The Nature of Managerial Work*, McGill University School of Management, Harper & Row

16 Our view is supported by the seminal research published by Scott Derue, of the University of Michigan, and others in *Personnel Psychology* in 2011. Their findings suggest that behaviour is by far the most important predictor of leadership effectiveness. Compare Derue, D. S., Nahrgang, J. D., Wellman, N., Humphrey, S. E. (2011). 'Trait and behavioural theories of leadership: An integration and meta-analytic test of their relative validity', *Personnel Psychology*, 64(1), 7–52.

17 Barsh, J., Mogelof, J. and Webb, C. (2010) 'The Value of Centered Leadership: McKinsey Global Survey results *McKinsey Quarterly*, October

18 Three notable models of psychological theories of leadership are: Scouller's Three Levels of Leadership model. See Scouller, J. (2016), *The Three Levels of Leadership: How to Develop Your Leadership Presence, Knowhow and Skill*, Management Books; Kegan, R. and Lahey,

L.L. (2009) *Immunity to Change*, Harvard Business Press; and the works of Manfred Kets de Fries at INSEAD.

19 Keller, S. and Price, C. (2011) *Beyond Performance: How Great Organizations Build Ultimate Competitive Advantage*, Wiley.

20 OHI (Organizational Health Index), McKinsey, 2010 (MID)

21 Cavanagh, R., Hesselbein, F. and Shinseki, E.K. (2004) *Be-Know-Do, Leadership the Army Way*, Jossey Bass.

## Chapter 2

1 McKinsey Leadership Development survey, 2016 (MID)

2 *Ibid*.

3 See for example: Bazigos, M., Gagnon, C. and Schaninger, B. (2016) 'Leadership in context, *McKinsey Quarterly*, January; Gurdjian, P., Halbeisen, T. and Lane, K. (2014) 'Why leadership-development programmes fail', *McKinsey Quarterly*, January; Alexander, H., Feser, C., Kegan, R., Meaney, M., Mohamed, N., Webb, A and, Welsh, T. (2015) 'When to Change How You Lead' *McKinsey Quarterly*, June; Barsh, J., Mogelof, J. and Webb, C. (2010) 'The value of centered leadership: McKinsey Global Survey results *McKinsey Quarterly*, October; Feser, C., Mayol, F., Shrinivasan, R. (2015) 'Decoding leadership: What really matters', *McKinsey Quarterly*, January; Barton, D., Grant, A., Horn, M. (2012) 'Leading in the 21st century', *McKinsey Quarterly*, June; Feser, C. (2016) 'Debate – Leading in the digital age', *McKinsey Quarterly*, March.

4 Gurdjian, P., Halbeisen, T. and Lane, K. (2014) 'Why leadership-development programmes fail', *McKinsey Quarterly*, January

5 Atabaki, A., Dietsch, S. and Sperling, J.M. (2015) 'How to separate learning myths from reality', *McKinsey Quarterly*, July

## Chapter 3

1 Gurdjian, P., Halbeisen, T. and Lane, K. (2014) 'Why leadership-development programmes fail', *McKinsey Quarterly*, January

2  Fiedler, F. (1964) 'A contingency model of leadership effectiveness', *Advances in Experimental Social Psychology*, 1: 149–190. New York, NY: Academic Press

3  Bass, B. and Bass, R. (2008) 'The Hersey-Blanchard situational leadership theory', *The Handbook of Leadership: Theory, Research, & Managerial Implications*, 4: 516–522. New York, NY: The Free Press

4  Vroom, V. H. and Jago, A. G. (2007) 'The role of the situation in leadership', *American Psychologist*, 62(1), 17–24

5  De Smet, A., Schaninger, B. and Smith M. (2014) 'The hidden value of organizational health and how to capture it', *McKinsey Quarterly*, April

6  McKinsey OrgSolutions, "The recipe is the recipe", January 2016 (MID); See also De Smet, A., Schaninger, B. and Smith M. (2014) 'The hidden value of organizational health and how to capture it', *McKinsey Quarterly*, April

7  Bazigos M. and Caruso, E. (2016) 'Why frontline workers are disengaged', *McKinsey Quarterly*, March

8  Readers seeking an online assessment of their organization's health quartile are invited to take McKinsey's nine-question quiz 'How healthy is your organization?' available at ohisolution.com

9  The four leadership styles included in the OHI are informative in their own right in terms of helping organizations increase their leadership effectiveness. Our OHI research shows, for example, that authoritative leadership and consultative leadership have minimum and maximum threshold levels. If organizations are not decisive enough to make decisions, their performance and health will likely suffer, but being too autocratic has limitations as well. The same goes for consultative leadership, where it is generally a good idea to consult employees, but not to the point where decision-making speed and quality suffers. On the other hand, for challenging leadership and supportive leadership, the research indicates that more seems to be better, especially when they work in concert. In most contexts, the best leaders seem to challenge people to do more than they thought possible, but support them enough to reduce fear and stress.

10 Psychologist Abraham H. Maslow contended that human needs are structured in a hierarchy; as each level of needs is satisfied, the

next higher level of unfulfilled needs becomes predominant. See Maslow, A.H. (1943) 'A theory of human motivation', *Psychological Review*, 50(4), 370–96; and Maslow, A.H. (1954) *Motivation and Personality*, New York: Harper & Brothers

11  Brenneman, G. (1998) 'Right away and all at once: How we saved Continental', *Harvard Business Review*

12  Organizational health in banks: Insights from an industry sample, McKinsey research, October 2014 (MID)

13  See for example, in the work of Jean Piaget, Commons and Richards, Kurt Fischer, and Charles Alexander

14  See for example, in the work of Erik Erikson, Jane Loevinger, Don Beck, Robert Kegan, and Richard Barrett

15  Talent Matters – McKinsey conference document (MID); Barton, D., Carey, D., Charan, R. (2018) *Talent Wins*, Harvard Business Review Press

16  McKinsey Global Institute publication, drawing on MGI and PWC sources

17  Dobbs, R. Manyika, J. and Woetzel, J. 'The four global forces breaking all the trends', McKinsey Global Institute available from: http://www.mckinsey.com/insights/strategy/the_four_global_forces_breaking_all_the_trends (accessed March 2018)

18  McKinsey 9 Golden Rules report, 2013 (MID)

19  Barton, D., Grant, A. and Horn, M. (2012) 'Leading in the 21st Century', *McKinsey Quarterly*

20  Webb, A. (ed) (2015) 'When to change how you lead', *McKinsey Quarterly*, June

21  McKinsey Transformational Change and Capability for Performance Service Line, *McKinsey's Ten Truths of Change Management*, (MID)

22  Heifetz, R. (1998) *Leadership Without Easy Answers*, Harvard University Press

23  Anderson, R.J. and Adams, W.A. (2015) *Mastering Leadership: An Integrated Framework for Breakthrough Performance and Extraordinary Business Results*, Wiley, page 156

24 Anterasian, C., Resch-Fingerlos R.S. (2010) 'Understanding executive potential', https://www.spencerstuart.com/research-and-insight/understanding-executive-potential-the-underappreciated-leadership-traits (accessed July 2018)

25 Birkel, F., Kelly C.L. and Wlech G. (2013) 'Survival of the most adaptable', SpencerStuart, available from: https://www.spencerstuart.com/research-and-insight/survival-of-the-most-adaptable-becoming-a-change-ready-culture (accessed July 2018)

26 Bureau of Labor Statistics, available from: https://www.bls.gov/news.release/tenure.nr0.htm (accessed December 2016).

27 Gray, Al. (2016) 'The 10 skills you need to thrive in the Fourth Industrial Revolution', World Economic Forum, available from: https://www.weforum.org/agenda/2016/01/the-10-skills-you-need-to-thrive-in-the-fourth-industrial-revolution/ (accessed March 2018).

28 Barsh, J., Mogelof, J. and Webb, C. (2010) 'The Value of Centered Leadership: McKinsey Global Survey results *McKinsey Quarterly*, October

29 Barsh J. and Lavoie, J. (2014) *Centered Leadership*, Crown Business; see also 'How executives put centered leadership into action: McKinsey Global Survey Results' available from: http://www.mckinsey.com/business-functions/organization/our-insights/how-executives-put-centered-leadership-into-action-mckinsey-global-survey-results (accessed March 2018); Barsh, J. and De Smet, A. (2009) 'Centered leadership through the crisis: McKinsey Survey results', available at: http://www.mckinsey.com/global-themes/leadership/centered-leadership-through-the-crisis-mckinsey-survey-results (accessed March 2018); Barsh, J., Mogelof, J. and Webb, C. (2010) 'How centered leaders achieve extraordinary results', available from: http://www.mckinsey.com/global-themes/leadership/how-centered-leaders-achieve-extraordinary-results (accessed March 2018); Barsh, J. and Lavoie J. (2014) 'Lead at your best', *McKinsey Quarterly*, April

30 Hunter, M. and Ibarra, H. (2007) 'How leaders create and use networks', *Harvard Business Review*, January.

31 Csíkszentmihályi, M. (2002) *Flow: The Psychology of Happiness,* Rider.

32 Kegan, R. and Laskow L.L. (2016) *An Everyone Culture: Becoming a Deliberately Developmental Organization*, Harvard Business Review Press

33 MBTI basics (2014) The Myers–Briggs Foundation, available from: https://www.myersbriggs.org/my-mbti-personality-type/mbti-basics/

34 Patton, B., Fisher R. and Ury, W. (1981) *Getting to Yes,* Random House Publishing

35 Bughin, J., Chui, M., Dewhurst, M., George, K., Manyika, J., Miremadi, M. and Willmott, P (2017) *Harnessing Automation for a Future that Works*, McKinsey Global Institute

36 McKinsey Global Institute, Independent work: choice, necessity, and the gig economy, October 2016, available from: https://www.mckinsey.com/global-themes/employment-and-growth/independent-work-choice-necessity-and-the-gig-economy (accessed March 2018)

## *Chapter 4*

1 McKinsey Leadership Development survey, 2016 (MID)

2 *Ibid.*

3 Barabasi, A-L (2002) *Linked : The New Science of Networks*, Perseus Publishing

4 Gladwell, M. (2000) *The Tipping Point*, Little, Brown Book Group

5 Kotter, J. (1996) *Leading Change*, Chapter 4, Harvard Business Review Press

6 Cross, R.L., Martin, R.D., and Weiss, L.M (2006) 'Mapping the value of employee collaboration, *McKinsey Quarterly*.

7 Heath, C. and Heath, D. (2007) *Made to Stick*, Random House

8 Return on Leadership – Competencies that Generate Growth, February 2011, Egon Zhender and McKinsey, available from: https://www.egonzehnder.com/files/return_on_leadership.pdf (accessed March 2018)

9 Keller S. and Meaney, M. (2017) *Leading Organizations: Ten Timeless Truths*, Bloomsbury

10 Retrieved from World Economic Forum's Future of Jobs report, available from: http://www3.weforum.org/docs/WEF_Future_of_Jobs.pdf (accessed March 2018)

11 See Handy, C. (2015) *The Second Curve*, Random House Business

12 Van Dam, N. Inaugural lecture, Nyenrode Business School, 25 November 2016

13 Johnson, W. and Mendez, J.C. (2012) 'Throw your life a curve', *Harvard Business Review*, September

14 Association for Talent Development (2016) State of the Industry, available from: https://www.td.org/research-reports/2017-state-of-the-industry (accessed March 2018

# Chapter 5

1 From the free search engine accessing the MEDLINE database of references and abstracts on life sciences and biomedical topics (PubMed)

2 Howard-Jones, P.A. (2014) 'Neuroscience and education: Myths and messages', *Nature Reviews Neuroscience*

3 Atabaki, A., Dietsch, S. and Sperling, J.M. (2015) 'How to separate learning myths from reality', *McKinsey Quarterly*, July

4 Whitmore, J. (1996) *Coaching for Performance*, Nicholas Brealey Publishing

5 Lombardo, M. M, Eichinger, R.W (1996), *The Career Architect Development Planner* Minneapolis: Lominger, p. iv.

6 Meaney M. and Keller S. (2017) *Leading Organizations*, Bloomsbury

7 Goldman-Rakic, P.S. (1987) 'Development of cortical circuitry and cognitive function, *Child Development*, pp. 601–622

8 Cunha, F., Heckman, J., Lochner, L. and Masterov, D. (2006) 'Interpreting the evidence on life cycle skill formation', *Handbook of the Economics of Education*, 1: 697–812

9 Rakic, P. (2002) 'Neurogenesis in adult primate neocortex: an evaluation of the evidence', *Annual Reviews Neuroscience* 3(1): 65–71.

10 Doidge, N. (2007) *The Brain That Changes Itself*, Viking); and (2015) *The Brain's Way of Healing: Stories of Remarkable Recoveries and Discoveries,* Penguin) Eagleman, D. (2015) *The Brain: The Story of You,* Pantheon.

11 Yerkes, R.M. and Dodson, J.D. (1908), 'The relation of strength of stimulus to rapidity of habit-formation', *Journal Of Comparative Neurology and Psychology*, 18, 459–482.

12 Gazzaniga, M.S. (2005) 'Forty-five years of split-brain research and still going strong' *Nature Reviews Neuroscience* 6(8): 653–9; Paschler, H., McDaniel, M., Rohrer, D. and Bjork, R. (2010) c. *Psychological Science in the Public Interest* 9, pp. 105-119.

13 Maguire E.A., Woollett K. and Spiers H.J. (2006) 'London taxi drivers and bus drivers: a structural MRI and neuropsychological analysis', published online 5 October at Wiley InterScience (www.interscience.wiley.com)

14 Hebb, D.O. (1949) *The Organization of Behavior*, Wiley & Sons

15 Salzman C.D. and Fusi S. (2101) 'Emotion, cognition, and mental state representation in amygdala and prefrontal cortex', *Nature Reviews Neuroscience*

16 McGaugh, J.L. (2004) 'The amygdala modulates the consolidation of memories of emotionally arousing experiences', *Annual Review of Neuroscience* 27: 1–28

17 See for example, Sylwester, R. (1994) 'How emotions affect learning', *Educational Leadership*, October, 52(2): 60–65; Pekrum, R. (1992) 'The impact of emotions on learning and achievement: Towards a theory of cognitive/motivational mediators', *Applied Psychology*, 41(4), October: 359–376

18 Nieoullon, A. and Coquere A. (2003) 'Dopamine: A key regulator to adapt action, emotion, motivation and cognition', *Current Opinion in Neurology*, Suppl 2: S3–S9.

19 Schultz, W. (1998) 'Predictive reward signal of dopamine neurons', *The Journal of Neurophysiology*, 80: 1–27

20 Kirschenbaum, D.S., Ordman, A. M., Tomarken, A. J. *et. al.* (1982) 'Effects of differential self-monitoring and level of mastery on sports performance: Brain power bowling', *Cognitive Therapy and Research*, 6: 335–41

21 Jones-Smith, E. (2013) *Strengths-Based Therapy: Connecting Theory, Practice and Skills*, SAGE Publications

22 See, for example, Kahneman, D. and Tversky, A. (1979) 'Prospect theory: An analysis of decision under risk', *Econometrica*, 47: 263–291; and Baumeister, R.F., Bratslavsky, E., Finkenauer, C. and Vohs, K.D. (2001) 'Bad is stronger than good', *Review of General Psychology*, 5: 323–370d

23 Robertson, I. (2012) *The Winner Effect*, Bloomsbury

24 Return on Leadership – Competencies that Generate Growth, report by Egon Zehnder International and McKinsey, available from: https://www.egonzehnder.com/files/return_on_leadership.pdf (accessed March 2018)

25 Corporate Leadership Council (2002), Building the High-Performance Workforce: A Quantitative Analysis of the Effectiveness of Performance Management Strategies, Washington, DC

26 McKinsey Quarterly Transformational Change Survey, January 2010 (MID)

27 Kegan, R., Lahey, L.L. (2009) *Immunity to Change: How to Overcome it and Unlock the Potential in Yourself and Your Orgnaization*, Harvard Business Review Press.

28 Fleming S.M., Weil R.S., Nagy Z., Dolan R.J., Rees G. (2010) 'Relating introspective accuracy to individual differences in brain structure', *Science* September 17; 329(5998):1541-3. doi: 10.1126/science.1191883.

29 Dweck, C.S. (2006) *Mindset: The New Psychology of Success*, Ballantine Books

30 Kahneman, D. (2012) *Thinking Fast and Slow*, Penguin Books

31 Schumpeter (2013) 'The mindful business', *The Economist* November

32 See https://vhil.stanford.edu/projects/, accessed March 2018.

33  Van Dam, N. and Van der Helm, E. (2016) 'The organizational cost of insufficient sleep', *McKinsey Quarterly*, February

34  See for example, Kegan, R. and Lahey, L.L. (2009) 'Immunity to Change', *Harvard Business Press*; Duhigg, C. (2014) *The Power of Habit: Why We Do What We Do in Life and Business*, Random House; Goldsmith, M. (2015) *Triggers: Creating Behavior that Lasts – Becoming the Person You Want to Be*, Crown Business

# Chapter 6

1  Schein, E. (1996) 'Culture: The missing concept in organizational studies', *Administrative Science Quarterly*, 41: 229–240; Ostroff, K. Kinicki, A.J. and Tamkins, M.M., 'Organizational culture and climate', in Borma, W.C., Ilgen, D.R. and Klimoski R.J. (eds.) (2003) *Handbook of Psychology* 12, Industrial and Organizational Psychology (pp. 565–593).

2  Lawson E. and Price, C. (2003) 'The psychology of change management' *McKinsey Quarterly*, June

3  McKinsey Quarterly Transformational Change survey; January 2010 (MID)

4  Harvard Business Review staff (2013) 'The uses (and abuses) of influence', *Harvard Business Review*; Cialdini, R.B. (2006) *Influence: The Psychology of Persuasion*, Revised Edition, Harper Business, 2006

5  Festinger, L. (1957) *A Theory of Cognitive Dissonance*, Stanford University Press

6  Paul, M.P. (2012) 'Your brain on fiction', *The New York Times*; Monarth, (H.) (2014) 'The irresistible power of storytelling as a strategic business tool', *Harvard Business Review*

7  Basford, T.E. and Molberg A. (2013) 'Dale Carnegie's leadership principles: Examining the theoretical and empirical support', *Journal of Leadership Studies*, 6(4): 25-47

8  Locke, E. A. and Latham, G.P. (2002) 'Building a practically useful theory of goal setting and task motivation', *American Psychologist* 705–717; and Sherif, M. (1966) In a common predicament: Social psychology of intergroup conflict and cooperation, Houghton Mifflin comp.

9 Argyle, M., Alkema, G., and Gilmour, R. (1971) The communication of friendly and hostile attitudes by verbal and non-verbal signals. *European Journal of Social Psychology*, I, 385-402

10 Chartrwhy and *et al.*, 'You're just a chameleon: The automatic nature and social significance of mimicry', *Natura Automatyzmow (Nature of Automaticity)*, 19–14

11 Pugh, S. (2001) 'Service with a smile: Emotional contagion in the service encounter', *Academy of Management Journal*, 55(5): 1018-1027

12 *Ibid*

13 Cialdini, R.B. (2009) *Influence: Science and Practice* (5th edition), Pearson Higher Ed

14 Skinner, B.F. (1961) 'Teaching machines', *Scientific American*, 205: 91–102

15 Pavlov, I.P. (1927) *Conditioned Reflexes: An Investigation of the Physiological Activity of the Cerebral Cortex*, Oxford University Press

16 Bandura, A. (1971) 'Vicarious and self-reinforcement processes', in R. Glaser (ed) *The Nature of Reinforcement*, New York: Academic Press 228–278

17 Kerr, S. (1975) 'On the folly of rewarding A, while hoping for B', *Academy of Management Journal*, 18: 769-783

18 McClelland, D.C. (1975) *Power: The Inner Experience*, Irvington Publishers

19 Deci, E. L. (1975) *Intrinsic Motivation*, Plenum Press; Robbins, S.P and Judge, T.A. (2009) *Organizational Behavior* (13th edition), Pearson Education

20 Hackman, J.R. (1980) 'Motivation through the design of work: test of a theory', *Organizational Behavior and Human Performance,* 250-279; Hackman, J.R. and Oldham, G.R. (1980) *Work Redesign*, Addison-Wesley

21 Burns, T. and Stalker, G.M. (1961) *The Management of Innovation*, Tavistock Publications; Robbins, S.P. and Judge, T.A. (2009) *Organizational Behavior* (13th edition), Pearson Education

22 McKinsey leadership development survey 2016 (MID)

23 Kirkpatrick D.L. and Kirkpatrick, J.D. (2006) *Evaluating Training Programmes: The Four Levels* (3rd Edition), Berrett-Koehler Publishers

24 Organizational Health Index database (n = 60,000) (MID)

25 McKinsey Quarterly Transformational Change survey, January 2010; June 2009 McKinsey Global survey results (MID)

26 Cernak, J. and Mcgurk M. (2010) 'Putting a value on training' *McKinsey Quarterly*, July

27 Bower, M. (1996) *The Will to Manage* New York: McGraw-Hill

## Chapter 7

1 Whitmore, J. (1996) *Coaching for Performance*, Nicholas Brealey Publishing

2 See Freedman, L. (2013) *Strategy: A History*, Oxford University Press

3 Strategies to Scale the Power Curve (McKinsey Strategy & Finance, September 2016) (MID); See also Bradley, C., Hurt, M., Smit, S. (2018) *Strategy Beyond the Hockey Stick,* Wiley

4 See Hall S. and Lovallo, D. (2012) 'How to put your money where your strategy is, *McKinsey Quarterly*; and see: Bradley, C., Hirt, M., and Smit, A. (2018) *Strategy Beyond the Hockey Stick: People, Probabilities, and Big Moves to Beat the Odds,* Wiley

5 Senge, Peter, *The Fifth Discipline: The Art and Practice of the Learning Organization,* Random House Business, 2nd edition, 2006

6 Kegan, R., Lahey, L.L., Miller, M.L., Fleming, A. and Helsing, D. *An Everyone Culture: Becoming a Deliberately Developmental Organization,* Harvard Business Review Press

## Chapter 13

1 See for example, Adair, J. (1987) *Effective Teambuilding: How to Make a Winning Team,* Pan Books; Belbin R. M. (2004) *Management Teams,* Routledge; Hill, L. A. and Anteby, M. (2006) *Analyzing Work Groups,*

Harvard Business School Publishing; Lencioni, P. M. (2005) *Overcoming The Five Dysfunctions of a Team: A Field Guide for Leaders, Managers, and Facilitators,* Jossey-Bass; and theoretical work by Belbin, Maslow and Tuckman

2 McKinsey Transformational Change Practice (MID).

3 Collins J. and Porras, J.I. (2004) *Built to Last,* HarperBusiness; (10th revised edition) November

4 Mandeville, B. (1957 edition) *The Fable of the Bees: Or Private Vices, Publick Benefits,* Oxford University Press. Mandeville's poem prefigures that of Adam Smith (invisible hand and division of labour) in this fictive account of a beehive.

5 Greiner, L. (1972) 'Evolution and revolution as organizations grow', *Harvard Business Review,* 37–46. The phases are growth through creativity, direction, delegation, coordination, collaboration and (a sixth, added in 1998) extra-organization solutions

6 McKinsey OrgSolutions, 'The recipe is the recipe', January 2016 (MID)

7 NHS, UK: *Developing People – Improving Care*: Evidenced-based national framework to guide action on improvement skill-building, leadership development and talent management for people in NHS-funded roles (2016), available from: https://improvement.nhs.uk/resources/developing-people-improving-care/ (accessed March 2018)

8 Gallup, 2015 (n=3956); See https://www.mckinsey.com/business-functions/organization/our-insights/revisiting-the-matrix-organization (accessed July 2018)

9 Fecheyr-Lippens, B., Schaninger B. and Tanner, K. (2015) 'Power to the new people analytics' *McKinsey Quarterly,* March

10 de Romrée, H., Fecheyr-Lippens, B. and Schaninger, B. (2016) 'People analytics reveals three things HR may be getting wrong', *McKinsey Quarterly,* July

11 See Björnberg, Å. and Feser, C. (2015) 'CEO succession starts with developing your leaders', *McKinsey Quarterly,* May

# *Chapter 14*

1 Manyika, J. (2017) 'Technology jobs and the future of work' McKinsey &Company available from: http://www.mckinsey.com/global-themes/employment-and-growth/technology-jobs-and-the-future-of-work (accessed March 2018)

2 World Economic Forum. (2016) The Future of Jobs: Employment, Skills, and Workforce Strategy for the Fourth Industrial Revolution, available from: http://reports.weforum.org/future-of-jobs-2016/ (accessed March 2018)

3 Van Dam, N. (2016) 'Learn or Lose', Inaugural lecture, 25 November, Nyenrode Business Universiteit

4 World Economic Forum. (2016) The Future of Jobs: Employment, Skills, and Workforce Strategy for the Fourth Industrial Revolution, available from: http://reports.weforum.org/future-of-jobs-2016/ (accessed March 2018)

5 *Ibid.*

6 Frey, C.B. and Osborne, M. (2013) *The Future of Employment: How Susceptible are Jobs to Computerisation?*, University of Oxford

7 'Automation and anxiety' (2016) *The Economist,* 25 June

8 Manyika, J. (2017) 'Technology, jobs, and the future of work', McKinsey & Company, available from: http://www.mckinsey.com/global-themes/employment-and-growth/technology-jobs-and-the-future-of-work (accessed March 2013)

9 Harress, C. (2013) 'The sad end of Blockbuster Video', *International Business Times*, 5 December

10 Live presentation by John Kao, 'The World in 2030', Athens, 3 December 2016

11 World Economic Forum. (2016) The Future of Jobs: Employment, Skills, and Workforce Strategy for the Fourth Industrial Revolution, available from: http://reports.weforum.org/future-of-jobs-2016/ (accessed March 2018)

12 Grothaus, M. (2015) 'The top jobs in 10 years might not be what you expect', *Fast Company*, 18 May

13  DESI indicator on digital skills (2015). Eurostat data available from: https://ec.europa.eu/digital-single-market/en/desi (accessed March 2018)

14  Gray, A. (2016) 'The 10 skills you need to thrive in the Fourth Industrial Revolution' World Economic forum, available from: https://www.weforum.org/agenda/2016/01/the-10-skills-you-need-to-thrive-in-the-fourth-industrial-revolution/ (accessed March 2018).

15  Deming, D. (2017) *The Growing Importance of Social Skills in the Labor Market*, Harvard University and NBER, August; graphic from *The Quarterly Journal of Economics* (2017) 132(4): 1593-1640

16  Gratton, L. (2011) *The Shift: The Future of Work is Already Here*. London: Collins

17  Van Dam, N. 'Learn or lose', Inaugural lecture, 25 November, Nyenrode Business Universiteit

18  Vuorikari, R., Punie, Y., Carretero, S. and Van den Branden, L. (2016), DigComp 2.0: The Digital Competence Framework for Citizens. EC, EUR 27948 EN.

19  Vuorikari, R., Punie, Y., Carretero, S. and Van den Branden, L. (2016), DigComp 2.0: The Digital Competence Framework for Citizens. EC, EUR 27948 EN.

20  Rashid, B. (2016) 'The rise of the freelancer economy' Forbes, available from:https://www.forbes.com/sites/brianrashid/2016/01/26/the-rise-of-the-freelancer-economy/#31a014e33bdf (accessed March 2018)

21  See Aghina, W., De Smet, A. and Weerda, K. (2015) 'Agility: It rhymes with stability', *McKinsey Quarterly*, December

22  Schwartz, N.D. 'The decline of the baronial CEO', https://www.nytimes.com/2017/06/17/business/ge-whole-foods-ceo.html

23  Puthiyamadam, T. (2017) 'How the meaning of digital transformation has evolved', *Harvard Business Review*, 29 May

24  Gratton, L. and Scott, A. (2016). *The 100 Year Life: Living and Working in the Age of Longevity*, Bloomsbury.

25  Senge, P. (2010) *The Fifth Discipline*, Random House

26 Watkins, Karen E. and Marsick, Victoria J. (eds.), (May 2003). 'Making learning count! Diagnosing the learning culture in organizations, *Advances in Developing Human Resources*, 5(2)

27 Kegan R. and Lahey, L.L. (2016) *An Everyone Culture: Becoming a Deliberately Developmental Organization*, Harvard Business School Press

28 For the interested reader, an assessment can be taken on www. reachingyourpotential.org

29 McKinsey Mind the Gap research (MID)

30 *Ibid.*

31 Barsh, J., Brown, L, and Kian, K. (2016) *Millennials: Burden, Blessing, or Both?* McKinsey & Co

32 See: Mind the Gap p15 (MID)

33 Van Dam, N. (2016) 'Learn or lose', Inaugural lecture, 25 November, Nyenrode Business Universiteit

34 Association for Talent Development (2016) State of the Industry, available from: https://www.td.org/research-reports/2017-state-of-the-industry (accessed March 2018)

35 *Ibid.*

36 Penfold S. (2016) 'Profile of the modern learner – helpful facts and stats (infographic)' Elucidat blog, available from: https://blog.elucidat.com/modern-learner-profile-infographic/?utm_campaign=elearningindustry.com&utm_source=%2Ftop-10-elearning-trends-to-watch-in-2017&utm_medium=link (accessed (March 2018)

## Appendices

1 For a more detailed review of a substantially similar list of such leadership behaviours, see Feser, C., Mayol, F. and Srinivasan, R. (2015) 'Decoding leadership: What really matters', *McKinsey Quarterly*, January

2 Psychologist Abraham H. Maslow contended that human needs are structured in a hierarchy; as each level of needs is satisfied, the next higher level of unfulfilled needs becomes predominant. See Maslow,

A.H. (1943) 'A theory of human motivation', *Psychological Review*, 50(4): 370–96; and Maslow, A.H. (1954) *Motivation and Personality* (first edition), Harper & Brothers

3   Herzberg, F. (1987) 'One more time: How do you motivate employees?', *Harvard Business Review*, 65(5): 109–120

4   For further details, see Bazigos, M.N. (2016) 'Leading for long-term performance: Matching the behavior to the situation', *Journal of Leadership Studies*, August

5   There are many sources of the GROW model (and variations of the model itself). See for example Alexander, G., Fine, A., Whitmore J. as well as Landsberg, M. (2003) *The Tao of Coaching* (Profile Books)

6   Maister, D.H., Green, C.H. and Galford, R.M. (2000) *The Trusted Advisor*, Free Press

7   Minto, B. (2010) *The Pyramid Principle: Logic in Writing and Thinking, 3rd edition*, Prentice Hall

8   De Bono, E. (1985) *Six Thinking Hats*, Little Brown and Company

9   Feser, C., Mayol, F. and Srinivasan, R. (2015) 'Decoding leadership', *McKinsey Quarterly*, January

10  Seligman, M. (1998) *Learned Optimism*, New York: Pocket Books

11  Pohlmann, T. and Thomas, N.M. (2015) 'Relearning the art of asking questions', available at: https://hbr.org/2015/03/relearning-the-art-of-asking-questions (accessed July 2018)

12  Covey, S.R. (2015) *The 7 Habits of Highly Effective People: Powerful Lessons in Personal Change,* FranklinCovey Co.

13  We measure speed by asking survey respondents how often they observed their leaders (and, separately, managers) making important decisions quickly and their organizations adjusting rapidly to new ways of doing things. We measure stability by asking respondents how often they observed their organizations implementing clear operating goals and metrics, setting clear standards and objectives for work, establishing structures that promote accountability, designing jobs with clear objectives, and devising processes to document knowledge and ideas. See Bazigos, M., De Smet, A. and Gagnon, C. (2015) 'Why agility pays', and Aghina, W., De Smet A. and Weerda, K. 'Agility: It rhymes with stability', both *McKinsey Quarterly*, December

14  *Ibid.*

15  *Ibid.*

16  Rogers, E. and Van Dam, N. (2014) *You! The Positive Force in Change*, Lulu

17  Jezzard P., Matthews P.M. and Smith S.M. (2001) *Functional MRI: An Introduction to Methods*, Oxford University Press

18  Ophir E., Nass C., Wagner A.D. (2009) 'Cognitive control in media multi-tasker', PNAS, 15;106(37):2

19  See for example, Foerde, K., Knowlton, B. J. and Poldrack, R. A. (2006) 'Modulation of competing memory systems by distraction' PNAS, 10: 11778–11783; Rubinstein, J.S., *et al.* (2001) 'Executive control of cognitive processes in task switching' *Journal of Experimental Psychology* 27: 763–71; Czerwinski, M., *et al.*(2000) 'Instant messaging and interruption: Influence of task type on performance', Proceedings of OZCHI 356: 361.

20  Begley, S. (2000) 'The stereotype trap' *Newsweek*, available from: http://www.newsweek.com/stereotype-trap-157203   (accessed March 2018)

21  Steele, C.M. (2010) *Whistling Vivaldi and Other Clues to How Stereotypes Affect Us*, W.W. Norton & Company, Inc.

22  Dweck, C. (2006) *Mindset: The New Psychology of Success*, Random House

23  Blackwell, L. S., Trzesniewski, K. H. and Dweck, C.S. (2007) 'Implicit theories of intelligence predict achievement across an adolescent transition: A longitudinal study and an intervention', *Child Development*, 78(1): 246–263.

24  Kahneman, D. (2012) *Thinking Fast and Slow*, Penguin Books

25  Van Dam, N. and Van der Helm, E. (2016) 'The organizational cost of insufficient sleep', *McKinsey Quarterly*, February

26  Goel, N. *et al.,* (2009) 'Neurocognitive consequences of sleep deprivation', *Seminars in Neurology*, 29(4):320–39; Verweij, I.M. *et al.* (2014) 'Sleep deprivation leads to a loss of functional connectivity in frontal brain regions', *BMC Neuroscience*, 15(88), biomedcentral.com

27  Williamson, A.M. and Feyer, A.M. (2000) 'Moderate sleep deprivation produces impairments in cognitive and motor performance equivalent to legally prescribed levels of alcohol intoxication', *Occupational and Environmental Medicine*, 57(10): 649–55, oem.bmj. com

28  Van der Helm, E., Gujar, N. and Walker, M.P. (2010) 'Sleep deprivation impairs the accurate recognition of human emotions', *Sleep*, 33(3): 335–42, journalsleep.org; Van der Helm, E. *et al.*, (2011) 'REM sleep depotentiates amygdala activity to previous emotional experiences', *Current Biology*, 21(23): 2029–32

29  McGlinchey, E.L. *et al.*, (2011) 'The effect of sleep deprivation on vocal expression of emotion in adolescents and adults', *Sleep*, 34(9): 1233–41, journalsleep.org

30  Macey, W.H. and Schneider, B. (2008) 'The meaning of employee engagement', *Industrial and Organizational Psychology*, 1(1): 3–30 and Stumpf, S.A., Tymon W.G. Jr. and Van Dam, N. (2013) 'Felt and behavioral engagement in workgroups of professionals', *Journal of Vocational Behavior*, 83(3): 255–64, available from: journals.elsevier. com/journal-of-vocational-behavior

31  See for example, Bryant, P.A., Trinder J. and Curtis, N. (2004) 'Sick and tired: does sleep have a vital role in the immune system?', *Nature Reviews Immunology* 4: 457–467 (June); Ayas N.T., White D.P/, Manson J.E., Stampfer M.J., Speizer F.E., Malhotra A., Hu F.B. (2003) 'A prospective study of sleep duration and coronary heart disease in women', *Archives of Internal Medicine*. 163(2):205–209. doi:10.1001/archinte.163.2.205; Alhola, P. and Polo-Kantola, P. (2007) 'Sleep deprivation: Impact on cognitive performance', *Neuropsychiatric Disease and Treatment*. October; 3(5): 553–567; Ferrie J.E., Shipley M.J., Akbaraly T.N., Marmot M.G., Kivimäki M. and Singh-Manoux A. (2011) 'Change in sleep duration and cognitive function: findings from the Whitehall II study' *Sleep*, 34 (5): 565–573; and 'How much sleep do we really need?' National Sleep Foundation, available from: https://sleepfoundation.org/excessivesleepiness/content/how-much-sleep-do-we-really-need-0 (accessed March 2018)

32  Van Dam, N. and Van der Helm, E. (2016) 'The organizational cost of insufficient sleep', *McKinsey Quarterly*, February

33  See for example, Kramer A.F., Erickson K.I. and Colcombe S.J. (1985) 'Exercise, cognition, and the aging brain', *Journal of Applied Physiology* 101(4):1237-42; Churchill, J.D. *et al.* (2002) 'Exercise, experience and the aging brain' *Neurobiology of Aging* 23: 941–55.; Cotman, C.W. and Berchtold, N.C. (2002) 'Exercise: A behavioral intervention to enhance brain health and plasticity'. *Trends in Neuroscience* 25: 295–301; Dillner, L. (2017) 'Is running the best exercise?' *Guardian*, available from: https://www.theguardian.com/lifeandstyle/2017/apr/24/is-running-best-exercise-reduce-risk-heart-disease?CMP=share_btn_link (accessed March 2018)

34  See for example, Ratey J.J. and Loehr J.E. (2011) 'The positive impact of physical activity on cognition during adulthood: a review of underlying mechanisms, evidence and recommendations', *Reviews in Neuroscience* 22(2):171–85; Scholey, A.B., Moss, M.C., Neave, N. and Wesnes, K. (1999) 'Cognitive performance, hyperoxia, and heart rate following oxygen administration in healthy young adults' *Physiology & Behavior*, 67(5): 783–789

35  See for example, Taras, H. (2005) 'Physical activity and student performance at school' *Journal of School Health*, 75: 214–18; Hillman, C. and Buck. S. (2004) 'Physical fitness and cognitive function in healthy pre-adolescent children', Paper presented at the Annual meeting of the Society of Psychophysiological Research; Summerford, C. (2001) 'What is the impact of exercise on brain function for academic learning?' *Teaching Elementary Physical Education* 12: 6-8; Hillman, C.H. Erickson, K.L. and Kramer, A.F. (2008) 'Be smart, exercise your heart: exercise effects on brain and cognition', *Nature Reviews Neuroscience* 9: 58-65 (January)

36  Singh-Manoux, A. PhD, Hillsdon, M. PhD, Brunner, E. PhD, and Marmot, M. PhD, MBBS, FFPHM, FRCP (2005) 'Effects of physical activity on cognitive functioning in middle age: Evidence From the Whitehall II Prospective Cohort Study' *American Journal of Public Health*, December 95(12): 2252–2258

37  Harada, T., Okagawa, S. and Kubota, K. (2004) 'Jogging improved performance of a behavioral branching task: implications for prefrontal activation', *Neuroscience Research*, 49(3): 325–337

38  Steinberg H., Sykes E.A., Moss T., *et al.* (1997) 'Exercise enhances creativity independently of mood' *British Journal of Sports Medicine* 31:240–245

39  Young, S.N. (2007) 'How to increase serotonin in the human brain without drugs', *Journal of Psychiatry and Neuroscience*, November, 32(6): 394–399.; Korb, A. (2011) 'Boosting your serotonin activity', *Psychology Today*, available from: https://www.psychologytoday.com/blog/prefrontal-nudity/201111/boosting-your-serotonin-activity (accessed March 2018)

40  Harber V.J. and Sutton J.R., (1984) 'Endorphins and exercise', *Sports Medicine*. Mar-Apr, 1(2):154–71; 'Depression guide' available from: http://www.webmd.com/depression/guide/exercise-depression#1 (accessed March 2018)

41  Sutoo D., Akiyama K., (2003) 'Regulation of brain function by exercise', *Neurobiology of Disease,* Jun, 13(1):1–14, McNary, T. (2017) 'Exercise and its effects on serotonin & dopamine levels' available from: http://www.livestrong.com/article/251785-exercise-and-its-effects-on-serotonin-dopamine-levels/ (accessed March 2018)

42  Medina, J. (2014) *Brain Rules*, Scribe Publications

43  U.S. Department of Health and Human Services, 2008 Physical Activity Guidelines for Americans, available from https://health.gov/paguidelines/pdf/paguide.pdf, accessed 29 April 2017

44  Tomporowski, P.D. (2003) 'Effects of acute bouts of exercise on cognition', *Acta Psychologica* (Amst), 112: 297–324

45  Levine J.A. (2002) 'Non-exercise activity thermogenesis (NEAT)', *Best Practice and Research: Clinical Endocrinology and Metabolism*, December, 16(4):679–702

46  Gómez-Pinilla, F. (2008) 'Brain foods: the effects of nutrients on brain function', *Nature Reviews. Neuroscience*, 9(7): 568–78

47  See for example, Edwards, S. (2016) 'Sugar and the brain', Harvard Mahoney Neuroscience Institute, available from: http://neuro.hms.harvard.edu/harvard-mahoney-neuroscience-institute/brain-newsletter/and-brain-series/sugar-and-brain (accessed April 2017); Barnes, J.N. and Joyner, M.J. (2012) 'Sugar highs and lows: the impact of diet on cognitive function', *Journal of Physiology,* June, 15: 590(Pt 12): 2831; Greenwood C.E. and Winocur G.

(2005) 'High-fat diets, insulin resistance and declining cognitive function', *Neurobiology of Aging*. December 2015

48 Carabotti, M., Scirocco, A., Maselli, M.A. and Severi, C.(2014) 'The gut-brain axis: interactions between enteric microbiota, central and enteric nervous systems', *Annals of Gastroenterology*, April–June, 28(2): 203–209; Galland, L. (2014) 'The gut microbiome and the brain', *Journal of Medicinal Food*, 1 December 17(12): 1261–1272 Mayer, E.A.,, Knight, R., Mazmanian, S.K. Cryan, J.F. andand Tillisch, K. (2014) 'Gut microbes and the brain: paradigm shift in neuroscience ', *The Journal of Neuroscience*. 34(46): 15490–15496.; Kohn, D. (2015) 'When gut bacteria change brain function', The Atlantic, available from: https://www.theatlantic.com/health/archive/2015/06/gut-bacteria-on-the-brain/395918/ (accessed March 2018); Andrew Smith, P. (2015) 'The tantalizing links between gut microbes and the brain' *Nature*, available from: http://www.nature.com/news/the-tantalizing-links-between-gut-microbes-and-the-brain-1.18557 (accessed March 2018)

49 Armstrong, L.E. et. al. (2012) 'Mild Dehydration Affects Mood in Healthy Young Women', *The Journal of Nutrition*,Volume 142, Issue 2, February 2012, available at https://academic.oup.com/jn/article/142/2/382/4743487 (accessed March 2018); Heid M. 'Your brain on: dehydration', Shape, available from: http://www.shape.com/lifestyle/mind-and-body/your-brain-dehydration (accessed March 2018)

50 See for example, American Psychological Association (2017) 'Many Americans Stressed about Future of Our Nation, New APA Stress in America™ Survey Reveals', available from: http://www.apa.org/news/press/releases/2017/02/stressed-nation.aspx (accessed March 2018); Fink, G. (2016) 'Stress: The Health Epidemic of the 21st Century', Elsevier SciTechConnect available from: http://scitechconnect.elsevier.com/stress-health-epidemic-21st-century/ (accessed March 2018); 'Stress facts', available from: http://www.gostress.com/stress-facts/ (accessed March 2018)

51 Lippelt D. P. (2014) 'Focused attention, open monitoring and loving kindness meditation: effects on attention, conflict monitoring, and creativity – a review', *Frontiers in Psychology*

52  Chiesa A., Calati R. and Serretti A. (2011) 'Does mindfulness training improve cognitive abilities? A systematic review of neuropsychological findings' *Clinical Psychology Review* 31(3), April

53  Geng L., Zhang D. and Zhang, L. (2011) 'Improving spatial abilities through mindfulness: effects on the mental rotation task', *Consciousness and Cognition*

54  Matthieu R., Lutz A. and Davidson R. (2014) 'The neuroscience of meditation', *Scientific American*, October

55  Tjan, A.K. (2015) '5 ways to become more self-aware', *Harvard Business Review*, February

56  Singleton, O. *et al.* (2014) 'Change in brainstem gray matter concentration following a mindfulness-based intervention is correlated with improvement in psychological well-being', *Frontiers in Human Neuroscience*, 18 February, frontiersin.org

57  Schumpeter, (2013) 'The mindful business', *The Economist*, November

58  Gelles, D. (2015) 'At Aetna, a CEO's management by mantra', *New York Times*, 27 February, nytimes.com

# Index